Making Ethnic Choices

In the series,
Asian American History and Culture,
edited by Sucheng Chan

Making Ethnic Choices
California's Punjabi Mexican Americans

KAREN ISAKSEN LEONARD

Temple University Press
Philadelphia

Temple University Press, Philadelphia 19122
Copyright © 1992 by Temple University. All rights reserved
Published 1992
Printed in the United States of America

LIBRARY OF CONGRESS CATALOGING-IN-PUBLICATION DATA
Leonard, Karen Isaksen, 1939–
   Making ethnic choices : California's Punjabi Mexican Americans /
Karen Isaksen Leonard.
      p.   cm. — (Asian American history and culture series)
   Includes bibliographical references and index.
   ISBN 0-87722-890-6
   1. Panjabi Americans—California.   2. Mexican Americans—
California.   3. Interracial marriage—California.   4. California—
Social conditions.   I. Title.   II. Series.
F870.P36L46   1992
305.891′420794—dc20   91-24482

Contents

Tables and Maps

Preface

This exploration of ethnicity in rural California began in 1979 when a former graduate student invited me to give a speech on "Women in Indian Culture" at Yuba Community College in northern California, where she was a counselor. I assumed my speech was an event of Women's Week; instead, it proved to be East Indian Week. I learned that Yuba Community College had a sizable enrollment of young Punjabis whose parents had recently immigrated to the United States. The campus counselors, concerned that young Punjabi women took no advantage of the career counseling they offered, wanted to know more about Indian women. The Punjabi women also had concerns that they hoped I could answer. They confided to me after the talk that their parents were sending them back to India for arranged marriages with Punjabi villagers (brides were being brought for their brothers); they wanted to know if arranged marriages could be happy ones, and if villages in India were modernizing rapidly!

I had been totally unaware of the recent large Punjabi immigration to rural northern California and of the operation of this marriage network linking Marysville and Yuba City with peasant villages back in the Punjab. At lunch, my education proceeded as a Punjabi faculty member at the college told me more of the background of the Punjabis in California. He said that his family, and others like them, had settled in the United States in the 1950s, and were "really American." For example, he allowed his daughter to become a cheerleader, earning the strong disapproval of more recent immigrants. And before him, there had been Punjabi immigrants—men called "Hindus" in rural California. There had even been some "Mexican-Hindu" families, formed by Punjabi men and Hispanic women.[1] These families numbered a mere handful, and most of them lived in the Imperial Valley, located along the Colorado River and California's border with Mexico. Fascinated, I listened to several stories illustrating the problems of cultural adaptation posed by the operation of these various marriage networks.

I had done research in India on marriage networks and economic resources,[2] and two years after my visit to Yuba Community College, I wanted to look more closely at the marriage networks and economic resources of the Punjabi immigrants in Yuba City. Finding, however, that others already were doing scholarly studies of the new immigrants there,[3] I decided to trace the handful of Mexican-Hindu families to see how these pioneer Punjabi men had transmitted Indian beliefs and behaviors to their descendants. That was my initial, simple preconception of the research project.

I also had a personal motivation, stemming from the deaths of my parents just before I began this research. Standing in a rural Wisconsin graveyard in 1980, I realized how little I had learned from my parents about their lives, particularly about the ethnic heritage that had been important to them. My father, the son of an immigrant from Norway, and my mother, descended from several generations of English, Irish, and Welsh in the United States, were buried in a Norwegian Lutheran church graveyard in Wisconsin farm country near Milwaukee. According to my mother, my father had wanted to be buried there, near a farm where he had lived as a child. Having become an honorary Norwegian, she too wanted to be buried there. Yet the place was completely strange to my brother, sister, and me; it meant nothing to us. As I began talking to older people in rural California about their lives, I thought about what it must have been like to grow up Norwegian in rural Wisconsin, in a time and place where ethnicity was an important determinant of social patterns, an important part of one's identity. I listened carefully when people spoke about their own ethnicity and that of their parents, trying to see the meaning it had for them in different contexts and at different times in their lives.

In his reevaluation of what scientifically conducted research should be like, Daniel Bertaux proposed that the last stage of research should not be the final writing and publication.[4] Instead, it should be the reading of the work, not only by other academics but by members of the general public, for whom good social science should expand sociohistorical knowledge and social consciousness. I agree with him. I am especially concerned that the people who helped me with the research read the result. With respect to the larger audience, I, like Bertaux, believe that research that produces only abstract theoretical discussion is useless because it fails to make scholarly work relevant and justifiable to society.

I do not believe that theory is a dead-end, but my own inclination and abilities lead me to affirm Bertaux's goal for social science, that of using descriptive narrative to develop a critical understanding of social history.[5] Many historians have returned to an emphasis on narrative, partly to communicate their research in a meaningful way and partly because the sharing of experiences of persons different from oneself can come about only by making those experiences accessible through good narrative. Storytelling structures the material in traditional, familiar ways. Oral history was an important component of my research. Descendants of the Punjabi men had thought about their experiences, and often the stories they told reflected not only their views but a multiplicity of perspectives. The whole social world of the biethnic couples and their children, from social relations to social thought, can be seen and analyzed in their stories.[6] Some chapters are filled with their words, counterpoints to some of the necessary quantitative material.

The book is dedicated to those who helped bring it about, and I hope they will enjoy reading it. The people who provided information appear in the bibliography; very few asked for anonymity. I welcome further recollections from readers. I want to thank those who read all or part of the manuscript and provided valuable insights: Joseph Anderholt, Sucheng Chan, James Ferguson, James Freeman, Mary Garewal Gill, Robert Khan, Bruce La Brack, Liisa Malkki, Duane Metzger, Robert Mohammad, Amelia Singh Netervala, and Pritam Singh Sandhu. Three colleagues accompanied me to the Imperial Valley and helped conduct some interviews: Ernesto Vargas in 1981, C. M. Naim in 1981, and Jayasri Hart in 1990. Lupe Beltran, a graduate student at the University of California, Irvine, and Tejinder S. Sidhu, of the Shields Library at the University of California, Davis, each contributed two interviews. Special thanks are due to my editors, Janet Francendese of Temple University Press and Sucheng Chan of its Asian American History and Culture series, for their help in making the final cuts. A series of small grants from the University of California, Irvine, helped fund the research. Finally, I thank my family

Part I

Introduction

1 Exploring Ethnicity

My original conception of the research project was simple: to study a community in southern California that had been fathered by Punjabi men in the early twentieth century. It was small, and has been superseded by new immigrant communities with families where both parents are Indian, but for at least a generation, the biethnic Punjabi–Mexican community was the model of family life for immigrants from India. I was curious about cultural transmission in these biethnic families. How were the children raised? Had the men taught Punjabi beliefs and behaviors to their descendants? What were the childhood experiences of children with names like Maria Jesusita Singh, Jose Akbar Khan, and Benjamin Chand, and what ethnic identity did members of the second generation espouse today?

Indians abroad have been noted for the tenacity with which they retain their culture and the importance they place on marriage alliances. I expected the Punjabi men in California to dominate their families, transmitting significant elements of Punjabi domestic culture to their children and trying to create a new endogamous group. All I knew about the women initially was that most of them were Mexican or Mexican American. The literature on the patriarchial Mexican family also helped shape my expectation that the women would be relatively passive, connected to one another only through the men and quite dependent on them.

When I did research in India, oral history was the only way to do family histories, but U.S. county records offer excellent information on vital statistics (births, deaths, marriages).[1] To get an idea of the shape and size of the community, I went to the office of the Imperial County Recorder. Family reconstitution through birth, death, and marriage certificates was my task, and I looked through the available index for the most common surname of the early Punjabi immigrants, Singh. Some 85 percent of these immigrants were Sikhs, and Sikh men all use Singh as part of their name; in the United States, almost all used it as their surname. By the second day of the research, I knew that the "handful" of Punjabi-Mexican couples numbered well over one hundred. These "dry" statistics provided other surprises: A single death certificate led to a dramatic murder case, and the marriage and birth certificates, when aggregated, revealed that sets of Hispanic sisters had married Punjabi men.

I supplemented the vital statistics with other local records and historical materials. The county criminal and civil cases (including probates and divorces) and the federal bankruptcy records showed that the Punjabi men's knowledge of U.S. laws and their access to agricultural credit were much greater than indicated in the contemporary literature about these immigrants. I turned to secondary literature on California agriculture and the history of the towns in the Imperial, San Joaquin, and Sacramento valleys. I also consulted contemporary newspapers and other primary sources for the towns, eager to learn about a society initially as unfamiliar to me as that of urban India had been when I began research there.

After I had some grasp of the rural California context and the structure of the Punjabi-Mexican families, I began attending local events and meeting people. The people I met in these California farming communities were diverse, ranging from Swiss farmers to a few old-timer Punjabis and many of the Punjabis' wives and descendants. They had important things to say about local society, past and present, about ethnic and race relations and specific family histories.

At this time, the problem of exactly how to refer to the people whose lives I was studying came up. Outsiders called the men Hindus, the old American misnomer for all people from India, regardless of religion, and called the families Mexican-Hindus. Members of the community most often called themselves Hindus (until 1947, when Pakistan was created), although the children also answered to Mexican-Hindu or "half and half." Most people, within and outside the biethnic community, called the Spanish-speaking wives Mexican, regardless of their birthplace; no one labeled them Latino, Chicano, or Hispanic, although the latter term conveniently includes all the Spanish-speaking wives (from Mexico, the United States, and Puerto Rico).[2] Of course, the confusion over name— multiple names, choices among names—is significant and is discussed in Chapter 8. Here I simply note the terms I use and my rationale for doing so. When using social science discourse, I call the couples Punjabi-Mexican, the Spanish-speaking women Hispanic, and the men Sikh, Muslim, or Hindu, because these terms denote ancestry most accurately. I use Mexican, Hindu, and Mexican-Hindu when citing or paraphrasing historical sources or informants, when the stance is clearly historical or the perspective local.

One of the first events I attended, the funeral of an old Sikh farmer in the Imperial Valley, well illustrates the ethnic complexities of the community. The old man died in the home of a daughter, Lupe Ramirez. One of his grandsons, a Christian fundamentalist minister, conducted a funeral service in an El Centro funeral home; afterward, there was another service in the Sikh temple in El Centro.

In the funeral home, people of all skin and hair colors, dressed in clothing ranging from high heels and short dresses to full Punjabi dress with its flowing trousers and shirts, sat around me. The grandson opened the service by asking us to stand for a brief prayer led by the Sikh *granthi* (temple priest). The *granthi*, a recent immigrant in full Punjabi dress with beard and turban, immediately ordered us in broken English to sit down and then disconcerted us by delivering a twenty-five-minute oration in Punjabi, replete with Urdu poetry. Finally, the grandson rose again and spoke impressively about his grandfather, who had stressed the work ethic. "Where you go?" the old man once asked him, in the broken English characteristic of these early Punjabi immigrants. Hearing that his grandson was going golfing, he rebuked him: "No, go work!" After the minister exhorted his predominantly Catholic and Sikh audience to be saved by Jesus, we proceeded to the Sikh temple for a brief service in Punjabi. Behind me, Punjabi-Mexican women giggled like girls about how little one of the Sikh elders, a crusty old pioneer from the 1920s, had changed since they had been youngsters coming to eat at the temple. After the service, I met descendants of early Sikh, Hindu, and Muslim Punjabi pioneers, some of whom had traveled from as far away as Sacramento for this funeral of one of the last survivors of the immigrant generation.

The people I met at this funeral, and at the Sikh temple in El Centro on Sunday afternoons, provided my initial research contacts. The surviving Punjabi old-timers in the Imperial Valley meet every Sunday at the Sikh temple for a brief service and long Punjabi conversations under the trees outside. The women who come with them do not all speak Punjabi; for that reason, and because of Indian custom, they usually sit separately and converse in English. I was placed with the women on my first visit and awkwardly expressed my interest in the historical experiences of the immigrants and their families. These women, two daughters of old-timers who were themselves married to older men from India and an Indian wife who had arrived in the 1950s, queried me about my family and my experiences in India. They gently parried my eager questions about the Punjabi-Mexican families formed in the 1920s; they wondered why I should be interested in them when most of them had proved to be "not really Indian." Slowly I recognized a conflict here: "Real Indians" did not acknowledge full kinship with the Punjabi-Mexican families and invariably claimed that they were few in number. I realized that my research would provoke ambivalent reactions from more recent immigrants from South Asia and that the recent immigrants might play a role in Punjabi-Mexican formulations of their ethnic identity.

Ambivalent reactions came from members of the Punjabi-Mexican community as well. Early in the research, I tried a mail survey, addressed to names taken from phone books, names like Joe Singh, Lucia Singh, John Mohammed, Ricardo Khan, and Jaime Chand. I received a few scattered responses to the questionnaire, and one request that I come and help fill it out, but the results were disappointing. Later, a very important problem with this survey became apparent. While the questionnaire was well designed in many respects, I had placed first the one question descendants were least able to answer accurately: From which village and district in the Punjab did your father come? Embarrassed that they did not know or did not know how to spell the village names, most recipients quickly put the questionnaire aside.

Other mistakes made in interview attempts proved helpful in correcting my initially romantic view of these marriages. After several productive visits with Hispanic widows of immigrant Punjabi farmers in the Imperial Valley, I became confident and stopped at a rural farmhouse without prior notice. But its occupant insisted that her *vida privada* was not my business, and later I learned that her marriage to a Punjabi had been long but difficult. Another prospective interview was to be arranged by an ebullient young woman whose godmother was the widow of a Singh. This Mrs. Singh, who lived in a small house in downtown El Centro, not only refused to talk to me or anyone else about the Hindus, she feared that if they even knew she had been approached to talk about them, they would come and burn down her house! In partial explanation, she told her goddaughter what had happened after her husband's death. She and he had lived in the town, away from the Punjabi-Mexican farming households, and they had run a restaurant together. When the husband died, a group of Sikh men came and forcibly removed his body from her house in order to cremate him according to Sikh religious practice. She was unable to recover his body and bury it as she has wished to do, in the Mexican section of the local cemetery. Clearly, the Punjabis had been powerful men, and not all experiences with them had been happy ones.

Other interviews, however, went well. As I traveled around California meeting descendants of the Punjabi pioneers, I found keen memories of childhood friends and a still-existing communication network. News of deaths and misfortunes traveled fastest, by telephone. Other news was passed on at the annual Mexican-Hindu dance in Yuba City or more randomly by casual visits or chance meetings (and by me, after a year or so of research, as people realized I often had recent news of their old classmates and friends). The shared experience of being Mexican-Hindu in the Imperial Valley produced bonds that have lasted a lifetime and across many miles, creating networks based on class, religion, childhood locale, school, and Hispanic kinship and *compadrazgo* ties. For those brought up in the Imperial Valley, being Mexican-Hindu has a special and lasting meaning.

All these research endeavors contributed to an understanding of the historical experiences of the Punjabi-Mexican families. They led me far from my original hypotheses about male dominance and cultural transmission. I soon found that the proud Punjabi male had more than met his match. Any facile assumption that ethnicity is determined by one's father proved spectacularly inadequate for an understanding of this biethnic experience. Not only were the Hispanic women individually strong, they had kinship networks of their own. The children of these marriages are also strong and independent minded. Toughened by prejudice expressed against them in their childhood, they are survivors, able to explain and use elements of three different cultures in their adult lives. With growing interest and respect, I listened to the life stories of the widows and children. That the women's role was central in structuring concepts of ethnicity became even clearer as I interviewed descendants of black and Anglo wives of Punjabis. Fewer in number and more frequently found in northern California, these descendants offered some striking contrasts to the Mexican-Hindus as they spoke about their lives.

Methods and Sources

Some social historians and sociologists have undertaken family reconstitution, the labor-intensive compilation of genealogies through record linkage and oral interviews, as a valuable alternative to the use of macro-level census data for the investigation of patterns of fertility and mortality, marriage and divorce, geographic and intergenerational mobility, and so on.[3] I used both official record searches and interviews to reconstitute the Punjabi-Mexican families. South Asian surnames from the centralized state death records, alphabetized and printed for 1905 through 1939, showed the pattern of settlement by counties for families and bachelors alike. California marriage certificates, consolidated statewide since 1949, provided alphabetized lists (indexed separately for brides and grooms for 1949 through 1959 and for brides and grooms combined from 1960 to 1969) that could be searched for South Asian surnames. Together, the statewide death and marriage records indicated which county record offices deserved a visit for more intensive research. Because California birth records have not been centralized for the pre-1956 period, it was necessary to go to the county record offices and use local surname indexes to locate birth certificates.

Interviewing was a crucial complement to official records. For the interviews, I contacted people through other people and through telephone directories and county and state records. Constructing genealogies from interviews showed that sometimes, especially in the early years, people may not have obtained official certificates for births and deaths. Some couples never did legally marry, while large numbers of others moved to California after marrying elsewhere. The interviews picked up many of these unrecorded people, but collecting genealogies from informants was also insufficient. County records were essential, particularly for the reconstitution of collateral lines.[4]

The community I have reconstituted undoubtedly includes a higher proportion of couples with children, and of couples with many children, than was the case. Couples who cohabited but had no children were less likely to marry and leave records; conversely, the more children an individual had, the more possible informants there are to record or report his or her existence.[5] Couples without children also had fewer links to the other families through either *compadrazgo* relationships or their children's friendships and marriages, so informants had fewer ways of recalling them.

Having family data from official records proved useful for the interviews. People in this community at first were highly suspicious of gossip; they preferred to hear that I had learned about them from county records. I compiled a list of "original couples" that I took around with me to show that I had done some advance homework. Far from discouraging informants from contributing information, the names stimulated memories. People looked carefully at this list, corrected it, added to it, and told me of relationships that were not evident from the records. In this way, I discovered many sets of stepsisters and sisters married to Punjabis, some of them living elsewhere in the southwestern United States.

I also found that I was performing a service for my informants. Some were not sure how to locate their own birth certificates or how to check on death dates or causes of death for deceased family members. In a few cases, there was uncertainty about birth order (e.g., of siblings who had died as infants) or about previous and subsequent marriages, so I was able to help people compile their own family histories.

Working with the county records often involved challenges, caused by the mistaken age estimates and misspellings recorded by county clerks. For example, after some time I realized that the Guillermo Singh and Rosa Bhagt Singh named on one birth certificate were the Bhagat Singh and Rosa Romero who appeared on several others. Table 1 illustrates the difficulties of reconstituting Punjabi and Hispanic families from these records; it follows family events recorded for one couple, with the variant ages and spellings of their names.

The death certificate of one Mohammed Abdulla likewise furnishes a good example of the uses and limits of county records. This man died in 1943 in Sacramento's County Hospital, and another Punjabi Muslim from the dead man's boardinghouse on K Street gave the coroner the minimal information that appeared on the original death certificate.[6] His race or religion was given as "Mohammed," his age "about 70," his occupation "laborer," and his birthplace "Punjab, India." The informant could not give the parents' names or birthplaces, and he gave Abdulla's length of residence as fourteen years in the United States and California and three

Table 1.   County Records for One Couple

His Name and Age	Her Name and Age	Date and Event
Amer Singh, 35	Mercedes Paiz, 20	1930, marriage
Ambro Singh, 40	Mercedes Paiz, 22	1931, birth of a child
Ambru Singh, 39	Mercedes Paiz, 24	1932, birth of a child
Ambon Singh, 47	Mercedez Paez, 24	1934, birth of a child
Ambrosio Singh, 40	Mercedes Pais, 28	1935, birth of a child
Ambrose Singh	Merced Paiz	1935, death of a child
Ambra Singh, 50	Mercedes Paez, 27	1941, birth of a child
Amber Singh, 53	Mercedes Bias, 25	1943, birth of a child

Sources: Birth, Death, and Marriage Certificates, Recorder's Office, El Centro, Imperial County, California.

years in Sacramento County. Later, another Punjabi Muslim, Rokn Din, came from Gridley and filled out an affidavit for correction of the death certificate, identifying himself as Mohammed Abdulla's cousin (Badar Din from Broderick also signed the affidavit). Din changed Mohammed Abdulla's race or religion to "Aryan," filled in his marital status as "widowed" and gave the wife's name, Rujjie (a Punjabi name). He gave the parents' names and specified Mohammed Abdulla's birthplace as the village of Nunglekhurd in the district of Ludhiana, Punjab, the same as the father's (he left the mother's birthplace blank). Finally, he corrected the length of residence in the United States and California to thirty years. With this further information, we know Abdulla's village origin, his correct arrival time in the United States (1913), and that he left an Indian wife behind and did not marry again. We know also that Mohammed Abdulla's death brought his cousin down from Gridley and that he thought it important to correct the inaccurate and incomplete death certificate. Clearly, official records could only reflect the knowledge of those filling them out, whether Anglo or Punjabi.

A final example of county record vagaries pertains to entries for race. A second-generation daughter gave birth in Yuba City in three consecutive years. In 1958 she was labeled "Hindu," in 1959 "Mexican-Hindu," and in 1960 "white." Although I did not make a count (I saw and copied some 1,800 to 2,000 marriage, birth, and death certificates), it is my impression that the most common term used for race was "brown."

Several little-known sources for this research should be noted. First is the Gadar Collection at the South and Southeast Asian Library at the University of California, Berkeley.[7] This collection includes miscellaneous early documents produced chiefly by the Punjabis in California and some valuable taped interviews with early immigrants. Second, and perhaps even more valuable at present, is the archival collection housed in the Hoover Archives, Hoover Institution on War, Revolution, and Peace, at Stanford University,[8] consisting of raw data from a "Survey of Race Relations" conducted by sociologists in the mid 1920s on the Pacific Coast. Only two volumes were ever published, but the typed interviews offer rich details.[9] Third, I found early telephone books, high school yearbooks, water district records, and many other useful research materials in the Pioneers Museum in the Imperial Valley.[10] This museum was established by the local Pioneers Society, originally an invitational group confined to early Anglo settler families that has now renamed itself the Imperial Valley Historical Society and broadened its membership significantly.

Theoretical Concerns

As a leading proponent of oral history put it, "Historians are not methodological purists, but jackdaws; given a problem, they will seize on any evidence they can discover, and make the best of it."[11] Having assembled a variety of evidence, I eventually turned to methods and theoretical perspectives from three different disciplines to "make the best" of the Mexican-Hindu experience. The "new social history"[12] led me to reconstitute families from local records, construct a statewide data set of marriages involving Punjabis and Punjabi descendants and do an endogamy analysis of it, and subject court cases and many other records to computer analysis. I looked at household composition, at individual life cycles, and at the way they fit with the family life course. All these analyses highlighted the crucial role of the women in domestic life and the socialization of children.

As I began active field work, concepts from sociologists interested in life stories suggested ways to analyze the interaction between individuals and the social system over time. I collected many life stories or life histories (the latter term is better because almost always these involved supplementary material from other individuals, public record offices, and various archival and secondary sources). To understand the life histories, it was important to understand their immediate social context—the social system in which the Punjabi-Mexicans lived. The small groups[13] to which they belonged—households, farming partnerships, neighborhoods, and even clusters of lawyers and bankers who worked closely with Punjabi farmers—were important mediating agents between society and individual. Beyond compiling the "collective biographies" of localized groups, the mapping of wider political and economic networks proved crucial to the analysis of the Mexican-Hindu experience. For both endeavors, written records failed to tell enough about relationships within the Punjabi-Mexican families or about relationships with others in society; oral history was thus essential.[14]

Field work also led me to the anthropological literature on ethnicity. I began to think in terms of ethnic groups and boundaries, trait lists, self-identification, and the perceptions of outsiders. That ethnicity is not genetically determined but is produced and changed through social relations is now widely accepted.[15] The notion that ethnic identity can be manipulated flexibly over the life course was particularly useful in clarifying the intersections between individual experience and the larger social system. Because of California's discriminatory laws, which constrained the participation of Asians in political and economic activities for many decades, the role of ethnicity in the distribution of economic, political, and social resources was an important one.[16] Comparative reading on other Asian immigrants who worked in California agriculture proved useful also. Both folk and scholarly categorizations include the Punjabis with the Chinese, Japanese, Koreans, and Filipinos to create an "Asian" group in rural California.

While the lack of historical work on ethnicity and the persistence of ethnic groups has been noted,[17] recent work on the historical construction of ethnicity and the "invention of tradition"[18] put the final theoretical underpinnings in place. An understanding of the Mexican-Hindu experience confirmed that ethnicity is both persistent and flexible, that ethnic identities are continually constructed and reconstructed by individuals and society. As Comaroff puts it, ethnicity is something to be explained, rather than something that can be used to explain other phenomena. Likewise, Clifford says that one's identity "must always be mixed, relational, and inventive." Clifford also speaks of the bias in studies of culture "towards rooting not travel."[19] One way to find out what people know and value about their place, their culture, and their identity is to follow them to a new place. In this study, not only the Punjabi men but many of the Hispanic women were immigrants in California, constructing their sense of self and community in a new context.

The new context played an important role in this process of construction. Following Comaroff, I believe that the marking of ethnic identities in relation to others, not the substance of ethnic identities, is primordial. He argues that this marking is rooted in "the asymmetric incorporation of structurally dissimilar groupings into a unitary political economy."[20] How the regional economic context and public policies helped determine the formation of ethnic identity is one of the major themes of this book. Power relationships in the California countryside, the placement of the Punjabis in the hierarchy of groups working in California agriculture, and federal and state laws governing immigration, citizenship, and access to resources all affected the Punjabis' identity. Delineating the variations within the Punjabi-Mexican biethnic community by regional context helped capture its full range.

A second theme is the differential construction and reconstruction of ethnic identity by individuals according to generation, gender, stage of life, and social class. As socioeconomic and political circumstances changed over time, the perception and use of ethnicity by the Punjabi men and the Hispanic women, and by members of the successive generations, changed as well. The same individual, over his or her life course, could choose to understand and use ethnic identity in several different ways. The children of these marriages, in particular, given their very incomplete inheritance of Punjabi culture, showed remarkable inventiveness and resilience as they continued to identify themselves as "Hindus" and as Americans.

A third theme is the articulation of gender power relationships and the problematic of ethnic identity *within* as well as outside the family. Certain stages of the family life cycle brought these gender conflicts into sharp focus; also, forces outside the family sometimes produced rifts along gender lines. We think of the family as a natural unit, a basically harmonious entity that responds to or influences larger social forces. Within this systematically biethnic community, however, ethnic markers and boundaries were contested and negotiated within marriages, within families, throughout the history of this social group.[21] I became particularly interested in the way adult children talked about their parents, often using ironic discourse that expressed both distance and closeness to their dual ethnic heritages. Anthropologists working on ethnicity in the United States have largely overlooked the world-building aspects of ordinary talk;[22] such talk was a valuable part of my research.

All three themes emphasize the interaction of individual and family life processes, that is, micro-level processes, with the political economy. Here was a community so small and idiosyncratic that the state took no official notice of it—a community that lasted only one, possibly two generations in any structural sense. Yet its history can tell us a great deal about the historical construction of ethnicity and its meaning to people across time, space, and context. In particular, its history offers insights into the nature of ethnic pluralism in the United States.

Part II

The World of the Pioneers

2 Contexts: California and the Punjab

The Punjabis were not the first immigrants from Asia to help develop agriculture in California, and by the time they arrived, "Oriental" was already a stereotype in rural California. Nor was the United States the first overseas destination for many of them, so they brought experiences and stereotypes of their own to California. To understand why the Punjabi men came from India, how they fit into the California political economy, and what resources they brought with them to the American West, it is necessary to review conditions in both California and the Punjab. Rural California at the turn of the century presented many contrasts to the Punjab province in India, but there were similarities as well. Fragmentary sources provide glimpses of Asian and Punjabi perceptions of their place in the California landscape.

California Agriculture and Asian Immigrants

The world of California agriculture was a highly competitive one, and Asians figured in its historical development from its early days. Before the discovery of gold in 1848, California was a pastoral, semi-isolated region, with cattle hides and tallow as its most profitable products. Then it became one of the world's centers of mining, a labor-intensive industry. The extensive cultivation of grain began after 1860, and California gradually developed a corporate, capital-intensive form of agriculture, in contrast to the small family-farm tradition in the East and Midwest that supposedly sustained "American" values. The construction of large-scale irrigation systems in California's valleys allowed fruits and vegetables to be cultivated commercially from the late 1870s onward, a shift well documented by Paul Taylor and Tom Vasey in 1936. The graphs in their study show the increased area of improved land and irrigated land, the rising value of crops, and the rising employment of farm laborers from 1889 to 1929.[1] In the twentieth century, as fruit growing and truck gardening increased steadily,[2] California agriculture also became labor intensive. Therafter, neither the centralized planning and development of irrigation nor the development of horticulture changed the basic pattern of land concentration or the commercialized and specialized nature of California agriculture.[3]

Although ethnic diversity has characterized California from its early days—Chinese gold miners were approximately a fifth of all gold miners[4]—little is known about ethnic groups in *rural* California. Research on rural areas has tended to focus on the big ranchers and landowners in the early period and, in the twentieth century, on farming communities without significant ethnic minority populations.[5] Paul Taylor still stands virtually alone, his early work on Mexican immigrants unrivaled in its rich social material.[6]

There has been some attention paid to the role Asian immigrants played in California agriculture. Taylor and Vasey included census figures for Mexicans and "Orientals" in the state from 1850 through 1930, stating that "each of the principal Oriental groups . . . has played an important part in agriculture." They did not discuss European immigrants who played important roles in agriculture because "as a group they graduated to farm ownership or operation more rapidly than any Orientals except perhaps the Japanese, and because the greater rapidity of their assimilation has made their presence among the general population less noticeable. Upon the basis of these racially distinct groups, the intensive labor crops have been developed in the state.'"[7]

The implication that cheap Asian labor was a basic determinant of the structure of California agriculture was given scholarly substance by Taylor's graduate student Varden Fuller in his 1934 dissertation, "The Supply of Agricultural Labor as a Factor in the Evolution of Farm Organization in California," which has had an important influence on all later work on this topic.[8] Fuller hypothesized that among the several factors affecting the evolution of California's farm structure, a social factor, the degree of homogeneity in the agricultural population, was very significant. Discussing homogeneity in terms of the differential entrepreneurial ability of members of the farming population and their differential access to capital resources based on race and ethnicity, he argued that the more homogeneous the population, the more similar in size farms would be; the more heterogeneous the population, the more dissimilar in size farms would be. In effect, the availability of cheap Asian labor initiated and perpetuated the development of California's large-scale agribusiness.

In this manner, the popular stereotype of Asians as cheap labor gained scholarly credibility. After Fuller, studies of California agricultural or farmworker history characteristically include a review of the Asian groups that, one after another, allegedly provided the backbone of agribusiness. As Table 2 shows, first came the Chinese and, after their exclusion in 1882, the Japanese. After the Gentlemen's Agreement in 1907 barred Japanese laborers, the Koreans and Asian Indians (our "Hindus") came and worked in the fields. After the 1917 "Barred Zone" Immigration Act stopped almost all Asian immigration, Filipinos with their peculiar status as U.S. "nationals" (and, of course, Mexicans) could still come into the United States to provide agricultural labor. The fact that many farmworkers were Asian has always influenced interpretations of California's agricultural development; for example, the move to exclude the Chinese from California has been viewed as an idealistic one, meant to assist the establishment of small family farms by preventing a kind of slavery from taking root in the new state.[9] Carey McWilliams, and after him other scholars of farmworkers, theorized that the successive employment of Asian and Mexican farmworkers helps explain the development of a pattern of systematic exploitation of all farmworkers.[10]

In a "history" that treats the various Asian "others" as functionally equivalent to each other, the Punjabis have been portrayed as just another group of Asian agricultural laborers. But challenges to this simplistic picture have recently appeared in the form of detailed, complex studies of each of the major Asian immigrant groups involved in California agriculture.[11] These studies can be used to compare and contrast the groups and demonstrate that they often functioned differently in the evolving agricultural economy.

Chan shows the Chinese building levees, reclaiming the peat soil in the Sacramento–San Joaquin delta, and then leasing large acreages there to grow potatos and other crops. They went into truck gardening and orchards in other counties, working as owner–operators, large- and small-scale tenants, laborers, fruit and vegetable peddlers, commission mer-

Table 2. California Asian Population, 1850–1950

Group	1850	1860	1870	1880	1890	1900	1910	1920	1930	1940	1950
Chinese	660[a]	34,933	49,277	75,132	72,472	45,753	36,248	28,812	37,361	39,556	58,324
Japanese			33	86	1,147	10,151	41,356	71,952	97,456	93,717	84,956
East Indian					202[a]	263[a]	1,948	1,723	1,873	1,476	815
Korean							304	772	1,097	1,088	621
Filipino							5	2,674	30,470	31,408	40,424

Sources: Paul S. Taylor and Tom Vasey, "Historical Background of California Farm Labor," Rural Sociology 1 (1936): 291; H. Brett Melendy, Asians in America: Filipinos, Koreans, and East Indians (New York: Hippocrene Press, 1981), 250, 253, 256; U.S. Department of Commerce, Bureau of the Census, Seventeenth Census of the United States: Population, 1950, California (Washington, D.C.: Government Printing Office, 1952), vol. 2, pt. 5, p. 57.

[a]Indicated by foreign birthplace; no entry for race.

chants and farm cooks.[12] The Japanese worked first as contract laborers and then gained strong positions as tenants,[13] growing rice in northern California and oranges and lemons in southern California from about 1900 onward. They soon specialized in intensive cultivation, particularly of crops like strawberries, and they did so well that they inspired passage of California's Alien Land Law in 1913 and amendments to it in 1920 and 1921, which barred aliens ineligible for citizenship from leasing or owning agricultural land.[14] The Koreans and South Asians, coming in the first and second decades of the century, worked all over the state as laborers, lessors, and owners; they too helped cultivate rice in northern California.[15] Much of this new research shows the extent to which Asians began to ascend the agricultural ladder despite legal discrimination; this is part of the Punjabi story too. Punjabi laborers and farmers fit into California's regional economies at several levels, although they had to battle ethnic stereotypes to do so.

One community study of rural California clearly outlines the "agricultural ladder," the progression from farmworker to tenant to owner. Hatch argues persuasively that until the agricultural depression of the 1920s, men could establish themselves and move up those steps; the key elements needed to ascend the ladder in the early decades of statehood were energy, determination, and luck.[16] The community Hatch studied was small and without minorities, but others have shown that Asians working in California agriculture could do well despite the numerous obstacles placed in their way.[17] After 1920, however, two decades of adverse conditions changed the situation for all agriculturalists. Even though World War II brought renewed demand for agricultural products and a price surge, movement up the agricultural ladder became increasingly difficult. Handicapped in the early decades by legal constraints (see Chapter 3), the Punjabis and other Asians could not seize opportunities when they were relatively available.

After World War II, technological advances narrowed the range of opportunities for individuals trying to enter agriculture. More capital was required for fertilizer and for tractors and other machinery. The increasing scale of farming also required more capital to buy or lease land; that, and the rising value of land, made inheritance the key element in the agricultural ladder. From the 1940s, the surest way to get a farm was to inherit one; those who began working up from the bottom had little chance of becoming landowners.[18] Given this important change, inherit-

SACRAMENTO VALLEY

Yuba

Glenn Butte

Yolo Placer Sacramento

Sutter San Joaquin

Colusa

San Mateo

Santa Clara

SAN JOAQUIN VALLEY

Fresno

Tulare

Kings

San Bernardino

Los Angeles

Riverside

Orange

San Diego Imperial

IMPERIAL VALLEY

Map 1. California counties and major agricultural areas of Punjabi settlement

ance and persistence—the continuing operation of a farm by children or widows—became crucial factors in the retention of landowner status in rural California.

Established family life, then, was a necessary and significant part of landholding in rural California after World War II. Here, too, Asians were at a disadvantage. Too little is known about the family and community life of the Asian immigrants—for most of these groups, research on economic and political activities has taken precedence[19]—yet the differences among Asians in these less public areas were, if anything, even more striking. Because of the timing of the different migrations and the passage of discriminatory immigration laws, the groups had very different sex ratios, although all were short of women (see Table 3).

Taking the sex ratios into account along with California's laws against miscegenation, or marriage across racial lines,[20] most Asian immigrants

Table 3. Asian Immigrant Sex Ratios in California
(number of men per 100 women)

Year	Chinese	Japanese	Asian Indian	Korean	Filipino	Total Population
1850	[a]					1,228.6
1860	1,858.1					255.1
1870	1,172.3	312.5				165.4
1880	1,832.4	1,620.0				149.3
1890	2,245.4	933.3				137.6
1900	1,123.9	1,735.6				123.5
1910	1,017.0	562.8	[a]	[a]	[a]	125.4
1920	528.8	171.1	[a]	260.7	1,307.4	112.5
1930	298.6	137.6	1,572.3	167.6	1,551.5	107.6
1940	223.6	127.7	N.A.	N.A.	N.A.	103.7
1950	161.9	116.0	N.A.	N.A.	N.A.	100.1
1960	127.8					99.5
1970	107.0					96.9

Sources: Paul S. Taylor and Tom Vasey, "Historical Background of California Farm Labor," *Rural Sociology* 1 (1936): 291; and Lucy Cheng Hirata, "Free, Indentured, Enslaved: Chinese Prostitutes in Nineteenth-Century California," *Signs: Journal of Women in Culture and Society* 5 (1979): 5.
[a]Fewer than 30 women.

found it difficult to establish a family life. Very few were able to bring wives from their own countries or to marry women in California. The Chinese had come as "sojourners," intending to return to their wives and families. The few Chinese women who came to the United States in the early decades were predominantly prostitutes; thus families were not common.[21] The Japanese fared better in this regard than other Asians, since more came with wives or soon brought them from Japan through the "picture bride" system.[22] Some Koreans brought wives in the same way, since Korea came under Japanese rule after 1910, and Koreans were treated similarly by U.S. immigration officials.[23] Most of the Punjabis, like the Chinese before them, were married but came without their families. Because family networks proved an important resource in rural California, different family structures and inheritance practices go far to explain the differential persistence of Asian farmers in California agriculture.

The Punjab and Punjabi Immigrants

The 6,800 or so Indians who came to the western United States between 1899 and 1914[24] were chiefly peasants from India's Punjab province, men from martial castes and landowning families. They were portrayed as illiterate and backward. The man in charge of the 1909 federal Immigration Commission's investigation of the East Indian laborers along the Pacific Coast said that "the Hindus are regarded as the least desirable, or, better, the most undesirable, of all the eastern Asiatic races which have come to share our soil." Furthermore, "the assimilative qualities of the East Indians appear to be the lowest of those of any race in the West . . . between one-half and three-fifths of them are unable to read and write."[25] The 1920 report of the California State Board of Control reiterated the theme: "The Hindu is the most undesirable immigrant in the state. His lack of personal cleanliness, his low morals, and his blind adherence to theories and teachings, so entirely repugnant to American principles make him unfit for association with American people."[26] Here "Hindu" was opposed to "American," with the suggestion that association between the two, much less assimilation of one to the other, was unthinkable.

Despite the unfriendly reception they encountered, within a decade of their arrival the Punjabi peasants were contesting their placement at the bottom of the rural hierarchy. They often dealt with their new circumstances with skill and confidence; much of their success can be credited to their experience under British colonial rule in India.

The situation in the Punjab at the turn of the century had prepared these men well for their experiences in rural California. The Punjab was a frontier area, marking India's northwestern border and lying in the path of invading conquerors for centuries. British conquest had been comparatively late, with the hard-fought Sikh wars (1846 to 1848) ending in annexation of most of the Punjab; only a few semiautonomous princely states remained outside the British Empire. Railway and road links and irrigation canals were developed under British rule from the 1860s onward, after which irrigated agriculture did well. The Punjab was a very flat region, much of it watered by the five rivers that give the region its name (*panj ab*, "five waters") and by a network of canals dating from Mughal times.

The peasants of the Punjab quickly earned a special place in the eyes of the British for their military ability and the way they valued and worked their land. Despite its relatively recent subjugation, the Punjab "held for the Queen" when British rule in India was challenged by the Mutiny of 1857, earning gratitude and preferential recruitment for its martial castes into the British Indian military service as a result. Although the people of the Punjab shared a common language, Punjabi, they belonged to three major religions: Just over half the population of the Punjab province was Muslim, some 30 percent were Hindus, and about 15 percent were Sikhs.[27] Sikhs, who were to constitute a majority of the immigrants to the west coast of the United States, were adherents of a fifteenth-century religious reform movement that drew important elements from both Hinduism and Islam. Sikhism is monotheistic, stresses the equality of all men, and has a long history as a brotherhood of fighting men, first against the Mughals and then against the British. (Sometimes Sikhs also fought against each other.) Today Sikhism's claim to an identity distinct from Islam and Hinduism is well publicized, but at the turn of the century religious distinctions were far less important in the Punjab. Oberoi has argued compellingly that caste, kinship, and locality were more important elements of identity than religion there until the turn of the century. In particular, he has shown that Sikh–Hindu boundaries were fluid and that a separate Sikh community began to be constructed only in the late nineteenth century.[28]

I was not able to go to the Indian Punjab for the present research project.[29] Among the many descriptions I read of Punjabi peasant society, that provided by the anthropologist Joyce Pettigrew most sharply evokes California's Punjabi farmers, albeit somewhat stereotypically. She identifies the major values in Punjabi culture: courage, a willingness to take risks, a capacity to impose oneself on others, and an absence of any concept of defeat and submission. Personal power based on landownership even legitimated killing and violence.[30] The Jat caste was the dominant land-owning caste throughout the Punjab, a caste with members from all three religions. In this patrilineal, patriarchial society, a Jat man's dearest possession was his land, which he was committed to secure and enlarge. This was his chief preoccupation, and connected with it were his concerns to arrange marriages for his sisters and daughters and to develop influential contacts.[31]

More significance was attached to family and faction than to village, while the value system was based on honor, prestige, independence, and equality.[32] India's caste system, defined as a religiously justified hierarchical system based on principles of inequality, was largely overridden in the Punjab by the principle of equality, expressed through competitive, nonexclusive relationships with many kinds of people. Since the Sikh and Muslim religions uphold an ideology of equality rather than hierarchy, they worked against caste in the Punjab. Caste did have negative solidarity, in that people did not marry, eat with, or visit the homes of persons of certain castes; but it provided little solidarity in terms of political organization, no horizontal ties other than marriage networks.[33]

Adapting to the socioeconomic structure of the Punjab, the British revenue settlements of the 1850s recognized the actual cultivators as owners and taxpayers, institutionalizing a peasant proprietorship system different from the land revenue systems in the rest of India. The revenue settlement was made with peasants as members of the village community, with few or no intermediaries.[34] There was a tradition of rugged individualism, of man-to-man paternalistic rule. This tone was set by the Lawrence brothers, who founded the "Punjab school" of British Indian administration and greatly respected the Punjabi peasantry.[35] Incorporated by colonialism into the world economy as petty commodity producers by the early twentieth century, Punjabi peasant proprietors not only owned and controlled the means of production, they had developed markets for their commodities, with land, labor, and credit freely available by purchase or exchange. According to Fox, ascriptive allegiances did not hinder individualized market involvement.[36]

The central Punjab was the core region of agricultural production and the chief sending area for immigrants to the Pacific Coast. It consisted of both British-administered territory and princely states, but the regional divisions of indigenous significance derived from the rivers (see map). According to which side of the Beas and Sutlej rivers the districts lay, the three regions were termed Majha, Malwa, and Doaba. Inhabitants of each region had distinct reputations, and people tended to marry within their own region. When marriages took place across regions, the highest prestige was given to the Majhails or the Malwais—the point is contested.

These regions had differing ecologies, histories, and political economies. The Doaba was a foothills region, where peasant proprietors produced valuable crops on small plots, relying only on rainfall for watering their plants. In Majha and Malwa, peasant production depended on well irrigation, although there was also some canal irrigation. Patrilineages controlled land, and men and their sons farmed together. Indebtedness and insufficient land forced many cultivators in the Doaba and Malwa into military service and wage labor abroad—the joint household often benefited from sending one son overseas for work. Kessinger has described this development in his study of landholding lineages over time in Jullundur district.[37]

Migration to earn wages was not a new strategy in the Punjab. The emigrants to Canada and the United States were overwhelmingly from the Malwa and Doaba districts of the central Punjab.[38] In the Hoshiarpur district in the Doaba, an area inhabited largely by Sikh Jats, the average cultivated holding was no more than four or five acres. Small holdings were the result of the large population and of laws of inheritance prescribing equal shares for each son. The land was fragmented further by a division of the inheritance so that each son got equal shares of every kind of land, each with a different soil; thus a man's holdings were usually scattered, not contiguous.[39] Population density was greater, holdings were smaller, and fragmentation was worse in Jullundur, the other Doaba district that produced many emigrants. Ferozpur, in the Malwa region, was the most heavily indebted district in the Punjab in the 1920s, and many of California's immigrants came from there. Ferozpur was thought to be the district in which the most alcohol was consumed, the most money paid for brides, and the most money spent on litigation.[40]

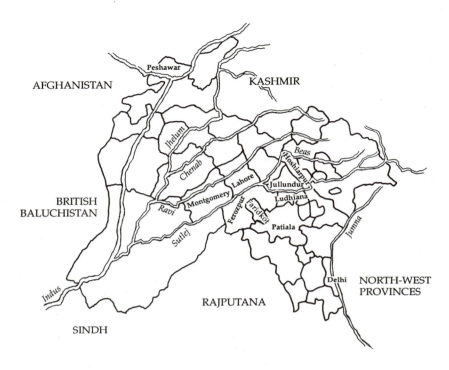

Map 2. Punjabi districts c. 1900. *Source:* Adapted from H. A. Rose, *Report on the Results of the Census of the Punjab, 1901* (Simla: Government of India, 1902), opposite p. 1.

In fact, all Punjabis were more prone to litigation, and litigation of a more serious nature, than Indians of other provinces. In 1922, a Civil Justice Committee Report noted that in proportion to the population, nearly twice as many suits were filed in the Punjab as in the United Provinces.[41] Punjabi cultivators, particularly the Jats of the central Punjab, also had a formidable reputation for pugnacity and dispute, as well as a predilection to violence.[42]

Military service had always been an honorable occupation for the Punjab's rural cultivators, and increased rural debt made it even more attractive. Men from the central Punjab sought military service as well as wage labor abroad. At the outbreak of World War I, more than 65 percent of Indian combat troops (100,000 of 152,496) came from the Punjab. By 1917, Punjab enlistments accounted for almost 50 percent (117,000 of 254,000) of the men recruited in India. Military service seems to have been most important in the central Punjab, and Sikhs enlisted far beyond their proportion in the province.[43]

The motives behind migration to Canada and the United States were primarily population pressure, subdivision of land, and rural debt. To these, McLeod adds a quest for status and adventure.[44] In the central Punjab by the 1920s, the flow of cash and export crops was well developed. Yet it was the areas of highest productivity that were most affected by heavy debts. There was migration within the Punjab to the new "canal colonies" in Lyallpur and other regions to the west, where major irrigation works had been constructed after 1900 by the British colonial government. These colonies were opened to productive agriculture, and they were worked by smallholders and their families much as in the central Punjab. In fact, many of the cultivators brought into the canal colonies were from the central Punjab. These peasant proprietors were mostly Jats, with some Arains, or gardeners; many Chuhras, or Untouchables, worked as laborers. The new canal colonies offered larger agricultural holdings than in the older areas. In Jullundur and Hoshiarpur, holdings averaged under 5 acres, but in the canal colonies they were 12.5 acres or larger.[45]

Punjabis preferred overseas emigration to migration to the canal colonies. Emigration was thought of as a temporary expedient, beneficial to the joint family, and at least in Jullundur district, emigration to the United States in particular was viewed favorably. It was thought that most of the emigrant men returned to India.[46] A 1916 source reported that men who earned 16 cents a day in India could earn $2 a day in the United States.[47] An emigrant from the Punjab to the United States who had returned to his village asserted in the late 1920s that in America a man could do as he pleased; there was plenty of land and plenty of money. In India, he said, one could not borrow, as no one would advance him money. This man and others in the Hoshiarpur district reported that moving to the new canal colonies in the Punjab was not as good an alternative because it took so much capital to buy land there and money could not be borrowed easily.[48]

Most of the men who migrated to Canada and the United States from the central Punjab were from the so-called martial "races" and from landowning castes. Although to other Americans these men were known collectively as "Hindus," almost none of them were *actually* Hindus. Perhaps 85 to 90 percent of them were Sikhs, and another 10 percent were Muslims, both members of monotheistic religions committed to the equality of all believers. Real Hindus, representatives of India's dominant religion with its many gods and caste system, were very few.[49] Within these religious groupings, there were further divisions according to caste or region of origin. Almost all the Sikhs were Jats, although there were also a few Chuhras (Untouchables). Among Muslims, there were Rajputs, Arains (gardeners), and even some Pathans (Pushtu or Pakhtun speakers from the northwest frontier and Afghanistan). The Hindus were Brahmans and Khatris from predominantly urban areas of the Punjab.

A significant proportion of the pre-1914 immigrants had served in the British military and police and had seen service overseas, in China, Southeast Asia, East Africa, Lebanon, and other places.[50] Even before their deployment in China in the Boxer Rebellion in 1900, Punjabi soldiers had served in China's treaty ports. Sikh platoons were stationed in Hong Kong, and a *gurdwara* (Sikh temple or church) was built there in 1910.[51] Punjabis serving overseas learned about the opportunities in the western United States. Steamships linked Hong Kong to the Philippine Islands and Canada, California, and Mexico. Men sailed from Calcutta to Hong Kong, a trip of about twelve days, and then boarded another ship to Canada or the United States. The latter journey took eighteen or nineteen days. One estimate put the cost of the entire trip from India to Canada at 300 rupees, an amount within reach by borrowing from relatives, pawning ornaments, or mortgaging land. Passengers got rations and did their own cooking, usually forming large groups to do so.[52]

Most men came on their own. Mazumdar has emphasized contract-labor recruitment as the cause of immigration to Canada and the United States, but I found only two accounts of such recruitment.[53] More typical was the background given by a Sikh immigrant to Canada, a Sergeant Singh, who produced a book of references from British army officers in India, merchants in Australia, and bankers in Hong Kong.[54] Another man, interviewed in Venice, California, in 1924, said: "I was born in the Punjab district of India and served on the police force in Hong Kong, China, for some years. While I was in China several Hindus returned and reported on the ease with which they could make money in America and so I decided to go."[55] One California Punjabi in his eighties named six relatives who had served in China and made trips to British Columbia and/or California from there, finally inspiring him and his father to follow them. Another man told me he had lost his mother at age fourteen and at eighteen had joined his brother in Shanghai; the brother was a policeman there, and the younger brother worked as a watchman before coming to the United States. Two more men went to stay with uncles in Shanghai (a policeman and a watchman), then came to the United States seeking better opportunities. Yet another, after two years in a Sikh regiment in India, followed older men from his village to Hong Kong, Vancouver, and the United States.[56]

The United States attracted the Punjabi men after Canada began tightening admission requirements.[57] As Punjabi immigration increased, prejudice was aroused, and it became more difficult for Punjabis to gain admittance to the United States. There was a rising rejection rate of Asian Indian applicants by the Bureau of Immigration and Naturalization. Before 1907, fewer than 10 percent of applicants for admission were rejected; in 1907, 28 percent were rejected; and in 1909, 1911, and 1913, 50 percent or more were rejected. A contemporary observer pointed to the immigration figures and remarked that "either a large percentage of those who applied for admission were unfit, or that the interpretation of the law was severe." He suspected both.[58]

Nonetheless, the Punjabi men continued to come. One strategy was to get admitted to the Philippines, then a U.S. possession, and subsequently enter the mainland legally from there. In 1913, a federal judge ruled that men who had been admitted to the Philippines could be detained and deported, rather than legally admitted to the United States.[59] This decision and restrictive practices effectively brought legal immigration to an end by 19ṛ4. The Immigration Act of 1917 was the final blow, with its "barred Asiatic zone" and literacy provisions.[60]

The difficulties Punjabis had with immigration produced bitter memories. One man stated in a rare early interview:

> I should like to return to India to secure a position in the immigration office so that I might treat some Americans as they have treated me. I have applied for American citizenship but this has been denied me. Were I in the immigration service in India, when an American would apply for entry I would refer him to his Consul, and that would be of no avail. He would then have to apply to Washington and even to London but it would avail him nothing.[61]

(Some of us, scholars who have survived the political turnings and twistings of U.S.–Indian relations and have gone through the application process for research visas from the government of India many times, think that this man has had his revenge!)

Asians in the California Landscape

In their first years in California, most Punjabis moved around the state in small groups, working on railroads, in lumbering, and in agriculture. A group of Muslims sold tamales and popcorn in San Francisco, but most of the men lived and worked in rural areas. They moved in groups, with a "boss man" who spoke English best and contracted for jobs on behalf of the group. They first found work in the orchards, vineyards, and sugar-beet fields around Marysville, Newcastle, and the Vaca Valley. Then they started working in vineyards in Fresno and citrus groves in Tulare, and finally, following the annual sequence of harvests, they picked cantaloupes in the Imperial Valley.[62] Old-timers recall stints of wood chopping in Oroville, piling and loading pinto beans along the Sacramento River, cutting asparagus in Stockton, digging potatoes in Alton, picking grapes in Fresno, and digging stones out of fields in Claremont.[63]

The Punjabis in California retained contacts with those settling in Canada and in the state of Washington.[64] Some moved from California to Texas, Arizona, New Mexico, Utah, and Colorado. Agricultural developments were the key to these moves. Rocky Ford, Colorado, for example, was at that time an important point for the sale of seeds and distribution of agricultural technology. Japanese farmers tried growing melons there in 1903. One Santa Singh is said to have grown cantaloupes for seed in Rocky Ford and distributed the product in California; he also owned a hotel there. Punjabis helped develop cotton in Canutillo, Texas, although their major efforts in cotton cultivation took place in California's Imperial Valley.[65] The Imperial Valley was one of the earliest areas of settlement for Punjabis in California, and it was there that the first Punjabi-Mexican marriages took place.

Racial and ethnic discrimination led to the settlement of Asians in the "foreign sections" of California's cities and towns. In Fresno in 1918, the Japanese lived behind Chinatown and kept roominghouses in which Hindus and other migratory farm laborers stayed. The Sacramento representative on the State Commission of Immigration and Housing observed in about 1919 that the Hindus usually patronized Japanese rooming-houses and restaurants. The Punjabi boardinghouses in Marysville were in the heart of Chinatown, next to the Bok Kai temple on the Feather River levee. In Brawley and El Centro in the Imperial Valley, Punjabis shared the foreign sections with other Asians and Mexicans.[66] A few men, "Hindu store men," owned groceries, bars, and boardinghouses in these sections and served as contacts for the men when they came to or through town. In Los Angeles, Punjabi pioneers owned land in the city as early as 1913; most men in Los Angeles resided in the vicinity of Little Tokyo and worked at a variety of occupations before 1918, as peddlers, interpreters, elevator operators, butlers, and "photoplayers" (actors).[67]

The Punjabis quickly gained distinct reputations, although these varied wildly according to region and speaker. Racial and ethnic groups almost always were compared with each other, particularly by employers of agricultural workers. In Sanger, the Hindus might be "the best of all classes of labor," while "the Armenians are the curse of the valley" and "white labor . . . is generally rotten." But in Colusa, the Hindus "have been generally disliked," while "the Japanese . . . are more generally liked." Similar fluctuating opinions were reported of the Japanese and many other groups, opinions highly dependent on local demographic configurations.[68]

Fragmentary sources give some insight into how the Asian immigrants saw themselves in the new land. In *Ayumi No Ato* ("Traces of a Journey"), Shiro Fujioka wrote about the Japanese in places he knew about in the early twentieth century. There are no historical narratives left by Punjabis, but interviews and later accounts can be used to reconstruct early impressions. While specific conditions of climate, soil, and topography in the new settings did not strongly resemble those in the agrarian regions of Japan or India from which they came, the immigrants' representations of their new homes stressed similarities and resemblances to their homelands.

Fujioka likened the leading early Japanese farmers of the 1920s in the Imperial Valley to rival Chinese kings in ancient times;[69] his account did not refer at all to the non-Japanese who controlled the political economy.[70] He imposed an Asian political geography on the Imperial Valley, with its three regions compared to the historical three kingdoms of China following the decline of the Han dynasty in the third century A.D.[71] The leading Japanese farmer in each region was termed a king, reigning over his own territory and contending with the others. The Imperial Valley was represented in this text in a way that made it familiar, beloved, and Asian—peopled by warlords, powerful Japanese to whom others owed allegiance. This helped create a collective identity and an attachment to the new land.

Like the Japanese, the Punjabis imposed familiar landscapes on the California countryside. Punjabi accounts come from two time periods. We have only one written account by an early Punjabi immigrant that comments on the California landscape, an account by Puna Singh, who moved to northern California from Utah in 1924. Here, too, Asian farmers had helped develop new crops: Chinese, Japanese, Koreans, and Punjabis cultivated rice in the Gridley–Colusa area after 1911. Agriculture had been established longer in the Sacramento Valley than in the Imperial Valley, but the socioeconomic structure was similar: Anglo growers, shippers, and bankers dominated, and Asian farm laborers had a hard time breaking in.

Puna Singh spoke of his first impressions: "On arriving in the Sacramento Valley, one could not help but be reminded of the Punjab. Fertile fields stretched across the flat valley to the foothills lying far in the distance. Most of the jobs available were agricultural and I found many Punjabis already working throughout the area."[72]

Descendants of the Punjabi immigrants who came in the first and second decades of this century made similar statements, telling me that their fathers and other old-timers claimed that the Imperial Valley or the San Joaquin Valley or the Sacramento Valley was "like the Punjab." The fields, the crops, the early farming methods, were all "just like the Punjab."[73]

The same emphasis on similarities appears in fuller written accounts from later Punjabi immigrants. One man who joined the older immigrant community in the Yuba City–Marysville region in northern California wrote about the "Land of Five Rivers" in an elaborate evocation of the Sacramento Valley as the Punjabi homeland. His title explicitly bestowed the name of the homeland on the new environment. He described Punjabis making a living there, mentioned the state capital, and relocated sacred landmarks, both Sikh and Hindu, in California, explaining his story thus:

> Almost all the details . . . match the description of the city of Rupar, in the Punjab. However, the name of the city I tried to describe, was Yuba City. . . . I should not have been so poetic. I left too much to the imagination of the reader. . . .
>
> In my story the Land of Five Rivers was Sacramento Valley. The river Sutlej was Feather River. The rest of the four rivers—American, Bear, Yuba, and Sacramento. My Bhakhra (Dam), the Oroville Dam. My Govind Sagar, the Oroville Lake. The city of Anandpur Sahib, the nearby town of Paradise. The Shivaliks, the Sierra foothills. There was Naina Devi, our Mount Shasta. And yes, the Jawalamukhi, the Lassen Volcanic Park. Obviously, I was carried away by my imagination. Yet, the reality was not left far behind. The water, like the water in the Punjab, had the same urge to run downward. The distant hills had the same charm. The fire in Jawalamukhi and in the Lassen Volcano has the same way to burn things![74]

Framing the new landscape in familiar images appears to have been a significant adaptive strategy for both Japanese and Punjabis. For both, Asian men were part of the landscape. The land was not unpeopled, it was being farmed by countrymen. Curiously, given that both Asian groups began as agricultural laborers and were deprived of citizenship and political power, in these accounts there were no other actors. Japanese and Punjabi farmers were depicted as kings and landowners in the Imperial Valley and the Sacramento Valley, with kingdoms and capital cities of their own. The white men who blocked them in reality had magically disappeared from the scene.

If one believes, with Comaroff,[75] that collective social identity entails some form of self-definition founded on a marked opposition between "we" and "others," it is striking that the immigrants in these written accounts situated themselves alone and in charge of the physical landscape. The Punjabis were cosmopolitan if not well educated, and they had undertaken their migrations very deliberately, so it is likely that when they and the Japanese thought of themselves as rulers on the land, they were denying not so much their own migration but the imposition of racial stereotypes that portrayed Asians as powerless workers in California agriculture.

3 Early Days in the Imperial Valley

The origins of the Punjabi-Mexican community lie in the Imperial Valley along California's southern border. Men from India's Punjab province stood out from the start among the pioneers who flocked there to work the newly arable land. Their fortunes, their legal status, and local opinion of them varied over the years. At first, South Asians could obtain American citizenship, but later they lost that right. Then not only the physical landscape but the political landscape and their place in it struck the Punjabi men as decidedly similar to their status in British India. They fought hard for their rightful place in society, and particularly for a place on the land, a very important component of Punjabi identity. The Imperial Valley was being transformed from a barren desert to a major center of agricultural production in California at the time the Punjabis arrived; the pioneer Anglo settlers there did not easily accept the Punjabis' claims to membership in the community they were building. Legal constraints and social stereotypes based on race and national origin helped determine the opportunities and working conditions the Punjabis encountered as they worked alongside others to develop the valley.

Settlement of the Imperial Valley

Turning the desert along the Mexican border east of San Diego into a fertile valley was made possible by diverting water from the Colorado River, an engineering feat first attempted in 1901. Attempts to close the break in the Colorado River finally succeeded in 1907, and Imperial County was officially marked off from San Diego County in the same year. The successful inauguration of the Imperial Irrigation District, the largest irrigation project in the United States (and the western hemisphere), followed in 1911; it covered 584,700 acres. Taming the waters was an engineering triumph, an achievement romanticized in Harold Bell Wright's 1911 novel, *The Winning of Barbara Worth*. The novel captured the adventurous spirit of the time, the robust combination of eastern money, engineering technology, and western frontier values. By 1919 there were six towns in the Imperial Valley with populations ranging from 1,000 to 7,000, where nine newspapers were being published. A local newspaper estimated the county population in that year to be 63,000, with 40,000 living outside the towns. (According to the census of 1920 this total was one-third too high.)[1]

The transportation system in the valley initially was oriented east and west, from Arizona to the California coast. Imperial Valley towns had good rail connections with San Diego and Yuma. After 1913, there were sections of plank road over the shifting sand dunes to Yuma, which were improved in 1916 and replaced by an oil-surfaced road in 1924.[2] North–south routes developed more slowly. Back in 1907, the first drive from Long Beach to Brawley took three days crossing the desert from Banning to Imperial Junction! Eventually, Highway 99 connected Calexico to Los Angeles, and a state highway went up the east side of the Salton Sea as well (see map). But the valley's early orientation was toward El Paso and the Texas border. When the telephone system was inaugurated, the first telephone call—which made the front page of all the valley papers—was from El Paso to El Centro, on June 20, 1911.[3]

The building of the American hemisphere's largest irrigation system drew ambitious men from all over the world. Asians were among the first to arrive: In 1901, the first and only house in the new town of Imperial was a tent hotel run by "a Chinaman."[4] Men of many nationalities came to work in the valley, but those who controlled it were white and English speaking. Among the first laborers, Cocopah Indians were prominent. Mexicans began moving across the border in 1910, while blacks were recruited from the South as cotton pickers. The 1920 census counted 43,453 people in the county, with many racial and ethnic groups represented. Mexicans (6,414), Japanese (1,986), and blacks (1,648) were especially numerous, constituting 14.7, 4.5, and 3.8 percent of the population respectively. They were followed by English-speaking Canadians (372), Swiss (245), Germans (237), English (193), Greeks (146), Italians (133), Irish

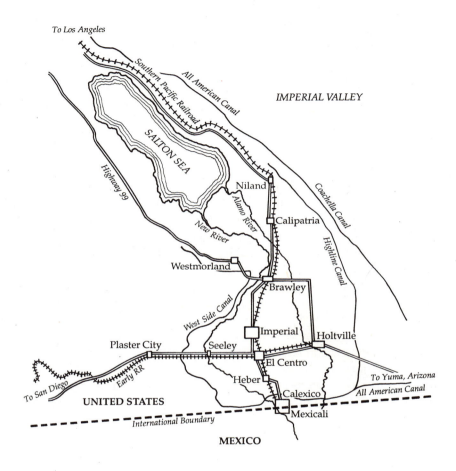

Map 3. Imperial Valley. *Source:* Adapted from Adon Poli, *Land Ownership and Operating Tenure in Imperial Valley, California* (Berkeley: U.S. Bureau of Agricultural Economics, 1942), and recent road maps.

(119), and Portuguese (99).[5] People from India were not counted separately in the 1920 census, but a count done by an educated Indian in
about that year put their number at 268, slightly more numerous than the
Swiss.[6]

Initially there was some ethnic specialization in farming. The Japanese
farmers specialized in brush-covered cantaloupes, tomatoes, and squash;
the Swiss opened dairies. "In Imperial Valley you could rent land and
buy cows on credit, the only qualification being was that you were a
Swiss." While there were a few Chinese on the American side of the
border, larger numbers of them were employed by the Sherman-
Chandler Corporation across the border in Mexico in the Mexicali Valley.[7]
The Punjabis made their first appearance as farm laborers in 1909 and
1910—the names of some Punjabis are unmistakable (although misspelled) in the 1910 *U.S. Census of Population.*

There were few women in the Imperial Valley in the early years. The
1910 census gives a sex ratio in the new county of almost 2 to 1: There
were 8,900 males and 4,691 females. By 1920 the population was 40 percent female, with greater imbalances among the immigrant groups. The
foreign-born whites (72 percent of them born in Mexico) were 37 percent
female and the Japanese were 28 percent female, while the American
blacks were 43 percent female. There were no women from India resident
there, and only 2 of the 88 Chinese residents were female.[8]

Many men came on their own and then went back for brides or sent for
them. The Swiss got "mail order brides" and the Japanese got "picture
brides." A vivid description of the arrival of the first Japanese woman in
the valley stresses the loneliness of the men there.[9]

> When the talk got around that Mr. Masanori Moriyama, the father
> of melon growers decided to take a wife from his native land after
> he made a fortune, the bachelors became excited. Because in those
> days there was not a single married man, so it was all bachelors'
> households. Cooking, washing and even mending were done by
> bachelors. Of course, for cooking, the dumpling soup or hot cakes
> were about the best they could cook. As for washing, they just
> rinsed the clothes with water. They mended the shirts, pants and
> socks with clumsy hands.
>
> Then the day came for Mr. Moriyama's bride to arrive. About 200
> farmers who heard this abandoned their spades and hoes and

rushed to the station and waited anxiously for the train to arrive. She was the first Japanese woman they would see since they came to America, so it was no wonder the expression in their eyes changed. Finally the train arrived, and the bride got off the train. The groom, who had been waiting hurriedly put his new bride on the buggy; sitting on the driver's seat he whipped the horse once, and the horse started trotting. At that moment a cry of "banzai" rose. Both the horse and the driver were surprised by the roar and speeded the pace. The delirious crowd did not wake up from their dreams easily, and they ran after the buggy.

When Mr. Moriyama saw this sight, he could not help having fear in his heart. Maybe because of this he taught his bride how to ride a horse first. The reason was because he believed that it was the only way to escape from danger in case a bunch of bachelors stormed their house. It is said that Mr. Moriyama had a shotgun ready in his bedroom every night. You may be able to imagine the warlike sight of the pioneer days.

Pioneer Anglo women set up the first library and began the school system in the valley. Most of these women shared fully in the hard work. One wife, indeed, "rode horseback and looked after 75 Chinese, thus saving the expense of a foreman." Accounts by the early Swiss women stress the difficulties posed by the hot climate, living in tents or dirt-floored shelters, the lack of ice, electricity, or running water, and the suspenseful fording of irrigation ditches in horse and buggy.[10]

Life was hard for the pioneers in the reclaimed desert. The daughter of a Belgian dairy farmer recalled that her mother married in Belgium in March 1912 and saw the Statue of Liberty on April 12, 1912. She had her first baby April 12, 1913, her second in 1914, twins in 1915, her fifth in 1916, and her sixth in 1917 (six babies in four years). The family lived in a home without running water but with its own electric generator. Another early resident, manager of a bank in Brawley from 1917 onward, first entered the valley at the age of thirteen, when his father sent him (instead of the employee who was to have taken them, who turned up drunk) with a trainload of cows from El Paso to El Centro. His dad gave him $1 for food on the three-day trip, and he drank milk from the cows en route.[11]

More settlers came, towns developed, and along with the towns came county government. Imperial became the first headquarters of the Imperial Irrigation District (which had been formed in 1911 and bought out all the other water companies by 1922), but the placement of the railroad gave El Centro the edge for the county seat. The county clerk and recorder presided over the land records, civil and criminal case records, and vital statistics in a striking courthouse with handsome burnished copper doors. The county sheriff's office and the jail were located nearby. Banks, dealers in cars and farming equipment, and stores selling farm supplies, groceries, and clothing proliferated.

With racial and ethnic diversity came segregation and discrimination based on both race and class. Like many other farmers, the Punjabis lived along the country roads and canals and came into town primarily for business or recreation. But they were not free to go where they wished, since prejudice resulted in segregated restaurants and hotels in Imperial Valley towns. A cattle rancher recounted incidents during the early 1910s: A Cahuilla Indian was refused a meal in a Brawley restaurant and a "colored" cowboy met critical comments from other guests in a roominghouse in Imperial, although "the old Chinese restaurant on Main Street was a reliable and hospitable place."[12] The towns in the valley developed "foreign sections" on the east side of the railroad tracks. One Punjabi old-timer explained, "There was discrimination then, in El Centro the same, even water; nobody served you. So the Mexicans, the Japanese, the China people opened places and served everybody."[13] Punjabis also owned bars in the foreign sections of Brawley and El Centro, and law-and-order enforcement was lax in those sections. A defense attorney for one Bishen Singh, charged with attacking Amar Singh with an ax in Brawley, alleged that Amar Singh provoked the attack by saying, "Before we were in town and now we're in Mexican town, so let's fight." Landmarks in the court case included the Chinese store and the Filipino Hotel.[14]

As families settled in the valley, the local school systems reflected the racial, ethnic, and class divisions, with separate schools serving the various sections of towns.[15] Only Holtville remained small and homogeneous enough to avoid this kind of segregation—few Mexicans, Japanese, or blacks settled there. Despite what outsiders perceived as short distances and similarities between them, the towns developed distinctively, and local residents tended to know only people from their own town.

Crops, Credit, and Land Use

The early days of Imperial Valley agriculture provided opportunities to many newcomers. Even small farmers without much capital could grow crops familiar to them from previous experience. Homesteaders could file for a maximum of two quarter-sections, or 320 acres.[16] Important early crops were alfalfa, barley, and cotton. The first cotton bales were ginned in the valley in 1909. Cotton cultivation took off spectacularly after 1913, when 20,000 acres produced 22,000 bales. In 1914, 50,000 acres produced 68,000 bales. By that year, too, there were sixteen modern cotton gins, three oil mills, and two cotton compressors. In 1918 there were twenty-two cotton gins, and in 1920, 126,081 acres were planted to cotton.[17]

Crops changed over the decades as new crops were tried. Most were field or garden crops; few permanent crops, such as citrus, were planted. Although alfalfa and barley were always of major importance, cotton had the largest acreage in 1920, and lettuce became the most important truck crop; it had the third largest acreage in 1930. Large acreages in the northern part of the valley were mainly in field crops such as alfalfa, barley, and cotton; large acreages in the southern part produced lettuce and cantaloupes. Cotton was risky because of fluctuations in the world market and its susceptibility to pests, and lettuce was risky because of the costly investment and the importance of "hitting the [eastern] market" when the price was right. Punjabi farmers were among the first to grow these risky but profitable crops.[18]

The transition from grain crops planted and harvested with work animals to cash crops grown with tractors and specialized irrigation equipment, fertilizers, and pesticides took place fairly rapidly. Individual and corporate landholdings became larger by the decade, a trend that escalated after 1940.[19] The specialized equipment owned by corporations and large individual landholders was rented out or used to do custom work for smaller tenants and owner–cultivators.

The agricultural industry quickly became dominated by big growers, shippers (shipping companies), and bankers. Small farmers were at a disadvantage, since they had no power to set the price. The timing of the harvest could not be controlled; when harvested, the crop had to be sold and shipped within a very short time. Shipping costs and the price the produce would bring at its destination could not be predicted. Only labor costs could be partially controlled by the farmer. Given this situation, access to labor and access to credit were crucial to farmers.

The Pacific Coast states relied more heavily on banks for agricultural capital than did other states throughout the decades of the 1910s and 1920s, and in the Imperial Valley small independent banks were a major source of credit.[20] Locally owned by people in the valley communities, such banks as the Holtville Bank and the Farmers and Merchants Bank of Brawley were run by bankers who knew the farmers well after a season or two, bankers who could set their own lending policies.

In addition to the crucial relationship with local bankers, farmers formed relationships with shippers from whom they could sometimes secure advances. Forward contracting, or "deals," was common, providing growers an assured market for their produce and ensuring shippers of a predictable supply of produce at harvest season. There were several kinds of contracts. In the early days, crops were sold on consignment. A shipper took produce on consignment to brokers in the East, leaving the farmer without any ability to set the price. The market rate for the crop could go down in the eight to ten days it took to arrive at its destination, and the loss was passed on to the farmer. The shipper was less vulnerable, since he subtracted his costs and packing fees (set beforehand at a fixed rate usually guided by the previous year's experience) before settling with the farmer. Any profit was split between the farmer and shipper according to a preseason agreement, usually 75–25 or 50–50. Here the farmers took the greater risk, but the shipper was also at the mercy of the eastern markets.

After the 1930 enactment of the Perishable Agricultural Commodities Act, a system of cash for sales at the time of shipping was initiated. Called F.O.B., or "free on board," this system allowed the farmer to negotiate a cash price when he delivered his produce to the shipper. The farmer still had to wait for his cash until the produce was sold in the East, but he would get the price agreed upon at the time of shipping. This kind of open-price contract accompanied by a minimum guarantee provision transferred some of the grower's risk to the shipper. Preharvest installment payments gave growers a primary source of operating capital, and the exact price was negotiated at the end of the season. Since the risks were greater in vegetable production than in field crops, commercial lending agencies preferred to channel credit through well-established shippers, who extended capital to growers by advances on contracts.[21]

Farm tenancy was a major form of land tenure in the valley. From 1910 to 1920, the proportion of tenant-operated farms and farm acreage increased sharply. In the mid 1920s some 60–70 percent of the land was owned by absentee landlords.[22] In 1936, tenants operated 53 percent of the farms and 47 percent of the farm acreage, while an additional 15 percent of farmland was leased by part-owners. Most leases were cash leases. In 1930, almost 70 percent of the tenant operators cash-leased 52 percent of the rented farmland, with the rest leased on share or cash-share rent basis. Nonresident private-individual owners leased the largest proportion of their land to tenants, with nonresident corporate owners leasing out the next largest proportion. It was more profitable for an absentee owner to rent his land to a garden crop grower because the rents were higher. Also, some farmers invested their capital in operating equipment rather than in land, so by leasing they could farm extensive acreages and use their entrepreneurial ability. Tenancy in the Imperial Valley was associated with undesirable features: It meant an unstable, highly speculative, specialized type of farming with high seasonal labor requirements. Tenancy also could mean insecurity and instability of land occupancy and ownership; most large companies leased for only three years at a time.[23]

Thus the Punjabi men entered a rapidly developing, highly competitive agricultural economy, one that would become a major if not the major producing region in California.[24] They entered it early and they settled down, although they were subjected to both social and legal constraints as they took up farming.

Unwelcome Immigrants

The Imperial Valley attracted Punjabi immigrants, but they were not welcomed. Early accounts about the arrival of Punjabis were apprehensive. In 1910, there was a "threatened importation of Hindus to pick cotton," when a company allegedly planned to bring in 500 "Hindus" from the north and several hundred Arizona Indians, in order to lower prices below $1.25 per 100 pounds.[25] In the same year, the *Holtville Tribune* printed a critical article on "the Hindu and his habits and why he should be prohibited at once from landing in California." Noting that a few Hindus had appeared on the street of Holtville, the writer opined that "cotton picking time is attracting a doubtful looking bunch of all shades and kinds," people who threatened the "college-bred population, its culture and refinement."[26]

After 1913, admission through legal channels was difficult, but men from India continued to arrive. One group of fifty-six "Asiatics" was lost in the desert between San Felipe, Mexico, and Mexicali in 1915. The party consisted of twenty Japanese, three Chinese, and thirty-three Punjabis; two of the latter reached their destination and a rescue by the Mexican governor was attempted, but only thirty of the fifty-six survived.[27] Then an "underground route for entrance of Hindus into the United States from Lower California" was discovered, and immigration officers paid close attention to natives from India in an effort to rid the valley of them.[28] In late 1914, the militant Ghadar party (of which more in Chapter 5) convened a political meeting in the valley, featuring a speaker from San Francisco who urged the men to return to India and fight the British. This resulted in the departure of some thirty Punjabis via the Picwick stage line to San Diego and thence by steamer to India, a departure noted with approval.[29] Following that, one Rulie Ram was arrested, "the ringleader of the plot to get Hindus into the United States from Mexico . . . one of the most famous fakirs in the Bengal district"; this stopped the "threatened invasion of Hindu undesirables."[30]

Imperial Valley residents, like others in California and the rest of the United States, showed an interest in the new immigration bill proposed in 1916. Earlier immigration restrictions had been forthrightly based on race (the 1882 Chinese Exclusion Act) or national origin (the 1907 Gentlemen's Agreement with Japan), but this bill correlated physical with cultural distance and expressly denied entry to immigrants from areas west of the 110th and east of the 50th meridian (Asia). Literacy tests were also included, but the Asiatic exclusion provisions would "especially bar Hindus," according to the local press. The bill passed as the 1917 Immigration Law; it was popularly known as the "Barred Zone" legislation.[31]

Despite the U.S. restrictions on immigration, Punjabis continued to come to the valley. By 1918, the press worried that they were becoming "a menace to the whole valley" for a new reason: The Hindu was "no longer a day laborer. He has quickly attained the point where he is only willing to farm [for] himself, and his low standard of living makes it impossible for the American to compete with him."[32] Also,

> according to a report received at the El Centro Bureau Tuesday, fifteen hundred Hindu and Mohammed farmers are headed for Im-

perial Valley with the purpose of buying and leasing land for farming. . . . Officials are trying to verify the report . . . the Hindus are
well supplied with funds, ranging from three thousand to five thousand in cash. The report is not being very well received. . . .
Farmers are very displeased . . . a British syndicate is backing the
plan. . . . At the present time . . . no Hindus own land . . . but about
75 leases for more than a year are recorded. The matter of the Hindu
invasion is causing some concern to the Sheriff's office, as considerable trouble has been caused, it is said, by these people already in
the valley.[33]

This represented a significant shift in local perceptions of the Punjabis.
Indeed, power relationships in the valley had changed markedly by the
1920s. The secretary of the El Centro Chamber of Commerce spoke for
Anglo farmers: "We need the labor of the Mexicans. They are not like the
Japs and Hindus. They don't come to stay. They are satisfied to labor."[34]
Certainly the Punjabis had moved quickly from their initial role as laborers. Almost immediately after they arrived, they appeared in a variety
of local records. Enumerated in the 1910 census as laborers, they began
sending foreign money orders from the Holtville post office between 1909
and 1913; they were listed as "ranchers" in local directories; and they
became telephone subscribers.

The 1910 manuscript census for Imperial County contains eighteen Punjabi names, many badly misspelled. These misspellings and the frequent
misrecording of their language as "Persian" or "Hindu" show the census
taker's unfamiliarity with the new group. Six of the seven households in
which Punjabis resided were in El Centro, four of them on Commercial
Avenue.[35] The seventh was in Holtville, where three Punjabi farm laborers lodged with an American family and one American lodger. Of the
eighteen men from India, two had come to the United States in 1903, the
rest between 1906 and 1910. Eight men can be identified as Muslims, four
as Hindus, and four as Sikhs; two, "Sende" and "Joe Bullard,"[36] remain
mysterious. All were farm laborers. Only three spoke English, and only
three were able to read and write (in any language, apparently). Only
two were listed as married. Their ages ranged from seventeen to fifty-
five, and they all lived in rented quarters, three alone and the rest in
groups ranging from two to eight. All lived with other Punjabis, with the
exception of the Holtville lodgers and another five men, who resided
with three Japanese laborers.[37]

Only two early post office books survive in the Imperial Valley, for Holtville, where Punjabis were growing cotton. Seven Punjabi names appear among the Swiss and English senders of foreign money orders. Foreign money orders were few in number (Mexico was not treated as a foreign country in these post office books), and Punjabis sent one-fourth of them from January 1909 to November 1910 and more than a tenth of them from July 1912 to December 1913. Frequently theirs were the largest money orders on a page. They sent money not only to India but also to Glasgow, Scotland, and Shanghai, China, reflecting the British imperial network. Within California, they sent money orders to Berkeley, Stockton, and Fowler, other early centers of Punjabi settlement.[38]

These early sources show that the Punjabi men were making enough money in agriculture to send large amounts back to India or elsewhere. They were recent arrivals, but one man (listed as illiterate by the census taker) had taken out papers for naturalization,[39] an indication that the Punjabis were moving into the local system.

In other parts of California, Punjabi men stayed in labor camps or roominghouses; in the Imperial Valley, they began to settle down. They lived on the land they were farming, typically in households of two to four persons, in wooden shacks. Better housing usually was not available to them or even desired, since many leased different acreage from year to year. Sometimes temporary workers stayed for short periods of employment with more prosperous Punjabi farmers, rather than stay in barracks.

Punjabi names first appeared in Imperial County records and directories in 1912.[40] The men's occupation in the early years was given as "rancher." The earliest names were Muslim: Komas Khan and Cain Deen. They were joined by Chiza Singh in 1915. The 1917–1918 directory listed 56 men from India, and the 1920–1921 directory 177.

Punjabis were among early subscribers to the telephone company as well. The directory for 1918 included twenty-seven men from India: seven in Brawley, thirteen in Holtville, three in El Centro, two in Imperial, and one each in Calexico and Calipatria. Eighteen of them were Sikhs, eight were Muslim, and one was Hindu.[41]

Early reports of Punjabis in the Imperial Valley ranged from stories of their curious and inappropriate behavior to notices of the business deals made by prominent Punjabi ranchers. Many newspaper stories stressing the peculiarities, real and imagined, of the Punjabis focused on the Sikhs, whose turbans caused them to be called "ragheads." A 1915 story, "Hindu Weps [*sic*] When Placed in City Jail Without Turban," told of a street fight between two Punjabis. In his haste to jail one Sikh, the acting marshal refused him permission to look around for his knocked-off turban.[42] A more serious issue arose when a superior court judge in 1920 became the first judge in the United States to force a Sikh to remove his turban in the courtroom. A Sikh missionary protested, but apparently the judge enforced his decision.[43] A number of comic newspaper stories also included details about turbans.

And Sikh funeral customs attracted notice. In 1918, when a man died near Imperial, his countrymen asked if he could be cremated. The county health officer approved, "but didn't expect them to stack a lot of wood in the middle of a field, lay the body of the departed on its top and do the oldstyle funeral pyre act. They were just touching the match to the stack when the officers arrived and stopped the weird funeral. The law says that human bodies may be burned by specially licensed crematories and not right out in the pasture, ala Hindu."[44]

Caste customs drew comment only when pointed to by the Punjabis themselves. Thus in 1915 one Nemo Partapa filed suit against Jawala Ram, alleging that the higher-caste man was appropriating his property according to "ancient Hindu custom." According to Partapa, Ram had taken bales of cotton, horses, harnesses, and other items.[45]

There were numerous press reports of violence among Punjabis and against them, as well as of incidents involving automobiles, overflowing drainage ditches, and the like. In 1915, initial headlines identified an "angered Turk, Gulam Isul," as the murderer of one Ma Ding. This religious fanatic turned out to be a "Hindu" named Ghulam Rasul and his victim was Amin Deen, another Hindu (and, as the names tell us, both men were Muslims). Another argument, over finances, among Punjabis led to an ax attack, headlined by the *El Centro Progress* as *Hindu Thinks Compatriot Is Cherry Tree.*[46]

Punjabis were also attacked by others, ranging from a Mexican worker with a monkey wrench to Anglo farmers. In one case, an Anglo was acquitted on a charge of murder, although "he killed a Hindu laborer while working near Seeley." In another case, one Jawala Ram was murdered by his Anglo neighbor with an ax. At first freed for "lack of evidence," the assailant was later indicted after the coroner refused to concur in the verdict.[47]

A vivid glimpse of the intersection of ethnicity, class, and climate comes from a novel set in the Imperial Valley.

> "El Centro's no place for a human being to work, or even an animal," the woman said. "There ought to be only machines, especially now, when we're getting on towards the Hundred Days. That's a part of the year don't show on the calendar. It begins when the first rag-head is found laying face-down in some culvert. A heat-suicide, the paper'll say, but likely the poor slob only walked down the street in a squeaky pair of shoes. At a hundred and twenty, he could even been knocked off for not squeaking."[48]

Other stories in the local press reflected favorably on the farming abilities of the Punjabis and noted the prominent among them. Thus, "B. K. Singh, well known Hindu rancher north of town, is going to remember his brother in India at Christmas time this year with an American talking machine . . . a $50 Victrola of the Imperial Valley Hardware Company."[49] And a sympathetic 1916 article about Asian Indian hopes for citizenship noted the El Centro superior judge's ruling that only certain castes were "white men" and eligible for citizenship, commenting that the decision "will be of interest to hundreds of Hindu ranchers and cotton pickers in the Imperial Valley, who have been counting on their ability to qualify for naturalization."[50]

Another indication that the Punjabi farmers viewed themselves as future Americans comes from their response to appeals for funds for the U.S. effort in World War I. Holtville Punjabis subscribed liberally to the Liberty Bond Loans in 1918. An appreciative article in the *Holtville Tribune* listed some twenty-nine Punjabi men who contributed a total of $1,500. Most of the Punjabis prominent in the local papers seem to have farmed near Holtville.[51]

Up the Agricultural Ladder

Certainly the Punjabis moved quickly into the leasing and owning of land. In 1919, Punjabis leased 32,380 acres in the Imperial Valley, slightly more than one-third of all the California land leased and owned by Punjabis at that time.[52] They secured credit from local banks and from individuals. A former president of the Holtville Bank thought that Punjabis brought more money with them than did Swiss laborers; the latter often spent years working for other Swiss before they had saved enough money to farm on their own.[53] But the keys to Punjabi success were probably length of residence in the same locality and the establishment of stable tenancy relationships with landowners (as has been shown for Japanese farmers in California around the same time).[54]

The earliest leases and chattel mortgages recorded for Punjabis in the valley were for cotton growing, and the earliest successful Punjabi ranchers grew cotton around Holtville. A Punjabi farmer recalled the richness of the new land in those early years, when a man could get three years' crop from one year's planting. He said that despite the many Punjabi bankruptcies in cotton in the early 1920s, bankers in the Imperial Valley wanted Punjabi farmers to stay and keep growing cotton, but many left, seeking better opportunities elsewhere in the state or in Arizona. Another farmer told of the differences between cotton farming in the Punjab and in the Imperial Valley, saying he and his partners had learned the new methods by watching the Anglo farmers.[55]

Imperial County leasing records from 1917 to 1923 show considerable activity on the part of the men from India.[56] Over that seven-year period, the number of recorded leases signed by men or partners from India ranged between sixteen and fifty-three per year, with some 56 percent of the leases signed by a single man, another 25 percent by two partners, and the rest almost equally divided between three- and four-man partnerships.[57] How these partnerships worked can be established from the lawsuits that sometimes resulted. In one instance, three men formed a partnership in 1917, each contributing between $1,500 and $1,600 to lease 160 acres for a three-year period. The man who contributed the most was manager, a second man kept the books, and the third stayed on the ranch throughout the summer while the other two worked elsewhere and reimbursed him. They went into debt for water rents and took a loan from the Imperial Valley Bank of Brawley, mortgaging their livestock to do so and causing a dispute within the partnership. A settlement was negotiated, requiring two translators from "Hindu" to English; the settlement agreement was signed in Punjabi script.[58]

Another partnership, the Hindustani Farmers Company, was formed in 1922 to plant, cultivate, and produce cantaloupes. The five partners, Murad Bux, Ali Farman, H. Ali, Moola Singh, and Golam Mohamed, were to have equal interests in the crop and pledged to contribute labor and one horse each. If a man could not work, he had to supply a replacement. Golam Mohamed was the manager of the partnership, and because Moola Singh failed to carry out his obligations, Mohamed had to hire a man and a mule. Ultimately Mohamed sued Moola Singh for the debts incurred ($366.84); the partnership took a loss in the venture.[59]

Partnership disputes often involved reimbursement for labor. Court records show that Punjabis cut hay crops for each other, rented livestock to each other, or simply did whatever labor was required. All agreements were verbal contracts and were subject to litigation when reimbursement did not follow as promised. In one case, the court helped set up an arbitration board with seven members elected by both parties; all were Punjabis from Calipatria (one Muslim, one Hindu, and five Sikhs). The defendant was indebted to the plaintiff for two years of labor performed, and in the end the sheriff sold the cotton crop to secure payment.[60]

Punjabis used the court system in the Imperial Valley very aggressively. Table 4 shows civil cases involving Punjabis; these cases were almost 3 percent of all civil cases from 1914 to 1919 and 2 percent of all civil cases from 1919 to 1931, although (using Ram Chand's count of 268 circa 1920) Punjabis were only about .6 percent of the county population.[61]

From the first Punjabi civil case in 1914 until 1919, Punjabis were involved in fifty-eight cases. Over 50 percent of them (thirty-one cases) pitted Punjabi against Punjabi, and almost all concerned land and labor agreements. In the other twenty-seven cases, they sued and were sued by others in nearly equal proportions; the "others" included a few Japanese and Chinese and many Anglos. Only one divorce case was filed before August 1919 (the first local marriage had taken place in late 1916).

From 1919 to 1931, Punjabis were involved in some 179 civil cases, and 30, just under a fifth, were against each other. In that period, the proportion of suits against Punjabis by others more than doubled. These were years of prejudice against Asian farmers, of discriminatory laws, and of bankruptcies for cotton farmers. Many Punjabis filed federal bankruptcy petitions. Certainly many Imperial County civil cases against Punjabis were filed by local banks and creditors during this decade. (The other big increase was in the proportion of divorce cases; there were twenty-five. Divorce is discussed in Chapter 6).

Cotton bankruptcies after World War I hit the men from India, along with other Imperial Valley cotton farmers, hard. They filed seventy-seven bankruptcy cases with the U.S. District Court in Los Angeles, cases that

Table 4.   Civil Cases Involving Punjabis, Imperial County

	1914–1919		1919–1931		Total N
	N	%	N	%	
Punjabi plaintiff/defendant	31	53	30	17	61
Punjabi plaintiff/other defendant	14	24	41	23	55
Punjabi defendant/other plaintiff	12	21	83	46	95
Divorces	1	2	25	14	26
TOTAL	58	100	179	100	237

Sources: Imperial County General Index to Plaintiffs, 1907–1919 and 1919–1931, and Imperial County General Index to Defendants, 1907–1931, Office of the County Clerk, El Centro. Surnames checked in the alphabetical indexes included those beginning with *A, B, C, K, M, R,* and *S.*

provide details unavailable elsewhere. The sources of credit to the Punjabis and the amounts of credit are somewhat surprising.[62] From 1919 through 1928, the heaviest period of filing, fifty-nine cases of bankruptcy were filed by Punjabis, thirty-eight by individuals and twenty-one by partnerships. The total amount of Punjabi debts was $721,090, with the average individual owing $8,526 and the average partnership owing more than double that, $20,279. Half of those with secured notes held loans for $10,000 or more; most were bank loans or bank loans plus loans from individuals. Over the nine-year period, the trend was from secured loans to unsecured ones, and local landowners were replaced by absentee landowners, indicating that big absentee landlords thought the Punjabis were good farmers and continued to lease to them. As the loans moved from secured to unsecured notes, however, the amounts did not decrease; 23 percent of all unsecured notes were for $15,000 or more. Most of the unsecured notes were, again, from a combination of sources: local banks, local Anglos, and other Punjabis (more loans were from local Anglos than from other Punjabis).

Most of these bankruptcy cases (86 percent) were handled by two local attorneys, James W. Glassford or Robert G. Hill. Punjabis usually paid these two lawyers with promissory notes; clearly the attorneys expected them to recover and profit from farming in the future. So while Punjabis in general gained a bad reputation for filing so many bankruptcies during these hard years, they had both local and absentee supporters.

Bankruptcy case details show the Punjabi farmers developing financial strategies. At first, the cases were straightforward. The men had few possessions, and the one item consistently retained as personal property was a blanket.[63] Later, however, Punjabis paid off their Punjabi creditors *before* filing, leaving the bank or Anglo farmer unpaid. A car might be put in a wife's name, and when challenged, the farmer would argue not only that she had bought it with her egg money but that it was mortgaged to a Punjabi friend and could not be seized. A case involving an automobile was even more complex. A creditor tried to seize Mota Singh's 1919 Dodge, but he had allegedly sold it to a second Punjabi for $800. That man had taken it to Oxnard for the summer and then sold it to a third Punjabi, again for $800. The third man had sold it back to the second man for only $250 (both the third man and Mota Singh were employed by that second man, who now leased the land formerly leased by Mota Singh). Finally, Mota Singh argued that the car could not be seized because it was frequently used by one Georgia May, the Anglo wife of yet a fourth Punjabi farmer! Land, more valued than cars, was safeguarded even more carefully. One Punjabi made a deal with a trusted Anglo storeowner, giving him a mortgage on the land and working for him on it so that it would not be lost altogether.[64]

These elaborate bankruptcy strategies reflected more possessions, increasing legal sophistication, and probably reactions to the growing discrimination against Asians. Certainly these strategies frustrated creditors and lawyers unused to working with Punjabi farmers. One lawyer billed the county far above the usual fee, stating that "the bankrupt is a Hindoo and very difficult to understand, necessitating extraordinary labor on the part of his attorney." The court referee sometimes had trouble finding a competent trustee who would serve, since "in practically all of these Hindu cases, neither I nor the trustee have been able to uncover any tangible assets." Indeed, it was often hard to challenge the Punjabis, who either kept no books or kept them in "Hindu." And it was often hard to collect awards. In one contested case, the man owing money was said to have gone back to India, but an Anglo disputed it, saying "no Hindoo ever leaves this country to go to India—they know they can't get back again." Another frustrated creditor testified, "In my opinion Moola Singh is very well covered up. I had a judgment against him and chased him all over the country without success."[65]

Legal Setbacks

In the middle of this period of bankruptcy cases, in 1923, the south Asians' battle for U.S. citizenship was lost. The Supreme Court decided against Bhagat Singh Thind, who had appealed the revocation of his citizenship. The judge held that while persons from India were Caucasian, they were not "white persons" in the popular meaning of the term, and therefore they, like the Japanese and other Asians, were "aliens ineligible to citizenship." The most significant consequence of this ruling was the application to the Punjabis of California's Alien Land Laws, devised to prevent the rapid Japanese progress in agriculture by prohibiting the leasing and owning of agricultural land by aliens ineligible for citizenship.[66] As an article entitled "Hindus Too Brunette to Vote Here" pointed out, many California county district attorneys welcomed the decision by filing actions to strip Punjabi landowners of their holdings.[67]

At least one absentee landlord with a very favorable opinion of his Punjabi tenants foresaw problems if the land law was applied to them:

> I have had a two years contact with the Hindu people in the relations of landlord and tenant and I am now employing four of them as foreman and laborers on a half section of land in the Imperial Valley. They are excellent farmers, very industrious, willing to work under trying conditions and I have found them scrupulous in the performance of their agreements.
>
> These men are Sikhs and come from the Punjab district of India, where they have had experience in growing the kind of crops we grow in the Valley. They especially favor the growing of cotton and when it comes to work, they are the original "men with the hoe." In the heat of summer they get up at 4 o'clock, work with their teams until about 10 A.M., then with the hoe until say 4 P.M. and then with their teams until 9 o'clock in the evening. *This, however, is when they are working for themselves. As day laborers I do not suppose they would do more than a day's work for a day's pay.* (Emphasis added.)[68]

The Punjabi farmers developed many defensive strategies to deal with the land law. A few moved to Arizona, New Mexico, Texas, or even Mexico. Then Arizona also enacted an Alien Land Law.[69] Only a few men were well enough educated to change professions, and the inability to become citizens hindered them as well.[70]

One immediate response to the implementation of the land law was violence. Pahker Singh had moved from soldiering in China to farming in the Imperial Valley, and he had done well. When the Alien Land Law was applied to Punjabis, he made a verbal agreement with Anglos to put his lettuce crop in their names. The men broke their word, harvested the lettuce in April 1925, shipped it east, and kept the money for themselves. According to testimony, Pahker Singh confronted two of them in the field and shot them dead, bashing their heads in with an ax for good measure. The case was a sensational one and aroused strong feelings; in fact, there was considerable sympathy for Singh, who had earned a good reputation in his end of the valley. Singh was eventually convicted of second-degree murder and sent to San Quentin.[71]

Many old-timers still recall the event vividly, and their accounts emphasize the resentment and anger felt by Punjabi farmers. They say the men called Pahker "a goddam Hindu."[72] Many versions of this story are still current. It made a strong impact on valley residents at the time and affected elections for county sheriff years later, because of the support Singh received in the north end of the valley and the threat his eventual parole seemed to present to voters around Holtville.[73] The murders may have affected the way in which Punjabi farmers were treated in subsequent years; some thought that the threat of violence ensured careful, honest dealings with the Punjabis, while others thought it led to an avoidance of dealings with them.[74]

Another way around the land law utilized relatives or friends to hold the land on a man's behalf. As one man said defiantly: "Two years ago I married a Mexican woman and through her I am able to secure land for farming. Your land law can't get rid of me now; I am going to stay."[75] This statement was technically incorrect, since a married woman's legal status was that of her husband. Although persons from Mexico were aliens eligible for citizenship in the United States, a woman marrying an ineligible alien became ineligible herself.[76] Such a legal technicality appears to have been either unknown or overlooked, however, since in the Imperial County land records from 1923 onward there are scattered instances of wives holding land on behalf of their Punjabi spouses. People stated that they or their fathers had indeed put land in the name of a wife.[77] The wife of one Punjabi Muslim farmer not only leased land for him but dealt with buyers as her husband's partner in the business. This woman had a fourth-grade education from the Yuma school system. She knew English well and kept the books, preparing written (but not recorded) leases for other Punjabi farmers as well.[78]

The strategy of putting land in one's Hispanic wife's name was seldom utilized, however (for reasons discussed in Chapter 6). Instead, most Punjabis worked out verbal understandings with Anglo farmers, bankers, and lawyers, who held land in their own names for Punjabi farmers. The director of the Holtville Bank did this, earning for his bank the name "Hindu Bank." Many lawyers and even judges held land for Punjabi farmers all over California and Arizona.[79] Anglo companies dealt with the Punjabi farmers and Anglo farmers fronted for them, handling all checks and banking on their behalf.[80] And, adopting a strategy pioneered by the Japanese all over California, the Punjabis formed corporations with Anglos, often outsiders, who arranged for them to farm the land.[81]

The final strategy, one not employed systematically in the Imperial Valley until a 1933 grand jury investigation and subsequent indictment by the district attorney imperiled the corporations, was to put land in the name of one's minor children and manage it as legal guardian through the probate court. In the 1933 case, four Punjabi and five Anglo farmers who had formed a corporation were convicted locally but won an appeal.[82] When the case was filed, most Punjabis in the valley with land registered immediately as guardians of their citizen children. The court in El Centro cooperated by scheduling all Punjabi probate reports "to be delivered by their lawyers for five minutes once a year."[83]

The Punjabis' Place

The Punjabis were farmers, and despite the application of the Alien Land Law to them, they continued to control land. Judges in the valley who held or leased land for Punjabi farmers were rewarded with live chickens at Christmas, delivered in gunny sacks. As one judge's daughter said, "Oh, how I hated to get up Christmas morning and see those gunny sacks flopping around under the tree!" Sometimes there were sacks of money as well.[84] Others who helped the Punjabi farmers were the big dealers in trucks and farm supplies. Roy Womack of Womack's Chevrolet habitually filled out blank checks, even signing the names of his Punjabi customers for them.[85]

Furthermore, the Punjabis were "Hindu" farmers, and "Hindu" became a local adjective and even a verb in the Imperial Valley. "Hindu farming" had characteristics apart from its profitability; it generally meant good but not tidy farming. Equipment yards tended to be sloppy, not well kept. Some say the crops often had weeds, in contrast to the crops grown by Japanese farmers; others say only the yards had weeds. One might refer to a "Hindu job," as in, "Well, I call that a Hindu job; do it over." An employer who maintained a camp for Mexican workers recalled telling them that "this looks like a Hindu camp," meaning that it needed cleaning. And the expression "that's been Hindued" meant that something had been quickly but temporarily fixed, perhaps with baling wire or string.[86]

Local stereotypes of the Hindu farmers also focused on their language ability, personal cleanliness, and distinctive diet. The men's ability to learn languages attracted favorable comment. The leading Chevrolet dealer in the valley recalled the time two Punjabis came in with a Mexican woman, and "one of them stood there and talked Hindu [*sic*] to his brother, Mexican [*sic*] to his wife, and English to me—they learned. I liked them for that."[87] Punjabi men seem to have rigged up showers and bathed noticeably more often than many of their neighbors. Neighbors also noticed the single Sikhs oiling their long hair after bathing (although the married men, and later almost all the men, cut their hair and shaved their beards).[88] Vegetable curries were the usual diet, sometimes supplemented by chicken or goat curry. A Swiss neighbor recalled that Punjabis bought milk and butter in ten-pound lots from his father's dairy, and they bought goat kids. Even though the men cooked curries for themselves, when Mrs. Brown prepared curry in the family restaurant in Holtville, Punjabis "came out of the woodwork" to patronize it.[89] Down at Tom Mallobox's bar on Broadway in El Centro, neighboring Anglo businessmen flocked in to eat Tom's curry.[90]

Many Punjabis married, some remained bachelors, but all were noted for their love of children and courtly treatment of Anglo women. They handed out silver dollars and had special smiles, hugs, and pet names for the children of neighbors or employers. They also knew how to please their employers' wives, leaving money with storekeepers for Mrs. X to buy a dress for herself or her child when she next came into the store. They depended on the female telephone operators to understand their broken English and assist them to place calls in the days before dialing, and they gave them candy at Christmas for their help.[91]

The reputation of the Punjabis improved gradually.[92] By 1924, Ram Chand, an interviewee articulate in English, reported his perception of a change for the better.

> I have, however, had the privilege of seeing a great change in the sentiment toward the Hindus in the Valley. A few years ago the lawyers in the courts would argue on the basis of race inferiority and would talk about the heathen Hindus and stuff of that sort. I called the attention of a number of lawyers to their woful [sic] lack of information and a great change has come over the courts. When a case involving a Hindu is tried now it is argued purely on its own merits. Some years ago when I walked about the streets of El Centro a number of persons would call me bad names and even spit on me. That was hard to bear, but now I am glad to report that a decided change for the better has come about. . . . During the time of the anti-Oriental agitation in 1918 the Hindustani Welfare Society was organized to be of assistance to the Hindu group. This Society gave assistance in the matter of contracts and gave out useful information. The occasion for this has now passed away to a considerable extent and so the Society does not function as it used to do. It now aids in case of sickness or other difficulties.[93]

Unfortunately, the implementation of the Alien Land Laws produced a resurgence of prejudice against "Asians." An Imperial County grand jury report in 1931 opined: "There is no doubt in the minds of the Jury that the Alien Land Law is being broken repeatedly in this Valley, but, due to the indifferent feeling toward sustaining this law, we doubt the wisdom of spending any money in attempting convictions that are not likely to be sustained."[94] By 1933, however, Punjabis as well as Japanese[95] had been indicted for conspiracy to evade the Alien Land Law. In the course of the 1933 trial all the old prejudices against Hindus were listed in a ten-point petition the five Anglo defendants presented requesting a separate trial from that of the four Punjabi defendants, beginning with the point that "Hindus are not Caucasians or whites but are members of the Aryan race of India and ineligible to citizenship." While undoubtedly overstated in order to obtain separate trials for the Anglos, this does indicate the damage done by the 1923 Supreme Court decision barring South Asians from citizenship.[96]

But despite legal setbacks and some prejudice, for many in the valley the once despised Hindus became good farmers and dependable neighbors. Other farmers hired out to do tractor work for Punjabis, doing it on credit or "half and half" pay (receiving half when done and the other half at Christmas). One person recalled that "when I did tractor work for Hindus, they didn't check on me much, coming by just once or twice a day so I didn't have to watch my lines carefully when I turned at the far end of a field." (When he worked for Japanese farmers, in contrast, they supervised the job closely, making him redo turns and requiring him to rent a plow rather than do tomato beds with a disc.) Another remembered a Punjabi farmer stopping and leaping from his truck to help deal with a leaking irrigation pipe.[97]

Most Punjabis were considered good credit risks (as the early bankruptcy cases receded in memory). Managers of the Holtville and Brawley banks recall only a small percentage of their Punjabi loans being lost during the difficult years of the 1920s.[98] During the depression, Anglo and Punjabi farmers helped one another out. One Swiss farmer told of the bad times when they all, Swiss and Punjabi alike, had to work for wages, and even those jobs became scarce. At one point, his father, prostrate with grief at the death of his eldest son, desperately needed money. Their neighbor, Mohamed Baksh, knew their situation and loaned them $1,000. Later, when times had gotten even worse, Mohamed Baksh twice sought loans from them to feed his family, and they found the money for him.[99]

The Punjabis helped themselves by their pride and self-confidence. Unable to speak or write English well, they hired lawyers and used the local courts extensively. When they wanted something, they asked for it. Subject to the same prejudices as the Mexican immigrants in many respects, the Punjabi farmers walked into the local banks and requested credit lines and loans; their Mexican in-laws could not or did not do that.[100] When the Mohammedan Club needed someone to type up its constitution, its president asked the daughter of the owner of Holtville's most popular restaurant to do it. When the Mohammedan Club needed a place to meet, the president asked a (German) Swiss farmer friend for the Swiss Club premises and got them, although some say the Italian Swiss were not welcome on those premises for many more years! (One activity that brought the Swiss and Punjabis together was wrestling, popular with both groups. Touring wrestlers came from the Punjab to California, and Swiss as well as Punjabis attended the matches. A Singh claims to have become the first non-Swiss wrestling champion in the Imperial Valley.[101])

The picture that emerges from their own accounts and those of others is that the Punjabis knew how to get what they wanted from the system. (I have argued elsewhere that their experience working with British magistrates and officials back in the Punjab helped account for their success in California.[102]) They were valued in the California valleys for their farming skill and often for their forceful personalities. One account from the San Joaquin delta describes Har Chand, a man who "mosquito-proof, man of energy and dreams, mighty reader and cyclist, was an empire builder at heart."[103] A southern California woman was moved to write a short story about the murder in the 1920s of a dynamic Sikh, a man of whom she had been very fond when she was a child. The murder occurred on a farm near Long Beach, where her mother was the cook. One of many Anglos with vivid childhood memories of individual Punjabi men, she still worries about the murderer's true identity.[104]

Documentary and other sources have filled in the landscape; no longer are Anglos and others absent from the rural scenes fragmentarily recalled by pioneer Punjabi immigrants. A story from the later decades demonstrates that Punjabi energies and skills had been successfully employed in building connections with those in political power in California. One determined old Punjabi in the Imperial Valley, denied a driver's license because of his failing sight, got in his car with his thirteen-year-old son and drove all the way to Sacramento, stopping in Stockton at the Sikh temple on the way to secure political assistance from Punjabis well connected in the state capitol. He came back with a driver's license.[105]

4 Marriages and Children

As the Punjabi farmers settled in the Imperial Valley, some began setting up households, usually joint households consisting of their partners in a farming venture. Unable to bring wives and families from India because of the tightened immigration laws, the men cooked and cleaned for themselves or hired local women. They also formed relationships with local women, and those who wanted a stable family life in the United States began to marry. The demographic patterns of marriage and childbearing are described in this chapter; subsequent chapters explore the social worlds of the men and women and the conflicts they experienced.

The First Marriages

For the Punjabi men, marriage was not a simple matter of choosing among the single women in the Imperial Valley, courting them, and marrying. There were customary and legal constraints even in this domestic arena. Thus the first few Punjabi marriages in the valley were front-page news, arousing concern and prejudice, even though the most wealthy and prominent men were the first to marry. Sher Singh, a Holtville cotton farmer, reportedly took out a license for a Mexican bride in March 1916. "While in doubt as to their legal right to marry under the laws of this state, the clerk . . . issued the license, thereby passing the responsibility up to any authorized person who performs the marriage ceremony." The reporter anxiously tried to ascertain whether or not the couple had been married.[1]

The strongest prejudice was against Punjabis associating with white women. When another well-to-do Holtville cotton farmer, B. K. Singh, married the sixteen-year-old daughter of one of his tenants in 1918, one headline read: *Hindu Weds White Girl by Stealing Away to Arizona*.[2] The article speculated that since Imperial County would not issue a license for a Punjabi and a white woman, it was doubtful that the clerk in Yuma had acted legally. California's anti-miscegenation laws prohibited marriages between people of different races, and Punjabis were generally classified as nonwhite. One Punjabi man recalled his love affair with a white woman around 1920; an offended Anglo neighbor rousted him out of her house with a shotgun and had him arrested. Even the employment of white women as house cleaners and cooks was difficult.[3]

Local Anglo opinion about Punjabi relationships with "Mexican girls" was somewhat more favorable—a prominent Anglo farmer and the county horticultural commissioner witnessed the first and fourth such marriages in the valley.[4] Marriage licenses soon were issued routinely to Punjabi men and Hispanic women.[5] These early marriages caused conflict with Mexican men in the area. In 1918, the *El Centro Progress* headlined *Race Riot Is Staged*. A fight between Mexicans and Punjabis in the cotton fields near Heber had resulted from a Punjabi's marriage to a Mexican woman and an oath of vengeance made by several Mexican men. The Mexican men went to the couple's farm to attack them, but Punjabi farmers got the better of them. Four years later, two Mexican men abducted two Mexican women, sisters, who had married Punjabis. They shot a man whom they believed to be one of the husbands and took the women to a cabin twelve miles across the border in Mexico, where they imprisoned them for several days and flogged them. Returning to their husbands, the women later described their captors and secured their arrest at Calexico.[6]

After the controversies of the first few marriages, a pattern was established, and many Punjabi-Hispanic marriages took place. Cotton was the crop that brought most couples together. Mexican families displaced by the Mexican Revolution were moving across the border into the United States, finding work in cotton fields from Texas to southern California. This was family labor, and women and children worked alongside the men.[7] Back in the Punjab, women had picked cotton, too; it was the only outdoor work done by Jat Sikh women in all three regions of the central Punjab.[8]

The labor market, and the Punjabi-Mexican marriage networks, began in El Paso, Texas, and extended to California's Imperial Valley.[9] El Paso was the most important entry point for Mexican immigrants. Mexican families and women on their own ended up in El Paso as they fled the 1910 revolution.[10] Some early Punjabi-Mexican marriages were performed in El Paso; others took place in Canutillo, Texas, where Punjabis were farming cotton.[11] Many marriages were performed in Las Cruces, New Mexico, because in Texas at that time there was a three-day waiting period between securing a license and getting married. In adjacent New Mexico there was no waiting period.[12] One marriage to a Punjabi led to others as the Mexican women called relatives and friends and helped arrange more matches.

Fragmentary records from 1913 show two Punjabis taking wives in northern California: Alice Singh, Canadian-born, married a Sikh in Sacramento; and Rosa Domingo, a common-law wife, was murdered by her Muslim husband in Contra Costa County.[13] The first Imperial Valley marriage was that of Sher Singh and Antonia Alvarez in 1916; the next year Sher's partner, Gopal Singh, married Antonia's sister, Anna Anita (photo 6). The weddings were civil ceremonies in El Centro, the first witnessed by a leading Anglo farmer and Gopal Singh, the second by the first couple. No attempts were made to carry out Punjabi marriage customs. One wife remembers that when she married, "another Hindu offered me money, but my husband did not accept, saying 'we are not in our country.'"[14]

The Alvarez family, consisting of Mrs. Alvarez, three of her daughters (Antonia, Anna Anita, and Ester), and a son (Jesus), had come from Mexico in 1916 via El Paso. The family lived on the Edwards ranch near Holtville and picked cotton for the Punjabi partners who leased the ranch, Sher Singh and Gopal Singh. At the time of the weddings, the men were thirty-six and thirty-seven and the sisters were twenty-one and eighteen. A fourth sister, Valentina, soon came from El Paso to join her mother and sisters. Valentina was older; she had been married already and had four daughters, whom she brought with her. She married Rullia Singh in October 1917, and a month later her fourteen-year-old daughter, Alejandrina, married a Sikh friend of his, a man who had taken the American name of Albert Joe. The youngest Alvarez sister, Ester, married another Sikh, Harnam Singh Sidhu, in 1919.[15]

The same pattern appears in the lives of another set of sisters who married Punjabis: women moving from Mexico to El Paso, close ties between mother and daughters, Punjabi partners marrying sisters, and a significant age difference between the men and their wives. A Mexican woman working for the Holtville cotton farmer Kehar Singh Gill told him about her eligible nieces in El Paso, and he took a train there at the end of 1917. He knocked on a door—as it turned out, it was the wrong door, but a pretty young girl opened it. Matilde Sandoval, her mother, and sister saw a tall, handsome man: "When we opened the door and saw him in that turban, we thought he was a Turk; but we asked him in anyway." After a few days, Matilde married him, and they all got on the train for El Centro. "But Gill, where is it?" the women wailed as they disembarked in the dusty center of El Centro, and they were equally dismayed on arrival at the ranch were Kehar and his partner, Sucha Singh Garewal, shared a small wooden house. They settled in, however, and four months later the younger sister, Lala, agreed to marry Sucha. The wedding party set out on the plank road for Yuma, Arizona, in a hired car driven by a Mr. Johnson. The day of the wedding, Sucha took off his turban and allowed Lala to shave his beard; she shaved his every day for the rest of his life. A third Sandoval sister, Macaria, then came from El Paso with her Mexican husband and children. The husband was employed by the Punjabi partners as a timekeeper, and later one of Macaria's daughters married a Sikh neighbor in Holtville. The mother of Matilde, Lala, and Macaria, Petra Quesada Sandoval, was a frequent visitor to the Imperial Valley, although she married and lived in Mexico for some time. She eventually was persuaded to take a Sikh as her third husband; he kept saying, "Tomorrow *caliiee*" (Let's go tomorrow), and so she married him.[16]

A third set of sisters also married Punjabis. A father and his eight children got a job picking cotton for Sikh farmers near Holtville. The eldest sister was courted by one partner, the second sister by another, and the third sister by yet another. The sisters married at ages twenty, twenty, and seventeen. Their father was not initially enthused about these marriages to foreigners—his children had been born in Texas and California—but he feared his daughters would elope and reluctantly gave his permission. When his fourth daughter *did* elope (at age twelve or thirteen) with a Sikh, he sought to annul the marriage.[17]

The women involved in these marriages often arranged marriages for their friends with their husbands' Punjabi partners or friends. After the Sandoval sisters, Matilde and Lala, married Sikhs and settled in Holtville, they wrote to the mother of Luz and Antonia Harper in El Paso and asked if the girls could visit them. Luz came first, and soon she eloped to San

Diego with a Sikh, with Lala Sandoval Garewal and Sucha Singh Garewal in attendance. She was only fifteen, but it seemed a good marriage.[18]

While the tendency of partners to marry sisters obviously owes much to convenience, it may not have been unusual for the Punjabi men. "The Hindus here married sisters, yeah, same as back in the Punjab; my father's mother and [uncle] Lalu's mother were sisters, in the Punjab," one man said.[19] Such arrangements could result in complex relationships, linking many Mexican women and Punjabi partners.

Household arrangements were complex as well, with partners commonly residing in joint households with their brides. The men and women lived in wooden buildings on the land they were leasing, out along the irrigation canals and country roads. The men took off their turbans but kept their iron wrist bangles, and the husbands or their bachelor partners taught the Hispanic wives how to prepare Punjabi-style vegetables and chicken curry. Some bachelor householders stayed on as helpful "uncles" when the children came.[20]

Patterns of Marriage and Settlement

Table 5 shows the distribution of marriages made by the Punjabis in California through 1949 by spouse and region.[21] The table places couples in the region where they first settled and where their initial children were born. It ends with 1949 because, after that date, it clearly was possible to bring wives or brides from India.[22]

Almost two-thirds of the couples lived in the Imperial Valley, where 93 percent of the wives were Hispanic. In the north, the composition of the community was different—only about half the wives were Spanish-speakers, while another 40 percent spoke English and 9 percent spoke Punjabi. Family and community life developed differently in northern, central, and southern regions.

These marriage networks were based in the Imperial Valley in the sense that most marriages occurred there or in adjacent San Diego or Yuma, and most children were born and spent their early years there, but the geographic range was initially very wide. Marriages involved Sikh, Muslim, and Hindu Punjabis from all over California, Arizona, New Mexico, Utah, Texas, and even Mexico and Canada for the first decade or so. The men traveled great distances for their own and others' mar-

Table 5. Spouses of Asian Indians in California, 1913–1949

Counties	Hispanic		Anglo		Black		Indian		American Indian		Total	
	N	%	N	%	N	%	N	%	N	%	N	%
Yuba, Sutter, Sacramento, San Joaquin	45	50.6	25	28.1	9	10.1	8	9.0	2	2.3	89	23.6
Fresno, Tulare, Kings	38	76.0	11	22.0	0	0	1	2.0	0	0	50	13.2
Imperial, Los Angeles, San Diego	221	92.5	12	5.0	6	2.5	0	0	0	0	239	63.2
Total	304	80.0	48	12.7	15	4.0	9	2.4	2	.5	378	100

Sources: Family reconstitution from county records (vital statistics, civil and criminal records) and interviews.

riages—at least seventy men married outside California but settled in California. Many of the women were recent immigrants from Mexico.[23]

A systematic age difference by sex characterized the marriages. For these first-generation couples, the average age at marriage for the men was thirty-five and for the women twenty-three; the median ages were thirty-four and twenty. A comparison sample of marriages of Hispanic women with Hispanic men in Imperial County from 1918 to 1923 gave an average age at marriage for those men of twenty-seven and for women of twenty-one; the medians were twenty-five and nineteen.[24] So Punjabi grooms were markedly older than Hispanic grooms.

Religious boundaries, important in India, were not tightly maintained in California: Sikhs, Muslims, and Mexicans witnessed one another's marriages frequently.[25] There were also a few early intermarriages, the first involving a Sikh man in the San Joaquin Valley and the daughter of Punjabi Muslim immigrants to Canada.[26] Most couples were married in civil ceremonies, although there were a few Catholic wedding ceremonies. The first marriages in the Imperial Valley show a small group of men, the first ones to marry, witnessing the marriages of the next ones and presumably playing some role in bringing those marriages about.[27]

While the twenty-five earliest marriages included a variety of spouses,[28] Table 5 shows that the balance shifted heavily to Hispanic women, for several reasons. A barrier to marriages with white women was posed by California's anti-miscegenation laws, voided only in 1948. In theory, they prohibited marriages between persons of different races; in practice, the clerk issuing the marriage license had to fill in the blank for race with the same word for the man and the woman. For the Punjabis and their intended spouses, clerks sometimes wrote "brown," sometimes "black," and sometimes "white," depending on the applicants' skin coloring and on the county. A clerk who judged the potential mates to be too different in skin color would not issue a license. In several instances, men took their intended spouses to another county, state, or even on the high seas for a ship captain's ceremony. One man recalled accompanying his friend and the intended bride, a "Spanish-looking" Mexican, to three Arizona counties. They went home unmarried, a license thrice refused because she was "too white."[29]

Then there was pressure from Punjabis against marriages with black women. The proportion of black spouses was highest among the very early brides in northern California. In the Imperial Valley, blacks had come in as cotton pickers about the same time as the Punjabis, but had settled predominantly in towns. The printed pamphlet of the Imperial Valley Hindustanee Welfare and Reform Association contained a clause warning the men not to marry "colored" women. One explanation of the Punjabi men's avoidance of black women stressed white prejudice against blacks: Why ally themselves with a group hated by whites, when the Punjabis had similar problems and could fight them better alone?[30] In northern California, however, the smaller and more diverse groups of wives included several black women who were respected members of their communities. Seven of these nine northern black wives were married to Punjabi Muslims, one to a Hindu, and one to a Sikh.[31]

A positive reason for marriage to a Hispanic woman lay in the tendency for women married to Punjabis to arrange similar matches for their female relatives. In southern California, at least 101 of the 239 wives had one or more female relatives married to Punjabis; these 101 women fall into 34 groups of related women. In the central part of the state, 6 groups of related women accounted for 17 of the 50 wives of Punjabis.[32]

Women came across the border, while their brothers tended to stay in Mexico or to return there. The Arias sisters who married Punjabis were born in Chihuahua; there were nine children in the family. One sister crossed the border and married a Sikh farmer. She brought several other sisters, who did likewise; their two brothers stayed in Mexicali. The Martinez sisters, born and orphaned in Mexico, were brought to the United States and married Sikhs, while their two brothers stayed in Mexico.[33]

The pattern was one of poor Mexican families with eligible daughters coming into contact with Punjabi farmers through agricultural field work. Often only one parent was present, usually the mother.[34] Not only Mexicans but others moving into the agricultural economy as laborers supplied brides. In Arizona, one pair of sisters from Puerto Rico married Punjabis—Puerto Ricans had been brought there to pick cotton in 1926.[35] Hispanic women who worked as cooks and house cleaners for Punjabis sometimes ended up marrying their employers.[36]

Most stories of these marriages involve some kind of courtship, some choice on the part of the woman. One woman told of her husband-to-be cavorting on his horse in the row ahead of her as she picked cotton, while his partner dropped a gaily colored handkerchief over her sister's hair. Another woman, whose uncle was weighmaster to Punjabi cotton growers, fell in love with the boss at first sight. And a daughter told how her mother met her father: "She worked for my father, although not very hard—she was a very beautiful woman!"[37]

Yet the situation often was one in which marriage was the best available option for these women, especially when the groom was one's boss or another man of the farmer class. As one man said of his parents' marriage: "Pakistanis were growing cotton on both sides of Dogwood. When they hired workers, my mother was among them. Tom whistled at her and she liked him. Lupe's parents were happy, she had married a boss." One woman told of her situation, deserted at eighteen with two children, and how she decided to make what turned out to be a successful marriage. "Through my sister and her husband, who was Hindu, I met my husband. I was thinking, now what am I going to do, left alone with two children and without being able to work. He was a nice person and single, so to get a father and home for my children I married him." There were stories of occasional bride purchase by the Punjabis, and there were stories of love matches; both were outnumbered by accounts that emphasized economic security as the woman's basic motivation.[38]

One daughter speculated about an instrumental motive when she said:

> I think in the old times the Mexican women were like an instrument to the Hindu people because they wanted children to buy properties in the childrens' names, because they could not buy any property in their own names. Neither could they marry with American women. But the same thing was happening with the Mexican women because they had the ambition to improve their lot for themselves and their children. So the marriage was a convenience for both partners.[39]

This allegation of a narrow economic motivation for the marriages needs to be dealt with, since it is a common characterization. New immigrants from India, anxious to explain marriages out of caste and community, told me that the wives could hold land for the men and often did so. As *India West* put it in a story about a praiseworthy pioneer: "To counter loneliness and to gain the rights of property-ownership he did not, like many others, re-marry Mexican girls here."[40] Anglos in the Imperial Valley also charged the men with acquiring land illegally through these marriages. Yet the initial marriages could not have occurred for this reason, since the men were not barred from owning and leasing land until 1923, when they lost access to citizenship and came under the jurisdiction of the Alien Land Laws. By that date, the biethnic marriage pattern was firmly established. Furthermore, wives acquired the status of their husbands upon marriage (although there is some evidence that both Punjabis and Anglos were unaware of this, and some wives held land for the men despite the law). Certainly the begetting of children who were citizens and could hold land was not the main motivation for these marriages, since most Punjabis in the Imperial Valley did not begin putting land in the names of their children until 1934, well after most marriages had occurred and many children had been born. They adopted that strategy only after the 1933 Imperial County indictment of some Punjabis and Anglos for conspiring to evade the Alien Land Law by forming corporations. Arizona had copied California's Alien Land Laws, but the Punjabis there only began using the guardianship strategy in the 1940s.[41]

So the temptation to label these marriages opportunistic attempts to secure land must be resisted. I suggest in Chapter 6 how the men thought about these marriages, and here we must remember that the Punjabi men were becoming permanent residents of the United States. They were making decisions not to return to India and their families there. An Indian student at Berkeley explained the marriages this way:

> Nevertheless during the war [World War I] economic and industrial successes brought some changes in their private lives. The "rice kings" in the north, however, were little affected in this regard, but the "cotton kings" in the Imperial Valley came under the enchanting influence of Maya, the female principle in the Cosmic System, and began to crave for a settled domestic life. Some of them married Mexican girls in the valley, and others, who had some higher education in colleges or universities, married broad-minded American girls. Soon a settled Hindu community drew up in that part of the state, with all its dependent Mexican and American members, and many of the single men, formerly accustomed to moving around the country, assumed new responsibilities as heads of happy families.[42]

Family life and the development of a Punjabi-Mexican community began and flourished best in the Imperial Valley, with settlement in other regions of California and the western states fanning out from there. The towns of Holtville and Brawley seem to have been the initial centers for these couples, but soon they resided all over the valley, moving from leasehold to leasehold. The collapse of the cotton market after World War I and then the depression in farm prices that began around 1924, followed by the Great Depression, sent some Punjabi-Mexican families elsewhere in search of a livelihood.

The settlement of Asian Indians in the southern San Joaquin Valley began in three counties, Fresno, Tulare, and Kings. In the latter two counties, Asian Indians cultivated cotton from 1928 to 1931. There were a few marriages before that period—to white, black, and Hispanic women and to Asian Indian women born in Canada. The large numbers of marriages with Hispanic women in central California, however, occurred from 1928 to 1931, when couples went to get married in the towns of Visalia or Tulare.[43]

Depressed agricultural conditions and labor troubles also caused many to give up cotton in the Imperial Valley and move north to Fresno County, where vineyards and orchards provided better livelihoods. Partnerships were less characteristic here. There were farm labor camps in Fresno, at least three of them run by Punjabis.[44] The proportion of married men farming on their own was lower than in the Imperial Valley; there were more bachelor laborers in labor camps. In Fresno, Chinatown or the foreign section was on the west side of town. As in the Imperial Valley, some bars, liquor stores, and grocery stores were owned by Punjabis.[45]

The ethnic origins of the wives in the southern San Joaquin Valley were fairly diverse. On occasion, all the wives of the local Punjabis gathered together, and communication was in English. Events such as a wedding or funeral, a court trial, or an eminent visitor from India drew almost all Asian Indians and their spouses. One of the few "real Indian" families settled near Fresno, although the family moved around a great deal and both spouses had died by 1934.[46] Then there were the Spanish-speaking wives, dominated as in the Imperial Valley by groups of sisters. Among the Spanish-speaking wives in the lower San Joaquin Valley, three unrelated sets of Garcia sisters provided fourteen of the thirty-eight wives.[47]

The Punjabi-Mexican couples in the lower San Joaquin Valley tended to have stronger ties to the Imperial Valley than to the north. The ties to northern California were weaker because of the southern origin of many of the couples and because of the smaller numbers of Hispanic wives in the north. Also, families from the south traveled through Fresno on their way to Stockton, but those residing in the north less often traveled south.

This pattern contrasted with that for bachelor migrant laborers, for whom the labor migration included the northern counties but stopped at the Tehachapi Mountains between Bakersfield and the Los Angeles basin. The center for single Punjabis remained in the north, where bachelor life in labor camps was the dominant pattern.[48]

In the 1930s, Punjabi-Mexican families moved to northern California and Arizona. There were few married couples in the north until the late 1930s, when a movement north from the Imperial Valley brought twenty to thirty Spanish-speaking wives into the Yuba City–Marysville area. Because of the ethnic diversity of the couples there, the language spoken by wives at gatherings of the Punjabi men was usually English, not Spanish. Despite this use of English, "Hindu" cooking was prevalent because the Anglo wives in the north prepared primarily Hindu food, while the Mexican wives prepared both Mexican and Hindu food. The other outpost established in the late 1930s was in Phoenix, Arizona, where several Muslim Punjabis went into truck gardening. Growing vegetables in Phoenix, they could market their own produce and avoid doing business with the close-dealing shippers in the Imperial Valley. One or two families were established there; in time, others joined them, seizing a chance to start over after the depression or the tuberculosis inspections of dairies in the Imperial Valley, which forced the killing of many cows. In Phoenix, most wives of the Punjabis were Hispanic, as was true in the adjacent Imperial Valley.[49]

Childbearing, Fertility, and Mortality

Punjabi-Mexican couples had many children. Sometimes records speak eloquently through their very starkness, and here I present primarily quantitative information about fertility and mortality. What it meant to be a child in these families, what people had to say about their childhood experiences, are matters taken up in Chapter 7.

Regional differences are evident in the patterns of childbearing as well. Looking first at the county records, the bulk of the births, and the earliest births, took place in the Imperial Valley. These births occurred in the home, with a midwife and sometimes a doctor in attendance.[50] The birth certificates give rural locations like "12 miles northwest of Brawley" or "Calexico, by the 10 foot drop." Few of these mothers resided in the same place for successive births; they moved about in accordance with their husbands' leasing arrangements. The names of the children and parents on the certificates usually were misspelled because others filled out the certificates; these parents were largely illiterate in English.[51]

The location of recorded births for the Punjabi-headed families before 1931 makes the concentration of the families in the Imperial Valley clear. Table 6 shows that few couples settled and had children in central and northern California before 1931.

A preference for sons, a strong feature of Punjabi culture in India, showed up in the recording of the California births and in stories about childbirth. Of the 126 birth certificates filed in the Imperial County record office from 1918 through 1930, only 53 were for girls. The underregistration of female children is confirmed by seven delayed birth registrations filed for Punjabi-Mexican children in Imperial County: five of these were for daughters.[52] And a dramatic story from Yuba City illustrates the preference for sons even better. The young Mexican wife of a Punjabi farmer giving birth to her first child kept telling the doctors and nurses that it had to be a boy, that if it was a girl, her husband would put the baby in a gunny sack and let it die. Her baby *was* a girl, and the mother left her in the hospital for many days, letting her get stronger before taking her home.[53]

Table 6.   Births Before 1931, Selected Counties

County	Births	Mothers	
Imperial	126	69	(64 Hispanic, 3 Anglo, 2 black)
Fresno, Tulare	26	18	(11 Hispanic, 3 Indian, 1 Anglo)
Sacramento, San Joaquin	9	7	(4 Hispanic, 2 Indian, 1 Anglo)
Yuba, Sutter	7	5	(1 Indian, 1 American Indian, 1 Hispanic, 2 Anglo)
Total	174	99	

Sources: County birth certificates, 1910–1931, Recorders' Offices. I have deliberately broken the northern counties into two microregions because that so clearly demonstrates the later arrival of Hispanic women in the Yuba–Sutter area.

Table 7.   Families Begun by 1931: Women and Births to Them

Births (N)	1	2	3	4	5	6	7	8	9	10	12	13	Total
Women (N)	12	9	5	7	10	2	6	2	8	5	2	1	69
Total births	12	18	15	28	50	12	42	16	72	50	24	13	352

The childbearing histories of the sixty-nine women who bore children fathered by Punjabis in Imperial County before 1931 are shown in Table 7, which gives the number of women by the number of known births to each of them; for example, twelve women had one child each, nine women had two, and so on. All children born to these women, before and after 1931, in the Imperial Valley and elsewhere, are included.

Clearly, most families were large ones. Over half these mothers (36) had five or more children. Eighty percent of the children (279) had four or more siblings; 42 percent (159) had eight or more siblings! But childbearing histories could not be completed for all sixty-nine mothers; twenty-one women, represented by at least one birth certificate in Imperial County before 1931, quickly disappeared from the official records. Of those bearing a single child, four immediately divorced the father, and one was widowed before her child was born. Four more women eventually divorced their Punjabi husbands, and of twelve others I found no further trace. The experience of these sixty-nine women, then, constituted from Imperial County records, points to large families but a significant proportion (30 percent) of unstable relationships in the first decade of Punjabi family life.

In order to establish a data set of women whose *complete* childbearing history was known, I again used Imperial County as the base, but dropped the twenty-one women whose childbearing histories could not be completed and added eighteen more giving birth there after 1930. This set of sixty-six women bearing children to Punjabi men could be followed to the end of their reproductive careers for a closer look at "maternal fertility." These were mothers, then, who had at least one live birth in the Imperial Valley and for whom I had records for completed reproduction; they were past age forty-five or their childbearing was disrupted by death (fifty-nine and seven cases respectively).[54]

The records of these sixty-six women show patterns characteristic of those families with children. Sixty-five of the women were Hispanic and one was Anglo. Forty of them (61 percent) had relatives married to other Punjabis, another indication of the significance of the female networks. The age difference between husbands and wives is apparent: The women's average age at first birth of a child by a Punjabi father was 23.2 years, while the men's average age was 38.6 years.[55] These sixty-six women did not all begin their childbearing with Punjabi men or in the Imperial Valley; twenty-four of them had children with other men before beginning their relationships with Punjabis.[56] Adding up their children by all fathers, or their total fertility, the sixty-six women had 425 children, an average of 6.4 children each.[57] This high figure is particularly striking when one remembers that seven women had their childbearing careers disrupted by death.

There was a significant number of stepchildren in these families. More than a third (twenty-four of the sixty-six) had had children previously, with an average of 3.2 children each. Fathered by Hispanic men and Spanish-speaking, these seventy-six children were brought into the marriages with Punjabi men. The Punjabi men were said by most to be "good stepfathers." They clothed and fed these children, even though they were not their own.[58]

Marital and premarital fertility were high. In thirty-four of the sixty-six cases, both the marriage certificate and a certificate of first birth to the couple could be located. In five of these cases, the first birth occurred before the marriage, and in three more the first birth occurred within eight and one-half months after the marriage.[59] Premarital pregnancy, then, was not uncommon. Children were wanted, and birth control was practiced seldom, if at all. In another sixteen cases, the first birth occurred within the first twelve months of marriage; only in less than a third of these cases did the first birth occur after a year of marriage.

By the close of the childbearing period for the sixty-six mothers, the impact of infant and child mortality was heavy. A comparison of all children born to those still living at the end of the women's reproductive careers shows that the average number of children living per woman at the time of the last birth to her was only 5.5. Since the average number of births per woman was 6.4, these couples lost, on average, one of every six or seven children born to them.

Statewide vital statistics for the Punjabis and their families show that

Table 8.   Selected Vital Statistics, 1913–1946

Regions	Marriages	Births	Deaths (1905–1939)		
			Child	Spousal	Men
North	17	68	14	2	295
Central	25	75	10	4	87
South	93[a]	277[b]	41	4	65
Total			65	10	447

Sources: Certificates from county record offices; statewide register, 1905–1939 (alphabetized and printed state records).

[a]Includes Yuma, Arizona, to 1940 only. (California couples went there for marriages.)

[b]Does not include San Diego or Los Angeles, where the public is denied access to birth records.

although more Punjabi men were living and working in the north (see Table 8), the families were forming in the southern end of the state.[60] Mortality data show that sixty-five infants and children of Punjabi immigrant fathers with registered death certificates from 1905 to 1939 died in twelve different counties, grouped in the table into northern, central, and southern areas. Fourteen deaths occurred in the northern, ten in the central, and forty-one in the southern counties. Some of the infant and child deaths in the north were of children born in the south but taken along on the migratory labor route by their parents. Most of the deaths of children occurred before the age of one year: twelve were stillbirths, eight were neonatal (defined by the state as occurring at 27 days or less), and twenty-four were infants (which I am defining as from 28 days to 11 months, 27 days).[61] Most deaths, twenty-nine, were due to disease; another sixteen were birth related, twelve were attributed to dehydration and malnutrition, and seven were accidental.[62]

Because of sex differences in children's health and mortality in India's Punjab region, which testified to a preference for sons,[63] I looked for patterns by sex in this data. But here males were overrepresented—thirty-seven were males, twenty-five were females, and sex was not indicated for three "Baby Singhs." It may be that, just as parents sometimes failed to register the birth of a daughter in Imperial County, they sometimes failed to register a daughter's death. Significantly, however, there was a sex difference in the expected direction in the percentage of female and male deaths that were stillbirths or birth related. Twenty-four percent of the female deaths but only 11 percent of the male ones were stillbirths; 38 percent of female deaths were birth related (this includes stillbirths), while only 14 percent of male ones were birth related. The numbers are very small, but there is one other finding connected with the sex-ratio issue that gives them significance. There was a higher proportion of birth-related deaths in the depression years. Over this twenty-three year span of records (the first Punjabi-sired child was born in 1917), eight of the sixteen birth-related deaths occurred in the three years from 1929 through 1931, four of them in 1929 alone.[64] The mothers may have been suffering from malnutrition and lack of prenatal care, or the care of female infants may have been deliberately neglected at this time, or both.

Death certificates for spouses number only ten during this same period (1905–1939).[65] The leading cause of death was childbearing: six deaths were caused by complications with pregnancies or childbirth. Two wives were murdered, and two died of tuberculosis or pneumonia. Breaking them down by the county groupings, four deaths occurred in the south, four in the central area, and two in the north. One wife was Indian, and nine were Hispanic. The Indian wife was forty-two; the mean age of the Hispanic wives at death was just short of twenty-six.

The vital statistics, the demographic parameters of Punjabi family life, have been given in some detail. They reveal important problems, some of which stem from the dominant society. Inaccurate names and ages tell of carelessness and ignorance with respect to these largely immigrant families. Births and deaths at home or without adequate medical attention tell of expertise and institutions denied to those with darker skins and less money. Problems also occurred within the marriages. One sign of instability in relationships between men and women was the difficulty of tracing almost a third of the women bearing children to Punjabis during the first dozen years of such relationships in the Imperial Valley. Even more striking is the high ratio of murders among the wives' deaths: small in numbers, two out of ten, but high in percentage terms.

5 Male and Female Networks

The Punjabi-Mexican families, wherever they settled in California, but particularly in the Imperial Valley, formed a community. Outsiders certainly viewed the men, women, and children as a community and called them Hindus, Mexican-Hindus, or Hindu-Mexicans. Within the community, men and women participated in collective activities—weddings, dances, holiday outings. Nevertheless, the activities of family members often were organized along gender lines. To a significant degree, male and female worlds were separate from one another and sometimes competed with one another.

The men developed networks through their experiences as immigrants, especially through working in California agriculture. Networks based on kinship, so fundamental to Punjabi society, were weak in California because usually only one or two members of a coparcenary group had migrated. But the men's places of origin in India, along with religion and caste, continued to be important means of identifying and differentiating them. Among the women, kinship was the most obvious basis of networks, and the *compadrazgo*, or godparent system, supplemented it; places of origin in Mexico were relatively unimportant.

Male Networks

Their work in California agriculture structured the Punjabi men's lives. In the northern and central regions of the state, independent "Hindu boss men" contracted with employers on behalf of their Punjabi crews. Large ranches in the Central Valley employed permanent Punjabi foremen who hired Punjabi crews on a seasonal basis. In the Imperial Valley, it was more characteristic for men to form partnerships and contract to farm together. All over the state in the rural agricultural towns, "Hindu store men" ran grocery and liquor stores, where the men could get special food from India and visit together. Both the boss men and the store men tended to speak English better than other Punjabis, so they often served as intermediaries with local officials..

Male work groups in California were formed in many ways. In the Imperial Valley, partnerships of two to seven members contracted to farm specific acreages for set time periods. The partnership agreements were usually short term, although some sets of partners farmed together for years. Partners often married sisters and formed joint households, but partnerships also frequently broke up over disputed money and work obligations or fell victim to divorces, which split the sister sets.

Partnerships could be based on blood relationship; one involved a son, his father and uncle, and two of his "cousin brothers."[1] Men from the same village, or men who had gotten acquainted as shipmates on the voyage to America, might become partners. Those who arrived on the same ship, confined to steerage in close quarters for many weeks, formed lasting bonds. Descendants could name not only the men from their father's village but those who came on the ship with him. Probably, more partnerships were formed between shipmates than between village mates.[2] During the journey from Shanghai, Hong Kong, or Manila, the men shared worries about their reception by immigration authorities and advice about how to respond to questions. They exchanged information about where to go and whom to contact after being admitted to the United States. In later years, they vouched for one another's arrival on a "legal" ship, one sailing before 1924 (those who entered later were illegal aliens subject to deportation). Those who lived long enough to see the naturalization law change needed to supply the name of their ship and the date of its voyage on their petitions for naturalization. And while very few men came from the same village, several hundred came on the same ship, so shipmates were readily available.[3]

Outside the Imperial Valley, there were Punjabi partnerships, groups of bachelor workers with a "boss man" living in established labor camps, and migrant laborers for whom the labor camps were seasonal destinations.[4] While most migrant workers were bachelors, some family men went on the labor circuit, often with their teenage sons. In hard times, wives and children went along, and the whole family worked. Among these migrant laborers, Sikh and Muslim families worked together. The statewide network of boss men and foremen was vital to Punjabis who were unable to settle down and secure land and credit in a particular locality.[5]

The settled farmers among the Punjabis built local networks of Anglo landowners, bankers, and lawyers that were crucial to success in agriculture. Although often illiterate and always labeled Hindu, Punjabi farmers established themselves in their local communities as other good farmers did—by building credit records with banks, suppliers of agricultural equipment and fertilizer, grocery stores, and automobile dealerships. They developed strong personal relationships with landowners, shippers, and attorneys, relationships that enabled them to continue farming after the 1923 application to them of the California Alien Land Laws. (Those laws should have confined them, like other "aliens ineligible to citizenship," to the laborer role in agriculture.) In fact, the number of attorneys and even judges who held land on behalf of Punjabis in defiance of the law is surprising.[6]

Mola Singh told how he and his father got a Brawley judge, H. B. Griffin, to "give his name," and how they farmed with his help.

> My father put $2,000 in his bankbook, in Judge Griffin's name. Daddy Griffin, he was a long-time Brawley judge, you know. We farmed his place, share rent, for two years. He had to pay with his check, for labor, to prove we were working for him and not farming, see. When we sold some stock, we had to use his name too. If I wanted to buy something, we had to use his name, he had to pay for it, you know.[7]

Relationships with powerful Anglos in local society were characterized by a spirit of equality.[8] One Holtville Sikh farmer not only got loans from his local bank but made the bank's president guardian of his two sons and holder of his land; a Muslim farmer, in the desperate days of the depression, gave a crucial loan to his Swiss neighbor and later got two loans when he himself was in need.[9] Mola Singh's account of an El Centro landowner who "fronted" for him reveals the personal nature of the relationship:

> He was an honest man, with a cap, a little cap, eyeglasses, a cigar. He was single, still single, an old man. You know what he had? One room, maybe a 50-cent room, with all his checkbooks, two

boxes filled up, all his canceled checks in two boxes. I went to his room lots of times, we sat out there in the 50-cent room he had. He took one glass of beer, that's all. He didn't want to spend money. . . .

[Once we went together to a cotton gin in Indio through West-moreland.] We stopped in a restaurant, we ate, and they charged me 40 cents for the food we ate there. . . .

"Oh, my God," he said, "this is too much."

All the way coming and going from Indio to Brawley, he didn't forget that 40 cents. He said, "They charge too much. I spend 15 cents, 25 cents, and I eat all I want to, in El Centro."

I said, "Parker, that's a highway road, you know, they want to make money."

"No," he said, "that's too much."

But he was a very good honest man, honest. Two years we worked together. He liked me, but it was too much trouble, you know.[10]

Among the Punjabi men, daily afternoon work breaks formed important bonds. The Holtville park was perhaps the most famous site of such gatherings. Many townspeople recalled the men's pickup trucks, loud voices and boisterous joking.[11] All the Punjabis working in the area came together on the grass for at least an hour of rest and talk. Although the Punjabi-Mexican women and children did not go, because it was a men's work break and the conversation was in Punjabi, they sometimes made their presence known. The memories are fond, even playful. Once Sucha Singh Garewal, a leading Holtville farmer, removed his sweaty socks only to expose brightly painted red toenails, compliments of his Mexican niece. He had been napping with his shoes and socks off earlier that day, and she had adorned his toes.[12]

The Punjabi men formed local organizations, which typically bridged the lines of religion in rural and urban California. The Hindustani Welfare and Reform Society, founded in the Imperial Valley in 1918, was led by Ram Chand, Asa Singh, and Fazl Din (a Hindu, a Sikh, and a Muslim). This was for the mutual aid of farmers, and representatives of the society were called in as mediators in civil suits.[13]

The Punjabi men also formed statewide political organizations. These were somewhat loosely based on religion or regional origin, the nationalist movement back in India, or the drive for U.S. citizenship. First was the

Pacific Coast Khalsa Diwan Society, a Sikh organization founded in Stockton in 1912 that constructed a Sikh temple in 1915. A major function of this society was ensuring that Sikhs who died were cremated—usually the bodies were sent to Sacramento for that purpose. The temple had quarters for travelers. The working men took turns serving as *granthi*, or priest; the role is not a very specialized one in Sikhism, although it does require literacy to read the Granth Sahib, or Sikh "Bible." This temple served as a central meeting place for the Punjabis of California, and non-Sikhs came even on days of Sikh festivals and observances.[14]

Punjabi Muslims formed the Moslem Association of America in Sacramento in 1919–1920 but did not acquire a mosque until the mid 1940s. But the Muslims rented halls and met regularly, often in the Travelers Hotel. Most important, they bought a plot in Sacramento City Cemetery in which Punjabi Muslims from all over central and northern California were buried. Similar Muslim organizations, formed in El Centro and Phoenix, Arizona, also bought burial plots. These plots were known to the public as "Hindu plots"—in fact, all Hindus and Sikhs were cremated, and only Muslims were buried in the plots![15]

The most active early statewide organization was the militant anti-British Ghadar party, formed in California in 1913. Partly inspired by the American revolt against British colonialism, the party's membership included Sikh, Muslim, and Hindu Punjabis.[16] Its propaganda also protested British imperialism in China,[17] reminding us of the cosmopolitan background of many of the Punjabi immigrants. Early Ghadar party leaders were urban-based intellectuals and students who drew on the farmers for funds and support.

Because the Ghadar party's international alliances aroused the federal government's suspicion, it fell prey to government persecution. Internal dissent also marked its activities. The prominent Ghadar leader Ram Chandra was tried by the U.S. government in 1918, but his dramatic murder by a fellow Punjabi during the trial[18] caused great dissension, and the party was taken over by Sikhs from the Doaba. A Doaba Educational Society, formed to promote education (particularly of girls) in the Punjab, often met at the Stockton *gurdwara* in conjunction with Ghadar party meetings. As factional fighting increasingly characterized Ghadar activities,[19] Malwa men formed the U.S. American Malwa Sudharak Society, a nonprofit organization incorporated in Stockton in the late 1920s. The society's stated purpose was the encouragement of educational training, in Malwa in particular and in India in general, the promotion of Sikhism, and the teaching of respect and patriotism for both India and the United States. Malwa men from the Imperial Valley and Fresno were involved in this organization, too. As with the Khalsa Diwan Society, disputes within the organization over the proper election of leaders and the use of money led to several court cases.[20]

Statewide organizations were strongest and most active in central and northern California, where most Punjabis remained bachelors and were heavily involved in political activities throughout their lives. Over the years, the Imperial Valley gained a reputation as a refuge from political factionalism. The family life of the men there led to a decline of contributions, in both money and time, to political causes; many wives opposed the drain on family finances and accused Ghadar party leaders of using the funds for personal gain. But occasional political speakers did come through.[21]

Another important state and nationwide network for the men was built around the fight for U.S. citizenship. Sixty-nine persons of "Hindu race" had been naturalized before the 1923 Supreme Court decision (*United States* v. *Bhagat Singh Thind*) that made Asian Indians ineligible for U.S. citizenship.[22] The citizenship battle united urban and rural Asian Indians, and organizers collected funds from Punjabi farmers and workers all over the American Southwest.

Urban and rural Asian Indians also continued to be closely linked by economic constraints and opportunities in these early decades. Those who could still enter legally, university students from India, used to do farmwork during summers in Punjabi crews under Punjabi bosses. This pattern persisted into the 1950s.[23] Meanwhile, Indian lawyers and other professionals living in California's cities invested in farmland and employed Punjabi crews.[24] Some educated men who had difficulty securing appropriate jobs turned to farming.[25]

There were so many Punjabi men in California that it became necessary to differentiate between men with the same name. This could be done by adding a village or caste name—for example, Inder Singh Chajjawal and Inder Singh Chuhra. At least two new naming systems were devised as well. One relied on nicknames, Spanish in the south and English in the north. Thus two Sucha Singhs in the Imperial Valley were known as Sucha El Gordo and Sucha El Loco. The other system used the English alphabet to indicate the chronology of migration. For example, the first

Sucha Sidhu to arrive used that name, while the second added B, as in B. Sucha Sidhu, and the third would be C. Sucha Sidhu.[26]

The Punjabi men also utilized networks from India. Village, district, and regional origins in the Punjab served as reference points in the United States, but activities organized on the basis of them were almost always aimed at goals located in India. Most men knew others' villages of origin, and sometimes the village name was added to the man's name in the United States. Wives and children mastered these village names too, and they generally knew which men came from their husband's or father's village.[27] Village and district names often were the only identifying information on Muslim tombstones found in the graveyards from Sacramento to El Centro. Tombstone inscriptions were largely in Urdu, indicating the limited literacy in English and the audience to which they were addressed. Few even thought it necessary to put "Punjab" or "India"; the village and district names were sufficient.[28] Similarly, when the men were asked to record a place of birth or origin, frequently only a village name was given. This was still true decades after their immigration, on naturalization petitions filed in the 1950s and later.[29]

Despite the continuing identification of men by their villages, village ties seldom formed the basis of partnerships, marriages, or residencies in California. Perhaps this is not surprising, since nonrelated villagers in the Punjab competed in farming, and marriage rules required marrying outside one's own village; there would be no reason save common immigrant status for fellow villagers in California to cooperate in farming or to marry related women. There were scattered instances where fellow villagers were called on for court testimony, for jobs during the depression, and for care of a widow, but these were relatively few. Analysis of the men born in India who applied for U.S. citizenship in the Imperial Valley after 1946 shows that very few from the same village had settled in Imperial County.[30] Some fifty village names were given on these naturalization petitions; only eight villages had more than one man. These eight villages accounted for nineteen men, two or three from each village. Of the village mates who settled in Imperial County, there is only one instance of marriage to sisters, and those men were brothers and partners, not just village mates.[31] Other attempts to trace village mates found sets of them widely scattered.[32] Yet the Punjabis did keep in touch with their villages and their village mates, as at least one solicitation of villagers to build a school back in India shows.[33]

An exceptional instance of villager solidarity involved one of the few "real Indian" families in California—the family of Bakhshish Singh Dhillon.[34] A soldier for the British in Hong Kong, Dhillon reportedly made trips to California in 1887 and 1899; he returned to India for his wife in 1909. Dhillon was one of the few Sikhs in California from the village of Sursingh. Dozens of Muslims from Sursingh were in California, however, and Dhillon was close to both the Sikhs and the Muslims from Sursingh.

From the beginning, Muslim and Sikh fellow villagers were a strong presence in the life of the Dhillon family. Bakhshish Singh Dhillon and Rattan Kaur were bringing up their seven children as orthodox Sikhs, but the boys found it hard to take the teasing their long hair and turbans earned them from other children. (At this time they lived in Oregon, and snowballs were a wintertime threat.) Fearing his wife would not agree to cutting their hair, the father arranged for his Muslim fellow villagers to "kidnap" his boys for a picnic in the forest that included haircutting. Then the Sursingh men and boys returned to the Dhillon home, announcing that the external signs of Sikhism could not be maintained in their new home.[35]

Sursingh Muslims were helpful again when farming was not good in Fresno. Many of them had settled in the Imperial Valley, and the Dhillons went there and joined others in working for Muhammad Baksh (a spokesman for Punjabis, an educated man married to an Anglo woman in Holtville). Later, during the depression, the Dhillons went to Los Angeles, where a cousin, Lachman Singh, had settled near his Hispanic wife's family; he was not able to provide work, however.

Fellow villagers felt responsible for the Dhillon children following the death of their parents. Bakhshish Singh Dhillon died in 1926, leaving his wife with seven children, the oldest fifteen or sixteen, and one more on the way. Fearing they would be held responsible for the care of a Sikh widow and her children, many villagers proposed shipping the six younger children back to India. Bud, the second boy, had just returned from a Ghadar party attempt to take arms into India through Burma and Tibet.[36] He helped keep the family together in California, opposing the effort to send any children to India and rejecting the idea of arranged marriages. Again, at the death of their mother in 1932, fellow villagers offered advice and financial help. The Dhillon children were aware of pressures from their friends, men concerned not only to help them but to maintain reputations back in Sursingh, but they continued to live markedly independent lives, the older children caring for the younger ones.[37]

Regional origin was another possible basis of networks for the Punjabis in the United States. The Sikhs referred to themselves as Malwas, Doabas, and Majhalis, according to the three regions delineated by the Beas and Sutlej rivers in the Punjabi. (For the Muslims and Hindus here, these regional terms were less relevant; Muslims tended to come from farther west and the Hindus from towns.[38]) Initially, no organizations were formed based on Malwa–Doaba–Majha origin, but rivalry between the Malwas and the Doabas eventually split the Ghadar party.[39] Also, when their children grew up and some fathers sought to arrange marriages, regional loyalties were brought into play.

Most of the Hindus from the Punjab were urban men, both in India and in California, owners of town properties who had their own statewide network. The 1942 death of Ram Pershad Loroia, a liquor store owner in Brawley, activated that network. All his heirs were back in Jullundur City, his native place. But Karm Chand, who held power of attorney for Ram Pershad and was the preeminent "Hindu store man" in Marysville, was also from Jullundur City and had a brother, Labu Ram, in Brawley. Karm Chand petitioned the Imperial County court for appointment as special administrator of Ram Pershad's estate. A telegram from the widow in India arrived making the same request (an interesting coincidence!), and he was so authorized. Karm Chand journeyed to the Imperial Valley, sued two local Sikh debtors, and sold the business to another Hindu, Malawa Ram, from Brawley. A claim was filed on the estate by Paritem Poonian, a Sikh who ran a nursery business in Loomis in northern California, for a loan of $20 he had made to the deceased. The estate was then sold and the proceeds sent to the widow in India.[40] The network linking the small number of Punjabi businessmen in California was not only statewide but extended back to India.

For perhaps obvious reasons, the network least drawn on in California was that of marriage alliances back in the Punjab. The men did not always continue to send money back to their families in India, and many remarried in the United States. But one man's chief inspiration in coming to California was his brother-in-law (his older sister's husband), a foreman on a big ranch in Mendota, who wrote letters urging him to come on to California from Fiji, New Zealand, the Philippines, Guatemala, Panama, and Mexico.[41] Such affinal connections were rare among the immigrants.

Caste and religion could have been the basis of groups or networks, but evidence points to their relative unimportance for social relations among the Punjabis in California. In contrast to their usually sharp memories of village and ship names, Punjabi-Mexican children have difficulty correctly recalling caste designations used by their fathers. Table 9 contrasts the Punjabi and California versions of these social categories.

Descendants of Muslims named various groups: "Rajaputs (Rajputs)," "Raes (Arains)," "Khans and Afghanistans (Pathans)," and "Hindus who became Muslims." Descendants of Sikhs talked of "Pandits" or "Rams (Hindus)," "Mohameds," and "Singhs," and among the Singhs the Jats and Chuhras (Untouchables). Descendants of Hindus mentioned "Bohmans (Brahmans)," "Kathris (Khatris)," and "Juts (Jats)," along with Singhs and Mohameds. Most terms have been distorted slightly in transmission, but the social references are clear, and their fathers' opinions about them have persisted. The sone of a Khatri had this to say about the caste system: "I don't know about others. We were Kathris, the most educated and wealthy; there were some called Bohmans, and most were workers, the low-class Juts." The son of a Rajput Muslim spoke of "other Muslims, villager or Okie types we called Chachis, and those Khans from the frontier," while the son of a Pathan mentioned "Rajaput Muslims and other converts."[42]

Among the Sikhs, stories of caste origin in India invariably concerned Untouchables, or Chuhras. There were only two Untouchable Sikhs in the Imperial Valley, and they met with the other Punjabis in the Holtville park for afternoon talks. One of them, nicknamed "the Cowboy" because he dressed like one, always brought a striped blanket to sit on in the park. The other men teased him: "Who does he think he is, sitting on that special blanket while we're on the ground, and he's just a Chuhra, after all." The Cowboy did not marry in California. The other Untouchable lived in El Centro. He married but had no children, and even Anglos in the town noticed that he was somehow "different" from the other Punjabis. In Arizona, a "sweeper" (Chuhra) was remembered, a man who was educated and did not drink; he married a Hispanic woman and did not bring her or their son when he joined other Punjabi families at social gatherings.[43]

Thus caste and religious designations from India continued to be used, but they did not serve as the basis for organizing in California, for either the men or their descendants. The one possible exception is that of Sikh

Table 9. The Social Landscape

Terms used in India

Punjabis—from the Punjab, speakers of Punjabi

Sikh	*Muslim*	*Hindu*
Jat	Pathan	Brahman
Chuhra (Untouchables)	Rajput	Khatri (Urban merchants)
	Arain (Gardeners)	

Terms used in California and Arizona

Hindus or *Punjabs*[a]—from India, speakers of Hindu or Punjabi

Singhs	*Mohameds*	*Pandits/Rams*
Jat	Khans	Bohman/Brahma
Chuhra	Punjabi Muslims/Rajputs	Kathri
	Raes	Sikhs who became Hindus
	Chachis ("Okie" Muslims)	
	Rajputs who became Khans	
	Hindus who became Muslims	
	Pakistanis	

[a]an Arizona usage

and Muslim religious organizations. They played a role when a Punjabi died in the United States, and some of their importance lay in reporting back to India that the proper ceremonies had been performed. But even the Sikh temple in Stockton did not divide the Punjabis along religious lines. It played its most significant role as a multipurpose meeting place for all Punjabis in the American West, serving economic, political, and social ends as frequently as religious ones.

Female Networks

Female networks overlapped in some respects with those linking the Punjabi men, but in other ways were different.[44] Women's origins proved even harder to trace than men's, not because their origins were unknown or so badly misspelled that descendants could not trace them, but because they seemed unimportant; they were seldom mentioned or written down. The women from Mexico did not write or send money to families left behind. Sometimes they lost touch even with siblings just over the border. Racial and ethnic groupings in Mexico were more fluid than in India, and the women were drawn from geographically scattered places of origin. Even between women from the same place in Mexico, there seemed to be no special ties, although those from the same places in New Mexico or Arizona often were close.

The important networks for the Hispanic women were based on blood relatives and fictive kin, or *compadres* and *comadres*. The most significant structural linkage was between related women, usually sisters, married to Punjabis. Among Mexican Americans, the importance of the mother–daughter relationship and the closeness between sisters have been recognized; there is even a special term for unrelated men married to sisters.[45] Sometimes overlapping with that, but based to a significant extent on common residential location and time of childbearing, was the *compadrazgo*, or ritual kinship, system.

A large proportion of Punjabi wives were members of sets of related women. Of approximately 300 Hispanic women married to Punjabis, at least 114 belonged to such sets. Even among black and Anglo women, there were five or six sets of sisters or related women. There are several explanations for this phenomenon. Most of the Hispanic women entering these marriages were from the migrant labor class and saw marriage as a way to improve their status, since the Punjabis had relatively bright prospects as farmers (at least before the Alien Land Laws were applied to them). But Mexican men resented such marriages, and to some extent the women who made them placed themselves and their relatives outside the local Mexican communities. Yet a wife's parents, possibly even her brothers, might benefit economically from the marriage. Some parents accepted a payment for their daughter; other parents became part of a Punjabi farmer's joint household. In a few instances, a brother was employed by a Punjabi or was engaged to hold land on his behalf. Initially, then, there were potential economic advantages when women from a Hispanic family married the newcomers from India.

Once a set of marriages had taken place, the sisters often served as godmothers, or *comadres*, to one another's children, strengthening the ties among the women. These marriages did not always work out; in these instances, the entire set of sisters or female relatives tended to divorce and remarry non-Punjabis.[46] The women acted together, and their *compadrazgo*, or prior kinship ties, outlasted the marriages.

In the *compadrazgo* relationships, the majority of the godparents came from within the Punjabi-Mexican community. Non-Catholic Punjabi men were seemingly accepted as godfathers by Catholic churches in California and elsewhere, albeit they were sometimes given Hispanic first names on official documents (e.g., Miguel for Maghyar Singh). The reasons for this acceptance are not entirely clear, but it did not lead to conversions to Catholicism.[47] A Punjabi-Mexican child's godfather was almost invariably Punjabi, and the godmother was his Hispanic wife. Even when the godparents were not married to each other, godparents were usually a Punjabi man and a Hispanic woman. In a handful of instances, Hispanic relatives of the baby's mother served as godparents.[48] The *compadrazgo* system, then, functioned primarily to strengthen relationships between the Punjabi-Mexican couples and between the women, not to integrate the Punjabi men into local Hispanic or Catholic communities.

Most literature stresses the higher status of the godfather and his potential usefulness,[49] but the godmother was the pivotal figure. The factors important in choosing godparents point to this. Proximity was a major factor. Most godparents were members of the same rural community as the parents: Brawley, Holtville, Imperial, and so forth. After proximity, the timing of births was important. Women giving birth at about the same time, over the same span of years, tended to be godparents to one another's children.[50] Occasionally, Hispanic blood relatives living elsewhere were named godparents. Particularly close friendships between Punjabi-Mexican couples could bridge not only distance but religion—a Muslim could be godfather to a Sikh's child, and vice versa.[51]

It is difficult to ascertain how important *compadrazgo* ties really were. Among Punjabi-Mexicans, most emphasis was placed on the godparents at baptism with less attention given to confirmation, marriage, or the many other occasions for which godparents could be named.[52] Some children speak of their godparents with great affection, while others have forgotten who they were. Where other ties coincided—where the women were sisters or neighbors for many years or godparents to one another's children, or the men were long-time partners—godparents were clearly important.

Godparents were supposed to instruct their godchildren in the teachings of the Catholic church, but the relationships formed by Punjabi-Mexican families were not particularly religious. Most of the women involved in them did not attend church regularly, and some were in fact Protestants.[53] I know of no case where the men listed in official baptismal records converted completely to Catholicism (a few said they were both Sikh and Catholic) or attempted to offer religious instruction of any sort to their godchildren. They did give gifts of money, clothes, and toys to their godchildren, but they also gave gifts to other children.

While the women often had very close female relatives married to Punjabis, their more distant blood relatives constituted a somewhat weaker network. Some were a resource during the depression or when children needed care. Several families moved to Mexico to try to survive economic hardships, while others left one or more children to be brought up by maternal relatives in Mexico or in the United States. "Raised by the grandmother, Mexican style," typically happened when an infant's mother left or died, or when someone had an illegitimate child. When a Punjabi father was jailed on a murder charge, one of his children spent four years in Juarez, Mexico, with the mother's relatives; the little boy hardly spoke English when he returned, and a family photo of him in an embroidered Spanish cowboy suit bespeaks his thoroughly Mexican boyhood.[54] One man, whose wife had left him, kept his son but took his daughter across into Mexico and found a family to care for her. Some couples who were childless adopted the youngest, or "extra," child of another Punjabi-Mexican couple; some Hispanic women to whom children were entrusted temporarily wanted to keep them permanently.[55]

Wives of Punjabis learned little about the religious, caste, and regional networks stemming from the Punjab. The knowledge they gained about Punjabi society was superficial and often came from other wives or their husbands' bachelor partners. Securely based in female kin groups here, most of them had little curiosity about India. Examples of their comments are these: "My husband was a member of the Singh religion . . . he was twenty, twenty-one years older than me, but this race does not look old. . . . my husband's partner told me that if a Muslim came to the door, the Hindu would not let him in but would talk to him outside." "Oh, yes, we ate beef, but there was another kind of Hindu, called Mohammedan, and they didn't eat pork." "Her three husbands were all Mohameds, though I'm not sure, one couldn't eat beef and another pork." "My husband told me the Hindus and the Pakistanis do not like each other in India, but here they are all united."[56]

One Hispanic wife, asked by an American missionary woman whether she would like to visit India, reportedly responded: "I tell my husband his country too far away. Who know what they do so far off? . . . I was born in this country, and my mother and sisters before me. They live here now. Do you think I would leave them to go off with a strange man to a country where a man can have many wives and beat them all day long if he wants to? No! America is a good country for women."[57]

There were very few relationships between Hispanic wives and the few Punjabi wives in California. There were no women from India in the Imperial Valley, the stronghold of Punjabi-Mexican family life. In northern California, there were four wives from India, one in the Yuba City area and three others in Loomis and near Orangevale; the latter three were relatively isolated, from each other as well as from other Punjabi-fathered families. The experiences of these "real Indian" families in rural California before the late 1940s reveal that far from being centers of Punjabi community life in California, the families were isolated and set apart.

Of the five "real Indian" couples who raised families in rural California,[58] three were Sikh and two were Hindu. Of the latter, one was Brahman and the other was Khatri. The best-known family is that of Puna and Nand Kaur Singh in Yuba City. Nand Kaur was friendly with the Hispanic and Anglo wives of other Punjabis in her area.[59] Their seven children were brought up as Sikhs, but Nand Kaur adapted herself readily to American dress and customs. There is one poignant story of her at a Utah trading post (before the move to California). She saw other women, "tall and colored like us," with long black braids, and "I felt like going over to them and hugging them." But her husband told her they were American Indians. She went over to listen to them. He was right; they were not speaking Punjabi.[60]

Another Sikh family from India, the Poonians, who ran a nursery in Loomis, was typically Punjabi. Dhana Singh Poonian had come to California, leaving his married brother Chinta behind. Chinta died in India, and according to Punjabi custom, Dhana went back and married the widow, Raj Kaur. He brought her and her two sons back to California, leaving a daughter in India. The older of the two boys died at age eight, the younger survived. After Dhana himself died in 1934, Raj Kaur ran the nursery business with her son.[61]

The third Sikh family, that of Bakhshish Singh Dhillon in the Fresno area, has already been mentioned in connection with the Sursingh villagers and their involvement with the children after the deaths of both parents. After bringing his wife to California through Singapore, Hong Kong, and the Philippines, Dhillon moved around a good deal and settled longest near Fresno. Rattan Kaur rarely saw the other women from India. She had no one to help her when she delivered her eight children, no one to tell her what to eat or when to rest during and after her pregnancies. Rattan Kaur could not speak Spanish well enough to converse with the Hispanic wives who dominated the Fresno community. The Hispanic wives tended to be jealous of her; being one of so few women from India, she was treated with great respect and affection by all the Punjabi men. In Fresno, her closest friend was a Japanese woman. Without a common language, they sat in the kitchen together, giggling and talking in signs. While the sons of the family were instrumental to other Punjabi men because they were American citizens and were trusted holders of land for others, the mother and daughters were more isolated. This family had almost no contact with Punjabi-Mexican families until after both parents had died, and the contacts then were not close, since the children were nearly grown up.[62]

The Khatri family of Ramnath Puri ended up in farming too, although Ramnath Puri was an educated man who came to the eastern United States around 1902 to avoid being jailed by the British for seditious activities. He returned for his wife in 1906 and brought her to San Francisco, where he had become a U.S. citizen and published a nationalist newspaper in Urdu, the first Urdu newspaper in the United States. The three Puri children were born in the first two decades of the century. Older than others fathered by Punjabis in northern California, they grew up with few peers and had little to do with Punjabi-Mexican families.[63]

The fifth Indian family, the Sareerams, were Brahmans. They farmed in Orangevale near the Puris for some years. The mother died in 1946 and the father in 1951, leaving an older daughter to raise the younger children. Married to a Catholic, she raised them in her husband's faith. These children did know their Punjabi-Mexican peers, and at least one of them later attended school in the Imperial Valley.[64]

A few Sareerams and other children from the "real Indian" families married children of Punjabi-Mexican parentage (see Chapter 8). But some of the older children do not recall using any designation for the children of the Punjabi-Mexican couples, they had so little interaction with them. And with the exception of Nand Kaur, the wives from India were not well connected to the other wives of Punjabis and were geographically isolated from one another.

The strongest women's networks, then, were those initially based on Hispanic kinship ties, reinforced and expanded by marriages to Punjabis, settlement in particular localities, and childbearing accompanied by *compadrazgo* ties to other women married to Punjabis. Hispanic wives knew many other Punjabi men, men who could be employers or co-workers of their husbands and godfathers to their children. As dependants and sometimes as field workers themselves, the women knew more about the men's work networks than about other male networks. Those male activities related to India, in particular, remained separate and were not part of the female world.

Gender and Ethnicity

By some generally accepted measures of "ethnic maintenance," a Punjabi "ethnic subsystem" was well developed in California.[65] Economic activity continued to link Sikh, Muslim, and Hindu immigrants into the 1930s. Men knew the conditions governing leasing, farming, and labor throughout the state, and they used the Punjabi network as they moved about. The Sikh temple at Stockton, the only one in the state until 1947, certainly linked the Sikhs and all the Punjabi men in associational activities (theoretically emphasizing their cultural distinctiveness and affirming ethnic solidarity). The Ghadar party and the drive for U.S. citizenship mobilized

Punjabi men and money throughout the state. The Punjabi and Urdu languages were used in these activities. While a man's place of origin, caste, and religion served as points of social reference in California, and played a role in organizing activities related to India, the activities related to the United States included all the Punjabi men.

But this Punjabi ethnic group was an all-male one in many senses, and the disjunction between male and female networks means that even the seemingly natural social unit of the family must be examined closely.[66] It is clear that the women and children were not integrated into all the men's activities, even though some wives and children traveled with the men to agricultural jobs all over the state, many others went to the Stockton temple regularly, and most were familiar with Punjabi political leaders and economic brokers. But the female view of the men's activities was often different from the male view. The women and children have their own distinctive memories of the Stockton Sikh temple. For them, it was a stopping place on travels around the state, a place to sleep and eat Punjabi food, a place to see many "uncles" and other Punjabi-Mexican children. Here children from the Imperial Valley met those coming over from Phoenix and elsewhere to work in the northern California orchards. Usually the women and children went to the movies or for ice cream in downtown Stockton, while the men talked politics (in Punjabi) at the temple. At the temple, the women smoked together in the bathrooms and gossiped (in Spanish or English) while the children played.[67]

In the English-speaking arena, gender was also a significant barrier to female participation. The local Anglo network of landowners, bankers, and lawyers, of paramount importance to Punjabis of the farmer class, was a male network even more exclusive than the Punjabi-speaking ones. Hispanic wives seldom were acquainted with the Anglo men so crucial to their husbands' livelihoods. It was rare for a Punjabi farmer to introduce his wife to his banker or lawyer. Several wives, notably well educated for their time and class, kept the books and bargained with shippers on behalf of their husbands and other Punjabis. An even smaller number of wives, termed "educated" or sometimes "blond" Mexicans, were on social terms with Anglos in their communities.[68] But for the most part, Hispanic wives were excluded from local Anglo society in the early decades.

Punjabi men paid careful and respectful attention to the Anglo women they met, the wives of Anglo farmers and women in the stores in town. This contrasted to some extent with the way in which they treated their own wives and other Hispanic women in the Imperial Valley. Fear of arousing latent prejudice and respect for the dominant class shaped their behavior toward Anglo women, while they often shared the derogatory attitudes of the Anglo farmers toward "Mexican girls" and indeed toward all Mexicans.

The Punjabi men's relations with Mexican Americans and local Mexican American society were not close. It is true that ethnic similarities between the men and women were most striking at the time these marriages began to occur. Like Mexicans, the Punjabis were discriminated against by white society. At least half the women, like the men, were pioneers in a new country and from a group also entering the agricultural economy as laborers. The signatures of bride and groom alike on the marriage certificates testify to low levels of literacy. The men were learning Spanish to deal with Mexican agricultural laborers and to speak to their wives.

Despite these similarities, the men from India did not associate themselves with Mexican American culture or institutions. Relatively few were close to their wives' male relatives. Exceptions to that generalization occur chiefly in the very few families where the maternal parents-in-law lived and worked with the Punjabi-Mexican couple. In one case, a couple running a dairy had the parents-in-law, a sister-in-law, and all the children milking and caring for the cows. There were men, particularly those whose wives died and left them with children to raise, who "turned Mexican" as their wives' relatives and their own children socialized them through domestic life. But Punjabi male camaraderie did not include Mexican men. The all-male socializing and drinking groups that met in town parks, bars, and one another's homes featured conversations conducted in Punjabi and excluded all who could not speak or follow that language. Those their children recalled as their fathers' *compadres* invariably turned out to be other Punjabis.[69]

The Punjabi "boss men" and farmers may have taken wives from the growing population of Mexican and Mexican American agricultural laborers, but I found only one case of a Punjabi and a Mexican farming as partners (it ended in a lawsuit).[70] The Punjabis farmed together and saw themselves as landowners, not agricultural laborers. None of the Punjabis became members of the *mutualistas*, the social and economic welfare associations set up by Mexican immigrants that also served as bases for the union organizing of the late 1920s and 1930s.[71] Punjabi men were labor contractors initially for other Punjabis, but they continued to operate in later decades under the *bracero* program, although most Mexican Americans opposed the program because it caused unemployment among them.[72]

Punjabi men are generally conceded to have had some prejudice toward Mexicans in general (the question of how they regarded their own wives is dealt with more fully in the next chapter). One informant thought that "most if not *all* Punjabi immigrants were openly contemptuous of Mexicans and things Mexican." The Punjabis did achieve varying degrees of proficiency in Spanish, so they could communicate with their Spanish-speaking workers, but they were not necessarily popular with them. In the Imperial Valley, white farmers reported that when they referred Mexicans looking for work to Punjabi farmers, it sometimes elicited negative comments. Some Punjabi employers were reputedly stingy and mean, their relations with workers so poor that Anglo neighbors attributed the barbed-wire fences and barricades typically surrounding Punjabi houses to fear of worker retaliation. Of course there were exceptions, men who got along well with their Mexican workers and men who eloquently defended Mexican workers against Anglo employers.[73]

The Mexican community did *not* welcome the men from India, nor did most Mexicans approve of the women marrying these immigrants. Several of the wives, now widows, recalled the disrespect and derision with which they were treated by Mexican workers. One woman said that her husband's own workers had shouted *"Hindera"* (Hindu's women) at her and her sister, until her father threatened them with his shotgun. Another reported similar taunts shouted at her and her mother by Mexican workers being trucked back from a night of irrigating. A Mexican woman friend standing with them shouted back an insulting reference to their imprisonment in the high-barred truck: *"Adios, tigres en una jaula"* (Goodbye, tigers in a cage)![74]

The social distancing by other Mexicans experienced by the women who married Punjabis was also apparent from the tendency for *compadrazgo*, or godparents, to be chosen from among the Punjabi-Mexican couples. Had the Punjabis and their wives been "assimilating" into local Mexican American society, with the *compadrazgo* system facilitating social mobility and social integration, one would expect many godparents to be from the local Mexican American communities. This was not the case.

One Hispanic wife, relatively isolated in Arizona from other Punjabi-

Mexican families, found that she and her children were rejected and ridiculed by the Mexican American neighbors. Her children and many other "half and halves" experienced prejudice and discrimination from Mexicans as much as from Anglos. For better or for worse, the Hispanic women who married Punjabis became part of the men's social world.[75]

In Yuba City, the division between Punjabis and Mexicans was, if anything, even more pronounced. Mexicans migrated there only in the 1940s, being preceded by some Punjabi-Mexican families in the 1930s. A book about the murders allegedly committed by Juan Corona quotes Dave Teja, son of a Sikh pioneer married to an Anglo woman and the Sutter County district attorney at that time. When a reporter covering the trial pronounced his name "Tayha," as it would be in Spanish, Teja corrected him sharply, saying, "I'm not a goddam Mexican."[76] The prejudice was largely class based, since Punjabi farmers typically employed Mexican laborers, but it reflects some ambivalence toward the Punjabi men married to Hispanic women as well.

Given these different male and female networks and the difficulties the Punjabi-Mexican couples and their children experienced in entering both Anglo and Mexican American society, their dependence on the Punjabi men and on other couples like themselves increased. Lack of knowledge of Punjabi was one barrier to the women's full inclusion in the men's activities, even if the Punjabi men had wanted to integrate them more fully. Another barrier was class, which combined with sexism and racism to minimize the Hispanic wives' interaction with Anglo farmers and businessmen.

Class also produced divisions within the Punjabi-Mexican community, differentiating families whose women did field work from those whose women did not. Family labor put women and children in touch with other (Mexican and Punjabi-Mexican) families, not with the bachelor (Punjabi) crews. Predictably, lower-class Punjabi-Mexican families had more closely overlapping male and female work worlds. Such families were closer to Mexican American society than to the Punjabi bachelor society.

It seems clear, however, that the men from India were not even remotely "assimilated" into Mexican American society. Yusuf Dadabhay, a scholar who did field work about 1950, argued that the Punjabi men did assimilate to "the Mexican American subculture," that this was their route to becoming fully American, by which he meant adherence to the

for the equality of the sexes in both Sikh and Muslim religious ideology, and Islam permits divorce, in practice both Sikh and Islamic law place women firmly under the control of men.[2]

Some marriage practices in the Punjab resulted from a shortage of women. The Punjab had the lowest sex ratio in India of females to males, a partial consequence of female infanticide and inferior health care for daughters.[3] Thus some men never married, and others practiced polyandry, or the sharing of one wife by several men. This practice was noted particularly among Sikhs. Men were responsible for their brother's widow. (Even today, with the sex ratio lower still, brothers sometimes share a wife.) Another practice attributed to the dearth of women was the occasional purchase of brides.[4]

Punjabi women shared in the martial tradition of the frontier to some extent. There is no greater epic romance in India than that of Heer and Ranjha, whose marriage was opposed because they came from two different communities among the Muslims. After many adventures, the young lovers were united at last, only to be tricked and meet violent deaths. Another well-known story is that of Sharan Kaur, the young Hindu bride who converted to Sikhism and became a brave woman spy for Maharaja Ranjit Singh in the early nineteenth century. After obtaining military secrets from a Pathan ruler, she murdered him. Then she helped foil a British-Afghan attack on a Sikh fort, and when four Pathans captured her, she killed them in hand-to-hand combat. The Maharaja personally bestowed honors on her.[5] Ordinary women led far more circumscribed lives.

The separation of the sexes was one of the most immediately noticeable features of rural Punjabi society, be it Jat Sikh, Muslim, or Hindu. This separation reflected the strength of consanguineal bonds and male companionship and the weakness of conjugal ties. Women in the Punjab followed the concepts of *purdah* in many ways, veiling before men in public and completely separated from men when sitting, talking, eating, and moving about publicly. Women spent most of their time with other women.[6] Men socialized with other men in the evenings, calling out whenever they liked for food prepared by the women and drinking heavily. Men planned family alliances carefully, establishing links through the marriages of their sisters and daughters and placing a high premium on a woman's honor because it maintained the family's honor.[7]

Marriage arrangement in the Punjab had to do with families, not with emotional bonds between individuals. Sexuality and love generally were unconnected with marriage; in fact, they were threatening to marriages and family reputations. One Sikh immigrant to California said that when he left the Punjab in 1913, if a young girl had done anything to bring dishonor on her family, such as talking to a boy, her father would have felt it necessary to "kill 'um, kill 'um good."[8] The Punjabi and Pathan Muslims followed a code that based family reputation on control and exchange of their women, a code often harsh toward romantic love. Thus love stories from the Pathan area (the Afghan-Pakistani border) rarely end happily; most often, the lovers die.[9]

Over half the wives of Punjabis in the United States came from Mexico, where conflict between church and state in the nineteenth century had produced divergent norms and practices related to marriage and the family. Legal reforms deprived the church of its authority over marriage: After the 1850s, marriage was wholly a civil contract, and civil registration was required for a legal marriage. Religious ceremonies had no legal standing, though couples might repeat their vows in a church ceremony. People complied slowly with the new codes, and many continued to marry in a church or live in informal union rather than marry in a civil ceremony. Children born to these church or "free union" relationships were illegitimate after the reforms. Illegitimate births in Mexico rose steadily in the late nineteenth and early twentieth centuries, highly correlated with rural, poor, and Indian populations (the proportion of such births was 42 percent in 1900–1905, with great regional variation). The nineteenth-century reforms provided for legal separations and annulments, but divorce became possible only following the Mexican Revolution of 1910–1917.[10]

Comparison of the civil codes in California and Mexico shows stronger legal support for the marital union in Mexico.[11] California's civil code in the early twentieth century defined marriage as a personal relationship arising out of a civil contract, and divorce was possible. The Mexican civil code defined marriage as the lawful partnership of one man and one woman united in an indissoluble bond in order to perpetuate their species and to assist each other to bear the burden of life. The unity and stability of the family were reinforced, and the interests of children were safeguarded. In Mexico, impediments to marriage included want of legal age and want of consent of the person exercising the *patria potestad* (the father and, in his absence, the mother). Females under age twelve could not marry unless a dispensation was granted, nor could persons of either sex under twenty-one marry without the consent of their father, or, if no father was living or known, of their mother. (The legal ages at marriage were raised to fourteen for women and sixteen for men in the Federal Civil Code of 1928.[12]) The husband and wife were bound to reciprocal fidelity, the wife to live with her husband and obey him in domestic matters and in matters concerning the education of their children and the management of their property.

Divorce became possible under Mexican civil law in 1917. Grounds for divorce included adultery, particularly by the wife; a husband's proposal to prostitute his wife; abandonment of the conjugal home; extreme cruelty, threats, or grave abuse; false accusations; and refusal to provide support. When a petition for divorce was presented, a conciliation procedure was set in action by a judge. Upon divorce, male children over the age of three were to remain in the custody of the father and female children with the mother. Illegitimate or adulterine children (and there were many of the former, because of the prevalence of nonlegal unions) were protected in that the names of the parents could not be entered in official records. Further provisions of the code enjoined any living relative to protect any child, the father's kin coming first in line to assume responsibility.

In law, then, there were similarities between India and Mexico in matters of parental authority and the precedence given to the patrilineage, but Mexican law provided for divorce and for the care of illegitimate children. California law also provided for divorce with somewhat less attempt at conciliation. Both Mexican and California law provided for community property, a concept foreign to the Punjabi men. In practice, however, Mexican family life differed considerably from that envisioned by the legal codes, and in ways that conflicted strongly with Punjabi law and practice. The concept of romantic love in Mexican culture sanctioned courtship of brides (and men's extramarital affairs after marriage). At lower socioeconomic levels, many men and women entered into free unions, without benefit of civil or religious marriage.[13] The marital histories of the Mexican and Mexican American women who married Punjabis often featured multiple marriages or sequential marriages, producing children by several husbands (see Chapter 4). This pattern characterized many of their mothers as well, women who had married two or more times in Mexico or in the southwestern United States.

On America's western frontier, a shortage of women heightened tales of romantic love, and at the same time arranged marriages of one sort or another often proved desirable (thus the Japanese "picture brides" and the Swiss "mail order brides"). Relationships with women in the American West involved some very real adaptations and discomforts for the Punjabi men as they learned new relationships between love, marriage, and divorce. Above all, the men learned about women's rights to divorce. Mola Singh eloquently testified about his experiences:

> In this country, it's a different class of people. You can't force love here, women go where they want to, even if they're married, even with three or four kids. In India, you could only get a divorce after India got freedom. Here, women go away, here it's different. The woman is the boss in this country. A woman can have four husbands, a man can have two or three women. What you gonna do, that's the way with love. . . .
>
> Sometimes I feel like I'm suffering here, you know, trouble at home. Here, when you marry, you have woman trouble, kid trouble, not like in India. When I got here, I saw, you have liberty, women have liberty, you know. The way it is here, I've been separated, divorced. In India, you stay together all your life. In this country, you have love. When you love a person, you stay with her, with her kids and everything.
>
> I divorced Carmen, when she went away to Mexico. I couldn't do anything, so I filed for divorce. She had two more kids by then. My wife in India, she'd died already by that time. Yes, I knew about divorce. In this country, I no sleep. Everybody was divorced, I could see what they were doing. It's only normal, you see the customs of the country, and so you have to do that. Bhagat Singh divorced too.[14]

The same man gave a dramatic account of the breakup of his second marriage to a Hispanic woman in the course of an evening of drinking at his joint household:

> Then in 1934 or 1936, this Maria went away. She went to a man who worked for me, Galindo. We were having a big party, with my cousin Lalu (the single one, my cousin brother who farmed with me), and Buta Singh and his wife, and Mota Singh and Julia, and

my father. It was a big party, we all drank. And that Mexican boy . . . I wanted someone to make food, so I called Maria to get him to come in the kitchen to make food. She said, "Yes, he'll come, if I call him." And he did come, he made *roti* and other things. We ate, and we Hindu men all watched the lovers. We saw how they looked at each other. We all knew.

Mota said, "You know what she's doing, I won't let mine do that."

I asked her, "Do you love him more?"

She said, "Yes, I love him more." So I hit her, and I kicked them both out. They went to Mexico. . . .

She said, "Okay, this is my friend, I'm going with him."

I couldn't say, "No, you can't go."

In this country, when she wants to go, my wife, she says, "All right, sonny honey, I'm going," and I say, "I can't stop you." It's because of love, therefore I couldn't stop her.

The themes of Mola Singh's narrative—romantic love as the basis of marriage, men's inability to exercise effective control over women, the ever-present possibility of divorce—are borne out by measures of marital conflict and instability traceable in the public records.

Murder, Divorce, and Remarriage

Murders were the most violent resolution of marital conflict between Punjabi husband and Hispanic wife. A 1919 murder involved the first Punjabi-Mexican marriage in the Imperial Valley. Valentina, eldest of the Alvarez sisters, married Rullia Singh, and they had a baby boy within a year of the marriage. Her daughter, Alejandrina, also married a Sikh, Albert Joe (the American name he took),[15] and she too had a baby (see photos 8 and 9). Albert Joe and Alejandrina ran a dairy southeast of Holtville, next to the ranch of Albert Joe's brother, Gajjan Singh, and they visited Valentina and Rullia every Sunday.

But conflict between Rullia Singh and Valentina led to tragedy. In the spring of 1919, Alejandrina and Albert Joe went for their usual Sunday visit with the older couple. Valentina announced that she was leaving

Rullia and asked her daughter and son-in-law to take her and her infant son away with them. They all left together, with an irate Rullia Singh threatening Albert Joe's life if he did not return his wife. These threats were repeated in the presence of other Punjabi men in the Holtville park over the next few months. Rullia also visited Albert Joe and Alejandrina and told them to "return the mother," threatening in both Punjabi and Spanish. Valentina did not return. She and the baby moved to San Diego, and when Rullia tried to see them, she called the police and Rullia was fined $50 for molesting her. At the end of November, as Albert Joe worked in the milk house to separate the cream from the milk, a shot rang out. Alejandrina heard buggy wheels rattling off as she found her husband wounded. Following his orders, she picked up her baby and ran to his brother's adjacent ranch for help. The doctor came, but Albert Joe died on the way to the hospital. Rullia Singh was the only suspect in the case, and he was convicted of first-degree murder. Sher Singh and Gopal Singh, partners and husbands of Valentina's younger sisters, testified in the courtroom and then moved to Arizona following the trial.[16]

In this first set of marriages, when conflict arose, the mother fled to her daughter's home. Rullia Singh turned to Albert Joe, whom he had originally introduced to his stepdaughter as a "high-class man."[17] He expected the support of other Punjabi men in regaining control of his wife. They could not influence her, however. Albert Joe paid for it with his life.

In another early case, a young wife refused to cooperate when her husband of three weeks took her to his friends' ranches and offered to leave her for a day or two in exchange for money. She went home to her mother and asked for a divorce. Her husband agreed to give her one, but on the way to a lawyer's office in Brawley, he shot her dead (in front of a Japanese packing shed in the "foreign section").[18] By Mexican law, a husband's proposal to prostitute his wife was grounds for divorce; among Punjabi Sikhs, there was no divorce, and men sometimes did share women.

Two more murders in the 1930s show continuing tensions between Hispanic women and Punjabi men. Speaking of these murders and, more generally, of rural violence, one widow of two Imperial Valley Sikhs (sequential marriages) explained her reluctance to remarry another Punjabi: "I was always afraid, out there," she said.[19] These two murders also reveal diverging regional patterns of political integration for the Punjabi men and a uniformly inferior position for the Hispanic women in California.

The first case contrasts the Punjabi societies developing in the San Joaquin and Imperial valleys. Sher Singh Sathi, a young Sikh student involved in Ghadar party politics, was suspected of informing on illegals to U.S. law enforcement agencies. Threatened by fellow countrymen in the Fresno area, he fled to the Imperial Valley in 1933, where Ghadar party politics were less central to the men's lives. There, he and sixteen-year-old Amelia Valdez (photo 10), whose sister and mother were married to Sikhs, became sweethearts. One day, shots were heard, and Sathi and Amelia were found dead in her mother's house, a gun in his hand. His body was taken to Los Angeles for a cremation ceremony that was attended by Sikh men and their wives from all over the state. In Fresno and farther north, his death is remembered as an act of revenge by Ghadar party hitmen; several northern wives viewed it as the tragic death of a young man, a terrible result of the men's political activities. In the Imperial Valley, however, Punjabi-Mexican families viewed it as an ill-fated romance, a suicide pact carried out by a distraught young man who believed himself doomed to an early death at the hands of vengeful political enemies. Despite advice regarding Ghadar party politics forwarded to them from Fresno, Imperial Valley officials also decided on the tragic-romance theory. Amelia Valdez is remembered well by the wives and daughters in the Imperial Valley, but she does not figure in northern versions of this event.[20]

The other murder, this time of a Hispanic wife by her husband's friend and co-worker, took place near Sacramento in 1937. Here, too, the woman was sometimes forgotten, while the men involved in the case knew each other well. Twenty-three-year-old Isabel Ramirez Singh had three sisters married to Sikhs; another sister, Rose, was still unmarried in Sacramento. Isabel, her husband, and their six children were living in Walnut Grove, where many Punjabis worked in sugar beets. Milkha Singh, a fifty-year-old bachelor who lived in the other half of the house, lured Isabel into his quarters (presenting a bleeding finger for bandaging) and hacked her to death with an ax and two knives. His reason, he told the police officers, was that he had given Isabel $950 over several years to arrange his marriage with her sister, Rose, and she had not done so. In the seemingly perfunctory trial, the murdered woman's name was forgotten by the presiding judge, but the men involved all knew one another. The arresting deputy sheriff and the constable were brothers and were on familiar terms with the murderer and the murdered woman's husband. Milkha Singh was declared insane and sent to the asylum at Patton, but he was released five years later because he was "not insane." Isabel's oldest son, who had heard the struggle and had run to the fields to call his father, was in the first grade, but he was too shy to testify in English at the trial. Her last baby, born three months before her death, died before his first birthday.[21] The case illustrates the men's desire to marry and their expectation that sisters could arrange marriages. It also speaks to the fragility of the lives of women and children in the face of strong bonds between men.

Divorce was another way of resolving marital conflicts. Petitions for divorce were relatively numerous for these couples, at least according to popular notions of norms for rural Mexican Catholics and rural Indian Sikhs, Muslims, and Hindus. Scholarly generalizations about divorce in the United States also would predict low rates of divorce for them. For example, because the divorce rates in countries of origin are comparatively lower than in the United States, "the foreign born are culturally less inclined to seek divorce in case of marital discord. The frequency of divorce is particularly low among new arrivals because of their general distrust of courts and language difficulties."[22] Certainly the official divorce rate in both India and Mexico in the early decades of the twentieth century was lower than in the United States—in the case of India, almost nonexistent. All the men and most of the women forming the Punjabi-Mexican community were recent arrivals in the United States, and most were not proficient in English. Furthermore, these were rural couples, and divorce rates have always been lower in rural than in urban areas. In addition, most of the women were Roman Catholics, a group (in the United States) for whom the recorded rate of divorce has been thought to be lower than for the population as a whole.[23]

There were some 230 Punjabi-Mexican couples before 1946 in the Imperial Valley, and 29 of these couples had filed divorce petitions before 1946. Men and women filed divorce petitions in nearly equal proportions, and defendants frequently cross-complained.[24] The first divorce cases filed show that the men expected more obedience and household services from their wives than they were getting. It is equally clear, from the women's petitions and cross-complaints, that the women felt these expectations to be unreasonable.

Again, one of the early marriages illustrates these conflicts. Matilde Sandoval married Kehar Singh Gill in El Paso in 1918; her sister and mother also married Sikhs. But Matilde's marriage did not go well, and within a year Kehar filed for divorce. He alleged that she reviled him in the presence of friends and refused to keep house and cook as he wished; she did so "only as it suited her convenience." She also went shopping in the town, bought and used makeup, and went dancing. Worst of all, she continually threatened to leave and once *did* leave, going with her mother to New Mexico. The couple reconciled in 1919, but he filed again and secured a divorce in 1922.[25] In another divorce, a man reportedly tied his wife to the bedpost to prevent her going out in his absence![26]

Not only differing cultural expectations but disagreements about property and money caused conflicts. Many women complained that investment in land and farming was their husbands' first priority; one left after years of allegedly being fed little but cabbage. The men also sent money back to India, to the Sikh temple in Stockton, and to the Ghadar party, sometimes against the wives' wishes. Yet to the men, the women seemed spendthrifts. One Sikh put a notice in the local newspaper, reading "To Whom It May Concern: [She] Having left my bed and board, I am no longer responsible for the debts of my wife, Maria Juarez Singh."[27]

Divorce was common in the Imperial Valley Punjabi-Mexican community.[28] There were fifty-nine divorce petitions filed in Imperial County civil court from 1919 to 1969[29] involving first-generation husbands from India. Because of reconciliations or failure to complete the procedure the first time around, these fifty-nine petitions represented only forty-five couples.[30] About 39 percent of the petitions were contested, more than triple the national average of 12 percent. While nationally, some three-quarters of all divorce petitions are filed by wives,[31] among these fifty-nine cases, men filed thirty-four cases and women twenty-four (and one case was an annulment filed by a father). The Punjabi men in these marriages, then, were quite aggressive in seeking divorces.

The filers in these fifty-nine cases[32] were almost all Sikh men and Hispanic women, and three-fifths of the women were born in Mexico. Two Anglo women and one black woman also filed for divorce. About half the marriages had taken place in southern California and half in other states of the American Southwest. An astounding thirteen of the forty-five marriages involved broke up in less than a year, four of them in less than a month; the median duration of all forty-five marriages was four years. The causes of divorce generally conformed to a pattern of the men charging desertion and the women cruelty.[33] The men tended to claim that there was no community property, the women that there was (particularly when children were involved, and the women sought custody). The women sought alimony and child support, the men sought divorce without making those provisions. In five cases, guardianship of the property of minors was an issue in the divorce. One man stated that his property was not community property, it was his son's; his wife then sought custody of the son, whom she had not seen for four years. She argued that her husband was living with his housekeeper, was not a suitable father, and only wanted the boy in order to hold property in his name. The husband charged, in return, that she was a bargirl in El Centro and unfit to have the boy.[34]

All five adultery charges were made by men, the one "failure to provide" charge by a woman; four men charged fraud or misrepresentation and sought annulments. Eleven petitioners were repeaters, eight of them filing against the same spouse, and two men and one woman against other spouses. In six cases (three couples), one spouse had filed previously and later the other spouse filed for divorce. In sixteen cases, the summons had to be published elsewhere, substantiating charges of desertion; fourteen of these desertions were by women. As for results, the files are not always conclusive, but the male petitioners more often succeeded in getting a final decree.

The women's relatives were part of the problem in many divorces. In twenty-six cases, members of the woman's family appeared in the petitions: her parents, siblings, or children from an earlier marriage. Yet the proportion of women with relatives married to other Punjabis was slightly lower among the women involved in divorces than among all women married to Punjabis. From other sources, we know that seventeen of the women in these forty-five couples had female relatives married to other men from India, or 38 percent, compared to 43 percent of the women married to Punjabis in the Imperial Valley. So, if female relatives were also married to men from India, divorce was slightly less likely. The men's countrymen were mentioned in only nine cases. Full information did not always appear in court records, of course. One wife's official divorce petition was not very revealing, but the local press divulged that her husband was charging another Punjabi with petty theft and that his wife was one of the "articles" taken from the home![35]

Not only was divorce a frequent occurrence, it was often followed by remarriage. I have reliable marital histories for twenty-eight of the forty-five women in the divorce cases discussed here, and of the twenty-eight, eleven were petitioning for dissolution of a second marriage. Of the twenty-eight men with known marital histories among the forty-five, nine were seeking dissolution of a second and three of a third marriage. Many others in the Punjabi-Mexican community married more than once or twice.

One study of marital instability (commonly measured by the incidence of divorce, separation, and remarriage) found it more prevalent among blacks and Anglos than among Mexicans and more prevalent among women than among men. The study used "a presumed familistic structure among Mexican Americans" to explain their lower marital instability.[36] Again, the Imperial Valley Punjabi-Mexican couples offer a surprising contrast to these generalizations, as Table 10 shows.

The calculation of multiple marriages here is rough at best. I have defined all those relationships that were long term or that produced one or more children as marriages for purposes of this discussion, and I have included only relationships formed in the western hemisphere. While the multiple marriage rate for men would be raised considerably if I included first wives in India, I do not have reliable data for all the men.[37] On the other hand, I did include the women who recorded their status as "widowed" on the marriage license, since researchers on Mexican society recognize that term as a euphemistic one for women who had deserted their husbands or had been deserted.[38] So, for the men, there may be an undercount, but the women may represent an overcount of the kind of multiple marriages that indicate marital instability.

Of the 378 women marrying men from India by 1949, at least 115 were

Table 10.   Multiple Marriages

	Two Spouses	Three Spouses	Four Spouses	Five Spouses	Eight Spouses	Total Spouses
Women (N = 115)	92	15	5	2	1	267
Men (N = 57)	44	9	2	2		133

Table 11. Spouses of the Women

	Hispanic (N = 98)	White (N = 14)	Black (N = 3)	Total (115)
Punjabi Sikh	112	12	0	121
Mexican	65	0	0	65
Punjabi Muslim	16	9	5	30
Unknown	18	4	2	24
Punjabi Hindu	6	1	0	7
Anglo	7	5	0	12
Filipino	2	0	0	2
Greek	2	0	0	2
Punjabi-Mexican	1	0	0	1
Total	229	31	7	267

married more than once. For 92 of them, I found evidence of two husbands; for 15, three husbands; for 5, four husbands. Two women had five husbands, while one had eight husbands! These 115 women, all but 17 of them Hispanic, had 267 husbands, or 2.42 husbands each. Of the men from India, at least 57 of them had more than one wife in the United States; 44 had two wives, 9 had three wives, 2 had four wives, and 2 had five wives. These 57 men had 133 wives, or 2.33 wives each. The women's spouses were more diverse, as Tables 11 and 12 show.

Not all those who married several times bothered to get divorced. Many informants spoke of the playboy reputations of the Punjabi men, particularly the "wild Hindus of the Imperial Valley." Having found another woman, one man took his first Mexican wife to visit Mexico and then reported her as an illegal at the border so that she could not return and had to stay (and raise their youngest child) in Mexico. There were also stories about the Hispanic women. Just as some wives did not know if their husbands had been married in India or not, some husbands found out later that their wives had been married in Mexico. In one case, a Mexican husband and children turned up for the funeral of a Sikh's wife, surprising him greatly. He had not known that her previous marriage had never been dissolved, and he had not known about the children from it![39]

Table 12.   Spouses of the Punjabi Men

	Sikh (N = 49)	Muslim (N = 6)	Hindu (N = 2)	Total (57)
Hispanic	90	10	3	103
Unknown	8	1	0	9
Anglo	8	2	0	10
Indian	4	0	1	5
Punjabi-Mexican	4	0	0	4
Black	2	0	0	2
Total	116	13	4	133

One descendant provided insight into the way these immigrant couples may have thought about their remarriages. "My mother left her first husband and then when she married a Sikh she went through a civil ceremony, not a church one because she'd already married through the Catholic church. This marriage was Americanized, not Catholic or East Indian."[40] So in an important sense a marriage or remarriage in the United States was part of becoming American, just as, in Mola Singh's words, divorce was American, something one learned about and might do while becoming American.

Respect and Love

Despite the conflicts, there were stable, happy marriages among these couples. We can best learn about the successful marriages by listening to what the participants and their children said about them. First, the long-lasting couples successfully negotiated certain immediate obstacles. The joint households proved a shock to many Hispanic wives. When Genobeba Loya married Memel Singh, she was not prepared to cook and clean for several partners as well as a husband. But she persevered and persuaded her husband to get his own land, his own lease, and move the family to a nuclear household. And when Rosa Reyes married Jiwan Singh, she did not like the way her husband's brother called her a "wetback" and bossed her around. He brought other men and asked her to cook and wash clothes for them. She told him she was not married to him, and she told her husband she would not be a maid to her brother-in-law and other Punjabis: "Either he goes or I go." Her husband supported her, and the other men moved out. And there were sometimes other women in the joint households with whom relationships could prove difficult, particularly if they were not relatives. When her favorite sugar bowl was broken by another partner's wife, Lala Garewal took herself and her children to a house on a property her husband was about to stop leasing; he had to renew the lease because she refused to move back.[41] In these cases, the couples had children, and the husbands bowed to their wives' wishes; also, these men could afford to farm on their own.

Another obstacle that often proved contentious involved a man's Indian family. Relationships with Punjabi relatives in India varied greatly. Some of the women knew their husbands had been married in India; some found out later or preferred not to know. Some men had lost their Indian wives in the 1918 influenza epidemic but kept in touch with relatives and sent money to children. One man arranged for his brother in the Punjab to take over responsibility for his wife and daughter. Some husbands simply stopped writing to India, but many others told their California wives about their Indian wives and families and sent remittances for years.[42] The diversion of funds to India became an issue in some families, but most Punjabi-Mexican wives and children accepted that as a minimal fulfillment of family responsibilities. Relatives in India, distanced by law as well as geography, had little reality in the early decades of Punjabi-Mexican family life in California.[43]

Some degree of bilingualism was an important factor in the successful marriages, although few of the men were rated excellent speakers of Spanish and no wife really learned to speak Punjabi well (many understood it adequately). But mastery of a common language seemed relatively unimportant; in any case, many people argued that there were similarities between Punjabi and Spanish. "Spanish is just like Punjabi, really," they said, illustrating the point with examples of similar words and grammatical constructions. Not only language, but other aspects of Punjabi and Mexican culture were viewed as essentially similar, and the long-time spouses expressed respect for each other's cultures.[44] Unable to visit the Punjab in the early decades of their marriages, the women found it harder to learn about Punjabi culture,[45] but many men reported on similarities. Rather than emphasize or even mention the anti-miscegenation laws that played a major role in determining their choice of spouses, the men and their descendants talked about the similar physical appearance of the Punjabi men and Mexican women. Further, they argued that Mexicans and Punjabis shared the same material culture. As Mola Singh, who had thirteen children from three marriages with Mexican women, put it:

> I no have to explain anything Hindu to my Mexican family—cooking the same, only talk different. I explain them, customary India, same Mexico. Everything same, only language different. They make *roti* over there, sit on floor, all custom India the same Mexico, living custom; I go to Mexico two three times, you know, not too far. All same India, all the same. Adobe house, Mexico, sit on floor, to make tortilla, *roti*, you know, all kinds of food; eat here plate, some place got table, bench. India the same, eat floor, two board cutting, make bench.[46]

Not only did the men view the women as coming from a similar material culture, some of the long-time wives came to view themselves as "Hindu." They meant that they cooked Indian food, conducted their households in a "Hindu" fashion to suit their husbands, and were cut off from Mexicans and Mexican Americans. They did not mean they had changed their religion, but they identified themselves with their husbands and the other Punjabi men, rather than with any Mexican American community.[47]

Another important characteristic of the happy marriages was respect for both religions and mutual support of religious observances. The few men who converted to Catholicism also remained Hindu or Sikh in important ways. One man, Ganga Ram, secured certificates of baptism and marriage with the new name of Arturo Gangara, a name used only on those documents insofar as his daughter knew.[48] And the couples and their children in these long-lasting marriages voiced a strong belief that there was only one God. As Mola and Susanna Singh said,[49] Susanna speaking first: "Well, God gives a lot of different languages, you know, but I don't think so many Gods." Mola: "Only one God."

This belief in the unity of all religions was stated in different ways: The Sikh religion is just like the Catholic one; Sikhism is a composite of Islam, Hinduism, and Christianity; the Granth Sahib is just like the Bible; all Gods are the same, but they are called different names because languages are different; Sikhism has the ten *cruz*, or ten crosses, which are the ten gurus; the founding Sikh guru preached exactly what is in the Old Testament; Sikhs have all the commandments Catholics have; one can be Muslim and Catholic, or Sikh and Catholic, at the same time.[50]

These statements ignore religious differences and stress similarities, frequently using metaphors and analogies to erase distinctions. While there were many vigorously contested matters between Punjabi husbands and Mexican wives, the children's religious training was not one of them. The men encouraged their wives to continue their own religious beliefs and practices and themselves served as godfathers in the *compadrazgo* system, but continued to practice their own religions. The men wanted to inculcate respect for Sikhism, Hinduism, or Islam, while they encouraged their children to practice Catholicism (or whatever form of Christianity their wives practiced). Thus, when talking about religion, husbands and wives reconceptualized differences as similarities at a higher analytic level.

Love was clearly the most vital ingredient in the successful marriages. While not necessarily developed in Indian marriages, many Punjabis found love was an integral part of marriage in the United States. Furthermore, love was associated with an aspect of Mexican culture that long-time husbands tended to admire, the greater freedom granted to women. Again, it is Mola Singh's account that shows how Punjabi men came to think about love. Mola Singh learned the meaning of love in the United States, during an affair with an older white woman in the Imperial Valley. He said he learned that love could make you crazy (that early affair got him into trouble with an Anglo man). In 1919 he married Carmen, his first wife in America, because of love. In his personal life, he became committed to the idea of love between man and woman, initially based on sexual attraction, as the best basis for a relationship. Like many other Punjabi men in California, he became critical of India's arranged marriage system:

> In India, lots of time in India, I feel, the woman is a slave. I say, no, that's no good. You should have a duty to them, women have rights, even more than men. When you want to make a marriage in India, you never see the boy; the boy and girl never meet each other. That's no good. Maybe the boy's all right, maybe the boy's no good. Maybe he's blind, maybe he has an arm broke, maybe a leg broke. You never know, you see, the mother and the father ask

for him. Today I feel that it's more important to love. First you love, then you should marry. It happens too young over there. The relatives do it all, and they can make a mistake. No, I don't like that way. I like it when a woman and a man get together, fall in love, and marry.[51]

Talking about his fourth wife, Susanna, Mola Singh did not use the word love but the feeling pervaded his account of their long-lasting relationship (photo 11). His words about her show another very important element in these successful marriages: respect, especially for hard work.

When I met Susanna, she did sewing, she's a good farmer girl. She cut all the kids' hair, she made all their clothes. . . . I found Susanna in 1937, and then everything got good. Susanna, she didn't want to buy anything, she only wanted to buy groceries. She chopped cotton, she worked, she didn't even want to buy a dress. I went to the store, I bought her a dress. She didn't want to go to the store, I had to buy it. She did go shopping for something, a sewing machine. She was no dummy, she was very smart, that woman. She sewed. For all of our girls, she never bought a dress. She sewed, she worked hard, she didn't want money. She never cared about money, she didn't spend it.[52]

Other accounts stress love and loyalty between spouses. One son told of the love his father, Sant Ram, had for his mother, Ricarda, a beautiful, gentle, hard-working woman. When she became ill, Sant Ram took her to the Brawley hospital and then went to visit her after a few days, with their two little boys in the car. The boys saw their father come out and fall on the lawn, crying inconsolably. Ricarda had died of typhoid, and since Sant Ram had no telephone, the hospital staff had just waited for him to come in to tell him. Another couple took great pleasure in their many children. Nellie Soto Shine spoke of Inder Singh Shine's joy at the birth of each child, his smiles so broad that "all the neighbors knew Nellie's new baby had come." When I asked a widow how long she and her husband had been together, she answered quickly, "twenty years and nineteen days."[53] And a daughter said about her parents: "When my father and mother married . . . they only met for a very short time, I think it was only ten days. And it's gone on forty-eight years. . . . Father worked hard, he would go to the city council, sometimes he wouldn't understand at all, and he would come home and he would sit here and discuss it and mother would give him his strength to go out into this strange world that he doesn't really understand."[54] Despite the precariousness (from the Punjabi point of view) of reliance on love as the basis of a long-term commitment, many couples stayed together for decades. There was little concern for legal marriage, and people clearly thought of the ceremony in very different ways. For some Punjabis, marriage seems to have become an unnecessary or unwanted legal contract, a matter of government record, irrelevant and possibly threatening to personal freedom and property rights.[55] For others, Hispanic women and Punjabi men, a civil ceremony in the United States seemed to negate all previous ceremonies and signal a new commitment (see Chapter 5). By the time of his fourth relationship, with Susanna, Mola Singh seems to have viewed love as a passion that rendered marriage and divorce contracts irrelevant. Both he and Susanna (she was twice widowed) were content simply to live and work together. They finally married much later, for legal reasons (their 1962 civil marriage) and, on her part, religious ones (their 1975 Catholic marriage).[56]

For many women of Mexican descent, civil marriage was less important than a religious ceremony. As the wives grew older, they worried about their standing in the church and asked their husbands for a religious marriage ceremony. The men in long-lasting relationships commonly went through Catholic ceremonies late in life to please their wives, usually decades after the original civil marriage or the beginning of the relationship.[57]

The mixture of love, respect, and humor that characterized long-lasting Punjabi-Mexican marriages shines through the dialogue between Mola and Susanna Singh concerning their delayed marriage. Said Mola:

> After a long time, I married Susanna. I didn't want to marry, I'd have to pay for the divorce, I didn't want to pay for the divorce again. Two women, I'd already had to pay for divorces. But the Social Security man told me to marry.
>
> "You better marry, make it legal," he said, so we married.
>
> And for the citizenship paper too, I didn't want trouble. And our kids were not legal until we married, so I had to marry. . . .
>
> I've been with Susanna since 1937 but we never married. I wanted to keep free for other ladies, see, wanted to be able to throw

Part III

The Construction of Ethnic Identity

7 Childhood in Rural California

For the children born to these biethnic couples, cultural identity could be problematic, both within and outside the family. Socialization into an essentially Mexican American domestic culture marked their early years. This came from several sources: mothers, aunts and grandmothers, godmothers, and other children. Older stepchildren were present in many Punjabi households, and these half-sisters and brothers were important Spanish-speaking caretakers for the new children. Children outside the family also were important, since most Punjabi-Mexican children attended schools in which Spanish-speaking children predominated. Outsiders usually classified Punjabi-Mexican children as "Mexicans"; to this day, some in the Imperial Valley think of Singh as a Mexican American surname.[1] But the Mexican identification caused difficulties, including prejudice from Mexican Americans, and there were significant countermessages from the Punjabi men. Most Punjabi-Mexican children grew up taking great pride in their Indian heritage.

Names, Languages, and Religions

The babies' names, home language, and religious training all reflected the mothers' authority in the domestic realm. Almost all the children born to these couples were given Hispanic, rather than Indian, first names, so their names seem both strange and beautiful: Maria Jesusita Singh, Jose Akbar Khan, Armando Chand. While a few fathers gave their sons Indian names, either on birth certificates or through affidavits of correction years later, these Indian names were seldom used. One illiterate father went to an Anglo neighbor year after year to have his sons' Punjabi names written down again so that he could try to have those names learned and used by his family. A boy known to all as Francisco Singh grew up being called either Frank or Paco; only when he registered for the draft did he learn that on his birth certificate he had been named Najar Inder Singh.[2]

Religious differences among the men were sometimes evident in the names given to their children. For the Sikh Hispanic children, there was always Singh as a middle name or surname, obligatory for male Sikhs in India. But Kaur, the obligatory second name for Sikh females in India, was almost never used in California for daughters.[3] Many Sikh descendants, daughters as well as sons, have retained Singh as a middle name. Muslim-fathered children tended to have names like Ishmael, Abraham, Benjamin, Jacob, Rebecca, and Rachel. Such Old Testament biblical names were rarer among the children of Sikhs and Hindus. These differences receded in importance, however, because Spanish nicknames were commonly used for all the children in the Imperial Valley.

Children brought up in the Imperial Valley are still known by their Spanish nicknames. "Kishen? Oh, you mean Domingo"; "Mr. Singh's name I can't recall, but his children were Beto, Meli, and Lola"; "Gurbachen, that's Botcho"; "Oh, yes, La Prieta, we called her."[4] The children of Harnam Singh Sidhu are known as Chavella, Pancho, Mundo, and Pedro, and those of B. Sucha Singh Sidhu as Bepo, Otto, Mella, and Bolio.[5] The children also had nicknames for the Punjabi men and their wives. Inder Singh Shine was called El Curiosito, "the cute one," from accounts of his antics on horseback when courting his wife as she picked cotton in his fields. One man was called Bulldog (perhaps because he was hard pressed to bring up his children after his wife's death in childbirth).[6]

In central and northern California, naming patterns were more diverse because the wives were ethnically more diverse. Black wives gave their children such names as Verdie, Sidney Pearl, Jacques, Leslie Felix, and Rex; near Fresno, an Anglo mother named her little boy Roy Roger Singh![7] Perhaps because the Muslim names were themselves more varied and complex than the common Sikh name Singh, there has been more distortion by descendants of the names of Muslim pioneers: "Bleth Khan," "Buga Ali," "Glam Sul," "Netika," "Sultanly," "Joseph Abdullia," "Mamdali," and "Glam Heather" were among those remembered by the second generation.[8]

Use of alternative names was part of the family dynamics. The children's names could assert commonality or difference. Names could show mutual affection and respect; in one family, the mother used pet Punjabi names for the two children, while the father used their Spanish names. One boy remembers his mother using his Punjabi name when she was angry with him.[9] Sometimes the children's names reflected marital conflict. In a divorce case, the mother claimed custody of Tony, Alfred, Emily, and Albert; the father, insisting that the children were really named Gurbachen, Thacker, Mahanti, and Sohan, counterclaimed for their custody.[10]

In the home, most children spoke Spanish with their mothers and Spanish or English with their fathers; few learned to speak Punjabi. Older boys, prominent among them Mexican stepsons, who worked in the fields with "Hindu crews" did learn Punjabi appropriate to the work situation. Many children understood some Punjabi, but did not speak it.[11] A husband's bachelor partner taught one woman's boys to greet the moon with a Punjabi salutation: *"Sar sa ka i chand,"* she recalled. (This was probably *"Sat sri akal, chand,"* or "Hello, moon.") Two other women, a stepdaughter and a daughter, were taught to count in Punjabi, and they recalled the words their father used when other Punjabis came to visit as *"Salamal, kai ha, usabaitjo."* (This was probably *"Salam, kaisee hai, udhar baith jaaoo,"* or "Hello, how's it going, sit down over there.")[12]

Most of the Punjabi men who married and founded families in California deliberately deemphasized Punjabi language and culture. One reason was the demands made on their time by work. Thus Amelia Singh Netervala said revealingly, "My dad talked about India to his grandchildren; he had time then." But another reason was commitment to their new country. They accepted the restrictions on immigration as permanent and considered their children Americans. John Diwan's daughter Janie remembers her shock and sense of loss when he suddenly stopped the evening sessions of Punjabi lessons and stories about the Punjab. He announced that since his children were Americans, they had no need to learn his language and culture. Other fathers gruffly turned back queries about the Punjab and its language, stating that they were in America now, and there was no point learning about India.[13]

There were exceptions to this general pattern of Punjabi cultural loss. The children did learn some Punjabi kin terms and were encouraged to use them when addressing relatives among the Punjabi men. But this usage was instrumental and sometimes turned out to be inaccurate; that is, kin terms often were used for partners rather than for blood relatives, and only later did the children discover that there was no biological relationship. When one son went to the "home village" in India after his father's death, he was puzzled to find no knowledge of his father's "cousin" (his partner) in the United States. Another girl spent years defending her father's partner's mentally disabled grandson in school because she believed him to be a relative; she was mortified to find later that they were "not actually related" and she had "suffered for nothing."[14] But most children happily referred to the many bachelor Punjabis as "uncles," glad to receive the candy and other gifts the men customarily brought when they visited family men.[15]

Religious differences proved relatively unimportant. There was little or no transmission of Indian religious beliefs and practices to the next generation. Many Muslim, Hindu, and Sikh men did not even transmit correct English terms for their religious faiths to their children. Thus some members of the second generation continue to refer to all Punjabi men as Hindus without realizing it is usually a misnomer, and a few men are designated by such improbable names as Ali Singh or Ghulam Singh. (Ali and Ghulam are Muslim first names, while Singh is a Sikh name.) Others refer to the Singhs or the Mohammeds, knowing the men were not really Hindus but unsure of the correct religious terms (see Chapter 5). The lack of a common language between fathers and children helps explain such flawed transmission.

Children were socialized into the religion of their mothers. Baptism, along with the appointment of godparents in the *compadrazgo* system, emphasized the early orientation to Catholicism for most Punjabi-Mexican children. This was permitted and encouraged by the men, for several reasons. Few Punjabi men were able to read, teach, or explain their own religious texts. Furthermore, the children did not know the Punjabi language, much less Arabic, so that the beauties of the Granth Sahib or the Quran were inaccessible to them. Finally, the Roman Catholic church was clearly hospitable to these families, allowing the Punjabi men to stand as godfathers in church ceremonies and Hispanizing their names on baptismal certificates. In many cases, the Catholic church allowed the Punjabi men to be married in religious rites without any meaningful evidence of conversion to Catholicism.[16] There are only four instances of Punjabi Sikhs allegedly converting to Catholicism, but these men "also remained Sikh" and were cremated.[17]

The idea of religion continued to receive the men's support, in the best tradition of Indian tolerance. The men reasoned that the inculcation of religion was a woman's responsibility, so it followed that the children should be brought up in the wife's religion. In one family, the children thought their father was Catholic until they moved to Phoenix and began to associate with other Punjabi men and their families; only then did the father's Sikh faith come to their attention. Feelings of pragmatism and flexibility prevailed. Another Sikh father explained to his children that he had changed his name from Singh to Ram because, having taken off the turban and beard, he felt he was no longer a Sikh and did not want to dishonor the Sikh religion; he then converted to Catholicism, and his children were brought up Catholic.[18] Some of the men, unable to practice and support the religion of their birth, simply became general patrons of religion in their new locality, contributing to several local churches and charities regularly and encouraging their wives and children to participate in the religion of their choice. One old Sikh farmer, upon his death, reportedly left $25 to every church in the Imperial Valley.[19]

Most of the Punjabi men were not only unprepared to instruct others in their religion, they were working too hard to do so. Again and again, descendants stressed the long hours put in by Punjabi farmers in California. A Mexican American wife, with a Punjabi-Mexican son who had been brought up a Catholic, told of the problem her husband's work ethic posed to the family's Catholicism. He would not stop work on Sundays or let his Mexican laborers do so, although she pointed out the bad effect of his example on their children. First, he stopped work himself on Sundays, and finally he realized his workers would do better on Monday if he gave them Sunday off.[20] In another case, the half-Mexican daughter of an Indian Muslim pioneer, a woman who has married a Pakistani and has become a devout Muslim, tried to talk her aged father into taking time for the five daily prayers. He insisted that he had no time to wash properly for them and would not dishonor Allah by praying without washing.[21]

The families, by and large, followed Catholic practices rather loosely. Children were baptized when convenient, sometimes years after birth and all at once. One rare attempt at a Sikh baptism was performed in a small building near Holtville by "godparents" Lala and Sucha Singh Garewal. The recipient of this ceremony was brought up as a Catholic, however, and when she learned that her baptismal ceremony had been a Sikh one, she asked her godmother (by then widowed) to rebaptize her in the local Catholic church.[22] The more religious Catholic women did have their children baptized and confirmed more or less on schedule, and their sons were altar boys when the family resided close enought to a church for convenient attendance.[23] The Sikh fathers and Hispanic mothers carefully planned whom to ask to be *padrino* and *madrina* for baptisms and confirmations in order not to offend relatives; and the wives of the wealthier Punjabi farmers were obviously central in some *compadrazgo* networks.[24] Many popular customs associated with Catholicism in Mexico, however, were not observed by these families. There were no saints days and no *quinzanyero*, or fifteenth birthday celebrations, for girls. Such customs were labeled Mexican, not American, and the families did not follow them.[25]

Most of the external signs differentiating Sikh, Muslim, and Hindu in India disappeared. In outward appearance, the Sikhs initially had been marked by the beard, long hair, and turban required by orthodox Sikhism. Retention of these characteristics proved difficult in the face of American prejudice. Moreover, many wives preferred their men to be clean-shaven. Several women explicitly linked the giving up of the turban and beard to their wedding day.[26] "The labor camp men wore turbans and the family men took them off," said one daughter.[27] There was no case of a Sikh son of a Mexican mother wearing the turban, and even the sons of the two "real" Sikh couples in central and northern California did not wear turbans. A few differences between Sikh, Muslim, and Hindu centered on physical objects in the homes—Muslims tended to have *hookahs*, or water pipes. The daughter of a Sikh farmer first saw one of these when she and her friend Sarah Mohamed were pushed off a bus to Los Angeles because they were "darkies," and they retreated to Sarah's house in El Centro.[28] Here American racism brought together two "Hindu" daughters who had not yet visited each other's homes.

Some Sikhs and Muslims maintained social distance based on religious boundaries stemming from India, while others did not; it was just as common for the children to pick up prejudices against other Punjabis in the same religious category as in different ones. For example, descendants of Muslims differentiated among the Muslims by language and caste (Pushtu and Urdu, Rajput and Arain), and I heard a great deal from descendants of Sikhs about ranking by caste and regional origin among them (Jat and Chuhra, Malwa, Doaba, and Majha).

The children of the "real" Hindus, Brahmans and Khatris by caste, were few in number. Their parents seem to have been least successful in transmitting beliefs and customs to the children. Most of the fathers were literate but made no attempt to teach their religion; they were as content as the others to have their children brought up Catholic. One told his son about "Krishna the young prince and the Sikh gurus"; that man did not eat beef himself, but his family did. Isolated in the United States, these Hindu men had almost no reinforcement from others of similar background.[29]

Important differences in religious practice that did affect family life in California for members of the second generation centered on two things: dietary prohibitions and death rituals. For Muslims, pork was forbidden, and the meat they did eat was supposed to be ritually slaughtered. Muslims were not supposed to drink intoxicating liquor. Most Muslim Punjabis seem to have observed the prohibition of pork, and some took care to obtain kosher meat from Jewish suppliers.[30] Many Muslim fathers drank, however. For the Sikhs and Hindus, beef was the meat to be avoided, although many descendants said their fathers ate it.

The children's memories of funerals are vivid, since this was one occasion when Indian custom was carefully followed. In the early decades most of the Muslim burials were in Sacramento, where a building was finally purchased for a mosque in the 1940s. Other Punjabi Muslims came and prepared the body for burial, stripping it, washing it, and shrouding it in clean white linen. Verses from the Quran were read as the coffin was lowered into the ground, and the men jumped down into the grave and filled it with dirt, paying no heed to the soiling of their best suits. The burial service ended with the distribution of fresh fruit to family members and guests.[31]

The Punjabi Sikhs were equally strict about the proper disposal of the body after death. When a Sikh died, orthodoxy was honored in two ways. First, his photograph was taken with a turban placed on his head, whether or not he had worn one in the United States. (By the early 1940s the rarely worn turban marked a "most religious" Sikh in California.[32]) In the photo, the dead man's partner or wife stood behind the coffin, and friends surrounded him (photo 14). The photo was sent home to the dead man's family in India, as proof of his orthodoxy as well as his death, although the bare heads of those in the background must have raised questions. Then, the Sikh's body was cremated, being sent for that purpose to Sacramento, Los Angeles, or Yuma, Arizona, and his ashes were sent to India or put into the Salton Sea or the Pacific Ocean.[33]

The practice of cremation by Sikhs and Hindus was not insisted upon for their children. The Catholic women believed cremation was a sin, and many widows wished to bury their husbands where they themselves would be buried, in the Mexican Catholic section of the local cemetery. In this they rarely succeeded, but when it came to infants and children, the men gave in—there are many children's gravestones marked *Singh* in California's rural cemeteries.³⁴ The Catholic funerals held for most children were attended by Sikhs, Muslims, Hindus, and Hispanic relatives and friends (photo 15).

According to their children, hardly any of the Muslim farmers observed the prescribed daily prayers and the annual month-long fast, or *Id*, in their early decades in the United States. Few Muslim farmers had copies of the Quran, fewer still had prayer rugs. Families usually gathered to commemorate the annual *Ramadan Id* ("breaking fast" together) even if they had not fasted, and those present who could read and explain the Quran did so. Fathers sometimes promised to "bring someone out from Washington, D.C." to answer their children's questions about Islam, and indeed for at least one Muslim's funeral, men did come from Washington.³⁵ For a short time an Arabic class was convened for the children being brought up in El Centro, an effort connected with the conversion of one Hispanic wife to Islam. This woman became an enthusiastic and zealous speaker for the religion in the Imperial Valley, but there are no other instances of a wife's conversion.³⁶

Finally, despite the presence of a Sikh temple in Stockton from 1912, the children perceived no institutions that divided the Punjabis clearly along religious lines. The Sikh temple was central in the lives of all Punjabis in California and neighboring states, and children of all classes and religious backgrounds remember going to the Stockton temple. Some talked about this as the Sikh Convention, held every January, or the Stockton Convention (some political meetings were held at Sacramento, Marysville, or Fresno as well). Children from the Imperial Valley who attended this event recall the reading of the "Bible" for three days and three nights, and the long, loud Punjabi discussions carried on by the men.³⁷ A Punjabi wife, Nand Kaur from Yuba City, described this "convention" as a three-day sequence of meetings, with a meeting of the "Indian Lady Educational Society" or Doaba Educational Society on the first day, a Ghadar party meeting on the second day, and then the celebration of the birthday of the tenth guru, Guru Gobind Singh, on the third day.³⁸

To most members of the second generation, however, the Stockton temple was where one met "other Hindu kids." Asked about it, one woman responded, "The Stockton temple, that's where we met the Khan kids every year, coming over from Phoenix to pick peaches." It was where families stayed overnight on their journeys up and down the state, where women shopped and talked as they took their children for movies and ice cream in the town.[39] Families in Arizona made these journeys less frequently. One descendant said, "When Dad finally took us to Stockton, that place where he'd sent a hundred dollars so often, even when the family was in need, we children saw that it *did* exist." Another described an event held there in connecton with her father's death as "a kind of a reunion, I guess you'd call it."[40] The Stockton temple was a central Punjabi institution, but memories of political and social events there outweighed those of religious ones for members of the second generation.[41]

Class and Ethnic Identity

Despite the domestic socialization into Hispanic culture and the relatively little Punjabi culture transmitted by the fathers, members of the second generation tended increasingly to identify themselves as Hindu or East Indian. Sometimes they contrasted themselves with their mothers: "Mother's interest in Dad's country was only in the food." But sometimes it was said that mothers also "became Hindu, not really Mexican anymore"; "my mother was both Hindu and Mexican." "All four older sisters married non-Christians to get away from their strict father. My mother too, she was very Indian, being the youngest sister she kept going to the Hindu homes of her older sisters. She married [a Hindu] at fifteen and never learned Mexican cooking." "Our foundation roots are East Indian; to her [our mother], we don't ask much about the Spanish culture and the American Indian culture [her ancestry] . . . in our home, it's East Indian."[42]

While the positive reasons for this self-identification as Indian were strengthened as the children grew up (these reasons are examined later), there were also negative ones. In the childhood years, the negative reasons loomed larger. Prejudice was a major factor in the lives of these children. They met prejudice from the dominant culture and from Mexican Americans. In the early years they may have found it easier to "be

Mexican," but this changed gradually. As prejudice against the Hindus abated and as some Punjabi men did well in farming, those men and their families set themselves apart from the large, predominantly working-class Mexican American population in the Imperial Valley. Thus, despite the cultural content of their daily lives, claiming to be Hindu was claiming a higher status in the rural stratification system for many Punjabi-Mexican children. There was prejudice within the Punjabi-Mexican community along class lines as well, with the working-class families tending to be closer to (though never merged with) the Mexican American population.

Conditions for Mexicans in the Imperial Valley have been well described during the late 1920s (by Mexican, I mean those of Mexican parentage, following "the generally prevalent social classification" of the time). From 1917, Mexican labor had become a major factor in crop harvesting there, and the Mexican population had grown until it constituted at least one-third of the total county population of 54,500 in 1927. About half the Mexican population was settled in urban and half in rural areas of the county; the largest concentration was in Brawley, which grew almost half the valley's cotton in 1920.[43] While instability caused by the high proportions of tenancy and short-term leasing led to rough housing conditions for many people in the valley, housing conditions for agricultural laborers were the poorest. They ranged from "ditch-bank camps" consisting of tents along the irrigation ditches to permanent camps with shelters of various kinds. Mexicans were settling down in the valley and rapidly becoming homeowners in the towns, but they were *not* becoming owners of farm property. Very few Mexicans were even leasing agricultural land. Furthermore, the Mexican population was segregated, concentrated on the east side of the towns and separated from neighbors in rural areas as well.[44]

Most Imperial Valley schools were segregated by race and ethnicity, with schools for black and Mexican children on the east sides of the towns.[45] Mexican children formed 37 percent of the elementary school enrollment in 1927, although their percentage of high school enrollment was only about 4 percent. Mexicans and blacks were put together in segregated schools through the eighth grade in Brawley. In Imperial, the Mexicans were in a separate school through the fifth grade and the blacks through eighth grade; in Westmoreland and Calipatria, Mexicans and blacks were in separate schools through the early grades. In El Centro, the biggest town, Mexican and blacks were together in segregated schools all the way through high school.[46] Only Holtville and Calexico were exceptions to the pattern of segregation, Holtville because it had so few nonwhite school children and Calexico because of its large middle- and upper-class Mexican population and close links to the Mexican ruling class in Mexicali.[47]

The Punjabi-Mexican children, regardless of what school district they actually lived in, were directed to the "nonwhite" schools.[48] Here they found a Spanish-speaking peer group, but hostility as well. Stories included harassment in the outdoor privies, taunts and shoves on the school bus, and name-calling and fighting at school. Often, Mexican children were remembered as being more prejudiced than Anglo children. Some Punjabi-Mexican children had stones thrown at them by the children of their fathers' workers as they went down the lanes to school together.[49] While teachers and other students in the school systems in the valley may well have been prejudiced against all immigrants and their children,[50] the children of mixed marriages seem to have had an especially difficult time, as suggested by the Imperial County district attorney's telling comment: "The Japanese-Mexicans and the Hindu-Mexicans are the meanest children our teachers have to deal with."[51]

Some Punjabi fathers protested the assignment of their children to the east-side schools, others did not. Faced with three schools, "one Spanish-speaking, one black, and one American," one father went to the principal and insisted that his children were Caucasian and should attend the American school. In the same situation, another father let his children stay in the Mexican school.[52] In Brawley, one Singh family lived right across from the Barbara Worth (Anglo) School, but the children were sent to the east-side Hidalgo School. By the late 1940s, a Brawley junior high school opened, and all the town children attended it, save for the children from the Government Project Camp (a labor camp), who were bused over to the east side to a separate school.[53]

Not only school systems but public facilities such as restaurants, barber shops, movie theaters, swimming pools, and even many churches were segregated.[54] One daughter remembers her mother insisting on sitting in the Anglo part of Brawley's movie theater. Others among the oldest children remember being barred from a swimming pool or getting seats on public transport only after others were seated (and as a result sometimes being denied a place). Hospitals also discriminated against nonwhites, with some tragic results. One man spoke of the death of his young step-brother. The boy became ill while the family was working on the Imperial Dam near Yuma, but the Yuma hospital refused to admit the boy and told his mother to take him to El Centro; he died on the way.[55]

Mexicans and Punjabis had entered the Imperial Valley in the 1910s, equally disadvantaged and facing similar prejudice and discriminatory practices. By the late 1920s, the growing Mexican population ranked lower in the social world than the small Punjabi population. The Punjabis were still a conspicuous minority, perhaps even more so by virtue of their biethnic marriages, but they had carved out a place just above that of the Mexicans. Many Punjabis were moving out of the laborer class and leasing and purchasing agricultural land, a movement that earned them respect as well as resentment. In contrast, the Mexicans were settling in towns and acquiring urban property; they rarely leased or purchased rural property, and most of them worked as agricultural laborers. The biethnic marriages probably contributed to both Anglo and Punjabi perceptions that Punjabis ranked above Mexicans. Certainly in Punjabi terms, they had become wife takers from the Mexican population, not wife givers (hypergamy, the systematic giving of daughters to higher-ranking families, was practiced in parts of India, including the Punjab). Of course, the Punjabis in California had no women to give, but the circumstance must have reinforced Punjabi perceptions of their higher rank.

The Punjabi-Mexican children shared many cultural attributes with Mexicans, but often tried to distance themselves from Mexicans because of the latter's low rank in the socioeconomic system. One daughter said, "I thought we were middle class when I was young, but we were poor. But not so poor as the Mexicans—I spoke Spanish, but still, Mexicans spoke and still speak English to me, it maintains a difference, a distance."[56] This tendency was encouraged by the divisions developing between Punjabi-Mexicans. Children were playing important roles in the household economy, roles that differed by class within the Punjabi-Mexican community.[57] As the children came, families that were less well off continued to share households with other Punjabi-Mexican families or (rarely) with Mexican relatives. Families that could afford it split off from the joint households and leased places of their own (often with bachelor partners living nearby). As the children grew bigger, many families put them to work. In families where their labor was not needed, children began to play an important function as landholders—as American citizens by birth, they could own the agricultural land their fathers coveted.

The mid 1920s marked the application of the Alien Land Laws to the Punjabis in the Imperial Valley. Although the men continued to farm by working with and through Anglos (particularly their lawyers), public criticism of Punjabi land acquisition mounted in the early 1930s. At the time of the 1933 Imperial County grand jury indictments for conspiracy to evade the Alien Land Laws, the Punjabis who were doing well began to use the probate court to register as guardians of their minor children. They bought land in the names of their children and managed it as guardians through probate.

Punjabi names had appeared in the probate records before this, as men died and their estates were settled by court-appointed public administrators,[58] but in 1929 a Punjabi registered as guardian of his minor child. A second Punjabi registered as guardian in 1932, another in 1933, nine others in 1934, and an additional twenty-four by the end of 1944. Most of the appointed guardians were the fathers, although in four cases the parents were appointed jointly and in four cases widowed mothers were appointed. In one case (an application of Punjabi joint-property practices?), two brothers were appointed guardian for all their children.[59] Probate actions connected with deaths also changed. In contrast to seventeen earlier cases where Anglo public administrators had been appointed for the estates of deceased Punjabis, after 1923 unrelated Punjabi men, widows, and even daughters became executors in about half such probate actions.[60]

This changing use of the probate court reflects both the growth of a family society and the enforcement of the Alien Land Laws in Imperial County. The children's important new role in the family economy raises the possibility that some men might have married and had families in order to hold land through their children after 1933. These probate cases also force us to recognize that many men preferred to control their land through their minor children by using the probate court, rather than through their wives. Because the Cable Act had been repealed in 1931, most of the wives of Punjabis were again eligible for U.S. citizenship through naturalization and could hold land,[61] yet the men preferred to use their children. No doubt the high divorce rate in the Imperial Valley was responsible for this reluctance to put land in the wives' names—the probate records themselves evidence conflict within the families. In one case, a man used the probate court to register his Hispanic wife's birth in Imperial County many years earlier (her birth had not been properly recorded at the time), probably intending to put his property in her name once her U.S. citizenship was established. The couple divorced, however, and he promptly put his property in the names of his sons. In another case, a mother successfully registered as guardian of her children and manager of their land, only to be challenged by her ex-husband and forced to resign the position in his favor.[62]

Having secure control of land through their children, Imperial Valley Punjabis demonstrated their economic success by improving their homes and furnishings. Sucha Singh Garewal took pride in the new home he built for his family, installing chandeliers and carpets and lining his driveway with fine lemon trees and flowers. He even maintained neat laborers' quarters across the road. Similarly, Diwan Singh in Arizona was known for the relatively modern camp he ran for his farm laborers, complete with Catholic chapel. Nand Singh Chell, when he finally married, had a son and set up his wife in a *real* house; he moved the bachelor shack he had lived in for thirty years from the land he had formerly leased to his new land so that he could remember the difference between his old and new life.[63]

Class differentiation within the Punjabi community could be seen not only in the landholder–laborer split but in the linkage between the better-off farmers and urban Asian Indians who were better educated, held professional positions, and led the efforts to gain U.S. citizenship. A working-class Punjabi, Mola Singh, expressed distance from these efforts when he said, "Most of our people lived by labor; we were just farmers, common labor people, you know. Some people, educated ones, they used to live in other places, they knew about the national movement, our country. They came here, made a corporation, made it with white men." In contrast, a well-educated, more successful farmer insisted that his urban countrymen recognize the important negative impact on the farmers' livelihoods of the Alien Land Laws. Thus, when Bagga S. Sunga was approached for help, he said, "Citizenship is important, but we can't even make a living now; we have two goals, to get citizenship and to get farm land." He then joined a delegation to Los Angeles to talk to a judge there about political strategies and funding.[64]

While the children of the more prosperous Punjabi farmers grew up knowing all about the Alien Land Laws and the problem of owning agricultural property, the children of the landless were less aware, sometimes even unaware, of the laws. Some who grew up without land spoke of leading Punjabi farmers in their areas as "landowners," in contrast to their own fathers. Working-class fathers and mothers were more often illiterate in any language (although some illiterate men were quite successful); theirs were the children who sometimes lacked birth certificates. These fathers did not do well enough to send money home to India regularly, and they often failed to keep in touch with relatives there. They thought of themselves and their families as working-class Americans.[65]

Prejudices within the Punjabi-Mexican community derived partly from competition and rivalry between farmers, much like the situation back in the Punjab. Families were acutely aware of socioeconomic levels within the community. Commenting on a 1926 court case in which a Mexican father sued the Sikh with whom his daughter had eloped for $753 worth of fine female clothing and house furnishings, the daughter of a leading Punjabi farmer said, "But that girl didn't have a pair of shoes to her name!" Two or three of the better-off families used their clan or village names as a surname instead of Singh to set themselves apart from the many Singhs who were laborers. One woman recalled how a better-off girl of Punjabi-Mexican parentage made her miserable as a child by criticizing her friendships with Mexican girls. "We are Hindus, and we should not go with Mexicans," she was told repeatedly. Some Punjabi fathers warned their children against associating with the children of other Punjabis. In one small place in Arizona, a wealthy Punjabi-Mexican family did not speak to the children of a poor Punjabi-Mexican family. This hurt the poorer children more than the hostility of the local Mexicans. Sometimes the fathers' views were misattributed to religion. "We didn't have much to do with them, they were Muslims," one second-generation woman told me, and she was surprised to learn that "they" were Sikhs. Their surname not being Singh, she had thought her father's prejudice was based on religion.[66]

While the better-off Punjabis kept their children out of field work, many a working-class Punjabi-Mexican family depended on child labor to make ends meet. A tenant farmer in California agriculture could cut wage costs by using his children. Heavily dependent not only on the landowner but on the financing agent, whether that was a local bank or a shipping company, the tenant had to come up with capital, machinery, and other equipment; such costs were generally constant and beyond control, whereas labor costs were within the tenant's control and could be manipulated. The family could also contract out as a unit and work for others, on "family contracts."

The poorer Punjabi-Mexican families followed the migratory labor circuit. Some of their children were born outside the Imperial Valley, in
French Camp outside Stockton, for example, as they journeyed. Children
could be workers only in certain crops. They were used in picking cotton,
the Imperial Valley's first big crop, but they were generally not used in
lettuce, its second big crop. Children were useful in hops, peas, beans,
carrots, tomatoes, prunes, walnuts, and olives, and in the cutting of
peaches, apricots, and pears in the drying sheds; they were not used in
other highly specialized crops, such as cherries, citrus, potatoes, and
dates. Sometimes children picked grapes and did cannery work. Except
where there were hourly wages, in the cutting and packing sheds, children and adults were on the same wage scale.[67] Again, children contributed importantly to the household economy.

These working-class Punjabi-Mexican children attended schools all
over California, but they could not always attend regularly. By state law,
children were required to stay in school until the age of sixteen and were
not supposed to work during school hours, although Taylor comments
that Imperial Valley authorities had difficulty enforcing this law in the
late 1920s. In cotton, children generally picked only half a day and spent
the other half in school.[68]

In these working-class Punjabi-Mexican families, ironically, the sons
learned Punjabi best, from working on "Hindu crews" as they grew up.
Just as they learned Hindu ethnicity on the job, they also learned Mexican American working-class culture. These sons and daughters had
closer contact with Mexican Americans from working alongside them in
the fields and orchards. The upwardly mobile Punjabi families were criticized for keeping their places "too nice," and the working-class men
spoke proudly of their wives working with them, while other wives
"never worked." More of the working-class sons went into the service in
World War II; at least one prosperous Punjabi father arranged a marriage
for his son to avoid the draft. Fathers expressed strong preferences that
their daughters marry "working men," clearly identifying themselves as
working class.[69]

Hard Times in Agriculture

Changed cropping patterns and the economic depression from the early
1920s through the 1930s sent the poorer Punjabi-Mexican families out of
the Imperial Valley. The exodus began with the cotton bankruptcies after

World War I. Cotton cultivation declined as a result of boll weevil infestations in the Imperial Valley, and in Texas, but it expanded north into the San Joaquin and Sacramento valleys. This meant fewer jobs for children in the south, where lettuce, too, had become a major crop. Many Punjabis changed from cotton to dairy farming, and from dairy farming to migratory labor, as conditions turned against them. Children were useful in dairy farming, but the tuberculosis testing of the early 1930s decimated many herds in the Imperial Valley, and dairy farmers went bankrupt. Some men took their families north along with the cotton, responding to changing labor demands by moving to the San Joaquin Valley or north to the Yuba City–Marysville area, where grapes and other crops still used child labor. Thus they were part of a gradual northward movement of predominantly Mexican families that depended on agricultural labor.[70]

The depression intensified this trend. In Tulare County, for example, a number of Punjabis married in the late 1920s. But wages fell drastically there, and almost all the families moved north. Working-class Punjabi-Mexican children traveled the migratory labor routes with their families, harvesting peaches, prunes, and walnuts in the northern counties. The fathers frequently served as foremen and supervised Hindu crews, albeit on a seasonal basis; their sons found work with them or with Mexican crews.[71]

Families moved about the state, looking for employment; some even went to Mexico. Finally, in 1938 the federal Fair Labor Standards Act prohibited the employment of a child under fourteen years at any time.[72] Enforcement of this law spurred some final moves north or to Arizona, where some Muslim Punjabis clustered around Phoenix in the early 1930s. Many Phoenix Muslims were starting over again after losses in the Imperial Valley. This community consisted of about a dozen single men and a dozen families. There were many children in the Phoenix area: seven Dads and seven Muhammads, six Rahmatullas, five Niamat Khans, four Rustam Khans (and five Mondos in Glendale).[73]

These same years produced unprecedented labor struggles in the Imperial Valley and elsewhere in California. The 1920s had seen the rapid expansion of commercial farming and the establishment of labor bureaus by employers, county farm bureaus, and chambers of commerce. Union activity was slower to develop, but low wages, poor living conditions, and prejudice against farmworkers brought efforts to mobilize. In 1928, a newly formed Workers Union of the Imperial Valley opened the spring cantaloupe harvest with an attempt to negotiate better wages and working conditions; rebuffed, some of the Mexican workers struck. This strike failed to enlist Filipino or Punjabi workers. At the end of 1929, the Communist party began to organize farmworkers in California, and in 1930 a lettuce strike led by the Mexican Mutual Aid Society of the Imperial Valley was taken over by communist organizers and their Agricultural Workers Industrial League. This effort was more successful and incorporated Filipino workers.[74]

The most tumultous year was 1933–1934. Cotton wages in the San Joaquin Valley had fallen from $1.50 per 100 pounds in 1929 to 40 cents per 100 pounds in 1932. Workers had little to lose when cotton strikes erupted throughout central and northern California in 1933, followed by dramatic strikes and reprisals against the strikers in the Imperial Valley in 1934. There, as elsewhere, officials and growers (most officials in the Imperial Valley *were* growers, it seemed) joined to put down the farmworkers in true vigilante style. Imperial County growers formed an organization that helped control "disorders."[75]

Toward the end of 1934, the Imperial County growers' organization was combined with other county groups by the state chamber of commerce, Farm Bureau Federation, and Agriculture Department. The new statewide organization, the Associated Farmers of California, represented growers and such outside groups as Safeway Stores, banks, railroads, oil companies, along with others who wanted to keep prices (and labor costs) low.[76] In the Imperial Valley, the conflict escalated. A federal "labor conciliator" from the Department of Labor was sent to bring about a "permanent economic and social adjustment" of labor relations there. This conciliator, retired U.S. Army Brigadier General Pelham D. Glassford, spent two months in the valley and suppressed the California Agricultural Workers Industrial Union, which he considered a "communistic front." When Glassford tried to implement labor reforms, however, he found the growers uncooperative. He left after recommending a special state-supervised grand jury investigation into lawlessness in the valley.[77]

Despite the strong class consciousness within the Punjabi-Mexican community, Punjabi workers did not participate in any labor mobilization in the Imperial Valley. The Mexican mutual aid societies were the organizational base of the 1928 and 1930 strikes, but no Punjabis were members of those societies. Although they were not brought into the Associated Farmers by the Anglo growers, the Punjabis, like all growers, actively opposed union organizing. The bonds between the Punjabi men were stronger than their class interests; Punjabi farmworkers continued to look to Punjabi employers and possible patrons for their welfare.

But the bonds of the Punjabi men did not always prevail for their children, and class divisions produced different responses to the question of identity. In some families, the children considered themselves to be Mexican American, and paralleling cases where Mexican wives "turned Hindu," they thought of their fathers as "turning Mexican." One son said, "Our dad turned Mexican. He brought us all up after Mother died, six or seven boys and one girl. Dad didn't teach us much about India, when he said things we all just laughed at him, six or seven boys, not much chance." One father, Mola Singh, identified strongly with Mexicans as he defended them: "That foreman, he asked my countrypeople . . . he hollered at them, 'Hey, hey you.' I told him, 'Hey, don't come here, these are Mexican people picking. You don't holler at these people, let them work ahead, they work good.' "[78]

For Punjabi-Mexican families of this class, Hispanic-kin ties succumbed to economic forces as sister sets were broken up; in at least two instances, the "poor sister" moved north, leaving behind sisters married to more prosperous Punjabis in the Imperial Valley. In the late 1930s, Sikhs, Muslims, and Hindus were all represented among those who moved north on the migratory labor circuit. Punjabi-Mexican families helped one another; religious and caste distinctions from India became unimportant in the face of the common economic predicament. The Sidhu family (Sikh) exemplifies these working-class networks. Their neighbor Omar Din, a Muslim, drove north, taking most of the Sidhus with him. Only the smallest Sidhu boy was left behind, with a childless Sikh-Mexican couple. The rest of the family worked in the fields around Yuba City and Sacramento, where children were still employed. Young Alfred Sidhu went to school all over California in those years; he finally begged to be left for a year with a Punjabi-Mexican family settled in Yuba City so that he could finish school.[79]

Families that moved with their children on contract around the state encountered difficult living conditions. Living frugally, trying to save money to buy land, Mola Singh defended his children from his employer, a man for whom the family was picking grapes and on whose land they were living. When the Singhs had another child, a confrontation occurred:

The man said, "Oh this little baby kid, too many kids, Mr. Singh, you move."

I said, "No, how can I move, I got no place to go."

Then he shut off the light. He said, "Too many kids. After the grapes finish, you go."

I said, "I'll move when I get a house, otherwise how can I move?"

Then he shut off the light. Close, maybe 200 yards, his place and mine. So he shut off the light.

I said, "Why did you shut off the light?"

He said, "I want you to move."

I said, "Okay, but turn on the light. Listen," I told him, "you shut off the lights, but don't you shut off the water. You shut off the water, I'll put you in the penitentiary here. If any kid here die, no water, then I'm gonna sue you. When I get a place, I'll move. I got family here." So then he kept his mouth shut.[80]

As the poorer Punjabi-Mexican families moved north, the repercussions of some of Roosevelt's New Deal reforms sent several bachelor farmers from the north to the south. The 1933 production controls forced "alien" farmers to change crops and relocate, since they did not have the proper records to qualify for acreage allotments in crops coming under the controls. After 1923, when the Alien Land Laws applied to them, many Punjabi Muslim farmers growing rice around Biggs, Butte City, and Colusa had continued to cash-lease on the basis of verbal agreements, while crop-sharing leases were written and sometimes recorded in the names of trusted Anglos. The 1933 acreage controls applied to rice, so a farmer had to establish an acreage history by showing five years of production records. A rice grower who could only produce leases in the name of an Anglo friend could not get an acreage allotment. At this point, several bachelor Muslim rice growers in the northern counties left for the Imperial Valley and began farming all over again.[81]

Thus the hard years in California agriculture, the depression, and the federal enactment of child-labor laws and production controls combined to distribute the Punjabi-Mexican families more widely and to bring some bachelor farmers south. The earlier pattern of bachelor Punjabis in the north and families in the south was modified. The ecology and demography of each location shaped the socialization of the Punjabi-Mexican children. Those living at a distance from the centers of Punjabi-Mexican settlement inevitably presented variations on the Imperial Valley pattern; for example, Muslim Punjabis dominated the settlement in Phoenix, with Sikhs playing peripheral roles. Despite differences in local and regional patterns, Punjabi-Mexican children everywhere had to deal with their biethnic heritage.

8 The Second Generation Comes of Age

As the children of the Punjabi men grew older and took an active role in defining themselves, they constructed an ethnic identity that was strong and positive. They made choices that might set them at odds with their families but that gave them flexibility in the multiethnic, stratified world of rural California. They began to look critically at their parents, and in their accounts, it is the fathers who stand out. Fathers represented the families to the outside world and were perceived as "different" by that world—and by their children. Mexicans and Mexican Americans were numerous in the Imperial Valley by the late 1930s, but the Punjabi population stayed small, subject to tight immigration controls and still ineligible for citizenship. The fathers shared characteristics with the other Punjabi men, which presented problems for their adolescent children. As they made marriage and career choices, the children played a vigorous part in the family dynamics, provoking new conflicts and exacerbating old ones.

Growing Up with Punjabi Fathers

While there was individual variation among Punjabi men, common patterns of interaction characterized father–child relations in Punjabi-Mexican families. The children were raised primarily by the mothers, and a certain distance from the father often resulted. This partly reflected the men's work patterns. As one wife said, responding to a question about fathers who "never knew their own kids" because they worked so hard: "Well, that is right. Because they'd get up early in the morning before daylight and they'd take off. The children were still in bed. I say for myself, I get up in the morning and get them ready for school and take them to school and attend to all their functions in school because he couldn't leave the work, he was a farmer, a field worker, a laborer, he had to work to make a living."[1]

Other pressures contributed to a lack of closeness, especially in the Imperial Valley, where large numbers of Punjabi-Mexicans lived. One Sacramento Valley second-generation couple observed that "in the Imperial Valley, the children of the Punjabis distanced themselves from their fathers to avoid discrimination; only the boys who worked with their fathers understood the old-timers, their language, their feelings. Later some were sorry."[2] It is also possible that Punjabi-Mexican father–son relationships were similar to those of Mexican Americans. Penalosa characterizes these relationships as distant but respectful. They would have seemed natural to the wives and to many of the children.[3]

The fathers presented strong, proud images, commanding respect and obedience from their wives and children. "Women didn't really count," two descendants agreed, illustrating this with two stories. One said that his mother, "even though she was a Mexican woman, was always three feet behind him, and she shut up when he talked." The other told of a time when her grandmother was driving her grandfather, and he ordered her to drive down a one-way street the wrong way. She protested but he insisted, so she did it. Cars honked at them. She pulled over, looking at her husband. He then ordered her to turn around and pull onto a side street. "They never admitted they were wrong, they had total control and total responsibility and they just handled it." Sikh men taught their children that Singh meant lion and that lionhearts were "never afraid or wrong." Mike Singh grew up thinking he was never wrong; later, he went into the U.S. Navy, where he learned differently.[4]

"There's nothing to match the temper of an East Indian," one daughter said. Among themselves, the men's disagreements could end in fights, particular when they had been drinking. Children remember parties where liquor flowed and so did insults about unpaid loans or other men's women. On several occasions, fistfights erupted and chairs were thrown. But domestic violence, although sometimes threatened, was not common.[5]

To their children, affection and discipline were expressed with restraint. Fathers held their daughters on their laps and stroked their hair, but they never hugged or kissed them. Fathers seldom touched their sons and taught them not to cry, not to show emotion. "No crying unless you were alone, no laughing unless others were laughing," one son remembered. Most fathers were gentle men. "Dad never put his hands on me; he signaled me with his eyes, I always knew what he meant." Or, "Father never, never spanked us; he would speak to us in a way that you would feel, that we wished that he would spank us. Mother would spank us because we deserved it." The worst punishment was silence. One boy remembered getting a *D* in penmanship, despite his father's provision of a private bedroom, desk, and study lamp, and the reproachful silence with which the grade was greeted. The anger signaled by these silences was sometimes neither expressed nor explained, and passed only slowly.[6]

Other characteristics shared by the Punjabi men were honesty and fairness, with an emphasis on "giving your word." Written contracts, written agreements, were not needed. "Dad used to say, your word was like gold, it's all you have." Once this El Centro father drove forty miles late at night to return two cents. A Calipatria customer had paid him $1.25 for a livestock delivery, counting out the change in pennies and giving him $1.27 by mistake. At home, the father discovered the error and immediately got in his truck and drove back to return the overpayment. Another aspect of giving your word was that "if someone did them wrong, they could act, take the law unto themselves." The Singh murders in 1925 were cited as an example of this.[7]

Most of the men were very good businessmen. "They could deal in seconds in their heads, figuring came natural"; or, "He couldn't read or write, but he had a computer up there." Their pride sometimes interfered with doing business. Rosie Lusier recalled two partners fighting over $500 that one man owed the other but would not admit it. Finally, Rosie's grandfather Sucha Singh Garewal paid the one partner, and the other man paid him, a solution leaving everyone's pride intact and allowing the partnership to continue. When such innovative solutions could not be found, disputes could turn into court cases that went on for years.[8]

While they took tremendous pride in their paternal heritage, many children also shared certain negative perceptions about their fathers. Most Punjabi fathers were seen as strict disciplinarians, relatively uncommunicative, and tight with money. Consider the following comments: "He was hard, he didn't talk a lot to me." "Dad was hard to get to know, work-oriented; he was a strict authoritarian and didn't show his feelings." "Father was a very strict disciplinarian." "He was a grouch, all Punjabis are grouchy." Just as money was an issue between husband and wife in many marriages, it was an issue between fathers and their adolescent children. Notoriously reluctant to spend money on anything but land, Punjabi men kept the household money and doled it out as they saw fit. One son complained, "Those old guys, all they cared about was money." And the money was used for farming. Diwan Singh in Arizona said it well: "Everything I make from the soil goes back into it. Money is all right, but only when it can be spent to make the soil better. My farm is my bank, and my faith is in it." Sometimes wives and children had to earn their own money, raising chickens to sell eggs, for example. Sometimes they used other strategies. "Dad wanted to use his money for land. Mom had to wait until he went to sleep and then she went through his pockets to get us money for schoolbooks," one daughter remembered.[9]

Many of the Punjabi men had money. "The lower the pants, the richer the man," one daughter recalled, describing the paunches on those who ate and drank well. And the "money ritual" was a familiar one—the routine the men went through when their children asked for money. Body language was an important part of it; the immediate response was to turn away and draw out the money from the pocket, counting it folded in half so that no one could see how much there was. Reluctantly, the father would peel off a dollar, squinting at it, pinching it, and feeling it to make sure there was only one. "How much is the movie?" he'd ask, followed by, "Don't spend it all." The child would quickly add that he wanted some popcorn or a Coke too, to prevent his father from withdrawing the dollar and reaching into his other pocket for change. Fathers countered with, "If you want a drink, get water, get a drink at home." But generally they handed over the dollar—and expected an exact accounting later.[10]

Some descendants called Punjabi men frugal, most called them worse names, especially when talking of other people's fathers: "tightwad," "stingy," "mean bastard." I heard several lively discussions nominating "the meanest bastard" among the "old Hindus." People recalled one man whose woman got tired of cabbage and left him, and another who appeared poverty-stricken for years, but left his family lots of money when he died. Of course, there were exceptions. Some descendants proudly told of the "Hindu rice kings" near Gridley who spent money grandly or other men who indulged themselves and their families after a good crop. Just as members of the second generation were quick to poke fun at those who were misers, they were ready to joke about "big spender" claims. One women dubbed her son, the grandson of a Punjabi farmer, the "Donut King" of Huntington Beach![11]

For most children of Punjabi-Mexican marriages, the "rice kings" were part of a mythical past. Born during the 1920s and 1930s, the children grew up during years of depression for California agriculture. Punjabi fathers lost jobs or were forced to take less secure and less rewarding work then they formerly had. Many of these families went on the migratory labor circuit, and many women and children also worked. One daughter recalled going into the fields before daybreak to pick peas for the family before the pickers arrived, stealing from the crop they had grown themselves under contract. In such situations, fathers probably experienced some loss of authority.[12] For the Punjabi fathers, older than their wives by many years and doubly disadvantaged by discriminatory laws, the economic threat to their authority must have adversely affected family relationships.

Some of the sharpest observations of Punjabi men came from children separated from them during their early years, usually because of the mother's death. Punjabi men faced the problem of caring for motherless children in several ways. If there were enough older children to care for the younger ones, the fathers kept the family together and raised the children. If that was not the case, a father could try various alternatives. One man took his five children back to Pakistan when his Hispanic wife died and raised them there.[13] In another instance, two brothers lived together with their wives, who were sisters; one wife left, but the other three adults stayed together, and the youngest of the numerous children grew up thinking he had two fathers and one mother. Since the men found sons useful for work and inheritance, they tended to keep their sons with them, but let their daughters be raised by Mexican relatives. One man kept his son, but took his daughter over to Mexico and left her with a Mexican family, whose name he then forgot! Other fathers put their young children in boarding schools in Banning or San Diego. Although children who had grown up with their fathers sometimes said they were "just like other fathers, just like Mexican fathers, really," those who were brought into close contact with their fathers for the first time as teenagers found many things about them that were different or even shocking. Especially intriguing was the fact that many of the men had been married back in India and had children there.[14]

As adolescents, many Punjabi-Mexican children were curious about those Indian families, especially about half-brothers or sisters. One daughter recalled her father telling them about "our family that we never met." For many family men, however, Indian had receded in importance over the years, and fathers were reticent about their Indian families. The Punjabi-Mexican children, like other Americans, thought of Indians as poor inhabitants of an underdeveloped country. Alfred Sidhu's father had left a son in India and sent money to him for some years; then he stopped sending money, saying that the son had land and would be all right. Alfred worried about his half-brother and asked for his address, but his father wouldn't give it to him. During Alfred's World War II service, he wanted to go from Burma to India and find his brother, but he did not have the opportunity. Home again, Alfred wondered "how that poor fellow is over in India." He wrote a letter and put every place name on the envelope that his father had ever mentioned. Fifteen days later, he had an eager reply: His "Indian brother" wrote that he had been waiting for years to hear from his American family! He also wrote that he worked in the fields and was not doing well. Alfred enlisted his five brothers, and they combined to send $100 every month for three years, financing a new pump for the fields and other projects. This was done without their father's knowledge, and when he did find out, he was angry. But Alfred told his father, "Your boy's not in such good shape as you thought," and got his father to contribute as well.[15]

Despite an explicit Punjabi preference for sons, evident in childbirth statistics and stories and in some of the choices made by fathers left with motherless children, Punjabi-Mexican daughters often expressed great affection for their fathers. Sons presented stronger challenges to paternal authority than did daughters, on a wider range of issues and for a longer time. Although both daughters and sons clashed with their fathers over dating and choice of spouse, some daughters followed paternal advice with respect to marriage partners. Others escaped strict parental control by marrying young and leaving the household. A greater control over girls' movements in the dating years accorded with expectations in the mothers' culture too, so the daughters often faced both parents when dating was the issue.

When a mother did back her daughter against a very strict father, the Hispanic godmothers could be counted on for support. This female united front deflected a father's attention from the daughter. In contrast, sons did not turn to their godmothers and could not get support from their Punjabi godfathers when engaged in disputes with their fathers; sons faced their fathers directly, without allies to soften the confrontation. It is also possible that the Punjabi men expected their daughters to be more like women in the United States, whom they had observed to be different from women in India, but they wanted their sons to be more like themselves.

Sons were expected to work for their fathers and for other Punjabis. "From the time I was twelve, I worked in the fields; Dad sent me to help other Punjabis, and I seldom got paid for that." The standards set for work were high. "If you can't outwork those Mexicans," boys were admonished, and their fathers set an example by competing to see "how many Mexicans they could drop in a day," that is, how many Mexicans would rest or drop out while a Punjabi kept working. Boys were pushed to excel in school and in sports, and bets were laid that pitted sons against each other on occasion.[16]

Mike Singh remembers a foot race against the son of another Punjabi (both boys were state champion runners, one in California and one in Arizona).

> The old men were sitting around, drinking whiskey and boasting about their sons. . . . An Arizona man put $1,000 on a blanket, said I couldn't beat the Arizona boy. Dad threw in $5,000, then others put down money. . . . We kids were off shooting .22 rifles at tin cans.
>
> Dad came, took me aside, and asked me, "Who are you?"
>
> I could tell something was up. I replied, "Mehnga Singh [his Punjabi name, seldom used]."
>
> "Yes," he replied, "a lionhearted Sikh warrior. Nobody can beat you, run and win, you're going to race this boy."
>
> "Okay," I said, "I'll run. Where is it?"
>
> "No," he said, "run and *win*, that's what you're going to do." He pointed to a course along the canal. "You are my blood," he said. . . . The women ran out, Mother among them, to see what was happening, and she remonstrated with him; Dad hushed her, she shut up. There was one drunken old man, he shot off a .22 to start the race, he called out, "You *chobdars*, run!" in Punjabi. Dad stood there with a deadpan look. . . . I ran but the other boy was ahead of me most of the way. . . . Then I hit it and ran, a Sikh warrior, ran for my heart, and beat him by two yards. Father just stood there looking impas-

sive, elders all around him. Then he spoke, "As I said, no one can beat my son, he's of my blood and he's a Sikh warrior." The other boy's father didn't say a word to him and they left within thirty minutes.[17]

This emphasis on being a Sikh warrior was unusual, but the father–son relationship and the pressure to win evoked ready recognition from others of the second generation. Pritam Sandhu explained Punjabi fathers this way: "They were out to win, they didn't care how they played the game; they wanted to be the best. When I was growing up, I thought this was an isolated thing with my father, but later on, I saw it was a Sikh thing, a Punjabi thing. They never quit, and they wouldn't let us either." They worked hard, fought with one another, and argued vigorously with their sons. Robert Khan in Phoenix remembers how difficult it was to deal with one of the fathers there, a man so obstinate that "if he fell in the river, you'd have to look for him upstream."[18]

Punjabi fathers' expectations for their daughters were not nearly so well defined, but they centered on their marriages. If daughters worked outside the family, it was usually briefly, before marriage. Also, once married, a daughter ceased to participate in the family farming enterprise and was not viewed as waiting for her inheritance; sons were expected to keep working with their fathers in the family farming tradition. This issue of property and its transmission bore much harder on the sons than the daughters. One daughter observed that her father had no sons, so he had no need to own land,[19] the implication being that having sons increased the fathers' expectations of *themselves* with respect to acquiring land to pass on. Where families did acquire land, sons certainly expected to inherit it, but fathers and sons had different ideas about when the property was to be turned over to the second generation. Political events in both Great Britain and the United States also dramatically altered the situation with respect to possible heirs, just as the sons were coming of age.

Teenage Years in Rural California

Members of the second generation[20] socialized with other Punjabi-Mexicans on many occasions. A Sunday afternoon at the El Centro Sikh temple was a frequent family outing, with the men visiting for hours while the women cooked and the children observed, listened, and ate. The men sat in a circle, and "as each one left, the others talked about him, tore him apart." Men tried to be the last to leave![21] Families visited one another's homes frequently, and some observed holidays with big parties involving several Punjabi-Mexican families. There was always an Easter Sunday potluck picnic in the Yuba City area. Both Easter Sunday and the Fourth of July were marked by picnics in the Imperial Valley and in Phoenix, Arizona. Held in cool places—the beaches near San Diego in the south, the buttes just outside Yuba City in the north—these picnics were enjoyed greatly by the young people. One Easter Sunday picnic in 1944 at Jacumba (near San Diego) involved three Punjabi-Mexican couples and sixteen of their adolescent children and was written up in the Holtville paper.[22]

Friendships among second-generation teenagers were based on locality and class. In the Imperial Valley, Punjabi-Mexicans and Anglos in Holtville attended the same schools (there were few Mexicans and no blacks in Holtville). High school ties were close ones for Holtville youth, and the earliest high school graduates (1937–1940) among the Punjabi-Mexicans seem to have been from Holtville: Harry Sidhu, Mary Khan, Gurbashen Singh Shine, Bessie Dhillon, and Mary Garewal. El Centro was close behind, with Central Union High School graduating Elizabeth Deen and Frank Ram in 1938. Imperial graduated Punjabi-Mexican children from 1942 on, the earliest ones being Josephine Singh, Lupe Deol Singh, and Albert Baksh. Albert Singh, Robert S. Khattre, and Gloria Saikhon graduated from Brawley's high school in the late 1940s. Before 1951, the Central Junior College on the El Centro Union High School campus was the local college, and Mary Khan, Frank Ram, and Louis Sareeram graduated from there circa 1940.[23]

Early graduates experienced differing degrees of isolation as they moved through the school system. Punjabi-Mexicans, although characterized as handsome or beautiful, often were set apart by parental restraints. The children of Muslim fathers were unable to participate in weenie roasts in the desert, a favorite teenage recreation in the Imperial Valley. The prohibition on pork became a test of adulthood. One son, home after serving in World War II, tried to demonstrate his independence by ordering a pork dish at a family dinner in a local Chinese restaurant. His father rebuked him angrily, forbidding him to eat it, "not in front of me and not when I pay!"[24]

Both Punjabi fathers and Mexican mothers were strict about their daughters dating in high school. The story of Mary Khan is especially poignant. Stepdaughter of a leading Muslim farmer near Holtville, she was strikingly beautiful and a bright girl. Many young men tried to date her, but her father steadfastly refused to allow their attentions. Punjabi Sikh farmers, Greek growers, and Swiss farmers all vied for her hand, but all were rebuffed. Early admirers still remember her beauty, her intelligence, and her lonely inaccessibility.[25] The daughters were marked out by Mexican Americans too, not necessarily with favor. Mary Gill remembers a Mexican Independence Day dance in Phoenix where Isabel Singh was running for queen. The boy Mary was dancing with said, "If that Hinda thinks I'm going to vote for her, she's got another think coming!" Mary said, "I'm a Hinda too," and left him.[26]

Other important shared experiences for Punjabi-Mexican teenagers came through their work in agriculture. They remembered the Punjabi foremen who employed them on specific ranches, and they recounted their meetings every year with other Punjabi-Mexicans at labor camps, in fields and orchards. Girls from the poorer families worked just as their brothers did. The Rasuls, the Sidhus, the Singhs, the Kakars, and the Khans met every year when they were teenagers moving from crop to crop. They picked peaches in Yuba City and grapes in Fresno. Teenage crushes and marriage arrangements proposed by fathers that never came off are remembered with nostalgia from those years.[27]

Among the sons, there was an especially strong network built on working and socializing together all over California. Boys from the Imperial Valley went north for seasonal agricultural work and met the boys from Yuba City. Joe Mallobox, for example, worked around Yuba City in Hindu crews, where the foremen were older Punjabis. Joe and the Rasul brothers, Benjamin and Jacob, from the Imperial Valley worked with Paul Singh, son of Nand Kaur and Puna Singh of Yuba City, and Mario Dacca Singh in the peach orchards there, and the young men went together to the bars in Marysville. There were few Mexicans in Yuba City–Marysville in the early 1940s,[28] and the Punjabi-Mexican sons all got jobs through "Hindu boss men."

Making Marriage Choices

The daughters and sons of the Punjabis married young, and most of their partners were Hispanic or Anglo. There were still no women from India, and while there were enough Punjabi-Mexican children to form an endogamous group in the Imperial Valley, they showed no preference for marriages with each other. A few fathers did succeed in persuading their daughters to marry Punjabis, but these marriages did not usually turn out successfully.

Some nineteen Punjabi-Mexican daughters and at least five Hispanic stepdaughters married Punjabis, men much older than themselves who were friends of their fathers. Of the nineteen daughters' marriages, ten ended in divorce and only five proved lasting.[29] The girls married at ages fifteen to eighteen, while their husbands were on average twenty years older (photo 19). This repeated the first-generation age pattern. The first such marriages paired Imperial Valley daughters with well-off Punjabis in northern California in 1935 and 1937 (Cirilia Singh, daughter of Antonia and Sher Singh, married Karm Chand, the leading Punjabi store-owner in Yuba City; and Florence Din married Charag Mohammed, one of the popcorn and tamale wagon owners in San Francisco).[30]

Because the Punjabi-Mexican daughters were American citizens by birth and the Cable Act no longer assigned them to the status of their husbands (aliens ineligible for citizenship), these young wives could lease and own land. In several instances, farm property and checking accounts were immediately put in the wife's name. Control invariably remained with the husband, however, a circumstance some of the young wives resented and ultimately cited as partial reason for divorce. Others willingly held not only the property of their husbands but that of other Punjabi farmers as well.[31]

These marriages of young Punjabi-Mexican daughters to older Punjabis provided some surprises. One incident made the front pages of the local papers. A day after the wedding, a young bride asked her husband to drive her across the border to Mexico to visit a favorite aunt, and she begged him for cash to make a gift. In Mexicali, she took the cash, left him guarding the car, and never returned. Finally, he left the car to search for her, and his car with all the wedding gifts and her just-purchased clothing disappeared as well![32] The local press treated it as a joke, but one can imagine the bridegroom's feelings.

In another example, a daughter held her father's property in her name, and he farmed it as her guardian. Following her wedding to an older Punjabi who had moved to the Imperial Valley from Fresno, the bride tried to depose her "guardian" and handle "her own property." She was only sixteen, but her lawyer and her husband argued successfully in a

1939 civil suit that because of her marriage, she was no longer a minor. Her father fought back, and the case was much publicized.[33] Here one must sympathize with the father against the interloper Punjabi, trying to seize property by marrying his daughter.

Even among the successful marriages made by these nineteen daughters, there were occasions when the young American-born wives resented the jealousy and patriarchial control of their Punjabi husbands. One told of waiting in a car in Yuba City for her husband to come out of the Punjabi store when a high school friend, a Punjabi-Mexican boy from the Imperial Valley, passed on the street. They were excited to see each other, and she invited him into the back seat (it was raining) so they could talk. Even though she had taken care not to talk on the street or invite him into the front seat with her, her husband was angry. He was scarcely mollified when she explained that the boy was her father's partner's son and they had been high school classmates. Another young wife could not continue her education because others teased her husband by singing a Punjabi song about a girl who was "learning her letters, but to write to whom, perhaps to a stranger!"[34]

Other daughters refused to marry older Hindus, despite pressure from their fathers. "Marriage to a rich Hindu farmer was the idea he had for me," one said. Another added, "Father tried to fix me up with someone; he had land and we had land and that meant it'd be a good marriage." Several said their fathers feared they would be old maids and anxiously proposed man after man to them until they finally married someone. Some fathers did not pressure their daughters to marry Punjabis or Punjabi-Mexicans, but did want them to marry "working men." Alternatives to marriage were seldom considered for daughters, although one girl, disfigured by a childhood scar, was urged by her father to continue her education. Some daughters were encouraged to finish high school, others were not; some were encouraged to work, others were not.[35]

Not only fathers but "uncles" tried to arrange marriages for the Punjabi-Mexican daughters. One favorite "uncle" had often spoken of his California nephew to a Punjabi-Mexican daughter in Arizona, but the boy, one of the few with a mother from India, married someone he met in college. The marriage did not last, and while the girl's family was visiting northern California, the uncle introduced her to his nephew. They liked each other at once. Though their fathers were from villages only two miles apart in the Punjab, her father tried to prevent the marriage, insisting that his daughter graduate from high school first. He also warned her about the terrors of having an Indian mother-in-law![36]

For the first Punjabi-Mexican sons to marry, the possibility of a bride from India was a distant one until federal laws regulating citizenship and immigration changed in 1946. Even after that date, few sons seriously considered making such a marriage. Fathers wanted Indian brides for their sons more than the sons did. One son was shown photos of three girls in saris, girls selected for him by a friend of his father's on a visit to India. (Not wanting an arranged marriage, this boy joined the navy, and his father did not speak to him for several years.) In at least three instances, a father's strong wish that a son marry a woman from India was carried out. These fathers held strong prejudices against Hispanic wives, based on their own or their partners' experiences. In two cases, inheritance of the father's property was reportedly made contingent on marriage to an Indian woman.[37]

To Punjabi-Mexican children, distinctions of religion, caste, or race had to be pointed out strongly as they approached marriageable age. Not only should the children of Sikhs not marry those of Muslims, there were distinctions within the religious groups. One father pointed out that all Muslim Dins/Deans/Deens were not the same; some families stemmed from low-caste Muslims back in the Punjab, while he and his family were Rajputs. Sikh fathers delivered similar messages. All Singhs were not the same; there were Jat Sikhs and Untouchable Sikhs. There were also men from the three different regions of the Punjab—Majha, Malwa, and Doaba—and the children of one should not marry the children of the other, Sikh fathers insisted.[38]

Sometimes the mothers attempted to prevent marriages. In the Yuba City area, Hispanic women felt isolated and dissuaded their daughters from dating Anglos, telling them to marry other Spanish speakers. A mother might point out that although the intended spouse's Punjabi father was of the right caste or regional background, the mother was a black or white American and did not speak Spanish. Several matches arranged by fathers were broken up by mothers, some because the mothers did not get along with each other but more because, unhappy in their own marriages to Punjabis, they simply refused to allow their children to get into "the Hindu situation." After her husband's death, one mother broke off her daughter's tentative engagement to a Punjabi-Mexican son for this reason.[39] After 1946, when the Luce-Celler bill opened up limited immigration from India, the mothers particularly feared husbands brought from India, seeing them as the start of an invasion by new immigrants. As one daughter recounted: "Once my father's friend in India sent a 'loop of engagement' for my sister, but my mother did not accept, saying, 'Everybody is going to come over here.'"[40]

Most members of the second generation married to please themselves, sometimes across religious boundaries that were important in the Punjab. A list of early couples includes Cirilia Singh and Karm Chand, Carmelita Sidhu and Suba Khan, Eva Rasul and Ray Singh Tom, Lucy Singh and Ali Abdulla (see photo 20), Rosie Khan and Johnny Singh Garewal. (The first couple was Sikh-Hindu, and the rest Sikh-Muslim combinations.) Carmelita Sidhu, daughter of a Sikh, met the man she decided to marry working in the fields. Suba Khan was a Muslim name. "Why a Khan?" her father protested, throwing up his hands. But she went ahead. (To everyone's surprise, Suba Khan turned out to be a Hindu whose idea of social mobility had been to give himself a Muslim name in the United States.) The marriage took her out of field work because Suba Khan owned and operated a hotel in Sacramento, and her father eventually approved of the marriage.[41] Other children married across the Malwa-Doaba regional boundaries: Besente/Betty Rai and her sister Mary both married Doabas, against their father's advice. A few daughters, especially those growing up in Arizona and isolated from the large Punjabi-Mexican community, were fascinated with men from India. Two of these daughters became engaged to Indians; one eventually married a Parsi (a Zoroastrian and a non-Punjabi).[42]

Mothers usually supported their daughters' choice of spouse. "Dad wanted me to marry a well-established man eighteen (or twenty-eight?) years older than I. He tried three times to get me married, but mother said, 'No way!' It bothered him a lot that I made my own decision." And a mother arguing on behalf of a daughter who wanted to marry someone of the "wrong caste" burst out with, "What is this caste thing, we're all Americans here!" But mothers sometimes met such strong opposition based on religion or caste from their husbands that they had to give in.[43]

For both sons and daughters, the partners *least* chosen were other Punjabi-Mexicans. That is, there was no preference for endogamous marriages among members of the second generation—quite the reverse. One son said, "The fathers tried to pick the spouses, always pushing us kids at each other, but my brothers and I hated the Pakistani girls."[44] Among

Table 13.   Second-Generation Spouses

Brides	Grooms Indian	Hispanic	Mexican-Hindu	Anglo	Other	Total
Indian	1	1	2	1	0	5
Hispanic	1	0	52	0	0	53
Mexican-Hindu	17	64	11	37	2	131
Anglo	1	0	34	0	0	35
Other	0	0	1	0	0	1
Total	20	65	100	38	2	225

Sources: California marriage licenses, brides and grooms, 1930–1969.

Punjabi-Mexicans, as Table 13 shows, endogamous marriages were the least preferred (aside from "other"). Endogamous marriages were out-numbered by marriages with Anglos and Hispanics.[45] Even considering twenty-four marriages (not all included in the table) of daughters and stepdaughters to Punjabi men, a small percentage of the Punjabi-Mexicans married within the Punjabi ethnic or biethnic community. And no children of Punjabis, by either white or black wives, seem to have married another second-generation Punjabi-fathered person.[46]

Most wedding ceremonies were Catholic ones: "Dad arranged to marry me in India at seventeen but I wouldn't go; I married a Mexican in a Catholic ceremony, and Dad was there." "I was promised to a Pakistani girl but married [a Mexican-American], in Catholic, civil, and Muslim services." "We had a Catholic wedding, nothing Indian about it." But, for many, there *was* something Indian about it, in that the groomsmen and bridesmaids tended to be Punjabi-Mexicans or closely related to the community in some way. This was certainly true when endogamous marriages took place. In the case of the last speaker, five of her six brides-maids were Punjabi-Mexicans and the sixth was about to marry the stepson of a Punjabi, and all the groomsmen were Punjabi-Mexicans ex-cept for that stepson. The ringbearer and flower girl were also Punjabi-Mexicans.[47]

The problem of second-generation marriages was probably most acute for those whose parents were both Punjabi. These children's marriages are a poignant reminder of the difficulties of ethnic isolation. The Punjabi practice of patrilocal marriage combined with village exogamy meant that a bride was sent to the home of her husband. Rather than be sent to marry and live in India, some daughters chose to marry older Punjabi men in the United States; others found their own husbands.[48] For sons, wives could not be brought from India until 1946. Some sons married Punjabi-Mexican daughters, some married Anglo women, and some married Indian girls born in Canada (not always of the same caste or religion as themselves). With the opening up of limited immigration in 1946, some younger sons accepted Punjabi brides from India or Pakistan, but pressures for arranged marriages were generally resisted.

Second-Generation Careers

The sons entered a wider range of occupations than their fathers had. First-generation immigrants from the Punjab had worked primarily as ranchers (farmers) or agricultural laborers, persevering despite legal constraints and the economic discouragement of the depression. The sons, as they grew up, married, and began families, tended to work as truck drivers, installers of gas heating, freight agents, money exchangers, tractor drivers, mix men, caterpillar drivers, and at many other jobs.[49] Although these occupations are specialized ones in agriculture, many sons were employed by bigger farmers and did not farm on their own. There are several reasons for this. Changes in the agricultural business in the 1940s made it difficult for young farmers to acquire land of their own.[50] This was particularly true in the Imperial Valley, where land prices made inheritance almost the only way to own land. Sons who did become farmers usually continued to work for their fathers, waiting for an anticipated inheritance. Some tried partnerships with other sons of Punjabis, for example, the Sandhu–Deen partnership in the Calipatria area. Several of the sons are leading growers in the Imperial Valley today, their status confirmed by membership in the Rotary Club or similar organizations.

In fact, there were few alternatives to farming or occupations tied to farming in the Imperial Valley in the 1940s, and Punjabi-Mexicans were among those who left the valley for urban areas and new occupations. Following World War II, there was an outmigration from the Imperial Valley of people in the prime working-age group (25–44). Although the total population of the country increased by 11.3 percent from 1950 to 1960, that of the prime group decreased by .5 percent. Finley attributes this to the effect of large-scale seasonal unemployment and the slow growth of year-round jobs. Imperial County in 1960 ranked near the bottom of California's counties in manufacturing jobs, the percentage of workers in white-collar jobs, and the percentage of 14–17 year olds enrolled in school.[51] Median family income in 1959 was 18 percent below the statewide figure, population per household was higher, and average worker earnings were lower. The educational attainment level was significantly below that of the entire state, though this may be explained by the outmigration of younger people; it is *not* explained by the high percentage of Spanish-surname people there, as non-Spanish-surname persons in the valley did not compare well with the rest of the state in this measure either.[52]

The initiation of the *bracero*, or Mexican labor, program during World War II provided competition for jobs from Mexican nationals, displacing Punjabi-Mexicans (and many other American citizens) from the rural labor market. The *bracero* program undoubtedly contributed to the serious problems of poverty, dependency, illness, and crime in Imperial County by the 1960s.[53] It also increased the difficulties of organizing agricultural workers to obtain better wages and working conditions in California's fields. This competition and the low level of reward for agricultural labor encouraged people to move into nonfarming occupations and to urban areas.

Punjabi-Mexican sons could use kinship ties and their double ethnicity to move out of agricultural labor. When Alfred Sidhu hurt his arm in a farm accident, he recuperated with his sister Carmelita Khan in Sacramento; she advised him to get out of field work and take a job in a cannery. He went with their old Imperial Valley neighbor, Omar Din, to a processing plant and got a job at the Frosted Food Company, where the Mexican boss hired him thinking he was Mexican. Often it was the Mexican American relatives who moved north first and the Punjabi-Mexican in-laws who followed them.[54]

Daughters tended to work only locally before marriage, at the telephone exchange or in stores. Those who married farmers were fully employed on the family farm. Friendships formed on the job tended to be with Mexican American girls, and they were reflected in bridal showers, wedding parties, and many lasting friendships. Some Punjabi-Mexican daughters went to Los Angeles to business schools, where they enjoyed meeting students from India as they prepared themselves for secretarial and library careers (see photo 21). Many have taken up careers later in life and have done very well.[55]

There are many individual success stories among members of the second generation, but there are few discernible patterns. Farmers include both large and small operators. Professional people range from lawyers, educators, and civil servants to farming consultants with academic degrees. One son opened the second Indian restaurant in San Francisco, and others have owned Mexican restaurants or bars. It does seem noteworthy that several sons went into law enforcement and several daughters married sheriffs, attorneys, or judges.[56] Also, the few descendants of "real Hindus" whose fathers were not from farming backgrounds in the Punjab have exhibited striking social mobility, moving away from other Punjabi-fathered descendants in the process. Those fathers had been urban men, generally better educated than most Punjabi immigrants, but they did not prosper in California. In three such families, two with mothers from India, the immigrant men worked in agriculture but were unsuccessful or only moderately successful. The Puris, Khatris from Amritsar, tried farming in the north, but Ramnath Puri was not a good farmworker. Nevertheless, his son became a foreman in the Yuba City orchards at the age of sixteen and was the family's chief support; he is a wholesaler of agricultural produce in Los Angeles today. The Sareerams (again, both parents were Indian, Brahmans in this case) managed to buy 100 acres of northern California land but left nine orphans by 1951, one of whom became the first admiral in the U.S. Navy of Indian descent. A third Hindu immigrant, another Brahman and an urban, educated man, tried farming in the Imperial Valley, but he was something of a loner. His son now heads an irrigation district near Firebaugh, in the Central Valley.[57] In all three cases, the son's upward mobility has meant some loss of connection to the "Hindu" community.[58]

The children of the Punjabis were selective about their biethnic heritage, choosing some aspects but not others of the strong Punjabi identity presented by their fathers. Daughters generally respected their fathers and Punjabi culture as they conceived of it. But, particularly in the Imperial Valley, they had no Punjabi women to emulate, and they did have the support of their mothers and other Hispanic women if they wished to disregard their fathers' wishes. Sons were confronted with stronger pressures to "be Punjabi." Although they worked for their fathers because it was in their interests to do so, most sons did not want to marry women from India and made their own marriage choices. There were sharper and more frequent conflicts between fathers and sons than between fathers and daughters, yet the respect most sons held for their fathers was great.

The children received contradictory messages from the Punjabi men. On the one hand, Punjabis stood together, proud of their homeland and supportive of one another, using their ethnic network to seek success in American society. On the other hand, inherited prejudices and rivalries rendered the network less useful for those born into the biethnic community. As they heard the men talk about others, learned about the factions and feuds, and witnessed the fierce anger and occasional violence, the children saw obstacles to an easy transition from the first to the second generation. The men's qualities that had benefited the biethnic families— a devotion to work, an ability to save, a stubborn perseverance against all odds—were less attractive when turned against a young adult arguing for a change of farming strategy, a new technology or accounting method, or a personal choice that did not accord with a father's wishes. And there was some ambiguity about being Punjabi: Most children saw themselves as "Hindu," rather than Mexican, but it was not altogether clear that their fathers saw them that way. Children's perceptions of Punjabi identity were equally unclear. One son took the "Sikh warrior" as his ideal, describing the role as one in which the warrior helped women and children. For example, he would see to it that "children ate first, then the women, and last the men." Yet his own account of a typical family dinner, where one could not be late and waited for the father to lead the prayer and take the first mouthful, recognized the daily realities of family life.

9 Political Change and Ethnic Identity

Suddenly the world expanded, and the boundaries imposed by law, time, and space collapsed. The Luce-Celler bill, officially titled the India Immigration and Naturalization Act of 1946, passed after extensive lobbying efforts, making the Punjabi old-timers eligible for U.S. citizenship and activating a small quota for new immigrants from India. Then, in 1947, India and Pakistan became independent, an independence marked by communal (religious) violence. India became a secular state; Pakistan, created through the political mobilization of Muslim religious sentiment, became an Islamic theocracy. The Punjab was divided between the two new nations, a partition reproduced between Sikh and Muslim pioneers in California.[1] In California, new Sikh *gurdwaras* and Muslim mosques helped institutionalize the new division and served the slowly growing groups of new immigrants from India and Pakistan. Punjabi Muslims and their families in the American Southwest devised a new name, Spanish-Pakistani, for themselves. Names became important in other ways, too, as the Punjabi-Mexican children learned of clan surnames and their meanings. After 1965, even more sweeping changes came when U.S. immigration law redressed past discriminatory quotas against Asians, and the number of new immigrants from India and Pakistan increased dramatically.[2]

The long-sought access to citizenship and pride in their newly independent nations of origin confronted the Punjabi men with difficult choices. They could become U.S. citizens, providing they passed the literacy test in English and an oral examination in American history. Those who could afford it could travel outside the United States and legally reenter. Some men traveled to their home villages for a visit or to investigate retirement there. They could also sponsor the immigration of close relatives to the United States, family members from whom they had been separated for decades. Some men brought over sons, nephews, and grandsons. A few brought their wives, and several old men who were widowed, divorced, or had never married returned to South Asia for young brides. The families thus started formed the nucleus of new immigrant communities in northern California, which grew very rapidly after 1965.

New Identities and Institutions

The Luce-Celler bill provided that Indian nationals in the United States who had entered legally (i.e., before the Immigration Act of 1924) could become naturalized citizens. It also activated the quota set in the 1924 act of one hundred immigrants per year for India, a quota unused because Indians had not been eligible for citizenship.[3] Urban men led the fight for this bill on behalf of the Indian community, but contributions from Punjabi farmers and agricultural workers were important in the effort. One organizational effort was based in the Imperial Valley (the Indian National Congress Association of America, led by Dalip Singh Saund and J. N. Sharma), and congressional testimony for the bill featured success stories about the Muslim farmers near Phoenix.[4] Punjabi farmers everywhere shared in the triumph when the bill passed.

For the farmers, the most significant consequence of eligibility for citizenship was that the Alien Land Laws no longer applied to them. Immediately, Punjabi men took back their land, or tried to, from trusted Anglos, from the wives and children of other Punjabis, and from their own wives and children. This was a tremendously meaningful step for the aging pioneers, and the first hurdle was to establish title firmly in one's own name.

The men were not always successful in establishing title to the land they had controlled over the years. In Butte County, two partners who had acquired agricultural land in 1919 had successfully evaded the law for over twenty years by "conveying the land from time to time to third persons, taking back fictitious notes, mortgages and deeds of trust, thus lending a semblance of validity to their possession, use and ownership of the land." Unfortunately, in 1945 one partner conveyed the property to the Anglo wife of another Punjabi; whether or not he meant this to be a bona fide sale is unclear. At any rate, she and her husband contended that it was a bona fide sale and succeeded in establishing clear title to the land, although the surviving partner fought the case to the district appellate court after the death of one "seller" and the seizure of the property by the "new owners." There are other stories of loss of land at this stage, when transfer to its true owner finally became possible.[5]

Punjabi men took their savings and decided where they wanted to buy land, without worrying about the trustworthiness of the person holding it for them. At this time, a few men moved from the Central Valley to the Imperial Valley, thought to be the site of the wealthiest Punjabi farmers in the 1950s. The highest proportion of Punjabi landowners was there, and the amount of land Punjabis owned was impressive. In 1955, county maps showed Punjabi holdings totaling some 13,000 acres. Descendants wonder how much land their fathers would have acquired had they been free to do so when it was available and relatively cheap.[6]

With the extension of citizenship, these intensely political men plunged into direct participation in U.S. politics.[7] Despite lingering bitterness, even those who had once been citizens and had been stripped of their rights reapplied for citizenship. Men who were illiterate or barely literate took courses, in some cases studying for years to be sure they could pass the citizenship test.[8] In Imperial County, sixty-eight old-timers applied for citizenship after 1946. Their ages ranged from forty-eight to eighty-four years. From 1947 to 1953, there were only two applications per year, but from 1954 through 1958, forty-one men applied for citizenship.[9] It is certainly no coincidence that in 1956 the first U.S. congressman from India, Dalip Singh Saund, was elected from the Imperial Valley!

An educated man who farmed for a living, Saund had been one of the leaders in the Indians' fight for citizenship; his wife was an Anglo woman. He had the strong backing of his countrymen and others in the Democratic party, and he had been a justice of the peace in Westmoreland, in the northern end of the valley. He had learned public speaking as a member of the Toastmasters Club, and he told many good stories. A favorite concerned his campaign for justice of the peace, when one fellow came up to him and said, "When you're a judge, are you going to make us wear turbans?" His reply was, "I don't care what you wear on top of your head, it's what's inside that counts." The Democratic party was usually a minority party in Imperial County, at least in terms of actual voting.

But Singh's opponent was Jacqueline Cochran, the woman pilot, and she had fewer local ties and even more prejudices working against her. Saund ran as a judge with a strong record of putting down corruption in his region of the valley. He beat Cochran soundly and then won reelection twice, visiting India as a member of the Foreign Affairs Committee in 1958.[10]

A few old-timers retired to India or Pakistan after 1947, and others visited there. Some of the returns proved unsettling. Men who had sold or given away everything they owned in the United States preferred not to stay in their original homeland, finding the villages of their youth too old-fashioned. Not men to settle for a life they did not relish, they returned and started farming again in California. Some of those who visited South Asia took along tractors, cars, or other equipment they thought would be welcomed. They planned to sell these things or to use them in demonstration schemes, bringing modern agricultural technology to their home villages. One man who did this had all his imported equipment and seeds seized by Indian Customs officials; he could not get them back and had to request funds from his son to return to California.[11]

Political responses to the new South Asian nations took many forms. While the Punjabi pioneers had been generally accepting of American use of the term "Hindu" for all persons from the subcontinent, understanding it as a reference to their place of origin rather than their religion,[12] the communal violence that accompanied the last years of the nationalist movement and the partition of the Punjab made the term an issue. Yet many descendants proudly insist that polarization between Sikhs and Muslims did not occur in the United States and offer evidence of individual resistance to it. Thus Robert Mohammed's father, Fathe Mohammed, was one of the few Muslims to attend a 1947 banquet in San Francisco for Madame Pandit (Prime Minister Jawaharlal Nehru's sister and subsequently India's ambassador to the Soviet Union, Great Britain, the United States, and the United Nations). Also in San Francisco, Kartar Dhillon cooked one night for a Ghadar party reception for the ambassador from India and the next night for a reception for the ambassador from Pakistan.[13]

In the wake of Indian and Pakistani independence, long-established Punjabi institutions in California changed in significant ways, and new institutions were built. The Stockton Sikh temple, a favorite stop for visiting Congress party nationalist movement leaders, had been the meeting place for all Punjabis. One photo, taken at the temple in 1946, shows Madame Pandit speaking there and soliciting funds (see photo 22). There are Punjabi Sikhs, Muslims, and Hindus in the photo, and most of the women and children are Punjabi-Mexicans. Three new wives from India also appear in the photo, harbingers of future divisions within the Punjabi-Mexican community (but at this time welcome new additions to it). This photo is treasured because it symbolizes the unified community of the old-timers. The nature of that community is dramatically evident in another historic photograph, showing the wives of the old Hindus in Yuba City at Indian independence (photo 23). All but four of the women in this photo are Hispanic—there are three Anglo wives and one wife from India.

At the Stockton Sikh temple, political struggles over temple management were fierce in the late 1940s, with new leaders institutionalizing social and specifically Sikh religious reforms. Permission was secured from Amritsar in the Punjab to use chairs instead of sitting on the floor, and *prasad* (consecrated food) was served on paper plates with spoons and paper napkins.[14] Turbans and beards, discarded by most attenders, became an issue when the first clean-shaven temple secretary, Balwant Singh Brar from Yuba City, was elected in the 1940s. The second clean-shaven secretary was Nika Singh Gill (1947–1948). Both leaders were younger than most of the early pioneers. Balwant Singh Brar became a U.S. citizen by serving in World War II and was the first Punjabi from California to go to India and return with an Indian wife. His career in the Yuba City area was a distinguished one. Nika Singh Gill had come to the United States illegally over the Mexican border about 1929; he married a Punjabi-Mexican daughter from the Imperial Valley. Gill led a crusade to admit Dalip Singh Saund and his Anglo wife to temple membership (and Dr. J. N. Sharma and his English wife). The issue here was not choice of wife, but the admission of educated, modernizing political leaders. Dr. Saund's crusading reputation, in particular, aroused apprehension; there was some fear that his public career against corruption would extend to the Sikh temple, and he would try to clean it up too![15]

The new Sikh emphasis in the Stockton temple was only one sign of an interest in building religious institutions in California. Sikh men in the Imperial Valley decided to establish their own temple and purchased the Japanese Buddhist temple in El Centro in 1947. The Japanese in the valley had been evacuated to camps in 1942, and few had returned after their release. This purchase was perhaps the first assertion of Punjabi *Sikh* pride there, although Punjabi Muslims and other South Asians often visited at the temple.[16] The temple's establishment coincided with the Punjabi applications for citizenship and the election of Dr. Saund to Congress.

Punjabi Muslims in California moved to build a meeting place of their own, since political tensions decreased their participation in political and social activities at the Stockton temple (or *gurdwara*, the term now coming into use). After decades of meeting in hotels and homes, the Sacramento Muslims bought a lot at Fifth and V streets in 1946 and financed a building that was completed in May 1947. This was done through a newly created organization, the Muslim Mosque Association, formed in 1944 by a visitor from Detroit who found the California Muslims deficient in their religious life. But the building was little used at first.

The next step was the formation of a Pakistan National Association in Sacramento in 1950, after the first ambassador of Pakistan came to the United States in 1948 and visited there. He suggested that the northern California Muslims form a political organization, and Charagh Mohammed, a rice grower from the Butte–Gridley area, was its first president. Another Pakistani association was organized in 1950 in Yuba City among peach growers and their co-workers. Both organizations began celebrating independence day every year and sent money back to the "old country"—really the *new* country![17] After 1955, when Pakistani visitors arrived and stimulated local Muslims, the Sacramento mosque became active. The increasing tide of new immigrants supported religious activities, and in 1961 the Muslim Mosque Association sponsored an *imam* to serve at the mosque.[18]

In the southern part of the state and in adjacent Arizona, Punjabi Muslims also began establishing religious institutions. Muslims in the Imperial Valley had conducted home services during the annual *Ids* and had made occasional efforts to set up a mosque. They had concentrated on food and burial practices. Like efforts to ensure proper burials that produced the "Hindu plot" in Evergreen Cemetery (just outside El Centro, on the way to Holtville), efforts to secure kosher food resulted in some interesting cross-cultural connections. Niaz Mohammed, one of the leading Muslim farmers in the Imperial Valley, got kosher (which is the same as *halal*) food from San Diego from Jewish stores. A special friend of his in El Centro was also Jewish; that man sponsored him when he got his citizenship.[19]

Independence and the partition of India and Pakistan spurred Muslims in the Imperial Valley to set up a Pakistan House in El Centro on Broadway, near the Sikh temple. They bought a building and converted it into an Islamic Center in 1952, with the men meeting to pray while the women prepared food for families to share afterward. The upstairs room over Tom Mallobox's bar (the Mazatlan) had served earlier as a Pakistani center. With no significant influx of new immigrants, however, Imperial Valley Muslim activities declined. In Phoenix, Arizona, more Muslims had settled, and new immigrants arrived in large numbers. There, the Sacramento pattern was followed, and Muslim activities became well established.[20]

Just as the old-timers became landowners in their own right and began establishing Sikh and Muslim institutions, new immigrants from India and Pakistan, sponsored by the pioneers, began to alter the cultural orientation of the Punjabi population. Most of the Punjabi pioneers took responsibility for one or more new immigrants and continued to provide for their families in the United States. They tended to sponsor nephews, and a few nephews who came from the Punjab even married Hispanic women, as the pioneers had done. A few wives from India came in the late 1944s and 1950s, sometimes replacing divorced or deserted Anglo or Hispanic women. But change was slow until 1965.[21]

Many Punjabi men had little or no desire to reestablish contact with their relatives in India and Pakistan. They had cut themselves off decades earlier and had fathered large Punjabi-Mexican families to whose welfare they were devoted. They, and their wives and children, feared additional demands on their resources from needy relatives in a Third World country. Punjabi-Mexican wives and children who had willingly hosted the occasional visitor from India in the past began to refer visitors to new immigrant families or to an Indian restaurant in town. Bernice Sidhu told of a phone call in the middle of the night, from Punjabi truck drivers from Canada who had seen her name in the phone book and wanted Indian food. In the old days, such calls were so rare that her mother-in-law would have invited them home. Bernice suggested an Indian restaurant in El Centro.[22]

Slowly, the Imperial Valley old-timers began a selective importation of relatives. Three wives came from India in the early 1950s. One of them had been separated from her husband for some thirty years, and the other two were new brides; all three were from the same village.[23] These women were introduced to the community through the El Centro Sikh temple, where the old-timers met and talked in Punjabi every Sunday afternoon. Isolated in their new homes, these Indian wives learned some Spanish and adapted well to the Punjabi-Mexican women and children with whom they mingled. They bore children for their husbands, children to inherit the property and carry on the family line in the Imperial Valley.[24]

The coming of wives from India and the establishment of a Sikh temple in El Centro represented efforts to revitalize the Sikh religion and found a new Indian community in the Imperial Valley. Renovated by the Sikhs, the temple has a plaque inside the door that lists the contributors (see Appendix B). Twenty-nine men and one woman are listed, and their names are given in full. That is, after Singh appears not only a clan surname but a Punjabi village name, the only such list in the Imperial Valley to my knowledge. (Few Imperial Valley men ever used their clan surname, before or after the erection of this plaque, although clan names became commonplace in northern California with its large new Punjabi population.) There is only one surprise in the list of villages—the word *Kasagrande* appears after the names of Mr. and Mrs. Diwan Singh. This is Casa Grande, Arizona, where Diwan Singh farmed, and it speaks to his adoption of a new native place. (Diwan Singh was a spectacularly successful farmer there, so much so that he is mentioned in grade school textbooks in the Arizona school system.[25]) Also, his first wife was from Arizona, and after her death, he met his second wife in Casa Grande. This oblique reference is the only clue on the plaque to the Hispanic origin of many wives, all of whom are simply designated Mrs. so and so.

In fact, almost all twenty-nine men on the plaque had married in the United States, eight of them twice. Between them, these men had twenty Hispanic wives, five Punjabi-Mexican wives,[26] two Anglo wives, and at least six Indian wives. Although by 1952 there were six wives from India among those listed, all had come after 1946 and three had displaced Anglo or Hispanic women. Even at the time the plaque was placed, eight of the nineteen wives were Hispanic.[27]

New immigrants and Punjabi-Mexican families met at the El Centro Sikh temple. Nephews or other young male relatives were brought from India and sent to the Imperial Valley College.[28] The men took turns as heads of the temple and sponsored the immigration of a *granthi*, or priest, from India. Children were born to the new wives from India. One husband and wife were reunited after decades apart—the wife past childbearing age—so the couple sponsored and adopted a nephew and brought a bride from India for him. Only a few of the men with Punjabi-Mexican families in the valley participated fully in temple activities, however. Their children enjoyed the food and the companionship after the services, but did not increase their knowledge of Punjabi or the religious service.[29] Weddings held in the *gurdwara* were few; funerals were far more frequent.

There were disputes among *gurdwara* leaders, and between the old-timers, the second-generation Punjabi-Mexicans, and some of the young men from India. By the time an anthropologist of Indian ancestry came in the late 1960s to study the "Hindus" of the Imperial Valley (a group he took to be synonomous with the members of the Sikh temple), the numbers supporting the temple had declined. One pioneer leader stated bluntly that he intended to will the temple to the Amritsar administrative committee back in the Punjab, since the members of the younger generation could not be entrusted with its management.[30]

The same process of nephew recruitment went on in the north. Among the Muslims farming near Butte City and Willows, older bachelors brought over nephews and enrolled them in the local high schools or in the agriculture program at Chico State.[31] These young men adapted themselves to the society of bachelor Punjabis that still characterized the northern area. Several of them, and one or two of the old men, married Pakistani brides, founding families that became core members of the new mosques in northern California.[32] Sikh bachelors in the north also brought relatives, and the Sikh community in the Yuba City area grew rapidly. One Sikh father and son moved from El Centro to Yuba City and brought over the son's son in 1958, Didar Singh Bains. Bains was probably the richest Punjabi in California in the 1980s, with extensive peach and kiwi orchards in the Yuba City area and other holdings elsewhere.[33]

Second-Generation Responses

Members of the second generation celebrated their fathers' American citizenship and the possibility of renewed relationships with relatives in South Asia, but they had their own ideas about ethnicity and national identity. Imminent independence from Great Britain had produced political mobilization in California along religious lines in India, but members of the second generation tried to ignore the emerging national boundaries in favor of the community of their childhood. During 1946, they countered their fathers' authority and signs of political polarization between Sikhs and Muslims by forming an organization specifically for the children of all Punjabis. The Hindustani Club was founded in the Imperial Valley in 1946, and its center was in Holtville. Originally meant to be an Indian youth and senior club, affiliated with an organization called Good Neighbors, International, the young people decided against that affiliation and formed an independent Young India club instead. While the four organizers were from Holtville, Brawley, El Centro, and Calipatria, part of the inspiration for the club came from Kaipur and Blanche Dillon, "real Indians" from the Fresno Dhillon family that lived and worked in the Imperial Valley for some time.[34] A major reason for forming the club seems to have been a desire to escape parental control, along with learning some Punjabi and socializing with others like themselves. To keep out members of the older generation, the youngsters put an age limit of forty on membership. Their fathers allegedly disliked the Hindustani Club, saying one should not mix with Punjabis of other religious or caste backgrounds. Despite the generational problem, this club often met at the Sikh temple in El Centro.[35]

Members of the second generation absorbed their fathers' pride in the two new nations and shared in the recognition Americans accorded newly independent nations and their people. The local press began reporting Punjabi-Mexican marriages and christenings.[36] The young people represented the new nations in various local fetes. In Phoenix, Arizona, farmers paid train fare and hotel bills to bring Indian students from Los Angeles over for a musical performance, wanting their children to see something of Indian culture.[37]

By the 1950s, in both the Imperial Valley and the Yuba City–Marysville area, the "Hindu queen" was an important title for Punjabi-Mexican daughters to win. As public consciousness of ethnic and national groups increased, an International Festival of Nations was instituted at the Imperial Valley Midwinter Fair, and a similar event took place in Yuba City. In the Imperial Valley, Hindu and Pakistani queens were among the "ethnic queen" categories for the annual Midwinter Fair; others were Mexican, Chinese, Japanese, Filipino, Swiss, and "American." The "Hindu wives" met at the El Centro Sikh temple and picked a girl each year to be Hindu queen; the Pakistani queen was selected by the Punjabi Muslims in the valley.[38] In Yuba City, Hindu queens also seem to date from Indian independence in 1947 and reflect an annual celebration of that event confined to the Punjabi Indian community. Punjabi-Mexican daughters represented India at international theme fetes in the area (photo 24). In both parts of the state, Hindu and Pakistani queens were all Punjabi-Mexican daughters until the contests lapsed in the 1960s when new immigrants from both countries began to arrive in force.

Members of the second generation initially greeted newcomers from South Asia with enthusiasm, and many established direct contact with relatives. As landowners in America, some of them felt a family obligation to bring over poorer relatives and help them get started at school or in farming. They were also eager to learn more about their relatives in India. One descendant sent away for her father's birth certificate and got back a "true copy" of the 1880 birth entry in the police station at Dehlon in Ludhiana district.[39] Some young immigrant men provided husbands for Punjabi-Mexican or Spanish-Pakistani daughters.

Family names became a topic of interest, stimulated by the many surnames used by incoming immigrants. The Sikh descendants discovered clan surnames in the late 1950s and early 1960s, as new immigrant Sikhs added a full range of Punjabi clan surnames to local telephone directories all over California.[40] Some descendants learned about their "real" surnames, and there was speculation about the position of kinsmen in India with that name. Two people in the Brawley area said they had heard that Sidhu was a big political name in India, like Kennedy in the United States; another said that Sidhus, Gills, and Garewals were leading names in Punjabi society. Members of the second generation still had difficulty distinguishing between religious affiliations indicated by names, but more of them began to use their clan surnames, sometimes as middle names. A few parents corrected birth certificates by adding clan surnames at this time.[41] Reclaiming their "real" names meant reclaiming the land of their fathers and asserting a meaningful relationship with kinsmen.

A few Punjabi-Mexican couples even made tentative commitments to the new or revitalized Punjabi religious institutions, holding weddings or wedding receptions in *gurdwaras* and mosques. In the Imperial Valley, Gurdit Dhillon and Dharmo Kaur Singh were married in 1963 in a Sikh ceremony in the El Centro *gurdwara*, the first wedding held there. They did that because they respected their fathers' culture, they said, and they followed the ceremony with a dance at the Elks Lodge, where Dharmo danced in an American-style wedding dress and the Sikh men danced too. In Sacramento, an Arizona Spanish-Pakistani daughter, Olga Khan, married a newcomer from Pakistan in the mosque in 1949 and affirmed her commitment to Islam.[42] Another way of honoring one's father was to contribute to fund drives for the new South Asian religious institutions in California. One group of siblings, originally from the Imperial Valley, donated an entryway stone bench in memory of their father to the Sikh *gurdwara* built in 1969 in the Tierra Buena area of Yuba City. Other members of the second generation joined the Tierra Buena *gurdwara* and began to participate in its activities.[43]

Reassessments After 1965

The dramatic changes in immigration laws and subsequent pressures from Punjabi relatives brought immigrants from India and Pakistan. The composition of the rural Punjabi communities changed, particularly in central and northern California, where small holdings and family farming patterns fit best with the sponsorship and employment of immigrant relatives. The new Punjabi immigrants were part of a surge of immigration from South Asia. The decadal census shows the changed demographic picture for South Asians in California and the United States. In 1960, there were 1,586 Asian Indians in California; in 1970, 1,585; but in 1980, 57,901. The Asian Indian population in California declined slightly relative to that in the United States, and the rural population in California declined dramatically relative to the urban population in the state (see Table 14). In only one way did the presence of the pioneer immigrants have a statistically noticeable effect: In all other counties in the United States, Asian Indians accounted for 1 percent or less of the total population in 1980, but in Sutter County (the Yuba City orchard region) they were 4.95 percent of the population.[44]

As the balance in the immigrant community shifted decisively in most of California to the new immigrants from South Asia, many old-timers reassessed their social and cultural orientations. The Punjabi-Mexican community had been the dominant model of family life for more than four decades. Membership in that community had been chosen voluntarily by individual men, but in important ways it had also been deter-

Table 14.   Asian Indians in California and the
United States, 1910–1980

| Year | U.S. | California | | California cities[a] | |
		N	%	N	%
1910	2,544	1,948	77	73	3.75
1920	2,544	1,723	69	75	4.35
1930	3,130	1,873	59	122	6.51
1940	2,405	1,476	60	89	6.03
1950	2,398	815	34	249	30.55
1960	8,746	1,586	17	722	45.52
1970	13,149	1,585	16	546	34.45
1980	387,223	57,901	15	54,447	94.00

Sources: Brett Melendy, *Asians in America*, tables VII, VIII, IX; U.S. Bureau of the Census, *Census of Population 1980*, IB, General Population Statistics, PC80-10B6 California, 160–170.

[a]All California city figures include Los Angeles, San Francisco, and Stockton. In 1950, Oakland is included as part of metropolitan San Francisco; in 1960, Oakland and Long Beach are included as part of metropolitan San Francisco and Los Angeles; in 1970, census inadequacies do not permit comparable figures for the metropolitan areas, thus the apparent decline. The 1980 figure includes the standard metropolitan statistical areas (SMSAs) of Anaheim, Garden Grove, Santa Ana; Fresno; Los Angeles, Long Beach; Modesto; Oxnard, Simi Valley, Ventura; Riverside, San Bernardino, Ontario; Sacramento; San Diego; San Francisco, Oakland; San Jose; Stockton; Vallejo, Napa Valley; and Yuba City. In 1980, Asian Indians were not tabulated in SMSAs where their numbers fell below 400.

mined by the laws of the dominant society, laws that had limited the men's choice of spouses. Laws had also constrained the men with respect to political and economic resources, but the legal changes beginning in 1946 allowed Punjabi men and their families to claim land and American citizenship. And the 1965 immigration law changes allowed the men to reclaim their Indian families. Thinking it possible that a "purely Punjabi" family life could be constructed in the United States, some Punjabis reassessed their commitment to the Punjabi-Mexican families.

From the beginning, there had been prejudice against Hispanic wives and Punjabi-Mexican children. The urban, more educated leaders of the fight for citizenship had few personal connections to the rural Punjabi-Mexican community. Many bachelors and old-timers married to Anglo women had maintained some distance from these families, as had members of the few "real Indian" families. If a man wanted to leave his "Mexican" wife and children and acknowledge or begin a "Punjabi" family, there was support for him from the growing Punjabi community. And with respect to descendants of Punjabis, some Punjabi old-timers simply found the generational and cultural gap too broad to cross. One man resentfully stated that those in the next generation experienced no prejudice: "Everything was theirs by birth, while we Punjabi men met discrimination in everything, from haircutting to landownership." He was wrong—clearly the children suffered from discrimination too—but the Punjabi-Mexican children were virtual strangers to him. Others spoke of "bad Mexican blood" when problems arose with members of the second generation.[45]

Another source of prejudice was the new South Asian immigrant community itself. Coming in under a totally different set of regulations and able to bring their families, these people found the existence of a large community of "half-breeds" in California disconcerting. Back in the Punjab, individual tragedies had been acknowledged when a father remarried in the United States and founded a new family,[46] but the extent to which a Punjabi-Mexican community had been created had not been (and still has not been) acknowledged. Confronted with a Punjabi-Mexican, the reaction of the newcomers was one of consternation and disbelief. For example, at Disneyland, one Imperial Valley second-generation Punjabi-Mexican approached a family from South Asia and offered to show them around, explaining that he was a Hindu too. They apparently did not believe him and refused his help.[47] Such encounters made Punjabi-Mexicans sensitive to their reception by the new immigrants.

Growing tensions within Punjabi-Mexican families between the men and their wives and children were fueled by concerns about property and its transmission. As the Punjabi men took control of their land, often displacing their wives or children, there was a consequent shift in domestic power, no matter how slight. Trusted wives and children who had held land for other Punjabis became less important to the larger community of Punjabi men. Thus Harry Chand remembers his mother telling him that the day the Luce-Celler bill passed, she lost all her wealth—the men all came to put their property in their own names.[48]

The old-timers now thought about how they would leave their hard-earned property, property only recently secured in their own names. The

1, 2. J. Labh Singh and his son, Mola Singh, in the Philippines before leaving for California, 1912. (Courtesy of Mola Singh, Selma.)

3. Northern California Moslem Association, c. 1920 (tentative identification). *Front row, left to right*: Dr. Fateh Mohammed Khan, Janday Khan, Moulvi Rehmat Ali, Mrs. Pandit Ram (Padmavati) Chandra, Dr. Syed Hussain, Charag Mohammed, Gobind Behari Lal. *Middle row, left to right*: Mohammed Hussain, Mehboob Ali Khan, Babu Khan, Munshi Feroze Din, Mian Jalaldin, Mehndi Khan, unknown, Gouda Ram. *Back row, left to right*: Fateh Din of Gurka, Munshi Mohammed Ali, Fateh Din of Darian, Nathoo Khan, Hakum Khan, Adalat Khan, Ghulam Khan. (Courtesy of Mohamed Aslam Khan, Butte City.)

4, 5. Sikh men before and after discarding their turbans. *Top, left to right*: Saun Singh, Karm S. Sandhu, Charn S. Sandhu, Sadu S. Sandhu, c. 1925. *Bottom, left to right*: Charn S. Sandhu, a visiting wrestler, Karm S. Sandhu, Saun Singh, c. 1930. (Courtesy of Anna Singh Sandhu, Calipatria.)

6. Wedding photo, 1917. *Standing, from left*: Anna Anita Alvarez Singh, Dona Petra Alvarez, Antonia Alvarez Singh. *Seated*: Gopal and Sher Singh, Ester Alvarez. (Courtesy of Harry Chand, Live Oak.)

7. Mola Singh and Carmen Barrentos, wedding photo, Arizona, 1919. (Courtesy of Mola Singh, Selma.)

8. Valentina Alvarez and Rullia Singh, wedding photo, 1917. (Courtesy of Harry Chand, Live Oak.)

9. Alejandrina Cardenas Alvarez and Albert Joe, wedding photo, 1917. (Courtesy of Harry Chand, Live Oak.)

10. Amelia Valdez, 1933. (Courtesy of Mary Garewal Gill, Holtville.)

11. Mola and Susanna Mesa Rodriguez Singh, Selma, 1983. (By the author.)

12. Karm and Francesca Singh and baby, Bishan and Herminia Lozano Singh, Lucy and Billy, c. 1935. (Courtesy of Lucy Singh Abdulla, Fresno.)

13. Jon Bux Abdulla, Juanita (Jenny) Chavez Abdulla, and Ali, Brawley, c. 1928. (Courtesy of Lucy Singh Abdulla, Fresno.)

14. Funeral of Utam Singh, Yuba City, 1945 or 1946. (Courtesy of Isabel Singh Garcia, Yuba City.)

15. Funeral of Marian Singh (Memel and Genobeba Singh's daughter), Yuba City. The Mexican godparents stand behind the coffin, and the boy at the left is Robert Mohammed. (Courtesy of Isabel Singh Garcia, Yuba City.)

16. Raminder Garewal, Gloria Dhillon, and Fred Dhillon in the mountains near San Diego, 1938. (Courtesy of Mary Garewal Gill, Holtville.)

17. Mary Garewal, in a carrot field near Holtville, c. 1936. (Courtesy of Mary Garewal Gill, Holtville.)

18. Raymond Singh and Raymond Garewal, Holtville, 1950. (Courtesy of Mary Garewal Gill, Holtville.)

19. Anna Singh and Charn S. Sandhu, wedding photo, Yuma, 1940. (Courtesy of Anna Singh Sandhu, Calipatria.)

20. Lucy Singh and Ali Abdulla, wedding photo, 1949. (Courtesy of Lucy Singh Abdulla, Fresno.)

21. Helen Ram and Amelia Singh in Los Angeles, 1950s. (Courtesy of Amelia Singh Netervala, Los Angeles.)

22. Madame Pandit (Sister of India's Congress Party leader and first prime minister, Jawaharlal Nehru), soliciting funds at the Stockton temple, c. 1946. The first new East Indian women are in the front row. (Courtesy of Isabel Singh Garcia, Yuba City.)

23. The first Indian Independence Day in Yuba City, Jan. 26, 1948. *Back row, from left*: Josephine Romo Subhra, Della Spence Khan, Alejandra Beltran Singh, Inez Wiley Singh, Cruz Perez Singh Ardave, Isabel Sidhu, Cirila Singh Chand, Nand Kaur, Velia Riveria Sidhu, Dorothy Sexton Sahota. *Front row, left to right*: Socorro Singh, Margarita Singh, Mrs. Mildren Gina Bains, Rosario Virgen Singh Gill, Mariana Singh, Dona Antonia Alvarez Singh, Genobeba Loya Singh, Mary Singh Rai, Amelia Camacho Bidasha, Nina Singh Shine. (Courtesy of Isabel Singh Garcia, Yuba City.)

24. Daughters of Punjabis, c. 1964–65, at the Campfire Girls All States Nation Dinner, Marysville. *Left to right*: Isabel Singh Garcia, Carmelita Singh Shine, Stella Ardave Singh, Sally Singh dove. (Courtesy of Isabel Singh Garcia, Yuba City.)

25. Jiwan Singh and his grandchildren, Diana and Gary, at Disneyland, c. 1956. (Courtesy of Amelia Singh Netervala, Los Angeles.)

26. El Ranchero restaurant, Yuba City, owned by Ali Rasul, who was born in the Imperial Valley. (By the author.)

27. Alfred and Isabel Singh Garcia and Mary Singh Rai at the Old-timers Christmas Dance, Yuba City, 1988. (By the author.)

guardianship strategy could easily have led to inheritance by the children when they came of age; both sons and daughters were listed, and many of the fathers were old men by the time their children came of legal age. But the disposition of the property proved to be one of the most difficult questions facing Punjabi-Mexican families. Men who had remained bachelors in the United States could and sometimes did turn to one another or bring relatives from India. Those who had married in the United States could turn to their wives and children here. But since many old Punjabis had brought over nephews or grandsons, intending to integrate them into family life or simply get them established in the United States on their own, there were alternative heirs available. Few thought of institutions, but institutions—the Stockton *gurdwara,* the Muslim mosque at Sacramento—sometimes thought of them and solicited final donations. There were many choices and many interested parties.

The first problem lay in the fathers' unwillingness to turn over the property they had acquired for any reason except death. Some fathers tried to postpone their sons' marriages, wanting them to continue working on the family land and fearing that marriage would force an immediate division of the property. Even the thought of death and the eventual transfer of their property often caused the men to put conditions on the inheritance. There are several instances of a father telling a son he would get more if he went to India and married a "real Indian" girl. Other men fought with their Punjabi-Mexican sons, objecting to the marriages they made and to their attempts to share in the management of the farming operations. One aging Punjabi made an extended visit to India and left his son in charge of the farming. When he returned, the son proudly revealed that he had made some profit, used it to carry out a venture of his own, and wanted to use the profit from that venture to undertake more ventures on his own. Since the initial profit derived from the family property, the father forced him to turn over all the money to him. In another case, a father turned land over to his son, but later disapproved of the son's marriage and management of the land. When the marriage broke up, the father and his friend, the chairman of the board of directors of the National Bank of Holtville, testified that the father had resumed control of the land; since the son owed his father money, he had leased the property back to his father and thus, the father argued, increased alimony payments to the ex-wife were impossible. In perhaps the saddest case, one man felt so little obligation to the son who had worked with him all his life that he sold off his Imperial Valley land, took the proceeds, and retired to Pakistan, leaving his Spanish-Pakistani son and grand-children with nothing.[49]

Even men on good terms with their sons found it hard to give up con-trol over their land. One man planned to leave his property to his sons, but could not bring himself to set up trusts that would have preserved his estate from heavy death taxes, viewing that as a relinquishment of total control of his property. This man's increasing disabilities meant that he could no longer walk about on his land, but he was driven around it every day until he died. In a generous exception to these patterns, a Pun-jabi Muslim left his land to a former partner's Hispanic widow and retired to Pakistan. When he did not like Pakistan and returned, she gave him back his house and eighty acres, and he built up his holdings once again.[50]

Inheritance by widows was not routine in these families.[51] Partners and relatives sometimes got the property instead of the local wife and chil-dren. One woman, widowed after nine years when her first Punjabi hus-band died of sunstroke in his fields, married another Punjabi. This man was wealthier than her first husband, but when he died, he left his estate not to his widow and stepchildren but to his brother, who farmed and lived with them. Generally speaking, Hispanic widows whose deceased husbands left no wills did better than those provided for in wills, for the wills put many qualifications on a widow's ability to enjoy her inherit-ance. A lawyer whose firm handled many Punjabi estates in the Imperial Valley stated his impression that Hispanic wives were "inadequately pro-vided for" in their husbands' wills; sometimes a partner or distant rela-tive from India was made executor of the estate, rather than a wife of many decades. Other people knew of instances where male Indian rela-tives or former partners were named executors even when a widow and children inherited most of the estate. There are more extreme cases. In one, an aged partner tried hard to have himself recognized as executor of a former partner's estate at the expense of a Hispanic wife, arguing that his former partner had become senile and was being taken advantage of by the wife. (This was a very unusual case, since the plaintiff's adopted son was actually the other old man's natural son, so the plaintiff was trying to claim the estate for "the boy with two fathers."[52])

Many Punjabi men deeply distrusted their women, hating the thought that the land they had acquired might be lost through the widow's remar-riage. One person said it was common knowledge that "the Hindus never left anything to their wives, since they believed that all their life's work would then go to another man, the man who came 'round after their death." Even some Punjabi-Mexican children seem to have feared loss of their inheritance through a widowed mother's remarriage, though it seems to have been remarriage to another Punjabi that they feared most! At least once, children gave their mother "permission to remarry," provided their inheritance was not threatened.[53]

Contributing to the distrust of Hispanic wives in the 1940s were some unfortunate matches made by late-marrying Punjabis. Mexican women coming across the border during World War II were said to be different from earlier immigrants. The Hispanic wives and Punjabi-Mexican children referred to them as "wetbacks" or "nationals from across the line" and accused them of deliberately ensnaring old Punjabi men who were just becoming citizens and often had some property. These women were sometimes even willing to constitute a second, bigamous family for such a man, on either side of the border.[54] A new wave of migration did occur at this time, and many marriages made then broke up very shortly, with the Punjabi husband suing for divorce on the grounds that he had been used only to obtain citizenship.[55]

Tensions over property had caused problems between Punjabi partners and relatives in California earlier, but now such problems acquired international dimensions. In one case, Karm Chand's brother sold his interest to Karm Chand and retired to India, arranging to receive regular payments from the sale. Shortly thereafter, Karm Chand died. When his brother in India heard of the death, he collapsed and died too. My sentimental interpretation of this was dismissed by Karm Chand's son, who said that the old man in India had been owed some $7,000 to $8,000 by Karm Chand and realized that he would never get it; he was so angry that he died! But claims made from India on estates in the United States could succeed. In a San Bernardino County case, a man willed his property to his widow and two sons in India, one-third to each. One tried to come to the United States to administer the estate, but instead it was sold, and three checks were sent to India.[56]

Some cases involving South Asian relatives became very complicated. The few Imperial Valley men who brought over sons or nephews nearly always created problems for their local descendants. One Muslim brought over his grandson, son of the son he had left behind in India, and taught him about farming so that he could leave him a portion of his property. After this pioneer died, however, the Pakistani son came, kidnapped his son, returned to Pakistan, and filed a lawsuit against the Hispanic widow for all the property. Another unhappy tale hinged on the arrival in California of an alleged grandnephew, who might really have been the man's grandson. The newcomer posed a considerable threat to the man's Punjabi-Mexican son, who had recently married a Punjabi bride, partly to please his father. And in another lawsuit, brothers in India tried to enforce Punjabi customary law (brothers share equally in an estate) in the United States by suing the brother in California, who had been brought over to the Imperial Valley and inherited an old Punjabi's estate. The brothers in India sought an equal share in the U.S. inheritance![57]

In Arizona, nephews or grandsons from Pakistan also were regarded with disfavor by local Spanish-Pakistanis. In one case, Pakistani newcomers inherited an old-timer's property when he died and actually sent the old man's body back to Pakistan, not utilizing the plot he had paid for through the local Muslim cemetery association. In another case, the newcomers were given land, but then their sponsor, an old man, took it back. The old man died suddenly, leaving the newcomers a large inheritance. Local Spanish-Pakistanis were suspicious about the old man's death and urged a Mexican illegitimate son of the deceased to claim the property so that it would not go to "those Pakistanis."[58]

There were instances where several wives came forward to claim an estate. In one, two wives in India argued that both should inherit, since polygyny was recognized in India; the decision finally awarded the estate to both of them.[59] When there were competing spouses in two different continents, the American judicial system sometimes helped disinherit Hispanic wives, going to considerable lengths (with the help of local Punjabi men) to establish the legitimacy of the first, Indian marriage.[60] In perhaps the most complicated inheritance case in the Imperial Valley, three widows fought for a Sikh's estate. When he died, a Hispanic wife appeared to claim the estate; she was challenged by another Hispanic wife, whom he had evidently married earlier and had not divorced. Both widows claimed to be raising the children born to the earlier Hispanic wife. Finally, a widow and children in India sent a claim, and a local Punjabi agent appeared to argue it on their behalf. After lengthy correspondence and a detailed examination by mail of the widow in India, the estate was awarded to her.[61]

Another source of tension between the men and their wives and children resulted from the claims made on them by religious institutions in California, claims intensified by the religious nature of the partition in the Punjab at Indian independence. Thus, although the Stockton Sikh temple generally had been less a religious than a social center, Sikhs had contributed money to it regularly, and temple officials expected to be remembered after a man's death as well. The Muslim mosque in Sacramento had similar expectations. Representatives of the temple and mosque sometimes visited dying men, exciting suspicious wives, who worried about a possible deathbed diversion of funds from the family.[62] These visits heightened perceptions that the interests of the Punjabi-Mexican descendants and the new immigrant communities were diverging.

Those who had property worried about its disposal, but the propertied and those without property alike worried about the proper disposal of their bodies after death. As the aging men's concerns about impending death mounted, they tried to provide for their funerals. This often meant a significant strengthening of religious identities. Their Punjabi friends and their children knew what was religiously required and desired by the old-timers. Muslims wanted proper preparation of the body and burial in a "Hindu" plot, with Punjabi Muslim pallbearers; Sikhs and Hindus wanted cremation, followed by a dinner some weeks later. The Sikh men's ashes were put in the Salton Sea, in the ocean off San Diego, or sent to India. But the biethnic nature of the community, particularly the Catholicism of the wives that condemned cremation, made one's fate uncertain.[63] A death often brought heartbreak for family members. Widows usually wanted to bury their husbands in the Mexican Catholic section of the local cemetery, where they themselves would be buried and where deceased infants and children already lay, but they feared "having the Hindu nation down our throats." Some told of Sikhs whose bodies had been buried by ignorant or willful widows. The goddaughter of a Mexican widow told of the traumatic seizure of her godfather's corpse from his widow's house by Hindu (Sikh) countrymen.[64] One widow related:

> When my husband died his race arranged with his brother and with their ranch mate, and not with me, for the cremation of his body. We didn't want that cremation. Although he said that after he died he would not know if he were cremated or thrown in the land, so that did not matter to him. And then he said, "If they want to bury

my body, do it, nobody can usurp the right of my sons to bury me."
But you know how they are, in their race. So they did the cremation. . . . But the ashes we buried in a case in the cemetery. . . . But
we don't admit that we buried the ashes of my husband.[65]

Perhaps most poignant were the tales three Punjabi-Mexican sons told
of their fathers' fears and their own concerns about proper observances
after death. One son, ignorant about his father's culture, was aware of
the old man's impending death and his desire for a proper cremation and
ceremony. The son had never gone to the Sikh temple at Stockton or to
the one established later in El Centro; he had been asked for money by El
Centro temple officials but had taken his name off their list. When he saw
a death notice of another pioneer Sikh in the paper in 1981, however, he
attended the funeral in order to see what the ceremony should be like,
and he tried desperately to get back on the mailing list for the "Seeki"
temple he had not attended or contributed to for decades. Another
son told of attending, with his father, the funeral of a fellow Muslim
whose ignorant wife and sons had not made the proper arrangements.
His father took over, insisted on helping to carry the coffin himself,
and afterward suffered nightmares that the same thing might happen to
him.[66]

A third told a story of conflict with the older Sikh men who ran the El
Centro temple. When his father died, he knew what had to be done. His
father had told him: "Two things, cremation and the dinner thing, that's
all I care about, not the rest of it, but do those things and do them soon."
The son tried, approaching the Sikh men and requesting that arrangements be made, but he was put off repeatedly. When a priest was finally
brought down from Stockton, the Sikhs wanted to hold a committee
meeting to see who should pay the fare. Protesting that his father had
given money all his life to the temple and that no committee should debate the issue, the son immediately paid the fare. But then the dinner was
put off in a similar fashion. Finally, the son contacted the Stockton temple
directly and offered $500 for someone to "come down and hold that din-
ner." So the priest came and the Punjabi-Mexican son paid, bypassing
and humiliating the old Sikh men in the Imperial Valley by doing so. The
son has enjoyed turning down their requests for temple donations
since: "And to think that my dad gave them money regularly all his life. . . .
I haven't donated a penny since then, and I remind them why whenever

they come around asking, too," he stated emphatically. "Whenever they come for money, I throw that in their faces."[67]

These tales reveal the private nature of the old men's religious identity at the end of life, their fear and the intensity with which they communicated it to their children. These sons resolved to carry out their fathers' wishes despite considerable personal ignorance of what was required. The old men's religious beliefs had remained their own. They had not asked their wives to conform to their beliefs or transmitted them adequately to their children, but they voiced them loudly at the end of their lives, requesting the "proper" death rituals.

Another point made in the three tales of the Punjabi-Mexican sons is that whatever solidarity had existed earlier among the Punjabi men who bought plots together or arranged for one another's cremations and ceremonies, the men had not built religious institutions that were ongoing, in the sense that they included their descendants. All three tales feature sons who were more or less estranged from the religious institutions to which their fathers belonged.

In contrast to the men's strong preference for Punjabi customs at death, funerals for the wives often combined features of two religions. For example, the obituary of Alejandra Khan, widow of a Punjabi Muslim, announced recitation of a rosary in a Yuba City chapel, followed by a funeral service at the Sacramento Moslem Mosque. When Bessie Abdullia died in Placer County, her daughter asked Spanish-Pakistani men to carry the coffin, much as though Bessie had been a convert to Islam. But she was not a convert and was buried in the Newcastle District Cemetery, although her husband Joseph was buried in the Sacramento "Hindu" plot. Mary Mohammed in Yuba City had remained a German Catholic, but the night before her funeral there was an "Indian-style wake" in her home, where she had served as hostess for many a Punjabi Muslim gathering. In death as in life, these wives bridged two cultures.[68]

The late 1940s brought the welcome developments of access to citizenship and landownership in the United States and a meaningful reconnection to families in India. The Punjabi men and their descendants found themselves confronted with personal choices whose consequences sometimes proved painful. The names they called themselves, the names people called them, assumed new significance. These names could assert difference or similarity, could deny or claim ethnicity and identity. Being Hindu was called into question, and problematic notions of "real" names, and "real" families had to be dealt with by the descendants of the pioneers. "Hindu culture," as it existed in California, began to be challenged by the perceptions and practices of the new immigrants as they arrived from South Asia.

10 Encounters with the Other

"You always know who you are until people ask you about it, really, don't you? . . . So your identity doesn't get shaken until other people doubt it. One's identity has to be some sort of alliance between the way you see yourself and the way other people in the world see you." Hanif Kureishi, in an interview in 1990, explained that he saw himself as a British writer with an Indian background.[1] His words also capture the dilemma of the Punjabi-Mexicans in California.

The arrival of large numbers of immigrants from South Asia after 1965 irrevocably altered the context in which the Punjabi pioneers and their descendants constructed their identities. The Punjabi men, having striven throughout their lives in California to obtain their rights as Americans and to adapt themselves emotionally and behaviorally to American culture, reassessed their situation with respect to ethnic identity and family commitments at the end of their lives. They found that among the rights to which citizenship entitled them after 1946 was the right to become Punjabi again, particularly after the flood of new immigrants arrived and undertook the "reconstitution" and "revitalization" of Punjabi culture in California.[2] Sometimes this reassertion of Punjabi identity was extended to their wives and children—several were taken to visit India or Pakistan. Sometimes, however, it threatened the family established in California. New choices and uncertainties were reflected in family life and had a strong impact on wives and children.

Members of the second generation reassessed their ethnic identities. They experienced unsettling encounters with representatives of the growing South Asian immigrant population, encounters that often challenged their claims to a Hindu identity. Taken along with conflicts in

Punjabi-Mexican families over marriage and inheritance, feelings of ambivalence about being Hindu grew. This ambivalence was expressed in marriage choices (the lack of preference for others like themselves) and in the names chosen for use as adults. Descendants' relationships with new immigrants and with relatives back in South Asia were problematic too. Like many descendants of immigrants, even those descendants of Punjabis lucky enough to visit "the home country" often found that the experience reaffirmed their sense of distance from it. Yet most clung to an identity they defined as Hindu, the identity developed before the 1950s in rural California, although they increasingly emphasized the "American" components of that identity.

Unsettling Encounters

Since 1965, the descendants of pioneer Punjabis have found themselves confronted with new immigrants from South Asia who present many contrasts to the earlier immigrants. Their numbers are large, and they come from all over India, Pakistan, and Bangladesh. They are members of the most affluent, highly placed Asian immigrant group in the United States (in 1970 and 1980),[3] and they have settled in upper-class urban neighborhoods. Furthermore, most have come in family units, often with both father and mother holding good jobs. The children in these families already know English from their schooling back in India.

Beneficiaries of liberalized U.S. immigration laws, these South Asian immigrants come as needed professionals, and their relatives come under the system of preference to close relatives. Few of these immigrants know about the earlier immigrants from India to California, the largely illiterate men from farming backgrounds in the Punjab whose history we have been following. While discriminatory public policies affected marriage choices and landholding patterns for the earlier immigrants,[4] the newcomers express ignorance about earlier federal and state laws and move into good positions with relative ease.[5]

Not only have these immigrants moved into the American economy at a level that allows them to maintain a stable family life, they have established a whole infrastructure of economic, social, and religious institutions geared to the South Asian community. South Asian restaurants, sari shops, jewelry stores, and other ethnic businesses cater to the newcomers' needs. Associations have developed based on the many different regional languages and religious and sectarian groups. These smaller groups celebrate distinctive regional and religious occasions all over California. The current richness of South Asian cultural life in the United States was undreamed of by the pioneer Punjabis. Even restaurants reflect the diversity of the South Asian subcontinent by specializing in Punjabi, Gujarati, Hyderabadi, and other regional cuisines.

The new immigrants bring an idea of India that stresses its diversity and complexity, its urban, cosmopolitan culture. With no political, economic, or cultural constraints, they feel threatened by the Punjabi-Mexican descendants and are anxious that their own children remain "true to their culture." Their notions of South Asian ethnicity and identity deny the claims of second- and third-generation descendants. Descendants of the pioneer Punjabis encounter these notions of well-defined and restricted South Asian identity when they meet the urban, professional immigrants and when they meet new Punjabi immigrants to rural California, people who are very like the original pioneers and are from many of the same villages.

While there is pressure on their identity as Hindus everywhere, the descendants have been affected by the new immigrant communities somewhat differently in California's agricultural valleys because the newcomers have settled more densely in the north than elsewhere. The Imperial Valley Punjabi-Mexicans are more secure and self-confident, less shaken in their commitment to "being Hindu." The Imperial Valley has been less hospitable to new immigrants from India, largely because of its self-contained, isolated character, but also because of the size of the Punjabi-Mexican community there and the existence of several very prosperous second-generation Punjabi-Mexican ranchers. There has been ambivalence, even hostility, on the part of Punjabi-Mexican descendants to the newcomers. Refusing to answer persistent letters from India, one woman said, "We know that over there, they're starving . . . they would want to come, they would be a burden to us." Particularly after the lawsuits over inheritances in the valley, apprehensions have increased. Other valley residents also feel apprehensive about the "new Hindus," as opposed to the "old Hindus," of whom, in retrospect, many have become fond. Sentiment in the Imperial Valley tends to back the descendants of the old Hindus, not the few newcomers who try farming there.[6]

In central and particularly northern California, new Punjabi immi-

grants are numerically overwhelming and have done very well economically. Punjabi families from India have assumed dominance over the Punjabi-Mexicans. The problem is most acute in Yuba City, where aging
bachelor Punjabis sponsored many new immigrants; chain migration has
brought the Asian Indian population up to between 8,000 and 10,000. In
1947, 34 Sikhs owned 95.2 acres in Sutter County with an assessed value
of $185,774; in 1974, 260 Sikhs in the Sacramento Valley owned 7,145
prime orchard acres valued at $15,339,412![7] Large numbers of Punjabi
children have come as immigrants; by the 1970s, there were more Punjabis than mixed-blood descendants of Punjabi pioneers in the Yuba City
high school.[8]

In the Yuba City area, the two groups were diverging fast by the mid
1970s. Newcomers disapproved of the Punjabi-Mexican marriages that
had occurred and would not acknowledge descendants' claims to membership in the same community. The split was accelerated by the building
of a new Sikh temple in Yuba City, the Tierra Buena *gurdwara* (on Tierra
Buena Road). The temple opened in 1970, and a full schedule of Sikh
religious functions (such as had never been observed in California) developed during the first five years of its operation.[9]

Some Punjabi-Mexican descendants participated in the fund-raising activities of the imposing new temple. This fact is evident as one approaches the entrance to this Indo-Persian structure. There are two
benches on the front porch of the *gurdwara*, one of which reads, *In loving
memory of our father Harnam Singh Sidhu, 1891–1974, from children Isabel S.
Villasenor, Ray S. Sidhu, Frank S. Sidhu, Pete S. Sidhu, Beatrice S. Myers.* The
other, donated by recent immigrants, reads *In memory of my husband Sadhu
S. Chima from Surjit Kaur Chima and his children.*

One anthropologist tells about a conflict between Hispanic and Punjabi
wives at the new *gurdwara* as Sikh women from India increased in number and contested the presence of the non-Sikh women. It seems that the
Indian wives accused the Hispanic ones of poisoning the chicken curry,
and so the new Punjabi women took over the cooking for all temple occasions. The very telling of such a story is significant.[10] And it happened
despite the frequent assertion by Punjabi-Mexican descendants that Mexican women cook curry better than Indian women!

Prejudice against the new Punjabis in Yuba City also caused descendants of the old-timers to reassess and redefine their ethnic identity. Punjabi-Mexicans moved to differentiate themselves publicly. Some second-

generation couples in the area began to hold dances regularly, and from this informal beginning developed the annual Mexican-Hindu Christmas Dance. Initiated and widely publicized in 1974 as a reunion for descendants of Punjabi pioneers, from the first the dance betrayed the double ethnic identity of its sponsors. It featured mariachi bands and exuberant dancing and included many Mexican American friends and relatives, gradually becoming known as the "old-timers' dance."[11]

Antagonism toward the new immigrants mounted as their economic success aroused resentment. By the late 1970s, Euro-American prejudice against the new immigrants was an acknowledged problem. Sikh students were spat upon, and one young girl had her hair set on fire.[12] The Tierra Buena *gurdwara* initiated an annual parade in 1979, ostensibly to commemorate Guru Gobind Singh's enthronement of the Granth Sahib as the eleventh and last guru of the Sikhs, but also as a show of strength. Male Sikhs, in complete Punjabi dress with full beards and turbans, carried drawn swords down Main Street, followed by thousands of women, also in Punjabi dress and carrying signs in Punjabi.[13] This first parade made headlines, but aroused local apprehensions; it attracted many Sikhs from elsewhere in the United States and Canada and has continued to do so. The situation worsened after political disturbances in India's Punjab (the Indian Army's 1984 invasion of the Sikh's Golden Temple in Amritsar and Prime Minister Indira Gandhi's consequent assassination by her Sikh bodyguards) led to immigrant mobilization in the Indian conflict over greater autonomy for the Punjab.

Local and international developments sharpened the descendants' sense of distance from the recent immigrants. Descendants began to adopt a defensive, critical stance. Just as descendants who actually traveled to the Punjab, untroubled by a need to claim India as a homeland, do not acknowledge similarities of landscape, they do not acknowledge similarities between their fathers and the new Punjabi immigrants. They emphasize differences that begin with physical appearance and manner of self-presentation. They say their fathers were big men, commanding, proud, and light-skinned; the newcomers are small, obsequious, deferential, and dark-skinned.[14] Attitudinal and behavioral differences are stressed as well—the willingness of the old-timers to relinquish beliefs and practices inappropriate to the new setting, the ways in which the Punjabi newcomers are *not* becoming American. The Punjabi-Mexican descendants defend their claim to being Hindu by claiming also to be

American, by emphasizing characteristics that bridged differences of national origin and helped win acceptance in the dominant culture for their fathers.

Descendants' stories about their encounters help delineate the changing configurations of "we" and "other" over the years. Some unsettling encounters between old and new immigrants have already been recounted. Another occurred in Bill's Market in Willows between John Singh, son of an Imperial Valley old-timer, and Mohammed Afzal Khan, a Pakistani nephew brought over in the late 1950s who helped build a Pakistani immigrant community in northern California. Singh was a new man in town, having retired to Willows, but he knew a Hindu when he saw one. When he encountered Khan in the local market, he greeted him with an enthusiastic *"Sat sri akal,"* the Sikh salutation. Khan, a Muslim, was taken aback. "He looked Mexican to me," said Khan, telling about the incident.[15]

More prolonged encounters produced further distancing. As the story about cooking curry at the temple indicates, major differences between the two groups centered on religious institutions. Even when her husband was president of the Stockton temple, one Punjabi-Mexican wife sometimes overheard newcomers saying about her, "She's Mexican." And a very serious rift arose between pioneer Sikhs and their families and the newcomers with respect to Sikh practices in the temples. (La Brack describes the situation in his book on the new immigrants.[16]) Mola Singh talked freely about the many issues involved in the rift.

> About our churches here, everybody went to the Stockton one—Hindu, Muslim, everybody went. Afterward, these days now, I don't know what they're doing. Chenchel Rai [a Yuba City old-timer], I know him, he doesn't like that new group. I don't like people like that, I don't believe anything like that. The church started one way, it was for everybody, you just came and went to church. It belonged to everybody, the public, anybody could go. One thing I don't like, not for that new group, not everybody can go.
>
> Before, the Hindu men married women here. You know, everybody married white women, everybody married Mexican women, everybody went to church. And our people, everybody went and sat on chairs. That was before, not now. Then, everybody could sit on a chair. And for food, they gave it on a plate, with a spoon, and

paper to clean your hands. But after that, some Indian farmers and preachers have come. They want all the customs like India, and they've taken away the chairs, put people back on the floor again.

I went with my wife one time to Stockton, where they have lots of chairs in back. Me and my wife, we got a couple of chairs, we sat in the back.

"All right, man, sit on the floor, all right man, sit on the floor," someone said to us.

I don't care, people like that, people from India, why not have a church like other churches in this country? These India people are damn fools. Why have a church like before, why sit on the floor, why have no chairs, why have nothing? Today, it's different, twenty or fifty years have passed and today it's different.

"All kinds of people come here," I said to them. "I don't like the way you people do it. One woman over there, she's having a baby, you know, how's she gonna sit on the floor? How's she gonna get up with her stomach like that?"

They said to me, "That's the custom in India, people from India like customs like that."

Then they always want money. I got Bible [Granth Sahib], see, I believe that, but I say no, I won't go to the church if it's like that. This man came here, came by my home for money one day.

I said, "That's all right, if you want to make a church, put the chairs back. Everybody should sit on a chair, the women and kids and everybody, they can be on chairs. A woman sits on the floor, doesn't it shame you? Kids sit on the floor, doesn't it shame you people? Huh? You people are dirty," I said, "don't you change your mind? Today, yesterday, don't you see the world, people, all changing; everything, everyday, it all changes. In this country, women and kids, they change their whole ways, you know. And you people hate women like that, they should sit on the dirty floor? You have no shame, you people? You're dirty, you people."

I gave money to the church, but I don't like it now. I told one man here, "Shave 'em up, shave 'em good. Let the hair, the beard go. What do they mean? Nothing. If you're dirty inside, having hair or beard won't help you. Shaving them off won't hurt you. You people don't understand anything."

The Hindustanis, these people come; they get a little bit of money, but money doesn't mean anything. Money doesn't make you good, it doesn't make you clean inside.[17]

The same kind of rift has arisen between old and new Pakistanis. With the coming of new immigrants, customs in the Sacramento mosque have changed, and many Spanish-Pakistanis consider the old ways better. For example, Elizabeth Deen Hernandez's mother, Julia, was a convert to Islam, and the children considered themselves Muslims as well as Catholics. But when Elizabeth and her older sister Florence attended the funeral in Sacramento of Florence's first husband, the new immigrants insisted that men and women sit on separate sides and pray separately, and the sisters felt that the newcomers worried more about financial contributions to the mosque than about being respectful during the burial service. A Spanish-Pakistani daughter who is a regular member of the Sacramento mosque also testified to the changing customs there. Married to a Pakistani immigrant who heads the mosque committee, she has changed from dresses to dark pants when she attends services, to outfits more in keeping with the modest, dark-colored Pakistani clothes of the new immigrant women. And another Spanish-Pakistani daughter found it necessary to remind Muslim Association officials to keep her father's grave swept clean in the Sacramento cemetery—she felt she was asking a favor of newcomers, not reminding old friends of a responsibility temporarily overlooked.[18] In the Phoenix area, Spanish-Pakistani descendants still are officers of the Muslim Association of America, but they tend to be Catholics, Mormons, and Methodists. The function of that association is to dole out the few remaining plots purchased by the old Punjabis; there is no identification with the Muslim religious institutions being developed there by new immigrants. The pioneers did not plan to bury their wives beside them, and only three men purchased plots for their sons (who are the current officers of the Muslim Association).[19] There are some similarities in the Phoenix situation to that of the Sikh temple in El Centro, that is, there was no real provision for the continuation by the half-Punjabi descendants of Islamic institutions.

Encounters between old and new immigrants continue to take place. Some have occurred in my presence. At Mola Singh's Selma home in 1984, many of his and Susanna's children and grandchildren gathered to commemorate Mother's Day and to welcome a new bride from the Punjab into the family. One of Mola's sons had gone to India and had married a graduate of Amritsar University, who had arrived from India the day before Mothers' Day. The bride was dressed in a Punjabi two-piece costume and and spent much of the day making *chapattis* in the kitchen, while some thirty or forty descendants and their in-laws talked, mostly in Spanish. Some of the groom's sisters told me about their friendship with the groom's first wife, a Mexican American. The elderly parents-in-law were enthusiastic about this second wife, since their failing health necessitated a loving caretaker in the home, and they assumed the Indian daughter-in-law would fill that role well. The bride's English was tentative, and whether from exhaustion or culture shock or both, she seemed apprehensive. Her meeting with her husband on the occasion of their marriage in India clearly had not prepared her for this basically Mexican American family celebration.

I shared another memorable occasion breaking fast during the Muslim *Id* with Salim and Olga Khan in their Sacramento motel in 1982. As we talked, some Pakistani men staying there on a training program came down and asked for the loan of a cooking pot. Olga said she had none there. They would not accept this. They told her to call her daughter to bring one from home. She did so reluctantly, saying, "Do I want them using my pots?" "Oh, but they're from Pakistan," responded her immigrant husband. She smiled ruefully at me, indicating that this was not the first time she had heard that justification. For me, this exchange vividly evoked Prakash Tandon's insight in his autobiography into the difference between Punjabi and English concepts of "home life." Tandon, a Punjabi who studied in London in the 1930s, was struck by his English landlady's careful acquisition and care of furniture and ornaments for the home. He was even more struck by the little or no contact the family had with relatives, and he remarked on the Punjabi's frequent contact with relatives and reliance on such contract for a sense of "home."[20] I thought also of the Punjabi partners and bachelor uncles who had so often shared households and dinner tables with the Punjabi-Mexican families in California, and of the apprehension with which some family members began to regard the arrival of relatives from the Punjab after 1965.

So far, I have stressed encounters that show the descendants to be more cosmopolitan than their new Punjabi cousins, but at least one encounter shows society in the Punjab changing more rapidly than in rural California. Although the early Punjabi immigrants in California became enthusiastic about girls' education, sending their daughters through high school and sending money home for girls' schools in their home villages, few aspired to higher education for their children here. By the time of independence in India, however, some Punjabi village families desired higher education for their children (this is partly a function of the lower age for college in India, sixteen to eighteen, and the rising age at marriage). One Yuba City "real Indian" second-generation daughter expressed disappointment that India had gotten ahead of the pioneers in America: "They raised us with the basic values they had in the 1920s [and then they went to India in 1948 and saw the value placed on education in the Punjab]. India had kept moving . . . when they came back, they were totally different. They had stood still in time . . . they raised my sister so much different than they raised me, [she] just kept on going to school."[21]

The new immigrants in the Yuba City area exemplify these educational aspirations. Certainly Punjabi schoolchildren in Yuba City in the 1980s, while popularly thought to be "not fitting in," not taking advantage of the high school opportunities there, were in fact encouraged by their parents to aim for higher educational goals than were most of the Anglo students.[22] (And the Amritsar University bride at the Mother's Day event was certainly one of the few B.A. holders there.[23])

Another way in which the new immigrants claim superiority is through their marriage practices. Although Punjabi-Mexican daughters were encouraged to marry Punjabi men, there have been only two marriages of "real Indian" women to Punjabi-Mexican men, to my knowledge. One was the elopement of an Indian daughter born and brought up in California with an Imperial Valley boy. The other case is even more unusual, since it involves an Indian woman who came over as the bride of an old-timer in the 1950s. Eventually widowed, she met an older Punjabi-Mexican bachelor and married him. These isolated cases reveal a strong prejudice on the part of new Punjabi immigrants against Punjabi-Mexican sons as potential husbands for their daughters, and the "Indian daughters" who chose to "marry down" have no doubt suffered for their choices.[24]

All these encounters have led the Punjabi-Mexican descendants to emphasize their identity as Americans and to distinguish the old Hindus from the new South Asian immigrants. They feel indignant about the failure of the newcomers to adapt themselves to the United States. Unlike the pioneers, the new Punjabi men do not shave their beards and remove the turban, and the women continue to wear Punjabi clothing. In Yuba City, one descendant has lectured the immigrant women about the need to switch to dresses. She has also threatened to call the Health Department unless a new neighbor's aged mother begins to use the indoor toilet instead of squatting, village style, in the back yard. And Isabel Singh Garcia's indignant letter to the local newspaper complained about its failure to mention the Punjabi-Mexican group in a series on immigrants from India.

> I also wanted to let you know that the first generation of Hindus that came here married Mexican women and there are a large amount of half-breed children born from the marriages. The East Indian of today would like to forget we exist, because they are ashamed that their people came to this country and found the Mexican women very compatible with them. . . .
>
> Our fathers and mothers lived a very rich life. They raised us to be very proud, and gave us the best and the finest quality of life that one could ask for. . . .
>
> Our fathers with the help of our mothers became well-to-do in our community and were well known for what good people they were. They could take a piece of ground, and turn it into a rich farmland. . . .
>
> Our mothers allowed their husbands to bring their brothers, sisters and nephews in the 1950s and helped them to adjust to our way of life, and the cycle has repeated itself over and over and over. But the new breed did not keep the quality up.[25]

Thus, descendants who initially welcomed the new immigrants experienced disillusionment. Being Hindu in the earlier decades meant providing food and hospitality to Indian visitors. As their numbers increased and feelings of dissimilarity grew, this hospitality lessened. In Arizona, Amelia Singh's father stopped putting up traveling Punjabis when he caught some overnight guests siphoning gas from his tank the next morning! Like Isabel Singh Garcia, he found the newcomers did not "keep the quality up." Even descendants of the few "real Indian" families have found the new immigrants unsettling. George Puri, an agricultural products wholesaler in Los Angeles, resents the new Punjabi customers he gets because they demand that he speak Punjabi and lecture him when he says he does not speak it. Kartar Dhillon had never known a

Sikh who was not trustworthy and honorable until the 1960s, when, to her initial disbelief, she found a recent arrival from India to be a liar and a braggart.[26] Such experiences challenge the pride descendants take in the community spirit and ethical standards of the pioneer Punjabis and produce ambivalence about claiming to "be Hindu."

To Be Hindu

The notion that America was a pluralist society provided legitimacy to the descendants' choices of ethnic identity as they grew older. Unlike ethnic and racial identity in Europe,[27] ethnic and racial identity in the United States seemed fluid, something that could be changed in response to different situations and historical contexts. Members of the second generation made ethnic choices through the marriages they made, the names they used, and other indicators of their relationship to the Punjab and other Punjabis. There was an early tendency for daughters to marry older Punjabis or new immigrants, and there was some adoption of clan surnames when members of the second generation first became aware of them. But these tendencies were reversed in succeeding years, and encounters with the new immigrants from the Punjab undoubtedly influenced the reversal.

My analysis of California marriage certificates for members of the second generation with Punjabi surnames from 1930 through 1969 showed that only eleven girls and eleven boys (8 percent of the girls and 11 percent of the boys) married others like themselves. There was certainly no inclination to constitute a Punjabi-Mexican endogamous group or to merge with the growing new Punjabi community. Most of the daughters' marriages with Punjabis occurred in the 1940s, and the tendency neither continued nor extended to the sons.

Naming was a powerful indicator of ethnic identity in Punjabi-Mexican families. As noted, most names on birth certificates were Hispanic, so much so that the corrections filed by fathers giving Punjabi names stood in dramatic contrast. Naming patterns at birth were one thing, but as children of the Punjabis became adults, they often changed their names, sometimes using a Hispanic version, sometimes using an Anglicized version, and, rarely, using a Punjabi name. There was a slight tendency later on for families to add an Indian element, most often the clan surname, to their names. Boys sometimes added an Indian element as a middle name. Thus Sebastian and Richard Singh fathered children as Sebastian Juagpall Singh and Richard Juagpall Singh; the latter died as plain Richard Singh, however. A boy born as Francisco, whose father corrected his birth certificate to Gurdev, witnessed his brother's wedding as Frank. Indian names for boys did not become typical, despite the example presented by the new immigrants.[28]

Marriage license applications of the descendants give a set of names for analysis. Sometimes the ethnicity of the intended spouse seems correlated with the form of the name used on the license—that is, a Punjabi-Mexican son named Alfredo on his birth certificate would marry as Alfredo if his spouse was Mexican American or as Alfred if his spouse was Anglo. On the whole, however, the trend is simply toward Anglicization of the names regardless of the spouse's ethnicity. Thus a son who married more than once might be Domingo for the first marriage and Don for the second one.[29]

When names of members of the second generation appeared on the birth certificates of their children, again the names used could differ from those on their birth certificates. Boys born as Ramon, Alberto, Tomasito, Rodolfo, Juan, and Miguel called themselves Raymond, Albert, Thomas, Rudy, John, and Mike on the birth certificates of their children. Boys also varied their middle names in these records: Fred Singh Dhillon could also be Frederick Anthony Dhillon; Baldev Singh Dhalliwal could be Bill or William S. Dhalliwal; and Javier Singh Sidhu could be Harvey Singh Sidhu, Harvey Francis Sidhu, or Harvey Virgen Sidhu. Girls did not vary their names nearly as much, typically dropping the final *a*, as Margarita became Margaret, Paula became Pauline, and Manuela became Nellie. Or Carmen could become Karmen, and pronounciation could stress either a Spanish or English orientation (Julia, Genobeba). There was no increased use of Indian names for girls despite the new selection of Punjabi names brought by the post-1965 immigrants.

By the third generation, names of both boys and girls began conforming to popular American choices. Thus the first-generation wives Simona, Sara, Silveria might have daughters named Sally, Shanta, and Sheila, and granddaughters named Sheila Kay, Sandra, Sheri, Sharon, Shirley, and Susan. First-generation husbands Rattan Singh, Ram Singh, and Rollo Singh might have sons named Ramon, Raymundo, Roberto, Rodolfo, and Ruben, and grandsons named Reginald, Richard, and Robert, with a rare Rajinder or Rodolfo. Pride in one's grandfather or great-grandfather could be shown by retaining a Punjabi middle name, as in Davy Jiwan Singh.[30]

Some name changes were made officially for specific reasons. In one instance, strict Roman Catholic descendants involved in Chicano Democratic party politics have dropped Singh as a middle name because of a belief that it invariably signifies the Sikh religion.[31] In another instance, his closeness to older stepsiblings of pure Mexican ancestry and his immersion in Mexican American culture led a Sikh-fathered youngest son to adopt his stepsiblings' Hispanic surname. And in the north two or three young men completely changed their names in order to avoid identification with new immigrant Punjabis. There are also instances where a man's profession made it desirable to use his mother's maiden name rather than his Punjabi surname: A disk jockey on a northern California Spanish-language radio station, for example, uses his mother's name instead of Singh. There are fewer instances of boys using their Indian names as adults. The choice of an Indian name might be explained by an unusually insistent father (perhaps using inheritance as an inducement), a better education than others, pride in an independent India, and, sometimes, business reasons. Thus a businessman catering to new immigrants might use his Indian name, Gurbashen, forcing even childhood friends to drop the familiar "Botcho."[32]

One very complicated name change shows the multiple identities available to some children and the confusion that can result. One John Joe Labh Singh, also known as Fred Escobar Rodriguez, also known as Juan José Labh Singh, also known as John Joe Madrid, petitioned in 1958 to take the last of these names. He was born Fred Escobar Rodriguez, but his mother had remarried within a year of his birth and his stepfather, Labh Singh, had him baptized as Juan José Labh Singh. When his mother died, he stopped associating with his stepfather and became known as John Joe; because his surname was difficult to spell and pronounce, and because people thought he was an adherent of Hinduism, he decided to change it to John Joe Madrid.[33]

While sons have tended to move away from Punjabi names, some daughters and granddaughters have retained and emphasized their maiden names so that their Punjabi identity will not be lost. Thus we have Isabel Singh Garcia, and others like her, whose pride in their fathers shows in the middle names they use. A granddaughter, Yolanda Singh, has retained her maiden name after marriage to a Mexican American, contrary to current Mexican American custom. Yet Yolanda's father, Joe Romero Singh, does not see himself as a Hindu. He insists that he is 98 percent Mexican and knows "nothing, language or religion, of the Hindu race." Emphasizing the Romero in his name, he tells of the problems caused by having Singh as a surname. Strangers call him up and ask questions about India, such as, "What is that cloth thing they wrap around?" His first thought was of the sari, the characteristic women's garment throughout India, and that was indeed what the questioner meant, but Joe knew nothing about it.[34]

Some members of the third generation have consciously decided against the designation "Hindu." Some question it because of its inaccurate indication of their religious affiliation; others, particularly in the Yuba City area, do so because its derogatory connotations have been intensified by the prejudice against the new immigrants. These descendants generally choose "East Indian" as an alternative. "I'm American . . . but I'm East Indian. . . . I would be ashamed to say I'm a Hindu," one third-generation man told an interviewer.[35]

The Hindu ethnic identity is still powerful for most members of the second generation, and visits to India proved important in stimulating ideas about that ethnic identity. Identification as Hindu was especially strong in the few cases of children being taken as youngsters to visit India; those going at older ages sometimes have been ambivalent about the experience. Karm Chand took his son Harry to India when the boy was five or six, and Ali Abdullah went with his father when he was quite young. Pritam and Alice Sandhu went with their parents in the 1950s. Bessie Dhillon was taken to the Punjab by her parents for three years during the depression, 1929 to 1931. All these descendants strongly emphasize their Indian heritage in their adult life, and two of them espoused Indians in second marriages.[36]

Rattan Singh Dhillon, an educated farmer in the Imperial Valley, took his three sons to India. The boys identified more with India than others of the second generation in the Imperial Valley. They had been given Indian names and knew some Punjabi. Despite this, Dhillon and his sons had trouble farming together, and when Dhillon remarried a Punjabi woman (in the 1950s, years after divorcing his Hispanic wife), the troubles increased. The boys had been brought up solely by their father and were encouraged to think of themselves as Indian. After his death, they discovered that his handwritten will entirely omitted them in favor of the Indian wife. They could not believe it. They explained their omission as a final test by their father, who once told the youngest son, "If you want to leave someone out of your will, leave him $1; if you don't want to leave them out, leave him nothing." Like good Punjabis, they took the man at his word and interpreted this to mean that they must have been intended to inherit something, so they contested the will. Their story gains plausibility from the Yuba City account of a Punjabi who left one son his estate and willed $1 to each of his other children.[37]

Some children went to India as adults. LIke some of their fathers who revisited their homeland late in life, many felt they had money and advice to contribute to those in the old country. The Punjabi-Mexicans experienced varying degrees of culture shock. Mary Jane Mohamed, daughter of Niaz Mohamed of Brawley, went to Afghanistan with the Peace Corps. Despite the similarities to her father's "home village" of Quetta (capital city of nearby Pakistan's Baluchistan province), she had a difficult time adjusting to the role of women there, and her stories discouraged other family members from visiting the old country.[38] Perhaps the happiest visits were those of second-generation daughters traveling with their Punjabi husbands; like wives of the first generation who were fortunate enough to go, these women found a warm welcome in their husbands' home villages.[39]

A short but revealing visit to India was recounted by Alfred Sidhu of Sacramento. After his father's death, Alfred and his younger brother went to see the home village. They made the journey, not to take their father's ashes home, but to meet their half-brother and help "straighten out his farming business." Arriving at the New Delhi airport, an Indian policeman directed them to the line for returning nationals ("I knew he was wrong, but it was a shorter line," said Alfred). Sure enough, the Muslim Customs officer processed them anyway, with a warm "Welcome home, boys!" They rented a car and driver and journeyed to their village. Alfred Sidhu proudly told me how he had consolidated scattered plots, introduced American farming tools and methods, advised his half-brother's family against arranged marriages, and so on. They left after only a few days, but thought that they had accomplished a great deal. They also learned of a lost opportunity. Like many Americans, they had an image of India as a backward country and were dumbfounded to discover that there had been a telephone in their father's village for years.

No one in Sacramento had suspected that telephones existed in Budh-singhwalla. Alfred's father had never seen the son he left behind, but he could have spoken to him on the phone at any time in his last decade of life.[40]

Life-cycle events offer chances for descendants to affirm their Hindu ethnicity. Planning his fiftieth wedding anniversary, Joe Mallobox had his choice of three dates: those of his Catholic wedding, his Muslim wedding, and the Punjabi feast given for him by the men. He and his wife chose the last date for their commemoration in 1991.[41] And as a final indication of their Hindu identity, some members of the second generation are considering cremation after their deaths. These descendants of Sikhs, both men and women, want to honor their fathers, they said, and their remarks on this subject were volunteered, not solicited in any way. Their choice speaks to the importance placed by the old-timers on death rituals and to the powerful connection the descendants make between death rituals and ethnic identity. Religious affiliation plays a secondary role. Acquaintance with the Sikh religion did not produce this desire. Rather, the conviction was that this would be a tribute to one's father and would affirm one's identity as a descendant of the pioneer Punjabis.

Encounters, brief or sustained, produced as much or more misunderstanding and ambivalence than close identification between descendants of the Punjabi immigrants and new immigrants from South Asia. Undoubtedly the fact that the new immigrants tended to arrive as families played a large part in these interactions. Just as the coming of British *memsahibs* (wives) to India set up a wall between the Anglo-Indians and the British there, the coming of South Asian immigrant women helped create a boundary between the Punjabi-Mexicans and South Asians. Boundaries even materialized between the Punjabi-Mexicans and the new rural Punjabi immigrants to central and northern California, despite the apparent similarities between these newcomers and the original pioneers. The new Punjabi families settling in rural California mounted particularly painful challenges to descendants' claims to Hindu identity. Defensive and distancing reactions were many, and the dominant stance was to claim to be American as well as Hindu, to identify with a "modern" nation and its culture, rather than with a "backward" Third World country. The notion that the "old Hindus" had become Americans by being culturally flexible was an attractive one for their descendants, members of a systematically biethnic community and of a nation commonly conceptualized as a plural society. The descendants themselves could choose among different markers of ethnic identity as they progressed through life. Being Hindu had meant one thing in early childhood, something slightly different as the second generation came of age, and something entirely different as large numbers of new immigrants challenged that identity. If the childhood years had emphasized the Mexican or Hispanic component of identity and early adulthood the Indian or Hindu component, as they matured, Punjabi-Mexicans emphasized their identity as Americans.

11 Contending Voices

Members of Punjabi-Mexican families contested and negotiated ethnic identity within marriages, within families, and in arenas beyond the family over the decades. They voiced distinctive perspectives based on regional, generational, gender, and class differences within the biethnic community. A review of the ways in which outsiders have interpreted the history of this community contrasts outsider interpretations with those given by the Punjabi-Mexicans. Finally, the construction and transformations of Punjabi-Mexican American ethnic identity have significant implications for theories about ethnic identity in the United States.

Constructions of Ethnicity

Scholars who did field research on the Punjabi immigrant experience in California have drawn varying conclusions about the immigrants and cultural change.[1] Dhan Gopal Mukerji, one of many students from India who earned money by working short stints with "Hindu crews," came to the conclusion that the Punjabi men worked so hard that they had little time either to preserve Indian cultural values or to adapt themselves to their new environment.[2] Dr. Rajani Kanta Das, who taught economics at New York University, in a special study for the U.S. Department of Labor published in 1923, found that prejudice and discrimination against Indians precluded much meaningful interaction between them and others. But he observed that "a large number of the Hindustanees have . . . changed their customs" and was optimistic about Punjabi adaptation to American society.[3] William C. Smith, an interviewer for the Race Relations Survey project, liked the men he interviewed, but made no systematic analysis of their adaptation.[4]

In the late 1940s and early 1950s, soon after the 1946 Luce-Celler bill granted naturalization and an annual immigration quota of one hundred to Indians, a number of studies were done. Allan Miller, who carried out an ethnographic study in the Yuba City–Marysville area in 1947, was not interested in "acculturation problems," but he observed that few of the men had maintained strong ties with kin in India and that few were returning to India with their money.[5] Yusuf Dadabhay, who did his research at San Jose, Mountain View, Sacramento, and Stockton in 1951, believed that the Punjabi men were assimilating into American society by way of the Mexican "subculture." He thought this phenomenon was possible because Punjabis and Mexicans occupied the same position in the American color hierarchy, and both groups came from patriarchial family systems that subordinated wives and children. He concluded that the assimilation of the Punjabis was thus "bound up with the assimilation of Mexican-Americans."[6] Harold Jacoby interviewed 451 Indian men (including many non-Punjabi men living in urban areas) all over California in 1954–1955 and concluded that they were acculturating well in terms of material culture, personal habits, and to some extent, food and drink, but not as well in language, religion, and "crime and delinquency." Instead of amalgamating with Mexican Americans or Euro-Americans, he thought they were heading toward "a stabilization of their biological separateness."[7]

Several studies done between 1959 and 1967 found an aging, declining population of Punjabi pioneers, with scant attention paid to the second generation, whom many considered no longer "Hindu." Scott Littleton, who did field work in 1959 in Marysville–Yuba City, Sacramento, the Central Valley from Stockton to Fresno, and the Imperial Valley, was bothered by the fact that the second generation attended (Catholic) Mass and then went to the *gurdwara*. He felt that simultaneous exposure to "two radically different religious systems" led to apathy toward religion in general. As the first generation was dying out and the second seemed to be assimilating, Littleton saw the Punjabi communities as no longer "viable."[8] In contrast, Lawrence Wenzel, who studied the Marysville–Yuba City community in 1963–1965, found the Sikh religion to be the most visible characteristic of the Punjabis—whom he dubbed a "religio-ethnic" group—though he, too, thought acculturation was well under way.[9] Ann Wood's 1964 research at the Stockton temple argued that the Punjabis pursued pluralistic aims, promoting economic and political assimilation but maintaining social and religious separation and a strong group identity.[10] Leonard Greenwood, in an article published in the *Los Angeles Times* in 1966, declared that El Centro's Sikh community was dying out, some of the old men having been drawn away from their religion by non-Sikh wives and children, while others had merged with Euro-Americans around them.[11]

A lengthy and detailed study of the Sikhs in El Centro, carried out in 1967 by Robindra Chakravorti, claimed that "the most crucial feature of the community was the rapidly declining influence of its ethnic subsystem." He found clear differences between the two generations in language, naming patterns, religion, and other characteristics. Despite the fact that their "actual" identification with the Sikh subculture was "at best tenuous," Chakravorti reported that members of the second generation still identified themselves as "Hindus."[12] He interpreted this preference for an "identification with the Indian subculture from which they were divorced to identification with the Mexican subculture to which they were close" in the light of sociological theory about marginality and status anxiety.[13]

As new immigrants from South Asia increased in numbers and the Yuba City population in particular grew dramatically, scholarly attention shifted from the old to the new immigrants.[14] Two scholarly studies done in 1974–1975 and 1980–1981—Bruce La Brack's of the Yuba City Sikhs and Salim Khan's of the Pakistanis in the American West—used both archival and interview materials and included sections on Punjabi-Mexican families.[15] But others have used limited sources and come to strange conclusions. In 1972, a young Sikh of Indian parentage at Chico State University wrote that "the rules of endogamy and exogamy have been carefully adhered to among California Sikhs. In the entire community there are only about ten to twelve marriages involving a Punjabi and a non-East Indian."[16] In 1986, Juan Gonzales, Jr., came up with the interpretation that the Sikh pioneers were "unable to produce a second generation of American citizens" and that the "Sikh-Mexican" children were "lost to the Sikh community as potential harbingers of assimilation."[17] While one sees the perspectives from which such statements can be made, they ignore or contradict what the Punjabi pioneers and members of the second generation have said about their lives and their ethnic identity.[18] Recent scholarship on Asian Indians and Pakistanis in the United States is even further from acknowledging or examining the experiences of the early Punjabi immigrants.[19]

After 1965, ethnic boundaries were established by the incoming South Asians, boundaries that had been nonexistent or blurred by the earlier immigrants. The Punjabi men had married across national, linguistic, and religious boundaries. Their children did the same; they also transgressed Punjabi regional, religious, and caste boundaries. Yet most stressed the Hindu component of their ethnic identity when they became adults. The wives also crossed boundaries, frequently seeing themselves as "Americanizing" their husbands, and some wives came to view themselves as "Hindu" in important ways.[20] Husbands and wives stressed similarities between their languages, religions, and homelands as they built strong marriages and families.

"Being Hindu" had many positive components for the wives and children of the Punjabis. They had an idea of India and of what it meant to "be Hindu." To them, India was the Punjab, a rural place, and one's village was the home place and a key to identity. For most, the model of a typical Indian was the Jat Sikh (members of that farming caste constituted about 85 percent of the early immigrants). "Being Hindu" meant being a good farmer: doing hard work, saving to lease and buy agricultural land, perhaps even being tight-fisted, a "mean bastard," in the cause of becoming a landowner. It meant having pride: in one's native place, in the fighting history of Punjabis, in the efforts to secure freedom in India and citizenship in the United States.[21] It meant men who were honest and stubborn and fiercely loyal to one another, men who, when they stayed in sometimes tempestuous biethnic marriages, were strong, committed fathers who transmitted their values of hard work, pride, and independence to their children. "Being Hindu" meant chicken curry and *roti*, lemon pickles and Punjabi vegetables, and a reverence for the "holy book" from India, whether that was the Granth Sahib or the Quran. It meant a social life based on the men's activities: going to the "Hindu store" downtown in the "foreign section" or to wrestling matches or to the Stockton temple. It meant a passion for politics, from engaging in litigation with one another to listening to political speakers from the Ghadar party and, later, to Syed Hossain and Madame Pandit. Above all, "being Hindu" in the early decades meant opening one's home to other South Asians, Punjabi bachelor uncles and others, providing Hindu food and hospitality to visitors.

The "old Hindus" were all from one province, all Punjabi speakers. Furthermore, they were rural people, largely uneducated in any language. They made many adaptations to live and farm in the United States. They changed their dress and diet, learned new languages, and married wives from different cultural backgrounds. Colonial subjects, they founded a political movement and fought for India's freedom, setting themselves at odds with British officials in the United States and India so that they had little or no assistance from those officials in their fight against discrimination in the United States. They came to depend on local bankers, farmers, and storekeepers of diverse ethnic backgrounds for their livelihood. Anglo landowners and county officials witnessed some of the first weddings; and Anglo farmers, lawyers, and bankers held land for many Punjabis over the years.

These early immigrants and their families made a virtue out of necessity and called it being American. Given the barriers to meaningful relations with the Punjabi homeland, they were unconcerned with judgments that might be formed about them back in India and proceeded to become both "Hindu" and "American" in ways ranging from adopting new concepts of marriage based on romantic love to religious practices that treated men and women equally. The "Hindu" category in the United States included all the early immigrants. Personal names lost much of the religious and regional meaning they held in the Punjab, and religious differences receded in importance, particularly for the children. Most members of the second generation married outside the Punjabi-Mexican community. Despite these changes and the adoption of a strong "American" component of individual identity, most Punjabi-Mexicans retained an allegiance to an identity as "Hindus."

There were transformations of this Hindu identity over the decades. Some came as people traveled out of the agricultural valleys where Hindu meant something special. One man told me he had been called Mexican-Hindu all his young life, by everyone including the state authorities that issued driver licenses in the Imperial Valley. His was a migrant laborer family. Working near Sacramento when the United States entered World War II, he enlisted in military service, giving his race as "Hindu and Mexican." The clerk put him down as Caucasian. When he protested, she said, Well, if you're not Mongoloid or Chinese, you're a Caucasian, as far as the Feds are concerned." This was a shock to him, an introduction to a wider world and, in some sense, a loss.[22] Other transformations came as political events divided the homeland into India and Pakistan in 1947.

The descendants made ethnic choices over the course of their lives, speaking about these choices quite consciously.[23] More often than not, they distanced themselves from Mexican Americans (whose ethnic consciousness was heightened by and after World War II).[24] "We went to that wedding but we had never met the family before and didn't enjoy it; that man had become more Mexican than Hindu, we had no common interests," was one woman's judgment of another family. Some descendants faithfully followed the new political boundaries in South Asia and reclassified themselves: "Dad was an Indian but we've become Pakistani now, he was born there, on Pakistani territory." They tried to inform themselves about their heritage: "When I was thirteen I went through the whole beef routine, then decided against calling myself Hindu and used East Indian from then on." And again and again they came back to the label "American" to identify themselves, particularly when distinguishing their families from those of recent South Asian immigrants. "I'm East Indian—East Indian, Mexican, and American, and some are not lucky enough to know all three cultures."[25]

Outsiders are confused about the ethnic identity of families founded by the Punjabi men because of the combination of Punjabi and Hispanic names. Some outsiders perceive them as Mexican American, while others readily learn about "Hindu" names and assign that status to new immigrants with Muslim names.[26] The unusual combination startles people and signals complications that are not really there. One does not laugh at names like Ramona Williams, John Rodriquez, Janet Nakamura, or William Chang, yet people do laugh at Maria Jesusita Singh and José Akbar Khan, which deviate from the "usual" pattern. The familiar biculturalism or biethnicity denoted by the former names becomes complicated; the listener is unsure how to categorize the bearers of Punjabi-Mexican names. Laughter is provoked by a sense of the unusual, of the ordinary becoming exotic.[27] Yet the bearers of these names insist that they are ordinary, that their claim to a triethnic inheritance makes them no less, and perhaps more, "American" than others.

The post-1965 immigrants from the Indian subcontinent reacted much like outsiders, with confusion and startled laughter, when they met Punjabi-Mexican claimants to their homeland and ethnicity. Confronted by second-generation Punjabi-Mexicans in El Centro in 1967, Chakravorti talked about marginal men, as Dadabhay before him had talked about subcultures, in order to place the second generation firmly on the periphery. Newer immigrants have no understanding of the reasons for the early marriage choices or the ways in which the marriages stimulated the members of those families to think about their ethnic identities. The new immigrants are numerous enough to marry within their own religious, regional, and caste groups. Neither demographic nor legal constraints determine their choice of spouse. Most have come in family units, with women equal in numbers to men, a situation far more favorable to family life than that in India's own cities.[28] These immigrants have the means to import and support many aspects of South Asian culture. Well placed in the American economy and founders of their own immigrant networks, they have no compelling reason to recognize the rural, less well educated, half-Indian descendants of Punjabi peasants as "real Hindus" or "real" South Asians—and they have not done so. Just as the early Hispanic brides endured taunts of *"Hindera"* (Hindu lover) from others in their community, now men who married outside their community defend themselves against countrymen who criticize them for having married non-Punjabi women.

The relationships between Punjabi-Mexicans and the South Asian newcomers do not display the continuity often deemed characteristic of the immigrant experience. The newcomers do not need help in securing residences, jobs, or credit from those who arrived earlier; the newcomers are doing very well, moving with relative ease into professional positions and self-employment in urban California.[29] Even in rural California, the newcomers are now sponsoring newcomers. It is Didar Singh Bains, who arrived in the 1950s and became wealthy in northern California, not an Anglo patron or an old-timer Punjabi, whose signature may appear as a witness on marriage licenses for Punjabi couples there.

There is little interaction between old and new immigrant even where they are coresident, for the descendants of earlier immigrants are not recognizably South Asian. The Punjabi-Mexicans see themselves as exemplifying a positive trend toward participation in a broader American culture. Punjabi-Mexican descendants in Santa Clara County, for instance, intermarry with African-Americans, Koreans, and Euro-Americans, although they recall their South Asian ancestors with pride.[30] To most of the new immigrants, such assimilation is alarming.

Ideas about the homeland have been significant shapers of ethnic identity for both old and new South Asian immigrants.[31] There was a transformation in the concept of the homeland. Many early Punjabi immigrants who stayed in California gradually cut themselves off from British India and their families there, although it was always possible to return to India, and some gave up work, money, and prospects to do so.[32] Embedded in a new life in a country that talked of freedom and that initially offered them citizenship, Punjabis formed the Ghadar party to fight for India's freedom. They worked to liberate themselves from the burdensome stereotype of being "coolies" in a colonized India.[33] Resigned to more or less permanent separation from their families in India, they formed families in the United States, marrying the women available to them. Many sent money and advice back to their Indian families, but personal reunion seemed a remote possibility.

The political component of their self-image always played a major role in the pioneers' emotional life and that of their families. Despite an ideology of justice and equality for all in a multiethnic society, in the early twentieth century resources and privileges in the United States were distributed among different racial and ethnic groups. Not only did government laws and policies directly affect the formation and persistence of families by the Asian Indian pioneers, popular stereotypes adversely affected the men as they sought jobs and political rights. The legal setbacks—denial of citizenship, application of the Alien Land Laws—produced anger and resentment. Neither the conditions nor the emotions were new; they reproduced those the men had known back in India. Mola Singh explained the intersection of race, citizenship, and political power this way:

> Only a few people, Hindustani, were here and they had no right to anything then. See, these countrymen, 1,000, maybe 2,000 Hindus here, they should have had rights together. Rights to live, hold a job, work. Most of our people lived by labor, you know. We were just farmers, common labor people. Some people, educated ones, they used to live in other places, they knew about the national movement, our country. They came here, made a corporation, made it with white men [to continue farming after the 1923 application of the Alien Land Laws to them]. The white men said, "I'll keep the records, let the Hindu people work and suffer." Who got the pistol, he got the law. Who got the power, he got the law. No power, no law. . . . They [the British] kept records in India too, and when India got free the records showed what they did. The Government always keeps records.[34]

This central theme of deprivation of political rights spurred the Punjabi men to work harder to secure the rights they felt should be theirs. The context-specific patterns of ethnic interaction, developed in California's rural valleys in the early twentieth century, gave Punjabi farmers a place despite systematic legal discrimination at state and federal levels.[35] The help afforded by many in California's rural economy, the connivance to work around the land laws in particular, encouraged them to persevere and think of themselves as Americans. The early sense of an empty landscape—empty of American farmers—that had helped them feel comfortable and free gave way to knowledge of their neighbors and working relationships with them and other local people. The land was now peopled with members of a multiethnic society, at least some of them sympathetic and even essential to the economic well-being of the Punjabi farmers.

After access to U.S. citizenship was gained in 1946, many old-timers triumphantly claimed their new homeland. In Yuba City, Rattan Singh "Happy" Sahota cooked wedding dinners for the children of his bank manager and a local judge and then secured their help in straightening out his immigration status. When Mola Singh bought land in Fresno in 1950, he sent a crate of grapes to a superior court judge in the Imperial Valley; later, he took a box of raisins to the immigration official in Calexico who had helped straighten out his wife's immigration status. "I made friends with everybody, you know, I made friends," he said, and now he thanked them for their help. Pahker Singh came out of prison with the help of an Anglo landowner from San Bernardino, visited the Imperial County sheriff to whom he had sent Christmas cards throughout his incarceration, and began farming again; in the mid 1950s, the Punjabi Sikhs elected him president of the El Centro temple. Golam Mohamed gave a talk on naturalization to the fifth grade in Holtville as part of an Americanization program and told the children, "I would not take a million dollars for my American citizenship."[36]

Many stories featured the Punjabi men's eagerness to show what they had learned for their citizenship examinations. Rattan Singh Dhillon, an Imperial Valley farmer who had a master's degree in economics from Berkeley and who told his sons he was the most educated tractor driver in the valley, got "a big blue book" and spent many hours underlining and memorizing it. He sent canteloupes to the president and went up to Los Angeles to take his citizenship test. When he was put with two or three hundred people in a big hall and asked simply to raise his hand, he went up to the stage and demanded to be asked a question.[37] The Punjabi men's passionate relationship to the British and American political authorities, first resistant and then triumphant, is one of their most meaningful legacies to their descendants.

But the same Luce-Celler bill that enabled the men to become citizens abruptly brought the original homeland back into their lives. After 1946, and particularly after 1965, contacts with relatives in the Punjab resumed, and these posed certain risks. Relatives in South Asia were often more eager to resume connections and come to the United States than the men here were to bring them. (At least two of the old men brought over all their immediate family members *except* their Punjabi wives!) The reconnections also had ominous implications for Punjabi-Mexican wives and children, who found that the newcomers were not only rivals to the family property but viewed the Punjabi-Mexicans as a historical mistake, people no longer (if ever) part of the South Asian immigrant community. Newly arrived relatives claim "all the ground" when they sue American descendants for an inheritance—they are not willing to compromise, to share with people they do not consider "really related."[38]

Developments stemming from the new immigration laws added stress to that produced by socioeconomic stratification and rivalries within the Punjabi-Mexican community. The community was not homogeneous,[39] and members of the second generation responded differently to the choices open to them. Poorer families tended to identify more closely with Mexican Americans. In some of these families, conflict with the father or his countrymen produced lasting anger or fear, alienating descendants from their Punjabi and Indian heritage. Yet even where the Punjabi men were said to have "become Mexican," incoming daughters-in-law found a pride in Hindu ancestry that denigrated Hispanic ancestry. Only one Punjabi-descended farmer in the Imperial Valley renounced his "Hindu" name (Singh) and took up leadership of the Mexican Americans there.[40]

Few Punjabi-Mexicans have "invented a tradition" that glorifies their fathers and their heritage. They are realists; at best, there is a nostalgia for the old days when bachelor uncles came to family homes to eat, drink, talk, and play with the children. A shared identity is still taken for granted in the Imperial Valley, and some are fighting for greater recognition of their heritage. Punjabi descendants formerly were not eligible for membership in the Imperial Valley Pioneers, the "first settlers" historical association. Yet the words of its organizer certainly apply to the Punjabi farmers. He said that this was "the greatest of all Valley orders, the Imperial Valley Pioneers, the builders of our empire, competent to grade and irrigate Hell and make another winter garden of it." At least one Punjabi pioneer has made an effort to have the Punjabi pioneers commemorated. Many local roads are named after prominent people, and he advocates naming a major road "Singh Road"—it would, he pointed out, cover a great many Punjabis![41]

The contexts for the Punjabi-Mexican descendants are different in Arizona and northern California. Compared to the Imperial Valley, the Phoenix area is cosmopolitan; it boasts a well-established university and frequently hosts national conventions. The second generation there participates in an expanding urban and suburban culture that has supplanted the agrarian culture of the past. There is still a group feeling among them, yet their ethnicity no longer marks them as distinctive in the Phoenix area. They are rarely identified by others as Hindus or as Spanish-Pakistanis.[42]

In northern California, where Punjabi descendants and new South Asian immigrants still rely on an agrarian economy, the Hindu identity is sharply contested. Food and restaurants are important markers of ethnic and national identity, and descendants are proud of their Yuba City restaurant, El Ranchero. Run by one of the Rasul sons from the Imperial Valley, this is the only Mexican restaurant I know of in California that features chicken curry and *roti* (photo 26).[43] Also in northern California, descendants of Punjabi pioneers are ambivalent about the annual Yuba City Sikh Parade. They still hold their annual Christmas Dance, but they have broadened its scope to include all who went to school with the founders of the dance in Yuba City. Often called the old-timers dance, its organizing committee is primarily Mexican American. In 1988, only two of the eight organizers and about one-tenth of the attenders were descendants of Punjabis or related to them by marriage. That year, the theme was Hawaiian, with *Aloha* written on a banner above the band platform, and the invitation began *Hello/Ohio/Buenos Dias*, emphasizing cultural pluralism and the claim to be American. Those who attended this rousing evening with its lively band and delicious Mexican food did tell stories about the pioneer couples, mimicking the broken English of the men from India, but the dance itself was a thoroughly American affair, albeit with a Mexican American tinge (photo 27).[44]

Theoretical Implications

The Punjabi-Mexican experience strikingly demonstrates the historical construction and reconstruction of ethnicity. State policies set a context in which Punjabi men and Hispanic women "chose" to marry and create a biethnic community in the Imperial Valley. The differential incorporation of racial and ethnic groups into the rural California economy and the views of the dominant Anglo society toward those groups helped determine Punjabi and Hispanic attitudes toward each other over time, even *within* families. The provisions of California laws concerning divorce and access to agricultural land had an impact on power within the families, affecting gender and generational relationships. Finally, changes in federal laws regulating citizenship and immigration enabled the Punjabi men to exercise power over property at the end of their life cycles, power exercised perhaps more vigorously because it was so long withheld from them.

For the Punjabi-Mexican children, growing up and experiencing the consequences of internal and external pressures, ethnic identity was not fixed and bounded. Identified by others as Mexican-Hindus, most often they chose to define themselves as Hindu. But the meanings of Hindu and Mexican-Hindu, and the content of those ethnic identities, were unique to the western states. Hindu in California meant something totally different than Hindu in the father's homeland; Mexican was equally inaccurate, since half the mothers were not from Mexico. Yet Hindu is still a useful marker in parts of rural California, an ethnic identity with a history and force all its own. Class differentiation within the Punjabi-Mexican community did not prevent the intensification of the Hindu identity and indeed cannot reliably predict who will assert it.

When descendants talk about being Hindu or East Indian today, they do not mean objective criteria that link them to India or the Punjab, attributes such as an anthropologist might list. They have few or no experiential links to Punjabi and Indian culture and are non-speakers of Punjabi. But they possess a sense of place and history that is distinctly Punjabi nonetheless. The perceptions or creations of similarities with which the men framed their new lives continue to be voiced by their descendants. These perceived similarities, the senses in which the descendants feel themselves to be Punjabi, to be Hindu, in California today include their place in the political system and their ideas about Punjabi and Mexican material culture, language, and religion.

The children grew up, then, consciously drawing on three cultural traditions. There have been occasions for choice, some of them posed by the individual life cycle. As they left the Imperial Valley and other places where they were known, they were given new labels. As the external political context changed, they were presented with new labels and new choices. The case of the Punjabi-Mexicans dramatically illustrates the need to investigate carefully the ways in which individual life cycles, family life cycles, and public policies interpenetrate. It is relatively easy to see how changes in immigration and citizenship laws opened choices to family members, but it is harder to separate material interest from emotion when analyzing some of the family experiences. Why might a son begin to use his Hindu name as his father grew older, or why might a father turn to a fully Punjabi nephew or grandson rather than to his Punjabi-Mexican son when it came to making his will? Particularly when considering inheritance, it is problematic whether "material flow systems" shaped "cultural meaning systems" or the other way round.[45]

Changing contexts, changing local configurations of "we" and "others," stimulated the "old Hindus" and their descendants to make ethnic choices, to reconstruct their sense of place and society as they made this land their own. The immigrants' spouses were predominantly Hispanic women, yet many of the Spanish-speaking Catholic women actively contributed to the construction and maintenance of a "Hindu" identity in the United States, an identity necessarily very different from that being constructed now by South Asian wives of more recent immigrants.[46] Their experiences emphasize the *process* of identity formation, the flexibility of culture and ethnic identity, their relational nature, and the importance of context.

Here we need to confront the current debate in anthropology about culture and the process of sociocultural change. Older notions of bounded cultural units located in time and space and sometimes ranked with respect to one another are giving way to a recognition of the difficulties of defining and analyzing such units, particularly in the contemporary world. Anthropologists are turning their attention to issues of transformation and transition, to events and historical processes affecting not "cultures" but "connected social fields."[47] Earlier, the Punjabi peasant immigrants might have been seen as "archetypal natives,"[48] people drawn from their own place by capitalist needs for labor, experiencing social disorganization[49] in their new place (the more so because of the need to marry women of other backgrounds), and forced to accommodate, adapt, or assimilate to the dominant American culture. Yet the immigrants themselves, and their descendants, present a different account, one that highlights the choices they made over the decades.

The Punjabi-Mexicans do not deny or disguise the ways in which the "Hindu" identity brought discrimination, but they view their ethnic identity as a resource that they employed flexibly over the life cycle. James Clifford has called ethnicity a weak conception of culture, a conception suitable for organizing divisions within a pluralist state.[50] Along the same lines, John Borneman believes that in the United States, a state formed on pluralist premises, "diverse cultural standards and social strata were never subject to strong political or bureaucratic structures capable of or in need of bringing about a uniform performance standard." He is talking about horse breeding and sees the "denial of social difference and of hierarchy" leading to many separate but somehow equal cultural breed standards.[51] John Higham, explaining the fact that ethnic groups acted differently in different contexts in the United States, related the localization of power to the absence of a national core, the absence of a "state" in "the European sense" of the word.[52]

Weak or strong, conceptions of ethnic identity have served Punjabi-Mexicans well, permitting cultural flexibility for both individuals and collectivities in what they clearly conceive of as a plural society. True, scholarly discussions of ethnic pluralism have tended to shift from an emphasis on culture to an emphasis on power in recent decades, and there has been a deprecation of the celebratory tone of much of the work on ethnic persistence.[53] Some have charged that ethnic pluralism and democracy are not easily compatible, since ethnic pluralism in America evolved from systematic inequalities; thus the preservation of ethnic identity implies the preservation of class cleavages.[54] Yet the voices of the immigrants and their descendants in this study testify to an underlying consensus that pluralism means equality and diversity, rather than repression and delusion.[55]

I am arguing here against a possible alternative interpretation of the Punjabi-Mexican experience that would continue to impose such labels as "marginal" and "subcultural," or their current equivalents, "borderland" and "periphery."[56] Such impositions are especially tempting because of the mediating role played by many of the Hispanic wives. Following the lead of Gloria Anzaldua, a whole literature is developing on women as the inhabitants of borderlands, women speaking from the margins, alienated and deterritorialized beings who can move in the interstices between groups. If categorized as "minority literature," the Punjabi-Mexican discourse might be viewed as political in essence, a discourse created for a nonhegemonic audience. In this kind of analysis, because of their "multiple positionality," women and minorities are said to sustain contradictions, invent themselves, and transform their sense of individual oppression into collective resistance.[57] These are literary, expressive terms, but I do not see them grounded in the structures disclosed by this study or in the feelings expressed by the Punjabi-Mexicans.

Werner Sollors suggests that Americans take much for granted among themselves and dramatize their differences; in particular, they dramatize and invent ethnicity rather freely. For him, ethnic literary history and discourse best illustrates, not each writer's "ethnic perspective" or descent, but the cultural understandings and contacts the writers share with each other as they (and others) seize upon and exaggerate their differences.[58] Again, the voices of the Punjabi Mexican Americans stress the centrality of the American component in their history and experience.

Ironically, the new South Asian immigrants, particularly the Punjabi peasants among them, pose the most serious challenge to the "Hindu" ethnic identity in California as they try to deny the changes wrought by place and time. Far from being inhabitants of "zero culture" transition zones, people without culture as they became adapted to a new place,[59] immigrants are the creative producers of new identities,[60] agents in the shaping of our contemporary world. I cannot do better here than quote Salman Rushdie, whose writing often speaks to the immigrant experience. Defending *The Satanic Verses*, he says:

> It is a migrant's-eye view of the world . . . written from the very experience of uprooting, disjuncture and metamorphosis (slow or rapid, painful or pleasurable) that is the migrant condition, and from which, I believe, can be derived a metaphor for all humanity. . . . [It] celebrates hybridity, impurity, intermingling, the transformation that comes of new and unexpected combinations of human beings, cultures, ideas, politics, movies, songs. It rejoices in mongrelization and fears the absolutism of the Pure. Melange, hotch-potch, a bit of this and a bit of that is *how newness enters the world*."[61]

In the discourse of the Punjabi-Mexicans, I think it is noticeable that the dominant Anglo culture does not loom large. Although national and state policies and laws were important determinants of social action, the men and their families carved out their identities with reference to Mexican Americans, Swiss, Japanese, and other groups, as well as to Anglos. They claimed their place in the social landscape proudly, unconcerned to orient themselves entirely to any single model of what it was to be American. As one descendant said, "Dad was distant from Anglo culture, apprehensive; he never criticized directly but he laughed often at them, the *gooras* [whites]. He admired certain ones here, but there was respect and distance. . . . Never worry about what people think about you, he told us, because they don't, he said."[62]

Examining ethnic and racial groups in contemporary America from 1980 census data, Lieberson and Waters found that an increasing proportion of the U.S. population is of mixed ethnic ancestry and that higher proportions of people identified themselves in the 1980 census as "American" or "white" instead of specifying an ethnic group. Further, they found that people's reports of their ethnicity "appear to involve distortions" in that they are making choices from various ancestries.[63] These developments have led Lieberson and Waters to postulate a new "ethnic" group, the "unhyphenated whites," or the whites of mixed ethnic ancestry who do not identify with or know about their specific European origin. Their speculations about the meaning of this new category are of limited usefulness here because of their focus on the Euro-American population, but they expect "increasing distortion in the true origins of the population" and a growing "unhyphenated white" or "American" group (regrettably, they sometimes seem to use these terms interchangeably) to show up in the 1990 census.[64] I would assert that these phenomena are not restricted to the Euro-American population, that many Punjabi-Mexicans are part of this "unhyphenated" or American category, and that their choice of this identity is not a distortion.

The early Punjabi pioneers and their non-Indian spouses have important things to say to scholarly outsiders ready to impose identities on them, and to the post-1965 South Asian immigrants who have turned out to be "other" and outsider as well. Most Punjabi-Mexican families defined themselves as Hindu, working with the cultural elements available to them and proudly claiming both South Asian and American identities. These examples of Punjabi-Mexican wives and children who chose to be Hindu, and the examples of others who made different choices, point to the flexibility and permeability of the "boundaries" of ethnic identity and strengthen the need to look again at the large issue of culture. For the Punjabi Mexican Americans, changes have occurred in many domains once considered crucial to cultural and ethnic identity, particularly those of religion and language. Their experience dramatizes the changing content and form taken by ethnic identity as it crosses oceans, continents, and years. As long as there is pride in ancestry and heritage, however, immigrants can continue to relate to their countries of origin, and children to their parents, in meaningful ways. And pride is something the Punjabis and their descendants have in plentiful supply.

Appendixes, Notes,
Bibliography, and Index

Appendixes

Appendix A. Marriage and Residence Patterns

Comparing marriages to births and to child and spousal deaths by county of record (see table), it is clear that the two counties with the largest concentration of householders, Imperial and Fresno, were less than hospitable to these marriages. Family births and deaths occurred in homes—it is apparent that the couples married in counties other than those in which they resided.

To make sense of these marriage patterns, we need to know some facts about marriage laws and local prejudices in the western states. In 1927, at the end of July, legislation became effective requiring a wait of three days between application for a marriage license and its issuance in California. This resulted in a decline in marriages in California and a rise in Nevada and Arizona, particularly Yuma. Another decline in the California marriage rate came with the requirement of premarital blood tests in September 1939, again resulting in increases in Nevada and Arizona. During World War II, however, migration out of California for marriage was curtailed by gasoline rationing and by the repeal of the three-day waiting period in early 1943. At the end of the war, marriages rose again in Nevada and Arizona.[1]

Although couples were married in Imperial County, there were sometimes difficulties. San Diego was the closest alternative, with Los Angeles next, until the road to Yuma was completed in 1925 (and after 1927, there was no waiting period in Yuma). Many marriages took place in the vicinity of El Paso, Texas, especially Canutillo (where some Sikhs farmed

[1]Jacobson, *American Marriage and Divorce*, 52.

California Counties Ranked by Numbers of
Births, Deaths, and Marriages, 1916–1946

Births		Deaths[a]		Marriages	
Imperial	277	Imperial	37	San Diego	46
Fresno	62	Fresno	7	Yuma	30[b]
Sacramento	22	Sacramento	4	Imperial	25
Sutter	21	Tulare	3	Tulare	16
San Joaquin	19	Yuba	3	Sacramento	9
Tulare	16	San Bernardino	2	Los Angeles	8
Yuba	7	Placer	2	Fresno	7
				San Joaquin	3
				Sutter	2
				Yuba	1

Sources: Birth, death, and marriage certificates, county record offices. For men's deaths by region, see Table 8 in text.
[a]Child and spousal deaths only, 1905–1939
[b]Through 1940 only

cotton), and Las Cruces, New Mexico. In the Fresno area, Tulare County provided the haven.

In the central and northern valleys, Reno and Las Vegas provided quick marriages for an unknown number of couples.

Appendix B. Contributors to the El Centro Sikh Temple[1]

Karm Singh Bharana	$6,561
Sucha Singh Tallewal	1,500
Mr. and Mrs. Kehar Singh Gill Dhudike	1,200
Mr. and Mrs. Rattan Singh Dhillon Barsal	1,100
Mr. and Mrs. Nand Singh Bhikki	1,100
Mr. and Mrs. Fauja Singh Sabhra	1,052
Mr. and Mrs. Budh Singh Sursingh	980
Mr. Charn Singh Sandhu Bharana	850
Mrs. Harnam Kaur Sandhu Bharana	850
Mr. and Mrs. Sucha Singh Garewal Lalton	750
Mr. Bawa Singh Sangha Sakrooli	625
Mr. and Mrs. Indar Singh Sekhon Kaunke	600
Mr. and Mrs. Bagga Singh Sunga Chhajjawal	600
Mr. Naranjan Singh Takhanwad	600
Mr. Sundar Singh Ladhar	525
Mr. Kartar Singh Kotla	525
Mr. and Mrs. Harnam S. Dhillon Kasapur	500
Mr. Gurcharn Singh Boparai	500
Mr. and Mrs. Kakoo Singh Khandal	500
Mr. and Mrs. Nika Singh Gill Malla	500
Mr. and Mrs. Kehar Singh Sidhu Chuharchak	500
Mr. and Mrs. Toga Singh Sandu Manunke	500
Mr. and Mrs. Rala Singh Samra Pohir	500
Mr. and Mrs. Sucha Singh Man	500
Judge and Mrs. D. S. Saund Chhajalwadi	500
Mr. and Mrs. Sadhu Singh Namolia	500
Mr. and Mrs. Diwan Singh Kasagrande	500
Mr. Spooran Singh Sarholi	500
Mr. Inder Singh Kilibara	500

[1]Names and amounts as listed on undated plaque (ca. 1948) by temple door, Main Street, El Centro.

Notes

Preface

1. See Chapter 1 for a discussion of terminology.

2. Karen Leonard, *Social History of an Indian Caste: the Kayasths of Hyderabad* (Berkeley: University of California Press, 1978).

3. Bruce La Brack, *The Sikhs of Northern California 1904–1975: A Sociohistorical Study* (New York: AMS Press, 1988); and Margaret A. Gibson *Accommodation without Assimilation: Punjabi Sikh Immigrants in an American High School and Community* (Ithaca: Cornell University Press, 1988).

4. Daniel Bertaux, "From the Life-History Approach to the Transformation of Sociological Practice," in *Biography and Society*, ed. Daniel Bertaux (Beverly Hills: Sage, 1981), 42.

5. Ibid., 32–33, 42–43.

6. Samuel Schrager, "What's Social about Oral History?" *International Journal of Oral History* 4, no. 2 (June 1983): 76–98.

Chapter 1. Explaining Ethnicity

1. Two invaluable references were Owen C. Coy, *Guide to the County Archives of California* (Sacramento: California Historical Survey Commission, 1919); and Harold W. Hannah, *Law on the Farm* (New York: Macmillan, 1951).

2. The term Hispanic has been criticized as a tool of the bureaucracy. For example, Gloria Anzaldua views the term as "copping out," in *Borderlands/La Frontera: The New Mestiza* (San Francisco: Spinsters/Aunt Lute, 1987), 62. But many scholars and organizations do use the term. Alejandro Portes, in "From South of the Border: Hispanic Minorities in the United States," observes that this "minority" has depended more on "the actions of government and the collective percep-

tions of Anglo-American society than on the initiative of the individuals so designated" (p. 160). See Virginia Yans-McLaughlin, ed, *Immigration Reconsidered: History, Sociology, and Politics* (New York: Oxford University Press, 1990). I am using "Hispanic" because it conveniently includes women of Mexican, Mexican American, Spanish, and Puerto Rican ancestry.

3. Peter Laslett, *The World We Have Lost* (New York: Scribner, 1966); Peter Laslett and Richard Wall, eds., *Household and Family in Past Time* (Cambridge: Cambridge University Press, 1972); Daniel Scott Smith, "Parental Power and Marriage Patterns," *Journal of Marriage and the Family* 35, no. 3 (1973): 418–428; Tamara Hareven, "The History of the Family as an Interdisciplinary Field," *Journal of Interdisciplinary History* 2 (1971): 399–414.

4. Warren T. Morrill and Bennett Dyke, "Ethnographic and Documentary Demography," in *Genealogical Demography*, ed. Warren T. Morrill and Bennett Dyke (San Francisco: Academic Press, 1980), 6.

5. Ibid., 8.

6. Sacramento County, Recorder's Office, Death Certificates, b. 84, no. 1503.

7. This spelling is used by the Berkeley Library; elsewhere I use the more usual Ghadar. The Gadar Collection is not yet catalogued.

8. Sucheng Chan found this collection and made an index of relevant files for me while carrying out her own research.

9. Eliot Grinnel Mears, *Resident Orientals on the American Pacific Coast* (New York: Arno Press, 1978; first published in 1927); and William C. Smith, *Americans in Process: A Study of Our Citizens of Oriental Ancestry* (New York: Arno Press, 1970; first published by Edwards Brothers, Ann Arbor, Mich., 1937). The latter includes only material on the Chinese and Japanese. A third publication, *Orientals and Their Cultural Adjustment*, Social Science Source Documents, No. 4 (Nashville: Social Science Institute, Fisk University, 1946), publishes twenty of the documents, again only about Chinese and Japanese immigrants.

10. Joseph Anderholt, Holtville, introduced me to the museum collection and facilitated my use of it.

11. Paul Thompson, "Life Histories and the Analysis of Social Change," in Bertaux, *Biography and Society*, 290.

12. For the new social history and particularly family history, see *Journal of Marriage and the Family* 35, no. 3 (1973); subsequent work in *The Family in Historical Perspective* (1972–1974) and *Journal of Family History* (1976——); and James M. Gardner and George Rollie Adams, eds., *Ordinary People in Everyday Life: Perspectives on the New Social History* (Nashville: American Association for State and Local History, 1983). My introduction to this field stemmed from an excellent summer seminar at the Newberry Library conducted by Richard Jensen and Daniel Scott Smith in the mid 1970s.

13. Franco Ferraroti, "On the Autonomy of the Biographical Method," in

Bertaux, *Biography and Society*, 23–24, has proposed such primary groups as the unit of analysis.

14. See Paul Thompson, *The Voice of the Past: Oral History* (London: Oxford University Press, 1978), for a discussion of the way oral history democratizes history and changes the process of doing history by involving the researcher with her informants. See Schrager, "Oral History," 84–85, and Bertaux, "From the Life-History Approach," 37, for the ways in which informants re-create past worlds in their talk and stories.

15. Fredrik Barth, ed., *Ethnic Groups and Boundaries: The Social Organization of Cultural Difference* (Boston: Little, Brown, 1969); Ronald Cohen, "Ethnicity: Problem and Focus in Anthropology," *Annual Review of Anthropology* 7, no. 3 (1978): 379–403; and Charles F. Keyes, ed. *Ethnic Change* (Seattle: University of Washington Press, 1981).

16. Paul Brass, ed., *Ethnic Groups and the State* (London: Croom Helm, 1985), and Kevin Avruch, "The Emergence of Ethnicity in Israel," *American Ethologist* 14, no. 2 (1987): 327–339, usefully review current issues in this area.

17. G. Carter Bentley, "Ethnicity and Practice," *Comparative Studies in Society and History* 29 (1987): Norman Buchignani, *Anthropological Approaches to the Study of Ethnicity* (Ontario: Multicultural History Society of Ontario, 1982), 14–15. See Kathleen Neils Conzen, "Historical Approaches to the Study of Rural Ethnic Communities," in *Ethnicity on the Great Plains*, ed. Frederick C. Luebke, (Lincoln: University of Nebraska Press, 1980), 1–18, for a thoughtful review of the issues.

18. John L. Comaroff, "Of Totemism and Ethnicity: Consciousness, Practice and the Signs of Inequality," *Ethnos* 52, nos. 1–2 (1987): 301–323; Eric Hobsbawm and Terence Ranger, eds., *The Invention of Tradition* (New York: Cambridge University Press, 1983); and James Clifford, *The Predicament of Culture: Twentieth-Century Ethnography, Literature and Art* (Cambridge: Harvard University Press, 1988).

19. Comaroff, "Totemism and Ethnicity," 302; Clifford, *Predicament of Culture*, 10, 338. Cohen, "Ethnicity," also forcefully points out that ethnicity has no existence apart from interethnic relations; 389 et passim.

20. Comaroff, "Totemism and Ethnicity," 303–307.

21. I am grateful to Liisa Malkki for her comments on this theme. Arthur Wolf, "Family Life and the Life Cycle in rural China," in *Households*, ed. Robert McC. Netting, Richard R. Wilk, and Eric J. Arnold (Berkeley and Los Angeles: University of California Press, 1984), 279–298, emphasizes the importance of sorting out individual life cycles from the family life cycle, important here not only because of demographic factors similar to those that Wolf points to but because of the biethnic nature of the community.

22. Phyllis Pease Chock, "The Irony of Stereotypes: Toward an Anthropology of Ethnicity," *Cultural Anthropology* 2, no. 3 (1987): 348, makes this point about

ordinary talk. An exception is Virginia Yans-McLaughlin's use of oral interviews, "Metaphors of Self in History: Subjectivity, Oral Narrative, and Immigration Studies," in Yans-McLaughlin, *Immigration Reconsidered*, 254–290. (The Punjabis and Punjabi-Mexicans were more like her Jewish informants than her Italian ones; see esp. 275.)

Chapter 2. Contexts: California and the Punjab

1. Paul S. Taylor and Tom Vasey, "Historical Background of California Farm Labor," *Rural Sociology* 1 (1936): 285–292.

2. Howard S. Reed, "Major Trends in California Agriculture," *Agricultural History* 20 (1946): 253–255; and Ann Foley Scheuring, *A Guidebook of California Agriculture* (Berkeley and Los Angeles: University of California Press, 1983), 135–185.

3. Donald J. Pisani, *From the Family Farm to Agribusiness: The Irrigation Crusade in California and the West, 1850–1931* (Berkeley and Los Angeles: University of California Press, 1984), 440–452; and Cletus E. Daniel, *Bitter Harvest: A History of California Farmworkers* (Berkeley and Los Angeles: University of California Press, 1981), 19–39.

4. Sucheng Chan, *This Bittersweet Soil: The Chinese in California Agriculture, 1860–1910* (Berkeley: University of California Press, 1986), 48.

5. Walter Goldschmidt, *As You Sow* (New York: Harcourt Brace, 1947); Elvin Hatch, *Biography of a Small Town* (New York: Columbia University Press, 1979); and Robert Lawrence Griswold, "The Character of the Family in Rural California, 1850–1890," Ph.D. dissertation, Stanford University, 1979.

6. Paul Schuster Taylor, *Mexican Labor in the United States: Imperial Valley*, University of California Publications in Economics, vol. 6 (Berkeley: University of California, 1928–1930).

7. Taylor and Vasey, "Historical Background," 291.

8. L. Varden Fuller, "The Supply of Agricultural Labor as a Factor in the Evolution of Farm Organization in California," Ph.D. dissertation, University of California, Berkeley, 1939, printed in U.S. Congress, Senate, Committee on Education and Labor, *Hearings Pursuant to Senate Resolution 266, Exhibit 8762-A*, 76th Cong., 3rd sess., 1940, 19777–19898. Chan, *This Bittersweet Soil*, chap. 8, provides an excellent review of Fuller's work and that of others who followed his line of inquiry.

9. Daniel, *Bitter Harvest*, 24–32; Gunther Barth, *Bitter Strength: A History of the Chinese in the United States, 1850–1870* (Cambridge: Harvard University Press, 1964).

10. Carey McWilliams, *Factories in the Field: The Story of Migratory Labor in Cali-*

fornia (Salt Lake City: Peregrine Smith, 1978), 117–119; David Runsten and Philip LeVeen, *Mechanization and Mexican Labor in California Agriculture*, Monographs in U.S.–Mexican Studies, No. 6, (San Diego: University of California, 1982); and Walton Bean, *California: An Interpretive History*, 2nd ed. (New York: McGraw-Hill, 1973), 496.

11. The strongest challenge is from Chan, *This Bittersweet Soil*, who points to several major fallacies in Fuller's argument about entrepreneurial ability and access to credit to demonstrate that Chinese farmers were not invariably laborers. See also Sucheng Chan's bibliography, "Asian Americans: A Selected Bibliography of Writings Published Since the 1960s," in *Reflections on Shattered Windows*, ed. Gary Y. Okihiro et al. (Pullman: Washington State University Press, 1988), 214–237.

12. Chan, *This Bittersweet Soil*, chap. 3–8.

13. Robert Higgs, "The Wealth of Japanese Tenant Farmers in California, 1909," *Agricultural History* 53, no. 2 (1979): 488–493; Yuji Ichioka, "Japanese Immigrant Response to the 1920 California Alien Land Law," *Agricultural History* 58, no. 2 (1983): 157–178.

14. Japanese Agricultural Association, *The Japanese Farmers in California* (San Francisco: Japanese Agricultural Association, 1918); and Ichioka, "Japanese Immigrant Response."

15. H. Brett Melendy, *Asians in America* (New York: Hippocrene Press, 1981), 166, 231.

16. Elvin Hatch, "Stratification in a Rural California Community," *Agricultural History* 49 (1975): 33.

17. Chan, *This Bittersweet Soil*; Higgs, "Wealth of Japanese Tenant Farmers"; and Ichioka, "Response of Japanese Immigrants."

18. Hatch, "Stratification," 34.

19. See Chan, "Asian Americans."

20. Anti-miscegnation laws were on the books in California until 1948. A special act was passed in 1933 to make sure the Filipinos (termed "Malays") were included. The California Supreme Court abolished these laws in 1948: Melendy, *Asians in America*, 52–53.

21. Lucie Cheng Hirata, "Free, Indentured, Enslaved: Chinese Prostitutes in Nineteenth-Century California," *Signs: Journal of Women in Culture and Society* 5 (1979): 3–29; and Chan, *This Bittersweet Soil*, 386–402.

22. Emma Gee, "Issei Women," in *Counterpoint: Perspectives on Asian America*, ed. Emma Gee (Los Angeles: University of California, Los Angeles, Asian American Studies Center, 1976), 359–364; Harry H. L. Kitano, *Japanese Americans: The Evolution of a Subculture* (Englewood Cliffs, N.J.: Prentice Hall, 1976), 39–40; Yuji Ichioka, "*Amerika Nadeshiko*: Japanese Immigrant Women in the United States. 1900–1924," *Pacific Historical Review* 44 (1980): 339–357; Yuji Ichioka, "*Amerika-*

san: Japanese Prostitutes in Nineteenth-Century America," *Amerasia Journal* 4, no. 1 (1984); 157–178; and Akemi Kikumura, *Through Harsh Winters: The Life of a Japanese Immigrant Woman* (Novato, Calif.: Chandler and Sharp, 1981).

23. Melendy, *Asians in America*, 127; Sonia S. Sunoo, "Korean Women Pioneers of the Pacific Northwest," *Oregon Historical Quarterly* 79 (1978): 51–63; and Eun Sik Yang, "Korean Women of America: From Subordination to Partnership, 1902–1930," *Amerasia Journal* 11, no. 2 (1984): 1–28.

24. Emily Brown gives a cumulative figure of 6,656 for 1899–1913: "Revolution in India: Made in America," *Population Review* 25, nos. 1 and 2 (1982): 41. Gary Hess gives 7,300 for 1899–1920, "The Asian Indian Immigrants in the United States, 1900–1965," *Population Review* 25, nos. 1 and 2 (1982): 29. Bruce La Brack uses Rajani Kanta Das, *Hindustani Workers on the West Coast* (Berlin: Walter de Gruyter, 1923), and Jogesh C. Misrow's 1915 Master's thesis, subsequently published as *East Indian Immigration on the Pacific Coast* (San Francisco: R and E Research Associates, 1971), to arrive at a maximum of 6,400 between 1906 and 1920: *Sikhs of Northern California*, 78–79, 103.

25. H. A. Millis, "East Indian Immigration to the Pacific Coast," *Survey* 28, no. 9 (1912): 381.

26. California State Board of Control, *California and the Oriental* (Sacramento: State Printing Office, 1922), 115–116. John Higham, *Send These to Me: Immigrants in Urban America* (Baltimore: Johns Hopkins University Press, 1984), 194–195, discusses the concern for purity and pollution behind American nativism and racism from 1890 to 1924.

27. Government of India Census Report, 1931, figures cited by Paul Wallace, "Ethnic Identities in Transformation: Violence in the Punjab," paper given at the Association for Asian Studies, San Francisco, 1988, 3.

28. Harjot S. Oberoi, "From Ritual to Counter-Ritual: Rethinking the Hindu Sikh Question, 1884–1915," in *Sikh History and Religion in the Twentieth Century*, ed. Joseph T. O'Connell et al. (Toronto: Centre for South Asian Studies, 1988), 136–158. I found, as did Hew McLeod in his investigation of early Punjabi immigrants to New Zealand, that some individuals were difficult to categorize and that religion for Hindus and Sikhs was not necessarily an important marker. H. W. McLeod, personal communication, December 1986.

29. I thought of going to visit the home villages of the immigrants to California, but India's Punjab was frequently closed to foreigners because of militant Sikh activities in the 1980s. I did go to one ancestral village, Padhana, just outside Lahore, Pakistan, in August 1989.

30. Joyce Pettigrew, *Robber Noblemen: A Study of the Political System of the Sikh Jats* (Boston: Routledge and Kegan Paul, 1975), 59. She also discusses the historical and cultural legitimation of killing.

31. Ibid., 55.

32. Ibid., 18–19.

33. Ibid., 44. As McLeod points out, this horizontal relationship is most important and tenacious: H. W. McLeod *The Evolution of the Sikh Community* (Oxford: Clarendon Press, 1976), 89–90; and see his descriptions of the major Sikh castes, 95–103.

34. Tom Kessinger, *Vilyatpur 1848–1968* (Berkeley and Los Angeles: University of California Press, 1974), 31–34; and Dolores Domin, "Some Aspects of British Land Policy in Punjab After Its Annexation in 1949," *Punjab Past and Present* 8 (1974): 19–20.

35. Philip Woodruff, *The Man Who Ruled India: The Founders* (London: J. Cape, 1953), 1:334–343.

36. Richard Fox, *Lions of the Punjab* (Berkeley and Los Angeles: University of California Press, 1985), 35–39.

37. Kessinger, *Vilyatpur.*

38. Malcolm Lyall Darling, *Rusticus Loquitur, or the Old Light and the New in the Punjab Village* (London: Humphrey Milford, Oxford University Press, 1930), 28; and Fox, *Lions*, 47.

39. Darling, *Rusticus Loquitur*, 27; and Malcolm Lyall Darling, *The Punjab Peasant in Prosperity and Debt*, 4th ed. (New York: Oxford University Press, 1947), 26–28. See H. J. Habakkuk, "Family Structure and Economic Change in Nineteenth-Century Europe," *Journal of Economic History* 15, no. 1 (1955): 9, for the prediction that an increase in productivity in regions of equal division tends to exhaust itself in an increase in population and accelerates division of the land.

40. Darling, *Punjab Peasant*, 42–48.

41. Ibid., 67–69, citing pp. 7 and 500 of a 1925 Civil Justice Committee Report (no further bibliographic information). See also his comment on p. 68 regarding the litigious nature of Punjab peasants in the central districts.

42. Fox, *Lions*, 37.

43. For the figures, see Dewitt C. Ellinwood, Jr., "An Historical Study of the Punjabi Soldier in World War I," in *Panjab Past and Present: Essays in Honor of Dr. Ganda Singh,* ed. N. Gerald Barrier and Harbans Singh (Patiala, India: Punjabi University, 1976), 340–341. See Fox, *Lions,* 45–46, about violence in the central Punjab.

44. W. H. McLeod, "The First Forty Years of Sikh Migration," in *The Sikh Diaspora,* ed. N. Gerald Barrier and Verne Dusenbery (Delhi and Columbia, Mo.: Manohar and South Asia Publications, 1989), 36–37.

45. Darling, *Punjab Peasant*, 117.

46. Darling, *Rusticus Loquitur*, 178.

47. Lee M'Crae, "Self-Exiled in America," *Missionary Review of the World* 39 (July 1916): 526.

48. Darling, *Rusticus Loquitur*, 28–29.

49. On March 16, 1925, the British consul general in San Francisco wrote Professor Eliot Mears of the Survey of Race Relations, Stanford University, remarking that the California State Board of Control's 1920 figure of 2,600 British Indians in California, three-quarters of them Sikhs, did not jibe with the 1920 census's total number of departures from San Francisco for India: "Survey of Race Relations," box 36, no. 371, Hoover Institution Archives, Stanford, California. Brown, "Revolution in India," 42, says the "overwhelming majority" of the immigrants were Sikhs; La Brack, *Sikhs of Northern California,* 81, says the majority were single Punjabi Sikhs.

50. Estimates of the percentage of soldiers among the immigrants are vague. See Brown, "Revolution in India," 42, and La Brack, *Sikhs of Northern California,* 62. My own impression is that a majority of the immigrants had worked in the military or police or related imperial services before coming to California from many places, including Bombay, Calcutta, Manila, Beirut, and Honolulu.

51. *India West,* July 22, 1983, copied from Reuters in Hong Kong, reported that the Indian troops were used in the Opium Wars of 1841, than more than 2,000 Indians were in Hong Kong when the British flag was hoisted there, and that Muslims and Sikhs were recruited in the 1870s for Hong Kong's police force. For the *gurdwara,* see Mahinder Singh Dhillon, *A History Book of the Sikhs in Canada and California* (Vancouver: Shromani Akali Dal Association of Canada, 1981), 166.

52. Dhillon, *History Book,* 33–34.

53. Sucheta Mazumdar, "Colonial Impact and Punjabi Emigration to the United States," in *Labor Immigration under Capitalism,* ed. Lucie Cheng and Edna Bonacich (Berkeley and Los Angeles: University of California Press, 1984), 331–333. In Los Angeles in 1983, George Puri told me that his father, Ramnath Puri, had worked around 1909 at bringing in Punjabis under contracts. Kartar Dhillon's father told about circulating leaflets among Indian workers on behalf of American companies when he returned to China and India after his 1887 visit working for the merchant marine (letter of May 11, 1989). La Brack, *Sikhs of Northern California,* 60–64, found little or no evidence of recruitment by steamship companies or of indentured labor in California; and in New Zealand, McLeod, "First Forty Years," 70, found that few if any Doaba immigrants had come with indenture agreements.

54. Fred Lockely, "The Hindu Invasion," *Pacific Monthly* 17 "1907): 593.

55. "Survey of Race Relations," Sucha Singh, August 8, 1924, interview by William C. Smith in Venice, California, box 29, no. 46.

56. Mola Singh, Selma, 1983, and Charn S. Sandhu, Calipatria, 1984. The final two are Kakoo Singh, in Peter Odens, *Pioneerland Below the Sea* (Calexico: Calexico Chronicle, ca. 1970), 48–50; and Sardar Puna Singh, "My Early Years in America," *Sikh Sansar* 1, no. 4 (1972): 109.

57. Nand Singh Sihra, "Indians in Canada," *Modern Review* (Calcutta) 14, no. 2 (1913): 140–149; and Norman Buchignani, Doreen M. Indra, and Ram Srivastava,

Continuous Journey: A Social History of South Asians in Canada (Toronto: McClelland and Stewart, 1985), 204–205.

58. Figures from Harold S. Jacoby, "Administrative Restriction of Asian Indian Immigration into the United States, 1907–1917," *Population Review* 25 (1982): 37; and Millis, "East Indian Immigration," 381.

59. "Hindus Fight Exclusion," *New York Times*, December 7, 1913, seen in the preliminary National Endowment for the Humanities exhibit assembled by Jane Singh, "History of South Asian Immigration," Oakland, Calif., November 13, 1982. Jacoby, "Administrative Restriction," 38, points out that the Bureau of Customs administrators in the Philippines were not as anti-Asian as those in the mainland United States.

60. Jacoby, "Administrative Restriction," 39; and Charles Hartshorn Maxson, *Citizenship* (New York: Oxford University Press, 1930), 213. Joan M. Jensen, *Passage from India: Asian Indian Immigrants in North America* (New Haven: Yale University Press, 1988), 339, argues that immigration ended effectively in 1914.

61. "Survey of Race Relations," Inder Singh, May 31, 1924, El Centro, interview by W.C.S., box 29, no. 273. In my interviews, Charn S. Sandhu had no passport and paid $5 to get off the ship in San Francisco, while Mola Singh was put back on the ship because he answered questions wrong the first time and had to make the journey again (interviewed in, respectively, Calipatria, 1982, and Selma, 1983).

62. Millis, "East Indian Immigration," 384; Misrow, *East Indian Immigration*, 25–28; and Das, *Hindustani Workers*, 18–20.

63. For the San Francisco Muslims, interviews with Joe Mallobox, El Centro, 1982, and Robert Mohammed, Yuba City, 1983; other interviews with Charn S. Sandhu, Calipatria, 1982, and Mola Singh, Selma, 1983.

64. Dhillon, *History Book*, 155–158; and Buchignani, Indra, and Srivastava, *Continuous Journey*, 220–221.

65. Ali Abdulla (Fresno, 1983), for the Punjabi connection with Rocky Ford; for the Japanese, Shiro Fujioka, "Traces of a Journey," typed translation by Mabel Saito Hall of the Japanese *Ayumi No Ato* (Los Angeles: Kanko Koenkai, 1957), 470. I thank Sucheng Chan for a copy of this manuscript translation, which she commissioned. Also Paul Schuster Taylor, "Field Notes for His Book Mexican Labor in the United States, 1917–1930," ed. Abraham Hoffman, Bancroft Library, University of California, Berkeley, 61–66 (Along the Rio Grande El Paso to Brownsville) and 103–107a (Labor Contractors and Agencies) for cotton in Texas.

66. California State Commission of Immigration and Housing. *Report on Fresno's Immigration Problem* (1918), 9; California State Board of Control, *California and the Oriental*, 125; and for Marysville and the Imperial Valley, personal observation.

67. For the Los Angeles residences and occupations (checked for Singh only),

see the *Los Angeles City Directory including San Pedro and Wilmington* (Los Angeles: Los Angeles Directory Company, 1910–1918), in the University of California, Los Angeles, University Research Library (now on microfilm there). One Singh was an inmate at the county hospital. More entries appear after these early years.

68. The Sanger quote is from "Race Relations Survey," box 28, no. 90, interview with William Richardson, manager of the L. Powers Fruit Company and former foreman of the Lucius Powers ranch in Sanger, February 18, 1925; the other quotes are from Eliot Grinnell Mears, "The Land, the Crops and the Oriental: A Study of Race Relations in Terms of the Map," *The Survey* 56, no. 3 (1926): 148. In the American Midwest, there was concern about German and Scandinavian intermarriage and its consequences for the capacities of the farming population! Edmund deS. Brunner, *Immigrant Farmers and Their Children* (New York: Doubleday, Doran, 1929).

69. The relevant paragraphs read, in Fujioka, "Traces of a Journey," 465–466:

> After overcoming such stage of hardships, each engaged in the farming he liked. Needless to say some of them failed in spite of their hard work, and some were blessed by the god of luck and dashed forward on the road to success. Successful or not, they were trained by hardship, and there existed, so to speak, the rivalry of powerful warlords.
>
> If we follow the example of China's history of the Three Kingdoms and divide the Imperial Valley into three parts leaving out the cotton growers on the border, there was Mr. Kikutaro Nishimoto in the southern area, Mr. Shonan Kimura in the central part around Holtville and El Centro, and in the northern area around Brawley was Mr. Rika Takahashi. They were, so to speak, Wu Ti, Shu Han and Wei of the Three Kingdoms.

70. Karen Leonard, "Finding One's Own Place: The Imposition of Asian Landscapes on Rural California," in *Culture, Power, Place: Explorations in Critical Anthropology*, ed. James Ferguson, Akhil Gupta, and Roger Rouse (Boulder, Colo.: Westview Press, forthcoming).

71. The period from A.D. 220 to 317, a time of political disunity in Chinese history, inspired many works of fiction about the internecine wars of the Three Kingdoms. While Japanese history features several periods of two kingdoms feuding, it does not feature three. The Japanese immigrants were a relatively well-educated group and easily appropriated and used Chinese history here.

72. Singh, "My Early Years," 109.

73. Bobby Singh Sanga, Brawley, 1987 (by Lupe Beltran); Alfred Sidhu, Sacramento, 1982; Uttam Dhillon, San Diego, 1988 (with Gurdit and Dharmo Dhillon); Mola Singh, Selma, 1982.

74. Hari Singh Everest, "Letter to the Editor," *Sikh Sansar* 1, no. 1 (1972): 31.

He describes other similarities in the late 1960s. Everest came after citizenship and immigration rights were won through the Luce-Celler bill in 1946 and the 1965 Immigration and Naturalization Act. Another nostalgic account is by Gurnam Singh Sidhu, "Saga of the American Sikh," *Sikh Sansar* 1, no. 4 (1972): 102.

75. Comaroff, "Totemism and Ethnicity," 303–304.

Chapter 3. Early Days in the Imperial Valley

1. *El Centro Progress*, December 5, 1919, 33, 80, 44; Harold Bell Wright, *The Winning of Barbara Worth* (Chicago: Book Supply Company, 1911). The 1926 film starred Ronald Colman and Gary Cooper as the young civil engineers. The 1920 county population figure was 43,453. U.S. Department of Commerce, Bureau of the Census, *Fourteenth Census of the United States: Population, 1920* (Washington, D.C.: Government Printing Office, 1921–1923), 3:113.

2. William Irvin Darnell, "The Imperial Valley: Its Physical and Cultural Geography," Master's Thesis, San Diego State College, 1959, 82–83.

3. "Imperial Valley First," *Valley Grower* (El Centro), Summer 1982, 38, for the first drive from Long Beach and the first phone call.

4. *El Centro Progress*, December 5, 1919, 122.

5. U.S. Department of Commerce, *Fourteenth Census: Population, 1920*, 3:109–110, 112–117, 123–124. Imperial County had the highest proportion among California counties of people born in Mexico, 14.7 percent, followed by Ventura County with 14.1 percent and San Bernardino County with 9.7 percent: Allyn Campbell Loosley, "Foreign Born Population of California, 1848–1920," Master's Thesis, University of California, Berkeley, 1927, 114–115.

6. "Survey of Race Relations," no. 232, Ram Chand, p. 4, interviewed by W. C. Smith, June 1, 1924, El Centro.

7. Joseph J. Anderholt and Dorothy M. Anderholt, eds., *The History of the Imperial Valley Swiss* (Holtville: Imperial Valley Swiss Club, 1984), 10, 7–8.

8. U.S. Department of Commerce, Bureau of the Census, *Thirteenth Census of the United States taken in the year of 1910; Abstract of the Census with Supplement for California* (Washington, D.C.: Government Printing Office, 1913), 601, for the 1910 Census sex ratio; for 1920, U.S. Department of Commerce, *Fourteenth Census: Population, 1920*, 3:113, 131.

9. Fujioka, "Traces of a Journey," 464–465.

10. F. C. Farr, *The History of Imperial County, California* (Berkeley: Elms and Frank, 1918), 480; Anderholt and Anderholt, *Imperial Valley Swiss*.

11. Irma Wheat, El Centro, 1982; Carl Jacobson, Brawley, 1981.

12. Lester Reed, *Oldtimers of Southeastern California* (Redlands: Lester Reed, 1967), 11, 291–292, 225.

13. Mola Singh, Selma, 1982.

14. Criminal Case 987, Office of the County Clerk, Imperial County, 1921.

15. Kathryn Cramp, Louise F. Shields, and Charles A. Thomsen, "Study of the Mexican Population in Imperial Valley, California," University of California, Berkeley, Bancroft Library, 1926), 15–19. Mimeographed.

16. Darnell, "Imperial Valley," 90–91.

17. Mrs. Wiley M. Weaver, *Imperial Valley 1901–1915* (Los Angeles: Board of Supervisors, 1915), 5; Farr, *History of Imperial County*, 68; and Darnell, "Imperial Valley," 95.

18. See Darnell, "Imperial Valley," 95. Japanese farmers also claimed to be pioneers in these crops: Fujioka, "Traces of a Journey," 466–477, for lettuce and cotton; U.S. Government, War Relocation Authority, *Japanese Population of Imperial Valley* (Washington, D.C.: Community Analysis Section, 1945), 2.

19. Darnell, "Imperial Valley," 90–105; and Adon Poli, *Land Ownership and Operating Tenure in Imperial Valley, California* (Berkeley: U.S. Bureau of Agricultural Economics, 1942). For the escalation, see Robert L. Finley, "An Economic History of the Imperial Valley of California to 1971," Ph.D. dissertation, University of Oklahoma, 1974, 158.

20. Alvin S. Tostlebe, *Capital in Agriculture: Its Formation and Financing Since 1870* (Princeton: Princeton University Press, 1957), 219–228, provides statistics on sources of credit for the Pacific States, Delta, Corn Belt, Appalachian, Northeast, Lake, Mountain, Texas-Oklahoma, Southeast, and Great Plains.

21. See the discussion in Finley, "Economic History," 153–157; also Joseph Anderholt, Holtville, 1984. The F.O.B. system still provides for price adjustments dependent on the condition of the produce on arrival (giving an edge to buyers, many farmers feel).

22. See Poli, *Land Ownership*, 48, for 1910–1920; Cramp, Shields, and Thomsen, "Mexican Population," 2, for the proportion of absentee owners. With respect to Poli's figures for later decades, there is no discussion of the effect of the Alien Land Laws and possible Anglo leasing or owning of land on behalf of Asians.

23. Poli, *Land Ownership*, 49–51; Cramp, Shields, Thomsen, "Mexican Population," 2.

24. By the measure of value of production per acre, the Imperial Valley was the most productive: Howard F. Gregor, "Regional Hierarchies in California Agricultural Production: 1939–1954," *Annals of the Association of American Geographers* 53 (1963): 30.

25. *Holtville Tribune*, October 21, 1910.

26. *Holtville Tribune*, September 16, 1910.

27. *Holtville Tribune*, August 20 and September 9, 1915.

28. *Holtville Tribune*, October 6, 1915.

29. *Holtville Tribune*, October 10, 1914; *El Centro Progress*, February 2, 1915.

30. *Holtville Tribune*, October 6, 1915.

31. *Holtville Tribune*, March 31, 1916. *U.S. Statutes at Large, Sixty-fourth Congress*, vol. 39, p. 1, 2nd sess., December 1915–May 1917, chap. 29, "An Act to Regulate the Immigration of Aliens to, and the Residence of Aliens in, the United States" (Washington, D.C.: Government Printing Office, 1917), 876, for the specific meridians in the 1917 law. See also Jacoby, "Administrative Restriction," 39.

32. *Holtville Tribune*, February 4, 1918. As early as 1907, the *California Fruit Grower* predicted that men from India working in the Fresno vineyards would not long be satisfied to labor in the fields: "The Labor Problem," August 24, 1907, 1.

33. *Holtville Tribune*, January 24, 1918.

34. Robert Hays, in Taylor, "Field Notes," ca. 1928. Hays's own Punjabi tenant in 1924, Sucha Singh Dhalliwal, went on to become one of Holtville's biggest Punjabi farmers: Civil Case 9632, Office of the County Clerk, Imperial County, 1924 (for the owner–tenant relationship).

35. The continuity of residence on Commercial Avenue in El Centro is striking—boardinghouses in which some Punjabis lived and died were located there, and the Sikh temple is there today.

36. Was the latter Albert Joe? (See Chapter 6 for his murder.)

37. U.S. National Archives, Record Group 29, Census of U.S. Population, Imperial County, California, 1910 (manuscript census).

38. Joseph Anderholt told me about the post office books in the Holtville City Hall. U.S. Postmaster General, "Register of Money Orders Issued, Jan. 2, 1909 through Nov. 5, 1910, and July 16, 1912, through Dec. 18, 1913."

39. This man, if he was the Rahmatulla recalled later, was certainly literate and became one of the leaders of the Punjabis in Phoenix. Millis, "East Indian Immigration," 386, estimated that between one-half and three-fifths of the Punjabi immigrants were unable to read or write.

40. The land records are in the Recorder's Office, El Centro. The directories were consulted in the Imperial Public Library, now relocated in El Centro. Early issues were titled *Imperial Valley Business and Resident Directory* (1912–1913), *Thurston's Imperial Valley Directory* (1914–1921), and finally *Imperial Valley Directory* (1924–1926).

41. *Imperial County Pacific Telephone and Telegraph Company*, April 15, 1918 (in the Pioneers Museum, Imperial). In 1920, 39 percent of all U.S. farms had telephones, a percentage that dropped to 25 percent by 1940. Don F. Hadwiger and Clay Cochran, "Rural Telephones in the United States," *Agricultural History* 58, no. 3 (1984): 222. In 1925, only five Punjabis were telephone subscribers, a huge drop perhaps better explained by local implementation to the Alien Land Laws (leading to less secure tenancy) than to this nationwide decline. *Imperial County Pacific Telephone and Telegraph Company*, 1925.

42. *Holtville Tribune*, August 10, 1915.

43. *El Centro Progress*, July 16, 1920.

44. *El Centro Progress*, August 13, 1918.

45. *El Centro Progress*, March 19, 1915.

46. *El Centro Progress*, March 27, 1915, and later stories (e.g., March 28, 1915; October 21, 1920). It is probable that, as with other "Orientals," the offenses of Punjabis fell most often in the category of misdemeanors, and the men were not disproportionately involved in serious crimes. For this observation about Japanese and Chinese immigrants, see Walter G. Beach, *Oriental Crime in California* (New York: AMS Press, 1971; first published 1932), 92–95.

47. The murderer was Charles Stanton. *El Centro Progress*, July 7, 1920; *Holtville Tribune*, October 26, 1914, December 27 and 28, 1915, and January 3, 1916.

48. John Sanford, *The Land That Touches Mine* (New York: Doubleday, 1953), 41. She went on to say, "Now's the time the women start clearing out for Coronado and La Jolla—the ones with money. The others, the ones like me, we get ready to fry by shedding our clothes." The hot weather starts about the first of June, in the middle of the cantaloupe picking season. F. A. Stahl, *Rolling Stones* (Glendale, Calif.: Wetzel Publishing, 1928), also depicts local life well.

49. *Holtville Tribune*, October 16, 1915.

50. *Holtville Tribune*, October 18, 1916.

51. *Holtville Tribune*, May 4, 1918. The demographic differences among the valley towns were considerable. Aliens had to register at the local post offices in 1921. Of those who registered in El Centro, Japanese were by far the most numerous, while about half of the more than seventy who registered in Holtville were Punjabis and half were Swiss, with just a few Japanese. *Holtville Tribune*, July 29, 1921. In El Paso, Texas, the county agent observed that Japanese farmers there contributed to civic affairs, but the Hindus did not: Taylor, "Field Notes," 85–90.

52. California State Board of Control, *California and the Oriental*, 47–48.

53. Keith Savage, Holtville, 1981. In the El Paso area, Paul Taylor was told in 1927 that "all the Hindus farm for themselves." Taylor, "Field Notes," 61–66.

54. Higgs, "Japanese Tenant Farmers," 492.

55. Puron Sedoo, Fresno, 1982, and Mola Singh, Selma, 1983.

56. Sucheng Chan, University of California, Santa Barbara, made her notes on these leases available to me, but thought her information was incomplete. These leases, like other early sources, show the Sikhs arriving slightly later than the Muslims and Hindus from the Punjab. According to most estimates, only 5 percent of all leases made were recorded before World War I, a percentage rising to only 20 percent by World War II. Interviews with Joseph Anderholt, Holtville, 1981, and Jim Bailey, El Centro, 1981. (The same 20 percent estimate for the two decades before World War II was obtained independently by Sucheng Chan from the recorder of San Joaquin County. Personal communication, 1982.)

57. Tenants with partners were poorer than those without, in the Japanese cases for 1909 studied by Higgs, "Japanese Tenant Farmers," 492. He points out that partnerships were for those who *needed* to pool resources. Significantly, I think, the written partnership agreement between Ganga Ram, Dalal Singh, Bhama and Baryama of December 20, 1920 is typed on stationery from the Holtville Bank. Copy furnished by Helen Ram Walsh, Hercules, 1989.

58. *Rur Singh* v. *Puran Singh and Kartar Singh*, Civil Case 4746, Office of the County Clerk, Imperial County, 1918. The man who kept the books, the plaintiff, signed in English, as did the two translators.

59. Civil Case 8395, Office of the County Clerk, Imperial County, 1922.

60. *Moola Singh* v. *Georgia May Singh*, Civil Case 11015, Office of the County Clerk, Imperial County 1923.

61. These percentages are based on 58 of 2,400 and 179 of 9,300. Office of the County Clerk, Imperial County. See also notes 1 and 6. "Hindoo" or "Hindu" was a category in court records. In Calexico, the groups were Caucasians, Mexicans, Negroes, and Japanese-Chinese-Hindoos; in Imperial, they were Americans, Mexicans, Negroes, Portuguese, Japanese, and Hindoo; in El Centro, they were white, Mexican, Negroes, Japanese, Chinese, and Hindus; and in Brawley, they were Americans, Mexicans, Negroes, Japanese, and Hindus. Cramp, Shields, and Thomsen, "Mexican Population," 12.

62. U.S. Government, Los Angeles District Court, "Bankruptcy Records for Indexes I, II, and III (1907–1917, 1917–1925, 1925–1932)," Laguna Niguel Federal Archives. For one thing, the literacy rate was higher than the 50 percent rate shown in immigration statistics or the 17 percent rate recorded in the census of 1910 for Imperial County. Perhaps because the partnerships were represented by the best-educated man, 57 percent of the petitioners signed in a good English hand. Another 30 percent signed in ragged English or Punjabi script, while only 11 percent signed with an X. Corroborating the high level of debt, Fujioka, "Traces," mentions that banks would lend up to 80 percent of the amount needed to produce cotton (p. 477) and gives an instance of a Takasaburo Go, who went bankrupt and owed $750,000 to a Calexico bank (p. 481).

63. U.S. Government, "Bankruptcy Records," Punjabi claims. A blanket was a staple item for agricultural laborers, who were called "blanket boys" or "blanket carriers," e.g., the Japanese migratory fieldhands in Kazuo Miyamoto, *Hawaii: End of the Rainbow* (Rutland, Vt.: Tuttle, 1964), 219–220, as cited by Higgs, "Japanese Tenant Farmers," 492.

64. U.S. Government, "Bankruptcy Records," cases 6212, 4752, and 6160.

65. Ibid., cases 5985, 4352, 6121, and 6170 for the quotes.

66. Jacoby, "More Thind Against"; and Karen Leonard, "Punjabi Farmers and California's Alien Land Law," *Agricultural History* 59, no. 4 (1985): 549–562.

67. *Literary Digest*, March 10, 1923, 13.

68. "Survey of Race Relations," no. 408, E. Chandler to Mr. George Gleason, May 2, 1924.

69. Mary Gill, Lala Garewal, and Silveria Chell, Holtville, 1981; Harry Chand, Live Oak, 1982. Arizona enacted a similar discriminatory law in 1921. California State Board of Control, *California and the Oriental*, 69–72. Robert Mohammed remembers driving from Yuba City to Phoenix with older Punjabis for public meetings on this in 1934 (Yuba City, 1982). The *Arizona Republic* has many articles in August 1934 on protests against the growing number of successful Japanese and Hindu farmers, including Alien Land Law cases filed against M. Rahmatulla and A. R. Webster (August 21) and against C. Bicham Singh and Ana Marie Zuniga (August 26). The latter pair are C. Bishen Singh and his mother-in-law.

70. One unusually well-educated man, Ram Chand, stated: "The alien land law has made the future somewhat uncertain and so I am looking around for some other means of livelihood. I am now taking a commercial course by correspondence from the International Correspondence School. A friend of mine suggested that I take up the practice of law but it would now be impossible for me to practice in the courts. I should like to be a citizen of the United States and have made application but have not been granted any naturalization papers." "Survey of Race Relations," box 29, no. 232, Ram Chand, June 1, 1924, El Centro; interview by William C. Smith.

71. See Karen Leonard, "The Pahkar Singh Murders: A Punjabi Response to California's Alien Land Law," *Amerasia Journal* 11, no. 1 (1984): 75–87.

72. Mary Garewal Gill, Holtville, 1981; Fernando Singh Sanga, Brawley, 1981; Mola Singh, Selma, 1983.

73. Carl Jacobson of the Brawley Bank visited Pahker Singh in San Quentin; Singh sent Christmas cards to Jacobson and to County Sheriff Herbert Hughes. "Pahkar Singh was a Christian gentleman," Jacobson told me. Carl Jacobson, Brawley, 1981, and Herbert Hughes, Holtville, 1981 (with C. M. Naim).

74. Mary Garewal Gill, Holtville, 1981; Bagga S. Sunga, Brawley, 1981; Fernando Sanga, Brawley,1981; Pritam Sandhu, Calipatria, 1990.

75. "Survey of Race Relations, box 29, no. 273, Inder Singh, May 31, 1924, El Centro; interview by W.C.S.

76. The Cable Act, in effect from 1922 through 1931, provided that female (but not male) citizens marrying aliens ineligible for citizenship lost their citizenship: *U.S. Statutes at Large, Sixty-seventh Congress*, 2nd sess. vol. 42, p. 1, Public Laws, 1921–1923, chap. 411: "An Act Relative to the Naturalization and Citizenship of Married Women" (Washington, D.C.: Government Printing Office, 1923), 1021–1022. Section 370 was repealed in 1931.

77. Although perhaps this was not always overlooked, since one man placed his land in the name of his mother-in-law instead of his wife: C. Bishen Singh and Anamaria Zuniga, June 17, 1925. General Index, Book of Deeds, Grantors, Recorder's Office, Imperial County, b. 84, p. 83. According to Mary Garewal Gill

(Holtville, 1981), her mother held land from 1924 to 1933. Harry Chand (Live Oak, 1982) said his mother held land for several Punjabis. In the Index to Book of Deeds, July 1, 1923–July 1, 1927, Recorder's Office, Imperial County, couples and wives suddenly appear for the first time. Sawarn Singh, in Joe Applegate, "Fire in the Valley," *Reader* (San Diego) 10, no. 31 (August 6, 1981): 9, got land through his American-born wife, apparently just after the repeal of the Cable Act.

78. This farmer, Omar Deen, put up tents with hanging gas lanterns for his laborers. He preferred to employ Anglos who were Holy Rollers, but he also hired Mexicans and Filipinos. The laborers lined up on payday, and he and his wife paid them all in cash. He usually set up his own packing shed and hired Japanese or Anglo crews for that work. Elizabeth Deen Hernandez, Burbank, 1981.

79. Keith Savage, El Centro, 1981; Joseph Anderholt, Holtville, 1981; Bob and Karmen Chell, Holtville, 1981. Similarly, Bernice Sidhu, Brawley, 1981, about her father-in-law, Kehar S. Sidhu.

80. Inder Singh traveled to Los Angeles to ask a dairy owner to give him management of the Imperial Valley concern; Mola Singh went there to confront a big cotton company and demand that he, not the man in whose name the lease was written, be given the money. Anglos were used as checks on Hispanic relatives. When Mola Singh felt he had to turn to his Mexican brother-in-law to put a lease in his name, he gave an Anglo storeowner a second mortgage on the property, to prevent the brother-in-law from simply taking the property himself. Francisco Singh, Selma, 1983 (about his father, Inder Singh); Mola Singh, Selma, 1982.

81. There were at least four such corporations in the Imperial Valley. Bagga S. Sunga, El Centro, 1981.

82. The defendants had formed the California–Nevada Land Company: J. Labh Singh, Moola Singh, Mehar Singh, Rolla Singh, Ray Johnson, N.J. Robbins, Carroll L. Post, Fred J. Hauseur, and Eugene Kelly. Harold Jacoby reported that the "Hindustanee Welfare and Reform Society" officers raised money for their defense but turned down an offer to fix the jury, confident that they could get the (expected) conviction set aside by the state appellate court. The prosecution had not established the Punjabi defendants' ineligibility for citizenship in the course of the trial. Harold S. Jacoby, "East Indians in the United States: The First Half-Century," Manuscript, 1978, 390–391. Imperial County did not retry them.

83. Probate records, Office of the County Clerk, Imperial County; quote from Herbert Hughes (former sheriff of Imperial County), Holtville, 1981.

84. Elizabeth Harris, with Robert and Karmen Chell, Holtville, 1981; Herbert Hughes, Holtville, 1981 (on receiving live turkeys).

85. Roy Womack, El Centro, 1981; Joseph and Dorothy Anderholt, Holtville, 1981.

86. Keith Savage, Holtville, 1981; Dharmo and Gurdit Dhillon, San Diego, 1988.

87. Roy Womack, El Centro, 1981.

88. Allen Griffin, Brawley, 1981; Joseph Anderholt, Holtville, 1981; Lorelei Griffin Jacobson, Brawley, 1981.

89. Joseph and Dorothy (Brown) Anderholt, Holtville, 1982.

90. Joe Mallobox, El Centro, 1982.

91. Allen Griffin, Brawley, 1981; Lorelei Griffin Jacobson, Brawley, 1981; Elizabeth Harris, Holtville, 1981; Bob and Karmen Chell, Holtville, 1981; Irma Wheat, El Centro, 1981.

92. The low point may have been 1918, when a lawyer asked for a change of venue because of the strong prejudice caused by alleged perjury by Hindus in local trials: Criminal Case 705, Office of the County Clerk, Imperial County, 1918.

93. "Survey and Race Relations," No. 232, Ram Chand, June 1, 1924.

94. "Report of the Grand Jury of the County of Imperial, State of California, for the year 1930–31, filed November 30, 1931," 5. Office of the County Clerk, Imperial County.

95. The Japanese had been indicted in 1925. *Imperial Valley Press,* July 30 and August 4, 1925.

96. Criminal Case 2731, Office of the County Clerk, Imperial County, 1933. The other points are given in full in Leonard, "Punjabi Farmers." The grand jury reports for 1925 and 1933 are missing from the courthouse, and it is alleged that a legislator absconded with them about 1946. Harry Free, county clerk since 1952, El Centro, 1982.

97. Joseph Anderholt, Holtville, 1981; Keith Savage, Holtville, 1981 (about Sucha Singh Garewal).

98. Keith Savage, of the Holtville Bank, Holtville, 1981; Carl Jacobson, of the Brawley Bank, Brawley, 1981.

99. Grateful for this help, Mohamed Baksh later set up an advantageous land purchase for his benefactor's sons. Joseph Anderholt, Holtville, 1981.

100. Keith Savage, Holtville, 1981, and Carl Jacobson, Brawley, 1981. Despite their recollections, Mexicans were depositors: 50 in the 1st National Bank of Holtville (30 had under $25 deposited and only 3 had over $200) and 126 in the Bank of Italy, Brawley (for a total of $20,804.15) around 1927. Paul Taylor, "Collection of Notes, etc. concerning Mexican Labor in the United States," University of California, Berkeley, Bancroft Library, carton 1, file "Statistics for Imperial County, California"; letters to Paul Taylor from the Holtville and Brawley banks dated May 31 and June 21, 1927, respectively.

101. The "champion" was Sawarn Singh, as recalled by his son Mike Singh in Applegate, "Fire in the Valley," 9. Joseph and Dorothy Anderholt found no record of this in their research on the Swiss and speculated that it might have been an exhibition match; Joseph does remember attending Punjabi matches. Holtville, 1990.

102. Karen Leonard, "Political Skills on a New Frontier," *South Asia* 12, no. 2 (1990): 69–81.

103. Idwal Jones, "Mr. Har Chand," *Westways* 1 (September 1939): 16–17.

104. Loretta Berner, "Sketches from 'Way Back,'" Long Beach, n.d. Manuscript.

105. Robert Chell, Holtville, 1981.

Chapter 4. Marriages and Children

1. Perhaps because the March license could not be implemented, Sher Singh took out another license (for another woman, too) in November. *Holtville Tribune*, March 16 and November 10, 1916.

2. *El Centro Progress*, April 5, 1918.

3. Mola Singh, Selma, 1982.

4. The phrase was used by the judge in a bankruptcy case: "Your wife is a Mexican girl, isn't she?" U.S. Government, "Bankruptcy Records," case 6212 (speaking of Refugio Gonzalez, wife of Malla Singh Deol). The Anglo witnesses were the farmer Shephard and County Horticultural Commissioner F. W. Waite, in 1916 and 1917 respectively.

5. Taylor, *Mexican Labor: Imperial Valley*, 6, reported that six Hindus had taken Japanese wives, but in 1982 Taylor was unable to recall his source. A Punjabi informant said this would have been impossible, that a Japanese girl had been sent to Japan for being too friendly with non-Japanese. Bagga S. Sunga, El Centro, 1982.

6. *Holtville Tribune* clipping from 1918 (month torn off); and *Holtville Tribune*, March 9 and 10, 1922; confirmed by Janie Diwan Poonian, daughter of one of the women, Yuba City, 1982.

7. Rosalinda M. Gonzalez, "Chicanas and Mexican Immigrant Families 1920–1940: Women's Subordination and Family Exploitation," in *Decades of Discontent*, ed. Joan Jensen and Lois Scharf (Westport, Conn.: Greenwood Press, 1983), 63; Ruth Allen, *The Labor of Women in the Production of Cotton*, University of Texas (Austin) Bulletin 3134, 1931.

8. For the Punjab, see Pettigrew, *Robber Noblemen*, 48; Darling, *Rusticus Loquitur*, 175–176; and Michelle Maskiell, "Women's Work and the Household Economy in Panjab," Sixteenth Conference on South Asia, Madison, Wisc., 1987, 3 and 7. James F. Elliott, "Cotton: A Love Story Across Cultures" (about Diwan Singh and Isabel Cabanillas) also noticed this. Clipping from Barbara Quade Lang, no journal name, Tucson, Ariz., 1988. See also Michelle Maskiell, "Gender, Kinship and Rural Work in Colonial Punjab," *Journal of Women's History* 2, no 1 (1990): 35–72.

9. Taylor, "Field Notes," file on Labor Contractors and Agencies, 103–107a.

10. See the many autobiographical statements in Manuel Gamio, ed., *The Life*

Story of the Mexican Immigrant (New York: Dover, 1971). And the well-known film star Anthony Quinn, born in Chihuahua in 1915, was taken by his mother and grandmother to El Paso in 1916. *Los Angeles Times*, August 31, 1981.

11. In the El Paso valley, Taylor interviewed one "Jan D. Singh" (probably the "Juan Singh" I found in county records), who told him that there were forty Hindus there growing cotton and that thirty-five of them had married Mexican women. Taylor, "Field Notes," 61–66.

12. Interview with the daughter of migratory workers in Sherry Thomas, *We Didn't Have Much, but We Sure Had Plenty: Stories of Rural Women* (New York: Anchor Press, 1981), 84. Las Cruces was the site of an experimental station for cotton started by Bill Camp in 1921. William J. Briggs and Henry Cauthen, *The Cotton Man: Life and Times of Wolford B. ("Bill") Camp* (Columbia: University of South Carolina Press, 1983), 101.

13. Sacramento County marriage license 40:459 for the marriage of Alice Singh and Dayal Singh, May 15, 1913. Ali Khan murdered Rosa Domingo in October 1913 because, according to the *Contra Costa Gazette* of October 25, 1913, "she was playing with him and taking all the money." Harold Jacoby brought this story to my attention.

14. Teresa Garewal, Holtville, 1981; marriage licenses 5:164 and 5:388, Imperial County Recorder's Office, El Centro.

15. Marriage license 5:447, Imperial County Recorder's Office. Albert Joe and Alejandrina also married in Imperial: marriage license 5:472 (Alejandrina's age was given there as eighteen); Ester married in Arizona.

16. Mary Garewal Gill, Holtville, 1981; Lala Sandoval Garewal and Silveria Chell and Robert Chell, Holtville, 1981.

17. Nellie Soto Shine and Caroline Shine Resendez, Huntington Beach, 1982; and Civil Case 10740, Office of the County Clerk, Imperial County, 1926.

18. Lucy Harper Sekhon, San Diego, 1982; marriage license 44:68, San Diego County. Antonia came and was courted by several Punjabis, but she did not marry.

19. For the quote, Mola Singh, Selma, 1982. The Urdu term for men married to sisters is *hamzulf,* "same hair." Paul Hershman and Hilary Standing, eds., *Punjabi Kinship and Marriage* (Delhi: Hindustan Publishing, 1981), 188, gives an example of brothers marrying sisters. Veena Das, "The Structure of Marriage Preferences: An Account from Pakistani Fiction," *Man* 8, no. 1 (1973): 39, mentions sister sets in Pakistani novels.

20. Lala Garewal, Holtville, 1981; Lucy Sekhon, San Diego, 1981; Verdie Montgomery, Sacramento, 1982; Teresa Garewal, Holtville, 1981.

21. My categories are based on marriage, settlement, and social network patterns. Others have traditionally broken the Central Valley into the Sacramento and San Joaquin valleys. For my categories, this would leave Sacramento County

in the north with Yuba and Sutter and move San Joaquin County into the center with Fresno, Tulare, and Kings. Bruce La Brack used four divisions when he reanalyzed Harold Jacoby's data: the Imperial Valley, Fresno, Stockton/Sacramento, and the Northern Sacramento Valley. Note that the frequencies of "East Indian-Mexican" marriages in these last two divisions in La Brack, *Sikhs of Northern California*, are identical, supporting my combining of these two divisions into one and their separation from the Fresno or central category. Ann Wood found the Stockton *Gurdwara* congregation organized into four geographical regions, similar to La Brack's but with two additional regions: Stockton, Yuba City/Marysville, Fresno, the Imperial Valley, the Bay Area, and, after 1935, El Paso, Texas and Casa Grande, Arizona. Wood, "East Indians in California: A Study of Their Organizations, 1900–1947," Master's Thesis, University of Wisconsin, 1966, 85. Sacramento, with more Muslims than Sikhs, was not a *gurdwara* region.

22. Unable to publish the master list of couples in this book, I donated copies of it to three University of California libraries, at Irvine, Berkeley (the South/ Southeast Asia Library Gadar Collection), and Los Angeles. I define marriages here as relationships that were long lasting and/or produced children; most were legal marriages, although I made no effort to track down all marriage certificates. The 1946 extension of citizenship to Asian Indians (Chapter 9) meant that the men could bring their wives from India or travel to India and marry there. I have somewhat arbitrarily included couples through 1949 because it took a few years for these possibilities to become known. The table includes all wives of first-generation Punjabis through 1949.

23. According to other information, primarily naturalization petitions, thirty-three California Punjabis married in Arizona, twenty-six in New Mexico, nine in Texas, and one each in Oklahoma and Colorado. I also obtained twenty-eight Las Cruces, New Mexico, marriage licenses, and only half of those Punjabi grooms lived in New Mexico. Six lived in California (El Centro, Fresno, Marysville, Yuba City, and two in Calipatria), seven in Texas, and one in Arizona. Of the twenty-eight women, fifteen had been born in Mexico, seven in New Mexico, and six in Texas.

24. Computer analysis of apparent first marriages in this country according to marriage licenses yielded these figures (for 101 Punjabi men). The comparison sample was drawn from Imperial County marriage license books: six Hispanic–Hispanic marriages at six-month intervals from May 1918 through May of 1923, a total of sixty-six marriages.

25. Looking at a data set of 137 marriage certificates (109 from California and 28 from Las Cruces, New Mexico), one finds that the witnesses to the marriages were most often other Punjabi men, then Anglo men, then other Punjabi-Mexican couples, then Hispanic sisters, sisters' husbands or other male relatives, and last of all, Anglo women (perhaps clerks or wives of the performers of the marriages). Ages were not accurately recorded, usually being given younger for him and older

for her than indicated by other evidence (e.g., their death certificates, or their ages on their children's birth certificates). Misspellings were frequent, and the clerk always gave the bride her father's last name, in the American fashion. The men's occupations were typically farmer or rancher, the women's were seldom given. According to these licenses, some 15 percent of the men and 18 percent of the women were either divorced or widowed.

26. This Rosemary Khan bore at least three children to Ram Rattan Singh: San Joaquin County birth certificate 3950-288 of 1927 and death certificate 3950-485 of 1927; Tulare County birth certificate 22 of 1930; Fresno County birth certificate 17:275 of 1931. I failed to find any descendants.

27. For example, A. W. Khan of Brawley (whose wife, Catherine Murrietta, bore him a child in 1919) witnessed the wedding of F. Deen of Brawley and Catalina Estrada in 1917; F. Deen witnessed the wedding of Albert Joe (Sajjan Singh) and Alejandrina Alvarez in 1917; Gopal Singh, witness to the first marriage in 1916, was the third Punjabi groom in the valley and later was witness for Diya Singh and Maria Jimenez in 1918. Sources for the above in the order cited are Imperial County birth certificate 11:14 of 1919; Imperial County marriage licenses 5:238 of 1917, 5:472 of 1917, 5:164 of 1916, 5:388 of 1917, and 43:172 of 1918.

28. Some twenty-three marriages took place from 1916 through 1918. Of the twenty-five relationships before 1919 (including the two in 1913), fifteen were with women from Spanish-speaking backgrounds, six were with white women, and four were with black women. Of these twenty-five couples, all but six lived in the Imperial Valley; they married there or in San Diego, Los Angeles, Arizona, and Texas. Ten of these Hispanic women were born in Mexico, four were born in the American West, and one's place of birth is unknown. Of the white women, two were married in Oklahoma and brought to the Imperial Valley, three others married in the Imperial Valley, and one married in central California. Of the black women, two were Mississippi born but met their Punjabis in the Imperial Valley; two were born in California and married Punjabis in northern California.

29. For marriages by ship captain, see vol. 55OR, p. 403 of Yuba County marriage records and instances given in La Brack, *Sikhs of Northern California*, 175–176. Mola Singh remembered a friend's attempt to marry Mola's (then) wife's sister Julia Consuelo in about 1925 (Selma, 1982).

30. One Sikh did marry a black woman in Brawley, and they had a daughter, but he was run out of town by the other Punjabis. His wife divorced him, charging desertion. Years later, the daughter married a black sailor; she worked in San Diego and had changed her last name. Bagga S. Sunga, 1981; Imperial County marriage license 53:487 of 1921; Imperial County birth certificate 4:60 of 1922; Imperial County civil case 13372 of 1928 (divorce); Imperial County marriage license 1445 of 1962. See also Civil Cases 5007 and 5008, Imperial County, Office of the County Clerk, 1919.

31. This tendency for Muslims to marry black women allegedly began in Detroit, an early destination for Punjabi Muslims, and was carried over to California.

32. In the northern part of the state there was only one pair of (black) half-sisters at first; other sisters moved up from the South later. There were two sets of Anglo sisters and an Anglo mother and daughter among the wives of the northern Punjabis.

33. Mola Singh, former husband of Maria Atocha Arias, Selma, 1983; Lola Martinez Dhillon, Holtville, 1981. One Martinez brother came up to Detroit and worked with his sisters' Sikh husbands in the Ford plant in the 1930s, but he went back to Mexico.

34. For a minor, the father's signature was required on the marriage license; if there was no father, the mother's signature was acceptable. In three of the four marriages involving minor females, the mother's signature appeared (out of 28 marriage licenses from Las Cruces, New Mexico, and 109 marriage licenses from California). Mario T. Garcia notes that new immigrants and refugees crowded into the city after 1910 and that 19 percent of his sample from the 1900 census consisted of a mother and her children. Garcia, "The Chicana in American History: The Mexican Women of El Paso, 1990–1920—A Case Study," *Pacific Historical Review* 40, no. 2 (1980): 318–320.

35. Edwin C. Pendleton, "History of Labor in Arizona Irrigated Agriculture," Ph.D. dissertation, University of California, Berkeley, 1950), 160.

36. Among the few occupations listed by Hispanic women on their marriage license applications was "cook"; others were housework, domestic, housekeeper, cotton picker, and laborer. An account of a 1950 labor camp describes two women cooking three meals a day for 200 men, working from five o'clock in the morning until sunset. (The women were Gloria Moreno, who married Juan Corona, and her mother, who married a Sikh pioneer in the Yuba City area.) Ed Cray, *Burden of Proof: The Case of Juan Corona* (New York: Macmillan, 1973), 24; for the marriages, Isabel Singh Garcia, Yuba City, 1982.

37. Nellie Soto Shine, Huntington Beach, 1982; Janie Poonian, Yuba City, 1982; Rose Chell Canaris, Calexico, 1987 (interviewed by Lupe Beltran).

38. Interviews with Joe Mallobox, El Centro, 1982, Karmelita Kakar, San Jose, 1981; Teja and Kay Dillon, Fresno, 1982 (with Sarah Leonard); Lucy Sekhon, San Diego, 1982; Kishen Singh Deol, Corona, 1981; Lola Dhillon, Holtville, 1981. Sally Maynez Dhalliwal, Holtville, 1983, told of a Punjabi who gave her father money when he went to El Paso and asked him to bring back a woman; her dad spent the money and said he could not find one.

39. Norma Saikhon, Brawley, 1981 (interviewed by Ernesto Vargas).

40. Ramesh Murarka, "Pratap Singh Brar—Pioneering Spirit Overcame 37 Years of Loneliness," *India West*, July 3, 1981, 12–13. (Brar lived in Fresno.)

41. Before 1934, only three Imperial Valley farmers had registered as guard-

ians, in 1929, 1932, and 1933. Probate records, Imperial County, California, and Maricopa County, Arizona.

42. Khairiti Ram Samras, "Hindus in the United States: Their Part in the Economic Development of the West," Carey McWilliams Collection, University of California, Los Angeles, Minorities Miscellaneous File, Index 1, Box 16, 1936, 14.

43. Just as Yuma and San Diego seemed better places than El Centro for a time, Tulare County seemed better than Fresno for securing marriage licenses in the Central Valley. See Appendix A.

44. Interviews with Ali and Lucy Abdulla, Laura Sedoo, and Teja and Kay Dillon, all Fresno, 1982. Three Punjabi bosses were Pratap S. Brar, Ram Singh, and Puron Sedoo; the Giffen ranch and Clayton Anderson had Punjabi foremen.

45. These were owned by Tom Sarban Singh and Jean Singh. Teja and Kay Dillon, Fresno, 1982.

46. Laura Lightfoot Sedoo and Puron Sedoo, Fresno, 1982 (with Sarah Leonard) and Teja and Kay Dillon, Fresno, 1982. The latter was the family of Bakhshish Singh Dhillon (see Chapter 6).

47. These patterns were pervasive and continued into the second generation. Fernando Sanga, Brawley, 1981; Mary Garewal Gill, Holtville, 1981; Susanna and Mola Singh, Selma, 1982.

48. Allan P. Miller, "An Ethnographic Report on the Sikh (East) Indians of Sacramento Valley," South/Southeast Asia Library, University of California, Berkeley, 1950. Manuscript.

49. Robert Mohammed, Yuba City, 1988, for the food differences; Victor Dad and Ishmael Rahmatulla, Phoenix, 1988.

50. Two women delivered in the El Centro Hospital in 1921; the next hospital deliveries recorded for these couples were in 1937, when three wives delivered in hospitals. After that, again most first-generation wives delivered at home. In San Miguel County, New Mexico, 95 percent of all births in 1936 were attended by midwives. Fran Leeper Buss, *La Partera: Story of a Midwife* (Ann Arbor: University of Michigan Press, 1980), 114. Most Arizona Mexican wives also had midwives in attendance, until the 1952 Midwifery Practice Act required literacy in English or Spanish (so that a birth certificate could be filed), thus reducing the number of legally practicing midwives in the state to two! Margarita A. Kay, "Mexican, Mexican-American, and Chicana Childbirth," in *Twice a Minority: Mexican American Women*, ed. Margarita B. Melville (St. Louis: Mosby, 1980), 57.

51. Those attending births had to report them to the county recorder, and most were midwives. Most of the first dozen birth certificates in the Imperial Valley had to be corrected later by affidavit. Imperial County Recorder, 1917–1920, entries for Singh, Sidhu, and Shine. Birth certificates were changed in 1940 to delete years in occupations and add years in California, the county, and the United States for the parents; they were changed again in 1948 to delete occupa-

tions for women, years in residence for both parents, and residence for men. A further change in 1952 deleted very useful information, the number of previous births to the mother.

52. Imperial County Recorder's Office, birth certificates 1918–1930 and delayed birth registrations filed through 1949. Another reason for late registrations was ignorance of the legal requirement—Elizabeth Deen Hernandez (Burbank, 1981) remembers her mother telling another wife that she needed to register her children.

53. Isabel Singh Garcia, Yuba City, 1983 (she was delivering at the same time in the same hospital).

54. Ann Millard, "Women's Reproductive Histories and Demographic Change: A Case from Rural Mexico," Women in Development Working Papers, no. 8, Michigan State University, June 1982, also studied maternal fertility by looking at women forty-five years or older with one live birth.

55. I adjusted the ages given on the marriage and birth certificates by taking into account the whole series of ages at births and the ages of husbands and wives at the time of the last birth to them: Her mean age was 31.8, with a median of 31.3; his mean age was 48.6, with a median of 49.

56. Many of these earlier children had been born in Mexico or outside California, and I have no reliable data on their dates of birth or (sometimes) their sex.

57. Sex ratios for the children born to these sixty-six women cannot be accurately calculated because no birth certificates were available for many of the children.

58. Rose Chell Canaris, Calexico, 1987; Lucy Sekhon, San Diego, 1982.

59. Daniel Scott Smith and Michael S. Hindus use this measure in "Premarital Pregnancy in America, 1640–1966: An Overview and Interpretation," paper, American Historical Association, 1971.

60. Copies of Punjabi surname death certificates from the alphabetized and printed state death certificate indexes for 1905–1939.

61. I am differentiating between neonatal and infant categories, although the California vital statistics registration system includes neonatal as a subdivision of infant: California Department of Health Services, *Vital Statistics of California* (Sacramento: Department of Health Services, 1971).

62. Twenty children died aged one through ten years, and only one from eleven to eighteen. Dr. Mark Mandelkern, University of California, Irvine, helped categorize the causes of death. Infectious diseases included pneumonia, spinal meningitis, measles, influenza, and cholera; dehydration included colitis and gastroenteritis; accidental deaths included choking, burning, and drowning. One certificate gave no cause of death.

63. Government of India, *Towards Equality: Report of the Commission on the Status of Women in India, 1974* (New Delhi: Ministry of Education and Social Welfare,

1974); Barbara Miller, *The Endangered Sex: Neglect of Female Children in Rural North India* (Ithaca: Cornell University Press, 1981).

64. Computer analysis of the sixty-five California death certificates, 1905–1929.

65. Death certificates for women with Punjabi surnames drawn from California state death certificate files, 1905–1939. California has centralized, alphabetized, and printed death certificate data for this period.

Chapter 5. Male and Female Networks

1. Mola Singh, Selma, 1983. In the Imperial Valley, there were at least nine cases where brothers or cousin-brothers farmed together for many years.

2. There are well-known examples of both types. Sucha S. Garewal and Kehar S. Gill in Holtville were shipmates; Chenchel Rae and Lal Singh Rai in Yuba City were village mates and traveled together through Mexico to the United States; Harmon Singh and Kartar Singh in Holtville met only in the United States but were from nearby villages. Mary Garewal Gill, Holtville, 1982; Chenchel Rae, Yuba City, 1983; Oscar Singh, Holtville, 1981. Kakoo Singh in Brawley first farmed with an uncle and then with a village mate, Diya Singh. Odens, *Pioneerland*, 49–50.

3. For the 69 men in the Imperial Valley who filed naturalization petitions after 1946, 42 of the 50 villages named had only 1 man from each; the remaining 8 villages accounted for 19 men. But the following had come on the same ship: 7 men, 4 men, 2 sets of 3 men, and 5 sets of 2 men. Thus 9 ships accounted for 27 men. Dhillon, *History Book*, reproduces the passenger list for the ill-fated 1914 *Komagata Maru* voyage to Canada. Of the 376 Punjabi passengers, more than half (204) were the sole representatives of their village. Only 172 had village mates, ranging from 1 to 16, on the ship.

4. It is difficult to discover the bonds between these bachelor crew members, since most have died and did not leave descendants in the United States. Miller, "Ethnographic Report," did not collect this information in his 1949 investigation of Sikhs in the Sacramento Valley.

5. Raymond Ram, Firebaugh, 1983; Alfred Sidhu, Sacramento, 1982; George Puri, Los Angeles, 1984; Isabel Singh Garcia, Yuba City, 1982; and Karmelita Kakar, San Jose, 1982.

6. See Leonard, "Punjabi Farmers." Attorneys and judges who held land for Punjabis included R. B. Whitelaw and Mark McGee in El Centro, H. B. Griffin and H. Horton in Brawley, Jerry Barcelox in Chico, T. S. Johnson, Duard Geis, and Harry McGowan in the Yuba City/Willows/Butte City area, and R. C. Stanford (later governor of Arizona) in Phoenix.

7. When Mola Singh and his father were among those charged in 1933 with conspiracy to evade the Alien Land Laws, Judge H. B. Griffin posted bond for them. He also advised Mola Singh on how to handle his wife when the couple was having marital difficulties. Mola Singh, Selma, 1982.

8. At first I was tempted to label them patron–client relationships, with the Punjabis securing powerful local patrons, but that seriously distorts the Punjabis' perception of them. Pettigrew's discussion of the patron–client system in the Punjab, in *Robber Noblemen*, captures the essence of these relationships, which are reciprocal rather than assymetrical and vary from transaction to transaction. She contends that the inequalities of the Hindu caste system do not characterize economic relationships in the Punjabi countryside; rather, men compete in a spirit of equality, sparring for advantage in a flexible system that offers multiple opportunities for securing resources and building factions. Her emphasis on the importance placed on land, power, and violence, and most of all on pride and the refusal to act subordinate to anyone, "fits" the Punjabis all over California.

9. Those were Sucha Singh Dhalliwal and Roy Thompson, and Mohamed Baksh and John Anderholt. Keith Savage, Holtville, 1981; Joseph Anderholt, Holtville, 1982.

10. Mola Singh, Selma, 1983.

11. Keith Savage, Elizabeth Harris, Dorothy Brown Anderholt, Herbert Hughes, all from Holtville and all in 1981. In Brawley, men also met at the park in the town center or near the Alamo Real Store just outside town. Mary Garewal Gill and Silveria Chell, Holtville, 1981. In Calipatria, they sat on the curbside in the late afternoon. Anna and Charn S. Sandhu, Calipatria, 1982.

12. Mary Garewal Gill, Holtville, 1981.

13. A pamphlet put out by the association survives in the possession of Bagga S. Sunga of Brawley. Imperial County Civil Case 11015 of 1926 mentions mediation by other Punjabi association members as part of the court-mandated procedure, and a Punjabi's lease dated July 16, 1919, includes a condition that a representative of the Hindustani Welfare and Reform Society can enter to inspect with the landlord (another Punjabi). Index of Grantees, Imperial County, b. 7, p. 211 (reference provided by Sucheng Chan). See also Ram Chand's remarks, Chapter 3.

14. For the Stockton *gurdwara*, see the many references in Wood, "East Indians," and La Brack, *Sikhs of Northern California*, 127–134. Mayer and Dusenbery both remark on the many functions performed by Sikh *gurdwaras* in India and in Canada: Adrian C. Mayer, *A Report on the East Indian Community in Vancouver* (Vancouver, British Columbia: Institute of Social and Economic Research, University of Vancouver, 1959), 8–9; Verne A. Dusenbery, "Canadian Ideology and Public Policy: The Impact on Vancouver Sikh Ethnic and Religious Adaptation," *Canadian Ethnic Studies* 13, no. 3 (1981): 104.

15. Salim Khan, "A Brief History of Pakistanis in the Western United States," Master's Thesis, Sacramento State, 1981, 55; and personal observation of the cemetery office maps in Sacramento and El Centro.

16. In Urdu, *ghadar* means "mutiny" and refers to the 1857 Sepoy Mutiny in India against the British East India Company. The recently conquered Punjab stayed loyal to the British then, so Punjabis in California felt that they had a special duty to fight against colonial rule because of that historic "error." See Sylvia Vatuk and Ved Prakash Vatuk, "Protest Songs of East Indians on the West Coast, U.S.A.," in *Thieves in My House*, ed. Ved Prakash Vatuk, (Varanasi: Vishwavidyalaya Prakashan, 1969), 63–80.

17. A leaflet (n.p., n.d.) in the Gadar Collection at the University of California, Berkeley, protested the arrests of two Sikhs in Hong Kong and tried to arouse Chinese support for anti-British activities.

18. For the "seditious" label put on the party, see Mark Juergensmeyer, "The Gadar Syndrome: Ethnic Anger and Nationalist Pride," *Population Review* 25, nos. 1 and 2 (1982): 52–55; Jensen, *Passage from India;* and California Legislature, Senate, Fact-Finding Committee on Un-American Activities, *Seventh Report of the Senate Fact-Finding Committee on Un-American Activities,* "The Gadar Party" (Sacramento: California Senate Printing Office, 1953), 215–246.

19. Nand Kaur, "Interview, May 21, 1972" (Yuba City, with her daughter Jane Singh), 14–15; Kesar S. Dhillon, "Interview, October–December 1976" (Oakland, with Jane Singh), notes on tape 3, side 2, made by Jane Singh. The transcribed tape (the former) and notes on the tape (the latter) are in the Gadar Collection, South/Southeast Asia Library, University of California, Berkeley.

20. Civil Suit 25280, Office of the County Clerk, Stockton, San Joaquin County, 1932, which was appealed to the Supreme Court in 1936. *Pacific Reporter,* 2nd series, 54: 1099; and *California Reports,* 2nd series, 5:405. Many members of this Malwa Sudharak Society were still contributing money and fighting about its use in the late 1940s.

21. Bagga S. Sunga, Brawley, 1981. Charn Singh Sandhu, for example, was a Ghadar party leader in the north and Fresno until he moved to the Imperial Valley in 1937, where he married the daughter of another Punjabi and put land in her name. Charn and Anna Sandhu, Calipatria, 1982.

22. In 1926 hearings on this issue, of sixty-nine men listed as citizens, forty-five had already had their citizenship canceled, twelve cancellation cases were pending, and ten were "soldiers" against whom cancellation proceedings could not be instituted: U.S. Congress, Senate, *Ratification and Confirmation of Naturalization of Certain Persons of the Hindu Race, Hearings before the Committee on Immigration,* Cong., 2nd sess., on Senate Joint Resolution 128, December 9 and 15, 1926 (Washington, D.C.: Government Printing Office, 1926), 1–7.

23. Professors Emeritus Michael Goodman and E. T. Grether, Berkeley, 1982

(they were at the University of California, Berkeley, in the 1920s); C. M. Naim, interviewed in Los Angeles, 1981 (he came as a student to Berkeley in the 1950s). See also Dhan Gopal Mukerji, *Caste and Outcast* (New York: Dutton, 1923), 269–282, for his personal experiences in California's fields with Punjabi crews.

24. Sakaram Ganesh Pandit, whose appeal for citizenship succeeded, was a lawyer in good standing in the California and U.S. courts. He was married to a white woman from Michigan who owned 320 acres of land in the Imperial Valley. If his citizenship had been canceled, the Cable Act would have caused his wife to become an "alien" too and lose her land. U.S. Congress, Senate, *Ratification and Confirmation*, 11.

25. Dalip Singh Saund, later elected to Congress from Imperial County, had a Ph.D. in mathematics but farmed in the Imperial Valley; Rattan Singh Dhillon, with a Berkeley master's degree in Economics earned under Paul S. Taylor, also farmed there.

26. Mary Garewal Gill, El Centro, 1990, for El Gordo (her father) and El Loco; Alfred Sidhu, Sacramento, 1982, citing his father's response when asked what the B. in B. Sucha Singh Sidhu stood for.

27. Nellie Soto Shine and her daughter Caroline Resendez recalled arguing with Lola Martinez Dhillon about which villages were cleaner (evidenced by the personal habits of the men) and which produced better food (which men cooked better). Huntington Beach, 1982. One man could name other men from his father's village but could not recall its name (Rudolfo Singh, Imperial, 1981); similarly, a widow who had actually been to her husband's village three times could not identity it but listed five men from it, as well as three men from his ship. Sophia Din, Brawley, 1981.

28. A few put their fathers' names as well: personal observation of about fifty tombstones in El Centro's Evergreen Cemetery and about thirty early tombstones in Sacramento's city cemetery, Masonic Cemetery, and Odd Fellows Cemetery. In Phoenix, where a cemetery was started later (1938) and Urdu is not used, fathers' names and village names seldom appear. Ishmael Rahmatulla, Phoenix, 1988; personal observation, 1990.

29. Since many of the men were illiterate, their spellings of village names in English were uncertain, and many descendants are frustrated when trying to locate their "native place."

30. Mrs. Swingle arranged for the xeroxing of these petitions. Office of the County Clerk, Imperial County.

31. These were Bawa S. Sanga and Hajara Singh.

32. The five men from Soondh ended up in four different places: Puna Singh in Yuba City, Amar Singh in Arizona, Ghulam Rasul and Tom Mallobox in the Imperial Valley, and Waryam Singh in Colusa. Jane Singh, Berkeley, 1981. Bagga S. Sunga's eight village mates scattered widely. Bagga S. Sunga, El Centro, 1981.

33. Imperial County, Office of the County Clerk, Imperial County. See also Civil Case 26053, 1950, Imperial County, where money collected from fifty former villagers by Chet Singh for repair and construction of a temple back in Parangri village, Amritsar district, was allegedly misused after his death by the administrator of his estate, another Malwa man from the Imperial Valley.

34. "Real Indian" is used now by all descendants, and I cannot tell when the usage began. Family members used Singh as a surname in the early years and only later used Dillon or Dhillon. It was this family that a returned missionary finally located near Fresno in 1922, after searching for months for an Indian woman in California. Annette Thackwell Johnson, "The 'Rag Heads'—A Picture of America's East Indians," *The Independent* 109, no. 3828 (1922): 234–235.

35. Teja and Kay Dillon, Fresno, 1982.

36. Nepal's Rana Mahendra Pratap recruited participants for this unsuccessful effort in Marysville in July 1925. See Nand Kaur, "Interview, May 21, 1972," 5–6. Raja Mahendra Pratap, *My Life Story of Fifty-Five Years* (Dehradun: World Federation, 1947), 104 and 106, mentions Shamsher ("Bud") Singh and includes him in a group photo. The Punjabi men had collected $12,000 for Pratap's mission, and some 800 Indians heard his report when he later returned to Marysville. *Life Story,* 139.

37. Teja and Kay Dillon, Fresno, 1982; Joan (Mrs. Bud) Dillon, Oakland, 1982; Kartar Dhillon, Berkeley, 1987, and her "The Parrot's Beak," in *Making Waves, an Anthology of Writings by and about Asian American Women*, ed. Asian Women United of California (Boston: Beacon Press, 1989), 214–222; and Blanche Dillon, Vancouver, 1988 (the youngest child, she remembers little of this). This pressure from fellow villagers concerned about status in their place of origin is an instance of what James Ferguson calls "localism" (contrasted to "cosmopolitanism," as exemplified by the Dhillon children) in his study of men working away from their home villages in Zambia. Ferguson, "Cultural Style on the Zambian Copperbelt: Micropolitical Foundations of Localism and Cosmopolitanism," Social Relations colloquim, University of California, Irvine, October 1989.

38. Most descendants of the Muslims and Hindus were unfamiliar with these regional designations.

39. For Ghadar party history, see notes 16 and 18; Harish K. Puri, *Ghadar Movement* (Amritsar: Guru Nanak Dev University Press, 1983); and references in Jensen, *Passage to America.*

40. Probate Case 3347, Office of the County Clerk, Imperial County, 1942. Appraiser D.B. Roberts held land for Punjabi farmers.

41. Because of his affection for Sher Singh, Chenchel Rai kept coming, finally entering illegally from Mexico in 1933 with his village mate and partner-to-be, Lal Singh Rai. Chenchel Rai and Naranjan Singh Atwal (with Bob Singh), Yuba City, 1982.

42. The last three quotes are from George Puri, Los Angeles, 1984; Joe Mallobox, El Centro, 1982; and Ali Abdullah, Fresno, 1983. Other informants included Raymond Ram, Firebaugh, 1983; Mary Garewal Gill, Holtville, 1981; Robert Chell, Holtville, 1981; Elizabeth Deen Hernandez, Burbank, 1981; Isabel Singh Garcia, Yuba City, 1982; and Lucy Singh Abdulla, Fresno, 1983.

43. Mary Garewal Gill, Holtville, 1981; William Ewing, El Centro, 1981; and for Arizona, Amelia Singh Netervala, Los Angeles, 1988.

44. Buchignani points to the neglect of women's networks in the literature on ethnicity and social organization and says, about ethnic communities he has known, "Men and women formed partially distinct social networks, and information control between sex-based networks was substantial . . . yet [these features] are rarely mentioned." Buchignani, *Anthropological Approaches*, 15.

45. Arthur J. Rubel, *Across the Tracks* (Austin: University of Texas Press, 1966), 68–69.

46. The Romero sisters are a case in point. Yolanda Singh, Santa Ana, 1983.

47. Many people told me that non-Catholics should not be accepted as godparents, yet in the records of the Holtville Catholic church (opened to me by Father Waiches), Punjabi men's names were officially entered. See also Ina Rosenthal-Urey, "Church Records as a Source of Data on Mexican Migrant Networks: A Methodological Note," *International Migration Review* 18, no. 3 (1984): 767–781.

48. There was a regional difference. In northern California and Phoenix, Arizona, where there were fewer Punjabi-Mexican families, a higher proportion of godparents were Mexican Americans.

49. For the *compadrazgo* literature, see George M. Foster, "Cofradia and Compadrazgo in Spain and Spanish America," *Southwestern Journal of Anthropology* 9, no. 1 (1953): 1–27; Sidney W. Mintz and Eric R. Wolf, "An Analysis of Ritual Co-Parenthood (Compadrazgo)," *Southwestern Journal of Anthropology* 6 (1950): 341–368; and others mentioned in Hugo G. Nutini and Betty Bell, *Ritual Kinship: The Structure and Historical Development of the Compadrazgo System in Rural Tlaxcala* (Princeton: Princeton University Press, 1980), 1:405–428.

50. Sorting the birth certificates by date and locality produced close correlations with clusters of godmothers. For their close friends, women invariably named other women married to Punjabis, often their old neighbors and *comadres*.

51. In Phoenix, Arizona, Diwan Singh's daughter Jane had Gulam Mohammed of Holtville for her godfather; Ali Abdulla's father, Fazl John Abdulla, went to a Catholic church and was called *compadre* by those for whose children he served as godfather. Janie Diwan Poonian, Yuba City, 1982; Ali Abdulla, Sacramento, 1983.

52. The elaborate charts prepared by Nutini and Bell, for example, were not relevant to these families. *Ritual Kinship*, 52 et passim.

53. A number of wives who attended Baptist, Lutheran, or Fundamentalist

churches participated in *compadrazgo:* the Deols, Rasuls, and Sidhus in the Imperial Valley (Kishen S. Deol, Corona, 1981; Elizabeth Deen Hernandez, Burbank,
1981; Alfred Sidhu, Sacramento, 1982); and Lucy Singh's mother farther north
(Lucy Singh Abdulla, Sacramento, 1983).

54. Harry Chand, Live Oak, 1983; Isabel Singh Garcia, Yuba City, 1982; and
Janie Diwan Poonian, Yuba City, 1983.

55. See Civil Case 17775, Office of the County Clerk, Imperial County, 1939,
for the man who left his daughter with a family in Mexico (and later could not
locate the family). Ali Abdulla's youngest sister was adopted by Nellie Dean; Alfred Sidhu's youngest brother was kept for many years by the Punjabi ex-husband
of his grandmother and the ex-husband's second wife; Sant Ram's youngest son,
cared for by a Hispanic woman for years, had to be kidnapped back by his father;
and the youngest Diwan daughter, Connie, was raised by her grandmother, Celia
Moreno. Ali Abdulla, Fresno, 1983; Alfred Sidhu, Sacramento, 1982; Raymond
Ram, Firebaugh, 1983; Nora Singh Nichols, Casa Grande, 1989, and Janie Diwan
Poonian, Yuba City, 1983.

56. Teresa Garewal, Holtville, 1981; Lucy Sekhon, San Diego, 1982; Sophia
Din, Brawley, 1981; and Emma Smiley, Sacramento, 1982.

57. Johnson, " 'Rag Heads,' " 235.

58. I found a few other women from India in the rural county records who
evidently moved or had no children. Balwant Singh Brar mentions "six or seven"
early families and locates one in Utah, two in San Francisco, and one each in
Loomis, Fair Oaks, and Stockton. "The East Indians in Sutter County," *Sutter
County Historical Society News Bulletin* 17, no. 2 (April 1978): 18.

59. Isabel Singh Garcia, Yuba City, 1982; Jane Singh, Berkeley, 1981.

60. Puna Singh came in 1906, worked on the railroad, and ended up in Utah,
where he was one of six Punjabis to attain U.S. citizenship early in 1921. He set
out for India in 1922 to marry and bring in his wife; as a U.S. citizen, he was able to
do that. As a result of the 1923 *Thind* decision, which denied naturalization to
Indians, his citizenship was later revoked. His wife suffered from snow blindness
in Utah, so they moved to California in 1924, starting over again in the Yuba City
area. Puna Singh, "My Early Years," 109–110. The quote about the American Indian women is in Bruce La Brack's field notes, interview with Nand Kaur, p. 3
(1974–1975).

61. Janie Diwan Poonian, Yuba City, 1982. This Raj Kaur may be the woman
brought in 1923 (a sister of Bagh Singh Chotia) who sought further extensions of
her stay: "Race Relations Survey," box 37, no. 405, July 17, 1924, letter of H. V.
White to J. Merle Davis.

62. Teja and Kay Dillon, Fresno, 1982; Joan (Mrs. Bud) Dillon, Oakland, 1982;
Kartar Dhillon, Berkeley, 1987. The parents incorporated some Spanish words
into their everyday language during their stay of several months in the Philippines. For example, their American-born children, isolated from other women

(Hispanic or Punjabi) who did ironing, thought *plancha* was a Punjabi word for iron.

63. For the Urdu newspaper, Puri, *Ghadar Movement*, 40–41.

64. *India West*, April 7, 1989, 1, 31; Louis Sareeram, interviewed in El Centro, 1981.

65. Raoul Narroll specified measures for an ethnic subsystem in 1964: Group members should share fundamental cultural values, overtly realized in certain forms or institutions; members should share a field of communication and interaction; members should be self-identified and identified by others as a distinguishable category among other categories of the same order; and the group should be biologically self-perpetuating or endogamous. Narroll, "On Ethnic Unit Classification," *Current Anthropology* 5 (1964): 283–312. This Punjabi-fathered group did not satisfy the last requirement.

66. On androcentric approaches, see Jane Fishburne Collier and Sylvia Yanagisako, "Toward a Unified Analysis of Gender and Kinship," in *Gender and Kinship: Essays toward a Unified Analysis,* ed. Jane Fishburne Collier and Sylvia Junko Yanagisako (Stanford: Stanford University Press, 1987), esp. 25, where they make the point about the family.

67. Isabel Singh Garcia, Yuba City, 1982; Karmelita Kakar, San Jose, 1982; and Alfred Sidhu, Sacramento, 1982.

68. Carl Jacobsen, Brawley, 1981; William Ewing, Holtville, 1981. In another case, membership in a Protestant church (Holtville) was important.

69. Bobby Sanga and Rose Chell Canaris, Brawley and Calexico, respectively, 1987, about their fathers, Bawa S. Sanga and Kunda S. Chell; Francisco Singh, Selma, 1983, about his father, Inder Singh.

70. For the partnership between Molina and Sham Singh, Judge William Lehnhardt, Brawley, 1981.

71. Bagga S. Sunga, El Centro, 1982; Mola Singh, Selma, 1983; Charn S. Sandhu, Calipatria, 1982, Rose Chell Canaris, Calexico, 1987; and Mary Garewal Gill, Holtville, 1982.

72. California Labor Commissioner, *Licensed Farm Contractors of California* (Sacramento: Office of State Printing, 1966), listed six men, three in San Joaquin County and one each in Colusa, Fresno, and Imperial. Elizabeth Deen Hernandez, Burbank, 1981, commented on the impact of *braceros* on Mexican American workers.

73. Pritam Sandhu, Calipatria, 1987; Joseph and Dorothy Anderholt, Holtville, 1982; Rose Chell Canaris, Calexico, 1987; Mary Garewal Gill, Holtville, 1981; and Mola Singh, Selma, 1983.

74. Nellie Soto Shine, Huntington Beach, 1982; also Isabel Diwan, Arizona, in a clipping from an unnamed journal, April 1988, 5 (sent by Barbara Quade Lang, Tucson, 1989); Mary Garewal Gill, Holtville, 1990.

75. Karmelita Kakar, San Jose, 1982; Mary Garewal Gill, Holtville, 1981; Ray-

mond Ram, Firebaugh, 1983. Hema Gonzalez, Oakland 1982, an Indian psychological social worker married to a Mexican American, lived in El Centro for five years and viewed the women as having joined a Punjabi group.

76. Tracy Kidder, *The Road to Yuba City. A Journey into the Juan Corona Murders* (New York: Doubleday, 1974), 94. Punjabi farmers figured as employers in writings about the case, and Juan Corona's mother-in-law was married to a Punjabi farmer (a second marriage for both spouses).

77. Yusuf Dadabhay, "Circuitous Assimilation among Rural Hindustanis in California," *Social Forces* 33 (1954): 138–141.

78. Dorothy Anderholt, Holtville, 1982.

Chapter 6. Conflict and Love in the Marriages

1. Darling, *Rusticus Loquitur*, 182. This means, as Saint Nihal Singh pointed out, that the "greater percentage" of the Punjabi immigrants to the west coast were married men. Saint Nihal Singh, "The Picturesque Immigrant from India's Coral Strand," *Out West* (Los Angeles) 30 (1909): 45.

2. Government of India, *Towards Equality*, 38–45, 102–144.

3. Ibid., 10, 15. In 1901 there were 972 females per 1,000 males in India; in 1911, 964; and in 1921, 955. The Punjab figure was 821 in 1921—the Punjab had the lowest proportion of women to men of all the Indian states through 1971.

4. Darling, *Rusticus Loquitur*, 40–41; Darling, *Punjab Peasant*, 51; Pettigrew, *Robber Noblemen*, 53; and Hershman and Standing, *Punjabi Kinship*, 175 et passim.

5. *Sharan Kaur* is available in comic-book form from Amar Chitra Katha, India Book House Education Trust, 29 Wodehouse Road, Bombay, India. For *Heer Ranjha*, see Waris Shah, *The Adventures of Hir and Ranjha*, trans. Charles Frederick Usborne (London: Peter Owen, 1973).

6. Pettigrew, *Robber Noblemen*, 50–53; and Hershman and Standing, *Punjabi Kinship*, 173–175.

7. Darling, *Rusticus Loquitur*, 49–51.

8. Mola Singh, Selma, 1983 (as we watched a Hindi movie on his VCR that featured a hot romance).

9. See Fredrik Barth, "The System of Social Stratification in Swat, North Pakistan," in *Aspects of Caste in South India, Ceylon, and Northwest Pakistan*, ed. E. R. Leach (Cambridge: Cambridge University Press, 1960), 113–146. For love stories, see Wilma L. Heston and Mumtaz Nasir, *The Bazaar of the Storytellers* (Islamabad: Lok Virsa, n.d. [ca. 1988]). This is not to deny that couples in arranged marriages frequently fall in love after marrriage.

10. Woodrow Borah and Sherburne F. Cook, "Marriage and Legitimacy in Mexican Culture: Mexico and California," *California Law Review* 54, no. 946 (1966): 946–1008.

11. For this and the following paragraph, see Orfa Jean Shontz, "The Land of 'Poco Tiempo,' " *Journal of Social Casework* 8, no. 3 (1927): 74–76.

12. Borah and Cook, "Marriage and Legitimacy," 976.

13. Fernando Penalose, "Mexican Family Roles," *Journal of Marriage and the Family*, November 1968, 685; and Borah and Cook, "Marriage and Legitimacy," 988. The California legislature in 1923 voted testamentary power to wives over their half of community property and granted both widows and widowers all the community property when a spouse died intestate. The spousal share of separate property continued to be one-third if the couple had more than one child, one-half if there was one child or parents, and all if there were no children or parents. Carole Shammas, *Inheritance in America from Colonial Times to the Present* (New Brunswick: Rutgers University Press, 1987), 174.

14. Mola Sing, Selma, 1982.

15. Albert Joe was one of the first twenty-seven Punjabis in the Imperial Valley to be a telephone subscriber. *Imperial County Pacific Telephone*, 1918.

16. Mary Garewal Gill, Holtville, 1981; Criminal Case 773 Office of the County Clerk, Imperial County, 1919. Family tradition holds that he was innocent. Lydia Soto Sidhu, El Centro, 1990 (Lydia's sister was Rullia's second wife). Paroled in 1933, Rullia Singh went to the youngest sister's husband, Harnam Singh Sidhu, to ask about his son. Valentina had raised the child, Carlos, and Ruth Albert Joe, her daughter's baby, in San Diego (Alejandria remarried a Mexican and had more children). Sidhu told Rullia of the boy's death in a fishing accident in Baja California; Rullia then farmed in Phoenix, Arizona, and married one of three sisters from Puerto Rico.

17. Criminal Case 773, Office of the County Clerk, Imperial County, 1919.

18. *Brawley News*, April 16, 1921; Criminal Case 1031, Office of the County Clerk, Imperial County, 1921; death certificate 44: 4, Recorder's Office, Imperial County, 1921

19. Lucy Harper Sekhon, San Diego, 1982.

20. *Brawley News*, June 13, 1933; Mary Garewal Gill, Holtville, 1981; Teresa Garewal, Holtville, 1981; Laura Sedoo, Fresno, 1982; Isabel Singh Garcia, Yuba City, 1982. When the *Brawley News* called a Fresno newspaper, it implicated the Ghadar party. "Man and Girl Found Slain in Lonely Cabin," *Wide World Magazine*, January 1934, 336, reprinted the *San Francisco Chronicle* account (August 12, 1933), which also blamed the Ghadar party, terming it a combined communist and Hindu-smuggling organization battling authorities in the United States and India.

21. *Sacramento Bee*, March 8, 1937; Criminal Case 13651, Office of the County Clerk, Sacramento County.

22. Paul H. Jacobson, *American Marriage and Divorce* (New York: Rinehart, 1959), 101.

23. Ibid., 101–103; and Alfred Cahen, *Statistical Analysis of American Divorce* (New York: AMS Press, 1968), 56–60.

24. Imperial County Civil Cases, 1919–1946, Office of the County Clerk, Imperial County.

25. The grounds for divorce at the time required complaints beyond those in Kehar S. Gill's 1919 petition. In 1922 he alleged adultery and pregnancy with another's child. Matilde subsequently eloped with Ram Chand (a trusted friend who had drawn up wills for Kehar and his partner Sucha Singh Garewal), and they settled in Phoenix, Arizona, where both she and her baby died shortly afterward. Mary Garewal Gill, Holtville, 1981; Civil Cases 4715 of 1919 and 7937 of 1922, Office of the County Clerk, Imperial County.

26. Yolanda Singh, Santa Ana, 1982, speaking about one of her aunts. And some Anglo neighbors speculated that the men locked up their women and forbade them to speak to visitors.

27. Isabel Singh Garcia, Yuba City, 1983; and a *Holtville Tribune*, January 11, 1929, ad placed by Munsha Singh, whose 1923 divorce petition was not completed but whose 1948 successful petition stated that they had separated in 1924. Civil Cases 8736 and 24078 of 1923 and 1948, Office of the County Clerk, Imperial County.

28. Old-timers said that disputes over money were a major cause of the many divorces, and they also stressed the age difference, which became increasingly important. Chenchel Rai and Naranjan S. Atwal (with Bob Singh) Yuba City, 1983. The incidence of divorce was much lower where there were fewer Punjabi-Mexican couples; checks of civil case indexes for Los Angeles, San Diego, San Joaquin, Sutter, and Yuba counties and for Maricopa County (Phoenix, Arizona) show scattered cases mostly filed in the 1940s.

29. Civil Case Indexes, 1919–1969, Office of the County Clerk, Imperial County. In 1969, major changes in California's basic divorce law based dissolution on actual breakdown of a marriage without finding individual fault, so there are fewer interesting details in the records. Howard A. Krom, "California's Divorce Law Reform: An Historical Analysis," *Pacific Law Journal* 1 (1970): 156, 161.

30. All but seven of the couples had married before 1946–1947 (the year legal changes enabled Punjabi men to become citizens and bring wives from India), and thirty-eight of the divorce cases (representing twenty-nine couples) were filed before then.

31. Cahen, *Statistical Analysis*, 43, 60; Jacobson, *American Marriage*, 119.

32. Computer analysis of the relevant divorce cases, 1919–1969, Office of the County Clerk, Imperial County.

33. Cahen, *Statistical Analysis*, 39–40. Desertion is generally charged in the later years of marriage, more than four years; here, six of the fourteen wives charged with desertion left within a year of marriage. Nationally, two-thirds of all divorces involve childless couples (Cahen, *Statistical Analysis*, 112), and here 35/59,

or 59 percent of all petitioners, were childless, but there was a big difference by sex: 8/23 of the women were childless and 26/34 of the men. While Imperial County records often were unclear about petition results, it seems that the men requested custody of the children more frequently than the national norm. Of the Punjabi male petitioners, 8/34, who constituted 100 percent of those with children, requested custody, while one-tenth of those who get custody nationally were men. Jacobson, *American Marriage*, 131. Finally, while statistics on the interval between divorce and remarriage for all these cases cannot be computed and compared to national figures, in several cases, one or both spouses already had remarried before filing for a divorce.

34. Civil Case 17775, Office of the County Clerk, Imperial County; *Post Press*, June 24, 1939.

35. *Holtville Tribune*, June 12, 1931.

36. W. Parker Frisbie, Frank D. Bean, and Isaac W. Eberstein, "Patterns of Marital Instability among Mexican Americans, Blacks, and Anglos," in Frisbie and Bean, ed., *The Demography of Racial and Ethnic Groups* (New York: Academic Press, 1978), 149–153.

37. If a man's marriage license gave his marital status as "divorced," I included him in the table, but if it gave his status as "widowed," I did not, since the former indicated a marriage and divorce in the United States, while the latter usually indicated a wife in India who might not really be dead.

38. Silvia Arrom, *The Women of Mexico City, 1790–1857* (Palo Alto: Stanford University Press, 1985), 112–113, found that census takers used the term "widow" to include single women with children; only single women without children were termed "single." The notations on marriage licenses were only one source of marital history for the wives of the Punjabis; other information came from interviews with descendants and neighbors and from birth certificate notations about previous births to the mother (indicating prior relationships).

39. Nika Singh Gill, Holtville, 1981; Olga Dad Khan, Sacramento, 1982; Mary Garewal Gill, Holtville, 1981.

40. Rose Chell Canaris, Calexico, 1936.

41. Genobeba Loya Singh, recounted by her daughter Carmelita Shine, Chico, 1988; Rosa Reyes Singh (with Amelia Singh Netervala), Los Angeles, 1989; Lala Garewal, Holtville, 1981.

42. Mary Garewal Gill, Holtville, 1981; Kishen S. Doel, Corona, 1981; Alfred Sidhu, Sacramento, 1982; Mary Singh Rai, Yuba City, 1981.

43. Mary Garewal Gill, Holtville, 1981; Kishen S. Deol, Corona, 1981; Alfred Sidhu, Sacramento, 1982; Mary Singh Rai, Yuba City, 1981.

44. Mola Singh, Selma, 1983; Rose Chell Canaris, 1987; Savarn Singh, El Centro, 1984; Mrs. Ganga Singh Bhatti, taped in Live Oak, 1989, by Tejinder S. Sibia of Davis (thanks to him for the tape).

45. After the citizenship law changed in 1946, some wives visited their hus-

bands' home villages in India. Lala Garewal, Holtville, 1981; Sophia Din, Brawley, 1981; Mary Garewal Gill, Holtville, 1982; Anna Sandhu, Calipatria, 1982; Caroline Shine Sunghera Resendez, Huntington Beach, 1982; Laura Sedoo, Fresno, 1982; Irene Afzal Khan, Willows, 1988.

46. Mola Singh, Selma, 1981.

47. This sense of "being Hindu" is discussed in later chapters.

48. Baptismal certificate, Anthony, New Mexico, January 3, 1932, for Arturo Gangara, and his marriage certificate, April 2, 1932, Mesilla Park, New Mexico (copies from his daughter, Helen Ram Walsh, Hercules, 1989).

49. Mola and Susanna Mesa Rodriguez Singh, Selma, 1983.

50. These views were expressed in interviews with Mola and Susanna Mesa Rodriguez Singh, Selma 1983; Norma Saikhon, Brawley 1981; Rose Chell Canaris, Calexico, 1986; Elizabeth Deen Hernandez, Burbank, 1981; and Fernando Sanga, Brawley, 1981. Two newspaper stories also quoted old-timers who expressed such views: a recollection of Sunder Amer Dhutt Singh by his daughter Vicenta, in Diane Kulkarni, "Immigrant a Strength and Inspiration," *Ogden Standard-Examiner* (Utah), April 30, 1984; and an interview with Nika Singh Gill, "He Sought an Education," *Holtville Tribune*, January 30, 1975.

51. Mola Singh, Selma, 1982.

52. Ibid.

53. Raymond Ram, Firebaugh, 1983; Nellie Soto Shine, Huntington Beach, 1982; Sophia Din, Brawley, 1981.

54. Marianne Singh Andrews, daughter of Josephine Lucero Singh Bhatti (Mrs. Ganga Singh Bhatti), Live Oak, 1989, taped by Tejinder S. Sibia, Davis.

55. Thus Mola Singh, with his second American wife, Maria, did not bother with divorce for decades, although he had divorced his first American wife, Carmen (whose departure had caused him far more regret and anger). In 1937, when he met Susanna, his third American partner and mother of eight of his thirteen children, he did not bother with marriage.

56. Marriages in India are almost never civil ceremonies recorded by government; they are religious ones recorded by genealogists for families and castes, usually between partners of the same religion.

57. Among those who did this were Mola Singh and Susanna Mesa Rodriguez Singh (Selma, 1983); Isabel Gonzalez and Inder Singh (on his deathbed in 1963–1964, according to his grandson Uttam Dhillon, San Diego, 1988); Lola and Sam Dhillon, forty-one years after their civil marriage (Lola Dhillon, Holtville, 1981); and Sophia and Shahab Din (Sophia Din, Brawley, 1981).

58. Mola and Susanna Singh, Selma, 1983.

59. Nellie Soto Shine and her daughter Caroline Shine Sunghera Resendez, Huntington Beach, 1982. The other fifty-year couples are Puron and Laura Sedoo of Fresno, Mola and Susanna Singh of Selma (counting from 1937, when they got together—he died in 1989), Sawarn and Lucia Singh of El Centro, Mir and Sus-

anna Dad of Phoenix, Arizona, Jiwan and Rosa Singh, of Phoenix, Arizona, and in 1991, Josephine and Ganga Singh Bhatti of Live Oak.

Chapter 7. Childhood in Rural California

1. Duane Metzger, Irvine, 1982, reported an Imperial Valley student who knew lots of Singhs but no one of Asian Indian ancestry; Kenneth Bryant, who grew up in the Imperial Valley, "thought that Sandhu, though a little different, was a Mexican name, and the Sandhus spoke Mexican" (Vancouver, 1988).

2. Elizabeth Harris, Holtville, 1981, talking about her neighbor Naginder S. Garewal of Holtville; Francisco Singh, Selma, 1983.

3. Only three or four daughters had Kore or Core on their birth certificates—the name was not a familiar one. One girl, born Besente Kaur, was termed Bistcor by her mother on a divorce petition: Civil Case 23525, Office of the County Clerk, Imperial County, 1946.

4. These were the comments of, respectively, a Sikh's wife about another's son, a Muslim's daughter about neighbors, an Anglo classmate about the son of a Sikh, and the daughter of a Sikh about the daughter of a Muslim.

5. Alfred Sidhu, Sacramento, 1982.

6. Nellie Soto and Caroline Shine Sunghera Resendez, Huntington Beach, 1982; Mary Garewal Gill, El Centro, 1981. For nicknames as a mark of inclusion in a group among Hispanics, see Carlos G. Velez-Ibanez, *Bonds of Mutual Trust: The Cultural Systems of Rotating Credit Associations among Urban Mexicans and Chicanos* (New Brunswick, N.J.: Rutgers University Press, 1983), 92.

7. Verdie Montgomery and Emma Smiley, Sacramento, 1982; birth and death certificates from Sacramento and Fresno counties.

8. The last six names were probably Ghulam Rasul, (unclear) Khan, Sultan Ali, Yusuf Abdulla, Mohamed Ali, and Ghulam Hyder (Khan). These mispronounciations were not just characteristic of black American descendants but of other descendants as well.

9. Mary Garewal Gill, Holtville, 1982; Mike Singh, El Centro, 1990.

10. Civil Case 19314, Office of the County Clerk, Imperial County, 1940.

11. Conclusion drawn from all interviews.

12. Teresa Garewal, Holtville, 1981 (the bachelor partner was a superb cook and taught her to cook Punjabi food); Emma Smiley and Verdie Montgomery, Sacramento, 1982, for the salutations to visitors. *Sat sri akal*, the most common Sikh salutation (once part of a war cry), means "the timeless is true."

13. Janie Diwan Poonian, Yuba City, 1982; Amelia Singh Netervala, Los Angeles, 1988. When Memel Singh married, he said, "Forget about the old country." Carmelita Shine, Chico, 1988 (remembering her mother's story). Niaz Mohamed, Sr., told his son that Urdu was too difficult, Spanish would be more useful to him.

Niaz Mohamed, Jr., Brawley, 1981. Alfred Sidhu said his dad told them not to ask so much about the Punjab because he didn't want "to dig up old things" (Sacramento, 1982). Ester Sidhu Villasenor (daughter of another Sidhu) said her father often told them, "This is my country now."

14. Alfred Sidhu, Sacramento, 1982; Leela Rai, Yuba City, 1983. (Leela is third generation, through her mother Mary Singh Rai; the grandson in question arrived after the immigration laws changed in 1965.)

15. Blanch Dillon (Vancouver, 1988), youngest daughter of Bakhshish Singh Dhillon from Fresno, was one who resisted pressure from the Punjabi men and would *not* call them uncle.

16. Catholic church records, Holtville; examples from elsewhere from Karmelita Kakar, San Jose, 1982, and Helen Ram Walsh, Hercules, 1988. Marriages without conversion occurred in the Imperial Valley (Sally Maynez to Aya S. Dhalliwal) and elsewhere (Susanna Mesa Rodriguez and Mola Singh in Fowler).

17. Bawa Singh Sanga, Ganga Ram, Inder Singh, and Memel Singh were said to have converted, but all four were cremated: Fernando Sanga, Brawley, 1981; Helen Walsh Ram, Hercules, 1988; Francisco Singh, Selma, 1983; Isabel Singh Garcia, Yuba City, 1982.

18. Amelia Singh Netervala, Los Angeles, 1988; Helen Ram Walsh, Hercules, 1988.

19. Bagga S. Sunga, Brawley, 1981, speaking about Karm S. Bharana.

20. Bernice Sidhu, Brawley, 1981.

21. Olga Dad Khan, Sacramento, 1982.

22. Sally Maynez Dhalliwal, Holtville, 1983.

23. Nellie Soto Shine and Caroline Shine Sunghera Resendez, Huntington Beach, 1982.

24. Lala and Sucha Singh Garewal were the dominant couple in the Holtville area. Author's field notes on *compadrazgo* relationships.

25. Lala Garewal and Mary Garewal Gill, Holtville, 1981; Nellie Soto Shine and Caroline Shine Sunghera Resendez, Huntington Beach, 1982.

26. Lala Garewal shaved Sucha Singh Garewal on their wedding day and every day since. Lala Garewal and Mary Garewal Gill, Holtville, 1981.

27. Verdie Montgomery, Sacramento, 1982.

28. Mary Garewal Gill, Holtville, 1981. A photo of some Muslim men in Phoenix shows them gathered around a hookah. Robert Khan, Phoenix, 1990.

29. Raymond Ram (whom Sant Ram had told of the young prince Krishna), Firebaugh, 1983; Harry Chand, son of Karm Chand, Live Oak, 1982; George Puri, son of Ramnath Puri, Los Angeles, 1984. For the Sareeram story, Viji Sundaram, "Sareeram Becomes First Indian Admiral in Navy," and "From Salt of the Earth to a Rare Old Salt," *India West*, April 7, 1989, 1, 31, 33.

30. Niaz and Sally Mohamed, Jr., Brawley, 1981, mentioned that Niaz Mo-

hamed, Sr., went to a Jewish butcher in San Diego, and this man sponsored him on his citizenship application. When Niaz Mohamed visited his son's home in later years and found baby-food jars of strained ham and peas, he swept them into the garbage, to the horror of the struggling young couple; after that, they took unorthodox food to a neighbor's when warned of an impending visit.

31. Olga Dad Khan, Sacramento, 1982; Verdie Montgomery, Sacramento, 1982. Descendants cared for the graves, even though they might not be Muslims themselves. In Phoenix, the Muslim Association plot is administered today by two Christian sons, Ishmael Rahmatulla and Robert Khan (Phoenix, 1988 and 1990, respectively).

32. Miller, "an Ethnographic Report," photo caption, 153.

33. Isabel Singh Garcia, Yuba City, 1981; Mary Garewal Gill, El Centro, 1981.

34. Personal observation, cemeteries in El Centro and Brawley. See the insightful discussions in Terry G. Jordan, *Texas Graveyards: A Cultural Legacy* (Austin: University of Texas Press, 1982).

35. Olga Dad Khan, Sacramento, 1982; Verdie Montgomery, Sacramento, 1982; Niaz Mohamed, Jr., Brawley, 1990; Robert Khan, Phoenix, 1990. In later years, with prosperity and renewed contacts with India and incoming immigrants, some men returned to the Islamic customs of their youth in India and secured Qurans and prayer rugs. Olga Dad Khan's remark about Washington, D.C., probably refers to the Pakistani Embassy personnel there after 1947.

36. Julia Villa, a fourteen-year-old schoolgirl in Yuma, Arizona, became a passionate convert to Islam after marrying Omar Deen. She insisted that her nine children have proper religious schooling, just as she insisted that they go to the "white" school near their home instead of the "Mexican" school. Julia, however, died at the age of thirty-seven, just as her first daughter was married to an older Muslim from India who had a business in San Francisco. Elizabeth Deen Hernandez, Burbank 1981. Julia Deen is one of only two women buried in the old Muslim section of the Sacramento cemetery (personal observation). Robert Khan's mother, Maria, in Phoenix relinquished her Catholicism but did not formally convert. Robert Khan, Phoenix, 1990.

37. Bernice Sidhu, Brawley, 1981; Caroline Shine Sunghera Resendez and Nellie Soto Shine, Huntington Beach, 1982.

38. Nand Kaur, "Interview," 28–29.

39. Bobby Sanga, Brawley, 1987 (interviewed by Lupe Beltran); Caroline Shine Sunghera Resendez, Huntington Beach, 1982; Isabel Singh Garcia, Yuba City, 1982; Karmelita Kakar, San Jose, 1982.

40. Janie Diwan Poonian, Yuba City, 1983; Barbara Quade Lang, Tucson, Arizona, 1989 (telephone).

41. Conclusion drawn from all interview notes.

42. Ishmael Rahmatulla, Phoenix, 1988; Judge William Lehnhardt, Brawley,

1981 (about his mother-in-law, Guadelupe Mancillas Din); Carmelita Shine, Chico, 1988; Helen Ram Walsh, Hercules, 1988; and Marianne Singh Bhatti, daughter of Ganga and Josephine Lucero Singh Bhatti (Josephine was half Mexican American and half American Indian), Live Oak, 1989.

43. The quoted phrase was used by Taylor, *Mexican Population: Imperial Valley*, 19; see also 16–19. The black population arrived earlier and settled in El Centro and Imperial, older cotton-growing areas; the Mexicans went to the newer cotton areas around Brawley and Calipatria. *Ibid.*, 26–27.

44. *Ibid.*, 55–56, for the camps, and 19, 65–69, 41, 79–83. See also Cramp, Shields, and Thomsen, "Study of the Mexican Population."

45. A suit brought by Mexican Americans against four school districts in Orange County made school segregation based on ethnicity illegal in California in 1947. W. Henry Cooke, "The Segregation of Mexican-American School Children in Southern California," in *Racism in California*, ed. Roger Daniels and Spencer C. Olin, Jr. (New York: Macmillan. 1972), 220–228.

46. Taylor, *Mexican Population: Imperial Valley*, 76–77, 83–84. Taylor's estimate of 36.8 percent is based on a census of elementary school children taken February 1, 1927, using the method of population estimation developed by Louis Bloch in his "Report on the Mexican Labor Situation in the Imperial Valley," *Twenty-second Biennial Report of the Bureau of Labor Statistics of the State of California, 1925–1926* (Sacramento, 1926), 113–127. Their figures differ because Taylor was able to use Bloch's completed questionnaires, unavailable when Bloch went to press. See also Paul Schuster Taylor, *Mexican Labor in the United States: Racial School Statistics California, 1927*, vol. 6, no. 4 (1929) (Berkeley: University of California Press, Publications in Economics, 1929), 264, where the 36.8 percent is reported to be the highest proportion of Mexican elementary schoolchildren in California.

47. See Taylor, *Mexican Population: Imperial Valley*, 27–28. for the small numbers of Mexicans in Holtville.

48. In northern California, schools were small and said not to be segregated, although "the Japanese, Portuguese, and Hindu children were put in a separate room together." Emma Smiley, Sacramento, 1982. In Arizona, only the blacks were segregated. Amelia Singh Netervala, Los Angeles, 1990.

49. Rose Chell Canaris, Calexico, 1987; Mary Garewal Gill, Holtville, 1981.

50. Joseph Anderholt, Holtville, 1990, testified to prejudice against second-generation Swiss and others whose early command of English was poor. See Maxine Hong Kingston, *The Woman Warrior: Memoirs of a Girlhood among Ghosts* (New York: Knopf, 1977), 163, for traumatic experiences in school.

51. Elmer Heald, then district attorney of Imperial County, said that in 1927 or 1928. Paul Taylor, "Field Notes," 74–79.

52. Domingo Deol, Corona, 1981; Fernando Sanga, Brawley, 1981.

53. Bernice Sidhu, with Ernesto Vargas and Sarah Leonard, Brawley, 1981.

54. Cramp et al., "Study of the Mexican Population," 8–11; Taylor, *Mexican Population: Imperial Valley*, 87–89. Second-generation members commented that segregation was stronger in the time of their parents. The Hispanic women attending the Sacred Heart Catholic Church on the west side of Brawley were told by the priest to move to the back of the church; later another Catholic church, St. Mary Margaret, was built on the east side. Bernice Sidhu, Brawley, 1981.

55. Elizabeth Deen Hernandez, Burbank, 1981; Ishmael Rahmatulla, Phoenix, 1988; and for the death, Raymond Ram, Firebaugh, 1983. Cesar Chavez described his family's stay in the Imperial Valley in the late 1930s and the impact of the discrimination on him. Dick Meister and Ann Loftis, *A Long Time Coming* (New York: Macmillan, 1977), 111–112.

56. Helen Ram Walsh, Hercules, 1988.

57. When one absentee landlord in Los Angeles tried to charge $30 a month rent for a shack on the land Sucha Singh Garewal was leasing, his schoolgirl daughter carefully wrote out the letter her father dictated, refusing to pay and stating that the shack in question was not fit for human habitation. Mary Garewal Gill, Holtville, 1981.

58. In almost all these early cases, the men died without wills, and the estates were handled by the same lawyer and court-appointed administrator, J. W. Glassford and R. Edgar respectively; in only one case was another Sikh appointed executor according to the deceased man's will. In one, the sixteen-year-old Hispanic widow requested that an Anglo farmer be named administrator in her place (the exceptional cases are 774 and 775, Office of the County Clerk, Imperial County, 1919.

59. The first guardian was Sucha Singh Dhalliwal, the Holtville farmer who worked closely with the president of the Holtville Bank in his farming operations (case 1800). The two brothers were Kehar and Mota Singh of Brawley (case 3198). In Arizona, such appointments began in 1941. Probate records, Maricopa County, Arizona State Archives in Phoenix for the (Singh) cases.

60. Imperial County, Register of Actions Probate, 1907–1949, indexes beginning with *A, B, C, D, G, K, M, R,* and *S* checked for Punjabi surnames. Every January 31, the "trustee" or guardian had to file a written report with itemized accounts of expenditures, acquisitions, and profits with the county clerk and with the secretary of the State of California.

61. In 1932, Laura Sedoo of Fresno was examined by J. Edgar Hoover himself to regain her citizenship. He told her it was "the damndest law he ever saw" and asked her only one question, to see their baby (she had dreaded the examination, having heard he was tough and usually asked twenty questions). Fresno, 1982 (with Sarah Leonard).

62. Cases 2731 of 1937 and 2959 of 1939 for the first instance and 3177 of 1941 for the second. Office of the County Clerk, Imperial County.

63. Robert Chell, Holtville, 1981, for Garewal and Chell; "Diwan Singh, Pinal Farmer, Dies While Flying Home from India," newspaper, ca. May 19, 1956 (from Barbara Quade Lang, Tucson, 1988).

64. Mola Singh, Selma, 1982; Bagga S. Sunga, Brawley, 1981.

65. Elizabeth Deen Hernandez, Burbank, 1981; Alfred Sidhu, Sacramento, 1982; Ray Sidhu and Isabel Sidhu Villasenor, Yuba City, 1982.

66. Sources are, in alphabetical order, Mary Garewal Gill, Holtville, 1981; Karmelita Kakar, San Jose, 1982; Laura Sedoo, Fresno, 1982; Nellie Soto Shine, Huntington Beach, 1982; Helen Ram Walsh, Hercules, 1988.

67. James E. Sidel, *Pick for Your Supper, A Study of Child Labor among Migrants on the Pacific Coast.* For the National Child Labor Committee, June 1939, 32 (part of the Carey McWilliams Collection at the University of California, Los Angeles, sequence 1, box 11).

68. Taylor, *Mexican Population,* 75. Punjabis were among those fined for employing children in their cotton fields. For examples, *Holtville Tribune,* October 10, 1924; and *Imperial Valley Press,* October 23, 1925.

69. Isabel Sidhu Villasenor and Ray Sidhu, Yuba City, 1982; Alfred Sidhu, Sacramento, 1982; Karmelita Kakar, San Jose, 1982; Isabel Singh Garcia, Yuba City, 1982.

70. For the change from cotton to dairy farming and out again, see Joseph J. Anderholt, *Desert Dairies: Catalyst for the Development of Imperial Valley* (Imperial: Imperial County Historical Society, 1989). Mechanical milkers came in in the 1920s, lessening the utility of children. Mark Kramer, *Three Farms* (Boston: Atlantic Monthly Press, 1980), 31. For the Mexicans' permanent northward movement, see Paul Schuster Taylor, *Mexican Labor in the United States,* vol. 12 (Berkeley: University of California Publications in Economics, 1933), 18; and Paul Schuster Taylor and Edward J. Rowell, "Patterns of Agricultural Labor Migration Within California," *Monthly Labor Review,* 1938, 980–990.

71. For example, Alfred Sidhu's father invariably was taken on as a foreman on the Firebaugh Ranch in Mendota, and three or four of his sons worked in his crew. Alfred Sidhu, Sacramento, 1982.

72. Briggs and Cauthen, *Cotton Man,* 61.

73. Khan, "A Brief History," 45–46; Victor Dad and Ishmael Rahmatulla, both in Phoenix, 1988.

74. Daniel, *Bitter Harvest,* 102–103, 108–109, 111–112.

75. Ibid., 179, 228; and see James Gray, "The American Civil Liberties Union of Southern California and Imperial Valley Agricultural Labor Disturbances: 1930, 1934," Ph.D. dissertation, University of California, Los Angeles, 1966.

76. Meister and Loftis, *A Long Time Coming,* 35.

77. Daniel, *Bitter Harvest,* 242–249.

78. Francisco Singh, Selma, 1983; Mola Singh, Selma, 1982.

79. Alfred Sidhu, Sacramento, 1982.

80. Mola Singh, Selma, 1982.

81. Robert Mohammed and Lillian Palmer, Yuba City, 1982; Mohammed Afzal Khan, Butte City, 1988.

Chapter 8. The Second Generation Comes of Age

1. Josephine Lucero Singh Bhatti, Live Oak, 1989.

2. Ali and Lucy Abdulla, Sacramento, 1983.

3. Penalosa, "Mexican Family Roles," 686. He also states that the mother/daughter relationship is the closest of the four parent-child relationships: 687.

4. Mike Singh and Rosie Lusier, El Centro, 1990. The driving incident, which occurred in Los Angeles on the way back from a trip to Stockton, was confirmed by Mary Garewal Gill, Holtville, 1990 (Rosie is her daughter).

5. Irene Dhillon, El Centro, 1990; Mike Singh, El Centro, 1990; Pritam Sandhu, Calipatria, 1990. See Pettigrew, *Robber Noblemen*, 49, for discussion of the drinking and its function in the Punjab.

6. Mike Singh and Rosie Lusier, El Centro, Feb. 1990; the first quote is from Mike Singh, the second from Marianne Singh Andrews, interviewed with Ganga Singh and Josephine Lucero Singh Bhatti, Live Oak, 1989 (she is their daughter); and Parmatma Dhillon, El Centro, 1990 (about his D in penmanship).

7. The quotes are from Mike Singh, El Centro, 1990; Kartar Dhillon, Berkeley, 1987; and Amelia Singh Netervala, Los Angeles, 1988.

8. The quotes are from Mike Singh, El Centro, 1990, and Nora Singh Nichols, Casa Grande, 1989; Rosie Lusier, El Centro, 1990; Janie Diwan Poonian, Yuba City, 1983; Verdie Montgomery, Citrus Heights, 1982; Rose Chell Canaris, Calexico, 1987 (interviewed by Lupe Beltran); and Amelia Singh Netervala, Los Angeles, 1990.

9. Sources, in alphabetical order: Ali Abdulla, Sacramento, 1983; Harry Chand, Live Oak, 1983; Blanche Dillon, Vancouver, 1988; Isabel Singh Garcia, Yuba City, 1982; Fatima Mia, Pacoima, 1983; and Mary Singh Rai, Yuba City, 1983. The Diwan Singh quote is from "Diwan Singh—American," n.p., n.d. (ca. 1948), sent by his daughter Barbara Quade Lang, Tucson, 1988.

10. Blanche Dillon, Vancouver, 1988, for the quote; Mike Singh, El Centro, 1990, for the money ritual.

11. Making fun of the "rice king" claims was Caroline Shine Sunghera Resendez, Huntington Beach, 1982.

12. Irene Dhillon, El Centro, 1990, for the picking peas story. Mirra Komarovsky, *The Unemployed Man and His Family* (New York: Dryden Press, 1940), 98, makes this general point.

13. One son came back and married the daughter of a Punjabi Muslim in Arizona. Ishmael Rahmatulla, Phoenix, 1988.

14. Salim and Olga Dad Khan, Sacramento, 1982; Bobby Sanga, Brawley, 1987 (interviewed by Lupe Beltran); Uttam Singh Dhillon, San Diego, 1988; Fatima Mia, Pacoima, 1983; Kay Sigera Dillon, Sacramento, 1982; and Lucy Singh Abdulla, Sacramento, 1983. Karmelita Kakar's father was "just like other fathers except he brushed his teeth with a cottonwood twig." San Jose, 1982. Civil Case 17775, Office of the County Clerk, Imperial County, 1939, for the man who took his daughter to Mexico.

15. Alfred Sidhu, Sacramento, 1982.

16. Mike Singh, El Centro, 1990; Pritam Sandhu, Calipatria, 1990.

17. Mike Singh, El Centro, 1990. Perhaps relevant is Glen Elder's discussion of fathers whose powerlessness (in this case, dependence on others for control of land) resulted in hostility toward their sons and punitive socialization, with possible outcomes in the sons of covert hostility toward their fathers, feelings of guilt, and pessimistic outlooks on life's prospects. Elder, "History and the Life Course," in Bertaux, *Biography and Society*, 84.

18. Pritam Sandhu, Calipatria, 1990; Robert Khan, Phoenix, 1990.

19. Fatima Mia, Pacoima, 1983. See Susan Carol Rogers and Sonya Salamon, "Inheritance and Social Organization among Family Farmers," *American Ethnologist* 10, no. 3 (1983): 534–535, for family farming concerns with inheritance.

20. In accordance with the literature, I term them "second generation," but several members of it call themselves "first generation," meaning the first generation born in the United States. The usage is contested.

21. Irene Dhillon, El Centro, 1990; Mike Singh, El Centro, 1990.

22. Isabel Singh Garcia, Yuba City, 1982; Domingo Deol, Corona, 1981; Mary Garewal Gill, El Centro, 1981; Amelia Singh Netervala, Los Angeles, 1990; *Holtville Tribune*, April 25, 1944 (reporting on the Harnam Singh Dhillon family picnic—others present were the Kunda S. Chells and the Karm S. Sandhus).

23. See the high school yearbooks in the Pioneers Museum in Imperial: *The Painted Desert, La Solana, The Oasis, La Ocatilla,* and *Mirage.* These sets were not complete when I saw them, so I have taken some information from the registrar's files for Imperial Valley College, which gives high schools and graduation dates for those who enrolled there. (For those descendants born before 1950, some 8 high school graduates from Brawley, 7 from Calipatria, 2 from Calexico, 32 from El Centro, 22 from Holtville, and 13 from Imperial went on to the community college.) The first non-Anglos in most of these high schools were Japanese girls; boys from farming families had erratic school careers because they were needed for work. Joseph Anderholt thinks the first Swiss farmer's son graduated from high school in 1930. Joseph and Dorothy Anderholt, Holtville, 1981. The Central Junior College was founded in 1922 and gave the AA degree from 1934. It was renamed the Imperial Valley College in 1951, the Imperial Valley Junior College District was formed in 1959, and the new campus was developed in 1962. *Imperial Valley College General Catalog 1981–82* (Imperial: Imperial Community College District, n.d.), 12.

24. Niaz and Sally Mohamed, Jr., Brawley, 1981. This prohibition extended to other pig products: Ishmael Rahmatulla had bought new pigskin gloves and had to throw them away when his father noticed them (Phoenix, 1988).

25. Joseph Anderholt, Holtville, 1981; Robert Mohammed and Lillian Palmer, Los Angeles, 1988.

26. Mary Garewal Gill, Holtville, 1990.

27. Isabel Singh Garcia, Yuba City, 1982; Karmelita Kakar, San Jose, 1982.

28. Some Mexican men first worked in Yuba City through their Punjabi relatives; later, the *bracero* program brought many Mexican workers to the northern area. Joe Mallobox, El Centro, 1982.

29. One was a second marriage, one involved the daughter of a Sikh by an Anglo mother, and in three of the five cases the marriage was the daughter's choice. (I have no information on how four of the marriages ended.)

30. The first marriage was a Sikh-Hindu one, the second a Muslim cousin-marriage (the daughter of a Muslim man and his Mexican wife in the Imperial Valley was married to a Muslim from San Francisco, her father's cousin). But in this "traditional" Muslim (civil) wedding, one of the two official witnesses was the Mexican wife of a Sikh farmer in the Imperial Valley. Marriage license, Recorder's Office, Imperial County, 1937, bk. 390, p. 407.

31. Caroline Shine Sunghera Resendez, Huntington Beach, 1982; Harry Chand, Live Oak, 1983.

32. *Post Press*, July 30, 1939.

33. *Post Press*, August 13, 1939. Santi Singh held land for other Punjabis as well, at least until she divorced her husband and left the Imperial Valley. Anna Sandhu, Calipatria, 1982; Caroline Shine Sunghera Resendez, Huntington Beach, 1982.

34. Mary Garewal Gill, Holtville, 1981; Caroline Shine Sunghera Resendez, Huntington Beach, 1982; Kartar Dhillon, Berkeley, 1987. See also Kartar Dhillon, "Parrot's Beak," 220.

35. Karmelita Kakar, San Jose, 1982; Fatima Mia, Pacoima, 1983; Isabel Sidhu Villasenor, Yuba City, 1982; Rose Chell Canaris, Calexico, 1987 (interviewed by Lupe Beltran); Amelia Singh Netervala, Los Angeles, 1988; Helen Ram Walsh, Hercules, 1988.

36. But she agreed to marry him; finally, her father approved. She did have a hard time, but they had chosen each other, she said, so it was a successful marriage. Janie Diwan Poonian, Yuba City, 1982.

37. Mike Singh joined the navy. El Centro, 1990. Jim Bailey, El Centro, 1981, and Isabel Singh Garcia, Yuba City, 1982, provided other examples.

38. Interviews with Elizabeth Deen Hernandez, Burbank, 1981; Mary Garewal Gill, Holtville, 1981; Kishen Singh Deol, Riverside, 1981; Mary Singh Rai, Yuba City, 1983; Karmelita Kakar, San Jose, 1982.

39. Isabel Singh Garcia, Yuba City, 1982; Elizabeth Deen Hernandez, Bur-

bank, 1981; Karmelita Kakar, San Jose, 1982; Mary Singh Rai, Yuba City, 1982; and Carmelita Shine, Chico, 1988.

40. Norma Saikhon, Brawley, 1981 (interviewed by Ernesto Vargas).

41. Alfred Sidhu, Sacramento, 1982.

42. Mary Singh Rai, Yuba City, 1982; Amelia Singh Netervala, Los Angeles, 1988; Helen Ram Walsh, Hercules, 1988.

43. Carmelita Shine, Chico, 1988; Elizabeth Deen Hernandez (quoting her mother), Burbank, 1981.

44. Victor Dad, Phoenix, Arizona, 1988. "Pakistani" came into use after 1947, with the creation of Pakistan.

45. These data are incomplete, since I did not check some seldom-found surnames in the California statewide database; I offer it only as illustrative of the patterns of second-generation marriages.

46. Two or three daughters of Anglos married pure Punjabis, but not half-Punjabis. Black and Anglo descendants (like others in the north) were harder to trace, but I found none married to Hispanics or Punjabi-Mexicans.

47. Bobby Sanga, Brawley, 1987 (interviewed by Lupe Beltran); Joe Mallobox, El Centro, 1982; Carmelita Shine, Chico, 1988.

48. Kartar Dhillon, "Parrot's Beak," 217. Another daughter eloped with a Punjabi-Mexican son, just a week before she was to be taken to India for an arranged marriage. Her father set out in his pickup truck with a shotgun when he heard about the elopement, but the bridegroom had worked alongside the bride's brothers in the orchards and they helped protect the couple. Some sons also eloped to avoid the pressures for marriage with a "real Indian."

49. First-generation occupations were variously given as rancher, farmer, or laborer on birth certificates of children. In several cases, the effects of the depression can be seen in changes from these occupations to field laborer or restaurant waiter. Son's occupational designations come from their children's birth certificates too.

50. Hatch, "Stratification," 33–34.

51. Imperial County ranked 54th, 56th, and 53rd (of California's 58 counties) on these measures. Finley, "Economic History," 93–94 (using the 1960 census).

52. Ibid.

53. Vernon M. Briggs, Jr., *Chicanos and Rural Poverty* (Baltimore: Johns Hopkins University Press, 1973), 28–29. For the impact on Imperial County, Jerome L. Schwartz, *Statistical Survey of the Aid to Needy Children Program in Imperial County, California* (Imperial County: Family Health and Welfare Project, 1961), 4–5. For the *bracero* program, see Bean, *California, an Interpretive History*, 498–501.

54. Alfred Sidhu, Sacramento, 1982; Lola Dhillon, Holtville, 1981.

55. Carmelita Shine, Chico, 1988; Mary Garewal Gill, Holtville, 1982; Mary Singh Rai, Yuba City, 1983; Amelia Singh Netervala, Los Angeles, 1988; Helen Ram Walsh, Hercules, 1988.

56. Harnam S. Dhillon opened the Taj of India in San Francisco after he had worked in the India House, run by Britishers. Teja and Kay Dillon, Fresno, 1982. For law-enforcement jobs, narcotics officer Bob Khan, Deputy Sheriff Mike Singh, Deputy Sheriff Dosant S. Sidhu, and Deputy District Attorney Fred Dhillon in the Imperial Valley; in Yuba City, Dave Teja was district attorney in the 1960s, and in Sacramento, Brar Sidhu is a deputy sheriff. In the Imperial Valley, Gloria Dhillon is married to Judge Donald Work and Sarah Deen to Judge William Lehnhardt (these men were once partners in a law firm); and in Yuba City, Eva Rasul married Sheriff H. P. Ollar.

57. George Puri, Los Angeles, 1984; Raymond Ram, Firebaugh, 1982; Sundaram, "Sareeram" and "From Salt of the Earth," 1, 31, 33, for Admiral George Sareeram. Ram Chand, an early well-educated resident of the Imperial Valley, did not do well in farming either and ended up running a small grocery store in Arizona. Robert Khan, Phoenix, 1990. Another family that fits many aspects of this pattern is that of Bakhshish Singh Dhillon, the well-educated political activist. His children, again with a mother from India, were orphaned early, grew up agnostic, and have followed diverse and interesting careers.

58. Perhaps it is the other way around, since all three families were somewhat marginally connected to the biethnic families. Two of the sons married Anglo women; the third, after a brief marriage to a Hispanic woman connected to the Punjabi-Mexicans, remarried a woman from Mexico.

Chapter 9. Political Change and Ethnic Identity

1. See Khushwant Singh, *Train to Pakistan* (New York: Grove Press, 1956); and Bapsi Sidhwa, *The Ice-Candy Man* (London: William Heinemann, 1988). Both contain graphic accounts of the violence that accompanied partition in the Punjab.

2. La Brack, *Sikhs of Northern California*, 272–274.

3. R. Narayanan, "Indian Immigration and the India League of America," *Indian Journal of American Studies* 2 (1972): 22. The McCarran-Walter Act of 1952 established a similar quota for Pakistanis.

4. Narayanan, "Indian Immigration," 13, 22, for the main provisions of the 1946 bill; U.S. Senate, Committee on Immigration, *To Permit the Naturalization of Approximately Three Thousand Natives of India, Hearings before a Subcommittee,* on S. 1595, 78th Cong., 2nd sess, September 13 and 14, 1944, 52–53.

5. *Laboo Singh* v. *Clara Banes*, December 6, 1954, cited in 129 CA 2d 395, Civ. No. 8012, 3rd District, 277 P2d 89. Johnny Khan and Kalu Khan, partners in Willows, allegedly had to buy back their property from the attorney who had held it for them over the years. Mohammed Afzal Khan, Willows, 1988.

6. Harmon Singh and Kartar Singh came to the Imperial Valley from the Fresno and Lodi area to purchase land. C. Scott Littleton thought there were some

eighty Punjabi men in the Imperial Valley in 1959 and all but three or four were landowners, with land ranging from forty acres to several thousand acres, whereas statewide only 70 percent were landowners. Littleton, "Some Aspects of Social Stratification Among the Immigrant Punjabi Communities of California," 109–110, in *Culture Change and Stability*, ed. Ralph L. Beals (Los Angeles: Department of Anthropology, University of California at Los Angeles, 1964). R. E. (Joe) Patzlof of the Wells Fargo Bank (formerly the Holtville National Bank) loaned me the 1955 Blackburn's Map of the Imperial Valley (Keith Savage, former head of the bank, remembered that it had that map). In the Imperial Valley, the Union Sugar Company books for 1950 and again for 1960–1961 show twenty-eight Punjabi farmers growing sugar beets for them, about a third of them on their own land in 1950 and a fifth in 1960. "Union Sugar Company Black Book of Field Sheets," 1950, 1960–1961. (Jim Bailey and Julia Youngblood, El Centro, let me see these, the earliest records available after 1946.)

7. A few had been active all along. Bakhshish Singh Dhillon had campaigned hard for Robert LaFollette for president, and Bagga S. Sunga in Brawley commented wryly that people often solicited his support for candidates and issues, not realizing he could not vote. Kartar Dhillon, Berkeley, 1989; Bagga S. Sunga, El Centro, 1981. The 1958 "Index to Great Register, General Elections, Sutter County," had eight registered Punjabi pioneers, six of them Democrats. Yuba City, Sutter County Library, Special Collection.

8. Jacoby, "More Thind Against," 8, predicted that most of the men would not apply for citizenship because they were so bitter. He was wrong. In Casa Grande, Arizona, Diwan Singh's friends helped him memorize facts and passages from the Constitution; he became the first Hindu to get U.S. citizenship at Tucson, passing an oral test shortly after Congress enacted the Luce-Celler bill. *Casa Grande Dispatch,* April 9, 1948, and May 1956, 8. In Yuba City, Fathe Mohammed and his German-Austrian wife, Mary, studied five years, and when they came before the board, neither one was asked a single question. They were well known and liked in the Yuba City area. Robert Mohammed, Yuba City, 1983. Mir Dad in Phoenix, Arizona, finally felt ready for the test in 1978 at the age of eighty-nine or ninety; his wife, who could read and write, had planned to take it with him but was too nervous. Victor Dad, Phoenix, 1988. Mohamed Rahmatulla in Phoenix took night school classes for four years and became a citizen in 1948. Ishmael Rahmatulla, Phoenix, 1988.

9. Naturalization Petitions, Office of the County Clerk, Imperial County, 1946–1980 (the age average at the time of application was sixty-six). Seven wives also became citizens, only two of them before 1965.

10. Dalip S. Saund, *Congressman from India* (New York: Dutton, 1960). For the story, "In Memory of the Honorable Dalip Singh Saund," *Sikh Sansar* 2, no. 3 (1973): 89. Saund is said to have had a Ph.D. in mathematics from Berkeley; he

did not wear a turban himself. Saund was a Ramgarhia (artisan caste) Sikh, the only one so designated to me, and perhaps for that reason seemed only loosely connected to the Sikh networks.

11. Those who retired or thought of retiring there included Babu Khan, Pir Miyan, and Bagga Singh Sunga; and in Arizona, Maluk Singh, Abdul Karim Khan, and Wali/Billy Mohamed Khan. Joe Mallobox, El Centro, 1982; Bagga Singh Sunga, Brawley, 1982; Amelia Singh Netervala, Los Angeles, 1990; Robert Khan, Phoenix, 1990. Among those who took equipment to South Asia were Mir Dad and Ramnath Puri. Victor Dad, Phoenix, 1988; George Puri, Los Angeles, 1984. The senior Puri went to India twice, and his son sent him money to come home the first time. The second time, he went despite his son's warning that he would not send money again, and someone else (the U.S. Embassy in India?) paid for his ticket home.

12. Some Muslims had resented being termed "Hindus," Salim Khan told me (Sacramento, 1982), and gave their place of birth as Afghanistan to differentiate themselves from the majority group of Sikhs from India. Khan came after 1946; I found it hard to check this statement, since descendants' versions of place names are not reliable.

13. Kartar Dhillon, Berkeley, 1987, and Robert Mohammed, Yuba City, 1982. Fathe Mohammed, Robert's father, had used "Bande Mataram" as a greeting to his Hindu friends (Karm Chand, Gouda Ram) in the 1920s; it was a nationalist salutation among Punjabis in California. Even after partition, the El Centro *gurdwara* served as a meeting place for Sikhs and Muslims.

14. Permission was received from the Shiromani Gurdwara Prabandhak Committee of Amritsar on April 13, 1946, according to Brar, "East Indians in Sutter County," 21. Brar mentions several progressive students who helped bring the change about; chairs were also installed in the El Centro temple. See also La Brack, *Sikhs of Northern California,* 223–224. The fact of permission was disputed later by new immigrant leaders in Yuba City.

15. Nika Singh Gill, Holtville, 1981; Brar, "East Indians in Sutter County," 21–22; Wood, "East Indians," 115–117.

16. Mohammed Aslam Khan, Butte City, 1988; Bagga S. Sunga, Brawley, 1981; and "Articles of Incorporation, Imperial Valley Khalsa Diwan, December 14, 1947," in the office of the El Centro *gurdwara*. See U.S. Government, War Relocation Authority, "Japanese Population of Imperial Valley," for an account of the evacuated population. Punjabis continued to patronize Japanese stores until their owners were evacuated, despite "advice" from others at this time. Bagga S. Sunga, Brawley, 1981.

17. Khan, "Brief History of Pakistanis," 63, 70–71. Mohamed Sadullah from Detroit wintered in California every year and initiated the mosque effort. Robert Khan, Phoenix, 1990.

18. Ibid., 56–58.

19. Niaz Mohamed, Jr., Brawley, 1981.

20. Ibid.; Joe Mallobox, El Centro 1982. When most of the Imperial Valley old-timers had died, the remaining members sold the property and divided the money among other California Islamic centers and mosques. The Muslims in Phoenix had purchased a cemetery lot much earlier, and they bought a building in 1980–1981. Khan, "Brief History of Pakistanis," 59.

21. La Brack, *Sikhs of Northern California*, 229–237; see also Bruce La Brack, "Overseas Sikhs and the Economy of Punjab: Remittances Before and After 1984," paper presented at the 16th annual conference on South Asia, Madison, Wisc., 1987.

22. Bernice Sidhu, Brawley, 1981.

23. These were Inder Kaur, the wife of Bagga S. Sunga, and Mohinder Kaur and Bachint Kaur, the new brides of Ripaduman Singh Samra and Toga Singh, respectively: Mary Garewal Gill, Anna Singh Sandhu, and Bachint Kaur, all in El Centro at the Sikh temple, 1981.

24. Chenchel Rai and Naranjan Singh Atwal, with Bob Singh, Yuba City, 1982; Bachint Kaur and Anna Singh Sandhu, in the El Centro Sikh temple, 1981 and 1984.

25. Jay Wagoner, *Arizona's Heritage* (Santa Barbara: Peregrine-Smith, 1978), 280; and his obituaries in the *Los Angeles Times*, June 3, 1956, *Casa Grande Despatch*, n.d. May, 1956, 1, 8, and *Trade Journal*, August 3, 1956, for his cotton-growing methods and career in Pinal County. Diwan Singh was one of the first to switch from horses to tractors, to practice "rough tillage," and to recirculate wastewater through a sump and pumps. He also had close ties to powerful political figures.

26. Of five wives on the 1952 plaque who were daughters of Punjabi pioneers, three went on to other marriages, one was in a second marriage, and the fifth stayed in the first marriage.

27. More women from the Punjab have come to the Imperial Valley since 1952, but more recent arrivals know little of earlier family histories. New immigrant families from India were not the nucleus of an expanding immigrant community in the 1980s, as were their counterparts in central and northern California. When I dropped in on Sundays from 1981 until 1985, the number attending varied between three to six women and six to ten men. Only for a funeral was there a larger number, and only then did more than two or three Punjabi-Mexican family members attend. By 1990, the numbers had doubled or tripled, with new immigrants accounting for the increase.

28. These boys included Billie Thind, Harnek Brar, and Jagdish Mann, in the Imperial Valley. Karmen and Robert Chell, Holtville, 1981.

29. When asked by some of the young mothers, the men refused to sponsor Punjabi lessons or pay for playground equipment at the temple, citing the expense. Mary Garewal Gill and Anna Singh Sandhu, El Centro, 1990.

30. Robindra Chakravorti, "The Sikhs of El Centro: a Study in Social Integration," Ph.D. dissertation, University of Minnesota, 1968, 73. The pioneer said he feared desecration as well as extinction of the temple.

31. In Yuba City, Nandu Singh's nephews from the Fiji Islands came over, and Memel Singh's nephew was brought from India at the expense of his daughter Carmelita Singh's college hopes, said Isabel Singh Garcia (Yuba City, 1982). (Carmelita herself said only that she helped bring the nephew over. Chico, 1988.) In the Willows–Butte City area, Kalu Khan brought his nephew Sadiq Khan over; then Atta Muhamed Khan, known as Johnny Khan, brought his brother's son Mohammed Afzal Khan, a boy of seventeen, to be his heir in 1957. Namat Khan and his farming partner, Fazal Mohamed, brought Namat's nephew Mohammed Aslam Khan in 1958. Fazal Mohamed was active in the International Rotary Club and Democratic politics and was on the Board of Governors of Chico State, where all three boys enrolled.

32. Johnny Khan married a Pakistani woman visiting the United States in 1958, and Fazal Mohamed's Pakistani bride came over with Mohammed Aslam Khan in 1958. Sadiq Khan and Mohammed Aslam Khan brought brides from Pakistan, and Mohamed Afzal Khan married an American woman whom he met at Chico State. These men provided the nucleus of the new Pakistani community. Salim Khan, Sacramento, 1982; Mohammed Afzal Khan and Mohammed Aslam Khan, in Willows and Butte City, respectively, 1988.

33. For Didar Singh Bains, see Dhillon, *History Book*, 492, and *India West*, December 19, 1980. In the latter story, Bains appears in a photo clean-shaven (he became an *amritdhari* Sikh in 1981 and a leader of the World Sikh Movement). His 6,500-square-foot ranch house has two tennis courts and a parking area for thirty to forty cars. His approximately 6,000 acres of orchards made him the largest landowner in District 10, the Yuba City area; at one time or another he owned almost 50 percent of the orchards there. *India West*, December 19 and 26, 1980. Singh farmed 10,000–15,000 acres of crops in 1989, and his 1964 marriage allegedly provided him with some of the capital he needed to expand. Richard Steven Street, "The Sikhs," *California Farmer*, January 21, 1989, 41. His wife is a third-generation Punjabi-Mexican descendant on her mother's side (Janie Diwan); her father was second generation and pure Punjabi (Paritem Poonian).

34. For the club's formation, see *Holtville Times*, April 11 and 18, 1946. These Dillons came to the valley from Fresno, Blanche with Kartar (her older sister) and Surat Singh Gill and Kaipur as a young adult. Blanche "wore red shorts and took a job in a liquor store in the black section" of El Centro. Kaipur married a Punjabi-Mexican daughter and is still remembered by Anglos in the valley as a militant organizer. Jim Bailey and Danny Danenberg, El Centro, 1982. Blanch (Vancouver, 1988) simply remembers working in a grocery store that sold liquor to both black and white customers.

35. Remembered variously as the East Indian American Club, the American Hindustani Club, and the Hindustani Club, this club also met at a Holtville location. Elizabeth Deen Hernandez, Burbank, 1981; Mary Garewal Gill, Holtville, 1982; Blanche Dillon, Vancouver, 1988.

36. The *Holtville Times*, July 21, 1949, for the marriage between a local boy, Peter Dhillon, and Susan Bans (Bains, a Punjabi-Mexican daughter from Fresno), and August 11, 1949, for the christening in Marysville of Mary Singh Rai's baby, with Mary's friend Nellie Sanchez from her telephone office job as godmother.

37. Amelia Singh Netervala, Los Angeles, 1990.

38. This custom may have stemmed from the Swiss "crown girls" and queen of the annual Swiss Swingfest, celebrated in Holtville from 1925 onward. Anderholt and Anderholt, *History*, 98, 176, 245. In 1958, Lucy Dhillon represented India and Nita Nell Mallobox represented Pakistan. *Holtville Times*, February 3, 1958.

39. Pauline Garewal, Yuba City, letter of March 7, 1988.

40. The 1980 Yuba City–Marysville telephone book had some 79 Punjabi Sikh surnames, of which only 8 were used before 1940 in the Imperial Valley.

41. Bernice Sidhu, Brawley, 1981; Norma Saikhon, Brawley, 1981 (interviewed by Ernesto Vargas); Isabel Sidhu Villasenor and Ray Sidhu, Yuba City, 1982. For a change of birth certificate, see Recorder's Office, Fresno County, 1937 b. 31, no. 222, corrected in 1976 by Petra Romero Singh Rompol and the son's spouse, Mrs. Sylvia (Frank) Singh Rompol, by adding Rompol to the names of father and son.

42. Uttam Dhillon (with Gurdit and Dharmo Dhillon), San Diego, 1988; Three others from Arizona—Louisa Khan, Lola Rahmatulla, and Mary Dad—married Pakistani men. Olga Dad Khan, Sacramento, 1982. Fatima Din Mia (Los Angeles, 1983) married a Bangladeshi Muslim.

43. La Brack, *Sikhs of Northern California*, 300. Caroline Shine Sunghera Resendez is listed in the 1972 *Register of Sikhs in the U.S. and Canada* (Redwood City: Sikh Foundation), 80. She is the only second-generation daughter included; there are about ten second-generation sons, including three of her brothers.

44. James Paul Allen and Eugene James Turner, *We the People* (New York: Macmillan, 1988), 198. After Sutter County came Fort Bend, Texas, with 1.01. There were 3,911 Pakistanis in California in 1980 (232), and Sutter County had the second-highest percentage in the nation for them with .20, following Fairfax City, Virginia, with .56.

45. Bagga S. Sunga, El Centro, 1981; Pritam S. Sandhu, Calipatria, 1990.

46. Professor Dave Singh, Economics Department, California State University, Long Beach, is a post-1965 immigrant from India whose grandfather left for the United States and never returned, leaving his wife and sons impoverished. They heard that he had married in Mexico. When he died about 1960, he willed

his property in India to his sons there, but they did not accept it. Telephone interview, 1987.

47. Joe Mallobox, El Centro, 1982.

48. Harry Chand, Live Oak, 1982.

49. Instances given by Rodolfo Singh, Brawley, 1981; Joe Mallobox, El Centro, 1982; Alfred Sidhu, Sacramento, 1982. And see Imperial County, Office of the County Clerk, Civil Case 26778, 1951.

50. Niaz Mohmed, Jr., Brawley, 1981, about his father; and Mohammed Aslam Khan about Babu Khan and the widow, Butte City, 1988.

51. For the literature on farmers and inheritance in the United States, see Mark Friedberger, "The Farm Family and the Inheritance Process: Evidence from the Corn Belt, 1870–1950," *Agricultural History* 57, no. 1 (1983): 1–13; he remarks that the spouse was the common choice as executor unless she was old and there were adult children (Hispanic wives were usually much younger than their husbands).

52. William Ewing, Holtville, 1981; Joseph and Dorothy Anderholt, Holtville, 1981; Lucy Sekhon, San Diego, 1982. Civil Case 38233, Office of the County Clerk, Imperial County, 1965 (for Harmon Singh's attempt to become guardian of Kartar Singh). Also, Oscar Singh, El Centro, 1981.

53. Karmen and Robert Chell, Holtville, 1981; Isabel Singh Garcia, Yuba City, 1982.

54. Elizabeth Deen Hernandez, Burbank, 1981; Joe Mallobox, El Centro, 1982. See La Brack's comments on bigamy in *Sikhs of Northern California*, 169–171. (I think he and Jacoby underestimate the number of Punjabis already married in India.)

55. Civil cases (divorce petitions), Office of the County Clerk, Imperial County, 1945–1958.

56. Harry Chand, Live Oak, 1982; Probate Case 11503 of 1935, Office of the County Clerk, San Bernardino County. In the latter case, the checks were signed for in Urdu by the sons and with a thumbprint by the widow.

57. Sophia Din, widow of Shahab Din; Civil Case 46651, Office of the County Clerk, Imperial County, 1976; Oscar Singh, Holtville, 1981.

58. Ishmael Rahmatulla, Phoenix, 1988; Robert Khan, Phoenix, 1990. And in the Imperial Valley, when some nephews came from India, Joe Mallobox's Yuba City children lost the eighty acres left to them by Babu Khan. Joe Mallobox, El Centro, 1990.

59. The case of Bir Singh in San Joaquin County, who died in 1945. 83 CA 2d 256, 188 P. 2d 499. La Brack, *Sikhs of Northern California*, 172, also discusses this case.

60. Retired Judge George Kirk, in his *Memoirs of a Cow County Judge* (n.p., n.d.), p. 6, tells of a "Hindu Estate" where a Punjabi "had left a wife in India and had married a Mexican lady here who knew nothing of his family in India. One of

the things in the will provided for a few thousand dollars to a daughter in India. I was able, through the American Consulate in India, to have the wife brought to El Centro . . . [and] through a good Hindu friend and client who came from the same village to establish that she [my Hindu friend] remembered the event of the Hindu marriage between the deceased and my client . . . since no divorce had taken place my client was the lawful heir." The judge does not date this, but we know from the key presence of a woman from India in the valley that it is after 1950. La Brack cites a New Mexico case that went the other way, dismissing the Indian marriage as one between children and awarding the estate to the Hispanic wife. La Brack, *Sikhs of Northern California,* 171–172.

61. Probate Case 4427, Office of the County Clerk, Imperial County, 1949. Possibly this is the case in note 60, with the judge's memory at odds with the court records. About estates awarded to widows in India, La Brack heard a story from retired Reverend C. H. Loehlin, Yuba City, in 1974. When serving in the Punjab as a missionary, Loehlin had several times observed women being taken to the post office by their husbands' male relatives, picking up a check from the United States, cashing it at the bank, and then giving the money to the men accompanying them.

62. Robert Chell, Holtville, 1981; Olga and Salim Khan, Sacramento, 1982.

63. By "one's fate," I mean that proper cremation of the mortal remains helped achieve proper placement in the next life.

64. The quote is from Isabel Singh Garcia, Yuba City, 1982, recalling her mother's words; Irene Brinkman, Imperial, 1981; Janie Diwan Poonian, Yuba City, 1982; Rose Chell Canaris, Calexico, 1987. There is a tombstone for Hari Singh (or, more probably, his ashes) in the Brawley cemetery, and in Selma's Floral Memorial Cemetery, Wacakha Labh Singh's ashes are buried, next to Josephine Gonzales Singh and with their photos mounted under glass. Personal observations.

65. Teresa Garewal, Holtville, 1981 (interviewed by Ernesto Vargas).

66. Rudolfo Singh, Brawley, 1981 (with C. M. Niam); Niaz Mohamed, Jr., Brawley, 1981 (with C. M. Naim).

67. Robert Chell, Holtville, 1983 (with John Leonard).

68. Alejandra Khan, *Valley Herald* (Yuba City), November 10, 1982; Verdie Montgomery, Sacramento, 1982; and personal observation of the Abdullia graves.

Chapter 10. Encounters with the Other

1. Irene Lacher, "No Fear He May Offend," *Los Angeles Times,* May 25, 1990, E6.

2. Bruce La Brack uses these words: "Immigration Law and the Revitalization Process: The Case of the California Sikhs," *Population Review* 25 (1982): 59–66; and La Brack, *Sikhs of Northern California,* 205, 272.

3. Harry H. L. Kitano and Roger Daniels, *Asian Americans: Emerging Minorities* (Englewood Cliffs, N.J.: Prentice-Hall, 1988), 169; Jacqueline Desbarats, "Thai Migration to Los Angeles," *Geographical Review* 69, no. 3 (1979): 302–318.

4. For the adverse impact of state policy on the formation and maintenance of ethnic groups, see Brass, *Ethnic Groups;* see also Karen Leonard, "South Asian Immigrants: Then and Now," *San Jose Studies* 14, no. 2 (1988): 71–84.

5. I have been interviewing recent immigrants for new projects and to check their reactions to the Punjabi-Mexicans. See Karen Leonard and Chandrasekhar Tibrewal, *South Asians in Southern California: Occupations and Ethnicity* (New Brunswick, N.J.: Transaction, forthcoming).

6. Bernice Sidhu, Brawley, 1981. Joseph and Dorothy Anderholt, Elizabeth Harris, and Carl and Lorelei Jacobson (of Holtville, Holtville, and Brawley, all 1981) were nostalgic about the "old Hindus."

7. La Brack, *Sikhs of Northern California*, 297; Gobind Singh Mansukhani, "The Sikhs Today," in *Sikh Sansar* 3, no. 2 (1974), citing La Brack's and Allan Miller's field-work reports.

8. Steven Erfle, University of California, Irvine, 1986, showed me his Yuba City high school yearbooks for those years.

9. La Brack, *Sikhs of Northern California*, 303–306; Wood, "East Indians," for religious functions and the frequency of their observance in the Stockton *gurdwara* (especially 74, 77, for the two times life cycle functions were observed there before 1947).

10. Bruce La Brack, personal communication, 1982, for the temple poisoning story. La Brack's interview with Alice Hitzfeld (field notes, June 5, 1974) gives another version, reporting that in the late 1950s the Mexican women had stopped cooking because of feuds between them and because Indian women were coming and "pushing them out of the way." The men then did the cooking, and one year they did not refrigerate the chicken and it spoiled, causing feuding Punjabi groups to accuse one another of a poisoning attempt.

11. Mary Singh Rai and her brother were particularly instrumental in starting these dances. The Christmas Dance is still held almost every year. I attended the 1988 dance, of which more in Chapter 11.

12. Margaret Gibson, "Punjabi Immigrants in an American High School," in *Toward an Interpretive Ethnography of Education: Educational Anthropology Today*, ed. George D. Spindler. 302–303 (Hillsdale, N.J.: L. Erlbaum Associates, 1987). Earlier, there had been jokes about Punjabi Sikhs, such as those reported by Peace Corps trainees. Marlin Christensen, Jim Thompson, and Phil Crump, "Four Day Community Study of Yuba City, California: A Report by Three Peace Corps Volunteers," University of California, Berkeley, 1966, 17. (Thanks to Bruce La Brack for this source.)

13. *India West*, October 23, 1981 (second annual Sikh Parade), and Oct. 19, 1990 (eleventh annual Sikh Parade). Guru Gobind Singh died in 1708.

14. Mary Garewal Gill, Holtville, 1982; Verdie Montgomery, Citrus Heights, 1982; Isabel Singh Garcia, Yuba City, 1982.

15. Mohammed Afzal Khan, Willows, 1988.

16. Janie Diwan Poonian, Yuba City, 1983; La Brack, *Sikhs of Northern California*, 198–321.

17. Mola Singh, Selma, 1982. For the reforms, see Wood, "East Indians," 116–117. By 1990, this had become an issue in El Centro as well, and newcomers requested that shoes be shed and heads be covered in the temple there. Personal observation.

18. Elizabeth Deen Hernandez, Burbank, 1981; Olga Dad Khan, Sacramento, 1982; and Verdie Montgomery, Citrus Heights, 1982, and Salim Khan, Sacramento, 1982, for sweeping the grave.

19. Ishmael Rahmatulla and Victor Dad, both in Phoenix, Arizona, 1988.

20. Prakash Tandon, *Punjabi Century 1857–1947* (Berkeley: University of California Press, 1968), 215–216.

21. Interview, in Beheroze Shroff, *Sweet Jail: The Yuba City Sikhs*, MFA film, University of California, Los Angeles, 1984.

22. Margaret Gibson, *Accomodation without Assimilation: Punjabi Sikh Immigrants in an American High School and Community* (Ithaca: Cornell University Press, 1988).

23. Another was Yolanda Singh, Santa Ana, who had come with me to Mola Singh's and was then a Ph.D. candidate at Stanford. Yolanda's grandmother had married and then divorced a Punjabi cousin of Mola Singh's and had brought up Yolanda's father to identity himself as Mexican. Yolanda and her sister Sylvia both earned degrees in Spanish at the University of California, Irvine.

24. The second couple met at one of the Mexican-Hindu dances. That bride had the support of her brother, Baldev "Bob" Singh, a professor at Yuba Community College.

25. Isabel Singh Garcia, *Valley Herald* and *Independent Herald*, April 1983.

26. George Puri, Los Angeles, 1984; Kartar Dhillon, Berkeley, 1987; Rosa Reyes Singh, Los Angeles, 1989. Of course there were countertraditions, such sayings as "Never trust another Sikh" and "When you shake hands [with a Punjabi], count your fingers!"

27. John Borneman, "Race, Ethnicity, Species, Breed: Totemism and Horse-Breed Classification in America," *Comparative Studies in Society and History* 30, no. 1 (1988): 45–47.

28. Francisco Singh, Selma, 1982; other observations from certificates.

29. Karen Leonard, "A Note on Given Names and Chicano Intermarriage," *La Red* 52 (1982): 4–5. I disagree with Edward Murguia's idea that non-Spanish "given names" (which he assumed were the names used on marriage licenses) encourage the espousal of Anglo Americans: "Given Names and Chicano Intermarriage," *La Red* 40 (March 1981): 2.

30. Comparison of birth, marriage, and birth certificates for members of the second generation; for Jiwan as a middle name in her family, Amelia Singh Netervala, Los Angeles, 1990. For comments on this issue from a Japanese-American perspective, see David Mas Masumoto, *Country Voices: The Oral History of a Japanese American Family Farm Community* (Del Rey: Inaka Countryside Publications, 1987), 89–98.

31. Fernando Sanga, Brawley, 1981.

32. Isabel Singh Garcia, Yuba City, 1982; Verdie Montgomery, Citrus Heights, 1982.

33. Los Angeles County, Civil Case 699527, Office of the County Clerk, 1958.

34. Yolanda Singh, Santa Ana, 1981; Joe Romero Singh, telephone interview, 1981.

35. Interview, in Shroff, *Sweet Jail*. The young man's wife, a Sikh from England, explains that in Yuba City "Hindu" is the equivalent of the British "Wog," both words used to insult East Indians. In that film, a local employer still refers to his Hindu workers as "boys" and explains that most were given the name "Jack" preceded by an adjective so that they could be distinguished from each other. East Indian was preferred by Uttam Dhillon, San Diego, 1988, because he is not a Hindu by religion.

36. Ali Abdulla, Sacramento, 1982; Anna Singh Sandhu, Calipatria, 1984; Harry Chand, Live Oak, 1982; Bernice Sidhu, Brawley, 1981. The Sandhu family is part Anglo, not Hispanic (Anna's mother was Anglo).

37. Uttam Dhillon, San Diego, 1988. After the Indian widow died, her niece and Dhillon's sons engaged in a court battle over the ranch. Parmatma Dhillon, El Centro 1990. Isabel Singh Garcia, Yuba City, 1982.

38. Mr. and Mrs. Niaz Mohamed, Jr., Brawley, 1981.

39. Anna Singh Sandhu, Calipatria, 1984; Mary Garewal Gill, Holtville, 1981; Caroline Shine Sunghera Resendez, Huntington Beach, 1982; Sophia Din, Brawley, 1981; Laura Sedoo, Fresno, 1982 (with Sarah Leonard). Others who have gone to South Asia are Rosemary and Julia Olk Singh, Yusuf/Joseph Deen, Elsie Dad, Robert Khan, Ray Sareeram, John Diwan Singh, and Kartar Dhillon.

40. Alfred Sidhu, Sacramento, 1982; and telephone, 1981.

41. Joe Mallobox, El Centro, 1990 (with Jayasri Hart).

Chapter 11. Contending Voices

1. Karen Leonard, "Historical Constructions of Ethnicity: California's Punjabi Immigrants," forthcoming. See also Karen Leonard, "Intermarriage and Ethnicity: Punjabi Mexican Americans, Mexican Japanese, and Filipino Americans," forthcomig, which compares the findings here about Punjabi-Mexicans to Chi-

zuko Watanabe, "The Japanese Immigrant Community in Mexico: Its History and Present," Master's Thesis, California State University, Los Angeles, 1983; and Barbara M. Posadas, "Mestiza Girlhood: Interracial Families in Chicago's Filipino American Community Since 1925," in Asian Women United of California, *Making Waves*, 273–282.

2. Mukerji, *Caste and Outcast*, 269–282.

3. Das, *Hindustani Workers*, v, 115–117. On the then-accepted meaning of American, see Masumoto, *Country Voices*, 61, where even after World War II a disgusted *nisei* (second-generation Japanese American, a citizen) veteran found that he needed an "American" or white (*hakujin*) to co-sign on a loan.

4. William Smith interviews, "Survey of Race Relations," box 28, no. 232; box 29, no. 237; box 35, no. 460.

5. Miller, "Ethnographic Report," 2. Miller was an undergraduate stuent of David Mandelbaum's at the University of California, Berkeley.

6. Dadabhay, "Circuitous Assimilation," 138–141. Dadabhay credited the American educational system with successfully orienting immigrant children to the larger society and believed there were "no ethnic schools" (p. 141). For California's Americanization efforts through the public educational system, see Gilbert G. Gonzalez, "The Americanization of Mexican Women and Their Families during the Era of De Jure School Segregation, 1900–1950," in *Social and Gender Boundaries in the United States*, ed. Sucheng Chan, 55–79 (Lewiston: Edwin Mellen Press, 1989).

7. Harold Jacoby, "A Half-Century Appraisal of East Indians in the United States," University of the Pacific Faculty Research Lecture, Stockton May 23, 1956, saw the offending behavior as largely intramural, due to the all-male nature of the group and to the violence used to maintain secrecy as protection against immigration and land laws (p. 17). For the "endogamy" (he worked when the phenomenon of some American-born daughters marrying older Punjabis was very noticeable), see pp. 30–32. Jacoby's figures on marital status and region from his "East Indians in the United States" are in La Brack, *Sikhs of Northern California*, 179–183.

8. Littleton, "Social Stratification," 113–115. Littleton's attention to religion is evident also in his terming the Punjabi concentrations in California "Muslim" (Sacramento) or "Sikh" (the rest).

9. Lawrence Allen Wenzel, "The Identification and Analysis of Certain Value Orientations of Two Generations of East Indians in California," Ph.D. dissertation, University of the Pacific, 1966; and his subsequent publication, "The Rural Punjabis of California: A Religio-Ethnic Group," *Phylon, Atlanta University Review of Race and Culture* 29 (1968): 245–256. Wenzel used a modified F. Kluckhohn questionnaire and found that the value orientations of both parents and students had important similarities to the dominant value orientations in American society. "Certain Value Orientations of Two Generations of East Indians," 133–135. Har-

want Kaur Khush's study, done at the same time, was more narrowly focused. "The Social Participation and Attitudes of the Children of East Indian Immigrants," Master's Thesis, Sacramento State College, 1965. She used the concept of the "marginal man" to explain the position of India-born students, but found that assimilation was proceeding.

10. Wood, "East Indians," 3. Wood remarks on the Stockton *gurdwara's* loss of uniqueness and centrality as other social and political organizations were begun after 1947 and on a tendency to bring wives from India after 1947. She, like Wenzel, anticipated only a slow population growth through new immigration.

11. Leonard Greenwood, "El Centro's Community of Sikhs Dying Out," *Los Angeles Times*, December 28, 1966, 1, 3, 8.

12. Chakravorty, "Sikhs of El Centro," 78–108; quote from 126.

13. Ibid., 122–129.

14. Helen Bradfield, "The East Indians of Yuba City: A Study in Acculturation," Master's Thesis, Sacramento State College, 1971; Richard Shankar, "Integration Goal Definition of the East Indian Student in the Sutter County Area," Master's Thesis, Chico State University, 1971; Elizabeth J. Carroll, "A Study: East Indian (Sikh) Women Students at Yuba College." University of Southern California, Ed He 690, May 1973; and Gibson, *Accommodation without Assimilation.*

15. Bruce La Brack, *The Sikhs of Northern California: A Socio-Historical Study,"* Ph.D. dissertation, Syracuse University, 1980 (subsequently published as *Sikhs of Northern California*); Salim Khan, "A Brief History of Pakistanis," 1981, 44. Khan drew upon the history of his wife's family to argue that Dadabhay was wrong, that the Hindustanis did not assimilate into Spanish-American culture but that the opposite was true. La Brack has also published a table comparing family life among Indian Punjabis, Canadian Punjabis, California Punjabis, "Sikh-Mexicans," and whites: "Evolution of Sikh Family Form and Values in Rural California: Continuity and Change 1904–1980," *Journal of Comparative Family Studies* 19, no. 2 (1988): 294–304.

16. Lal Singh Chima, "Sikhs Marriage in India and California," paper presented at the Southwestern Anthropological Association, Long Beach, Calif., March 29–April 1, 1972, 7.

17. Juan L. Gonzales, Jr., "Asian Indian Immigration Patterns: The Origins of the Sikh Community in California," *International Migration Review* 20, no. 1 (1986): 46–57.

18. Other recent researchers on the Yuba City Sikhs have minimized or completely missed the Punjabi-Mexicans: Patricia Josephine Santry, "An Historical Perspective of the Factors Preventing Sikh Assimilation in California, 1906–1946," Master's Thesis, California State University, Fullerton, 1981; Carol Cameron Kurtz, "The Sikhs of Yuba City, California: A Study in Ethnic Geography," Master's Thesis, California State University, Hayward, 1984.

19. For example, Iftikhar Haider Malik, *Pakistanis in Michigan: A Study of Third Culture and Acculteration* [*sic*] (New York: AMS Press, 1989), 50, 52; and Prakash N. Desai and George V. Coelho, "Indian Immigrants in America: Some Cultural Aspects of Psychological Adaptation," in *The New Ethnics*, ed. Parmatma Saran and Edwin Eames (New York: Praeger, 1980), 364.

20. Judith A. Nagata found that, similarly, some Malay and Indian women marrying Arabs in Malaysia became Arab. Nagata, "What Is a Malay? Situational Selection of Ethnic Identity in a Plural Society," *American Ethnologist* 1, no. 2 (1974): 345.

21. When Chakravorti asked members of the second generation in El Centro about their self- and group concepts, they identified Hindus as characterized by hard work and pride. Chakravorti, "Sikhs of El Centro," 127–129.

22. The man was Alfred Sidhu, Sacramento, 1982. Speaking of the Chico area, where she moved as an adult, Carmelita Singh Shine (Chico, 1988) said that nobody there knew anything about Mexican-Hindus, they had Portuguese and Italians up there. Another descendant tried to secure a marriage license in Los Angeles, but when she put down "Hindu" in the blank for race, the clerk refused to issue a license, since the intended spouse's category was Mexican; the match would have met with approval in the Imperial Valley, but the Los Angeles clerk felt that it was illegal.

23. Charles F. Keyes points out that individuals create and work with alternative versions of an ethnic identity. See "The Dialectics of Ethnic Change," in *Ethnic Change*, ed. Charles F. Keyes (Seattle: University of Washington Press, 1981), 10. See also Mary C. Waters' stimulating book, *Ethnic Options: Choosing Identities in America* (Berkeley: University of California Press, 1990), which came to my attention as this book went to press.

24. Gerald Nash, *The American West Transformed* (Bloomington: Indiana University Press, 1985), 126–127.

25. Isabel Singh Garcia, Yuba City, 1983; Ishmael Rahmatulla, Phoenix, 1988; Uttam Dhillon, San Diego, 1988; Mike Singh, El Centro, 1990.

26. At the Rotary Club in Brawley an Anglo confidently introduced me to a man whose "appearance and name" marked him as "Hindu," a man who turned out to be a recent immigrant from Egypt. Brawley, 1981.

27. My colleague Jim Ferguson suggested this interpretation.

28. This was pointed out by Kiran Ghei, "Hindi Popular Cinema and the Indian American Teenage Dance Experience," paper for the 17th Annual Conference on South Asia, Madison, Wisc., November 4–6, 1988, 14.

29. Thus the kind of immigrant continuity shown for the Chinese and Japanese by Ivan Light, *Ethnic Enterprise in America* (Berkeley: University of California Press, 1972), is lacking.

30. Karmelita Kakar, San Jose, 1982.

31. Karen Leonard, "Ethnicity and Gender: South Asian Identity in the United States," in *Ethnicity, Identity, and Migration,* ed. Milton Israel and N. K. Wagle (Toronto: Center for South Asian Studies, University of Toronto, forthcoming).

32. Jacoby shows three periods when many did in fact return, pulled primarily by the excitement of revolutionary politics and independence in India. Jacoby, *Half-Century Appraisal,* 10–11.

33. Vatuk and Vatuk, "Protest Songs," quoting a Ghadar party song, 72.

34. Mola Singh, Selma, 1982.

35. Here John Higham's exploration of nineteenth-century "localism" in America, a "condition of decentralization, enabling towns and other local districts to be largely autonomous communities" and "an attitude that such autonomy is the key to liberty" seems relevant. Higham, *Send These to Me,* 182. The extreme localism in the Imperial Valley has been remarked on in earlier chapters.

36. Ramesh Murarka, "Rattan Singh Sahota—Incredible Saga of One Man's Journey to America," *India West,* May 28, 1981; Mola Singh, Selma, 1983; Herbert Hughes, Holtville, 1981; Bagga S. Sunga, Brawley, 1981; *Holtville Tribune,* July 13, 1961.

37. Parmatma Dhillon, El Centro, 1990.

38. A 1990 trip to the Imperial Valley revealed several new cases involving Indian relatives claiming inheritances in this way.

39. Gary Okihiro has effectively debunked the tendency for ethnic scholars to assume the existence of communities. See his "The Idea of Community and a 'Particular Type of History,' " in *Reflections on Shattered Windows,* ed. Gary Okihiro, Shirley Hune, Arthur Hansen, and John Liu (Pullman: Washington State University Press, 1988), esp. 178, 181.

40. Joe Romero Singh, Santa Ana, 1981; Mrs. Otto Gil Singh, Woodland, 1982; Mrs. Francisco Singh, Selma, 1983; Fernando Sanga, Brawley, 1982.

41. Thaddeus Dale McCall, the organizer, quoted in the *Valley Grower,* Summer 1982, 48. The Pioneers has renamed itself Imperial Valley Pioneers Historical Society and has broadened its entrance criteria greatly. *Imperial Valley Pioneers Newsletter* 8 (March 1984): 5. Some representatives of the Pioneers (including a Punjabi descendant) point to a short street named Singh in El Centro. The street is not long enough to satisfy Bagga S. Sunga, whose November 22, 1978, letter to the *Brawley News* suggested that Dogwood Road be renamed Singh Road.

42. Robert Khan, Phoenix, 1990.

43. Another restaurant, Pancho's in Selma, closed after a brief career in the early 1980s; Pancho, or Francisco, Singh was from the Imperial Valley too. See Arjun Appadurai, "How to Make a National Cuisine: Cookbooks in Contemporary India," *Comparative Studies in Society and History* 30, no. 1 (1988): 3–24.

44. Personal observation, November 1988.

45. See Hans Medick and David Warren Sabean, "Interest and Emotion in Family Kinship Studies: A Critique of Social History and Anthropology," 11; and Alain Collomp, "Tensions Dissensions, and Ruptures inside the Family in Seventeenth- and Eighteenth-Century Haute Provence," 146. Both are in *Interest and Emotion*, ed. Hans Medick and David Warren Sabean, (New York: Cambridge University Press, 1984). The quoted phrases are those of Roy G. D'Andrade, "Cultural Meaning Systems," in *Cultural Theory*, ed. R. A. Shweder and R. A. Levine (New York: Cambridge University Press, 1984), 111–112.

46. Dorothy Angell Rutherford, "Bengalis in America: Relationship, Affect, Person, and Self," Ph.D. dissertation, American University, 1984, perceptively delineates this process for the new immigrants.

47. Sally Falk Moore, *Social Facts and Fabrications* (New York: Cambridge University Press, 1986), 4–5; Eric R. Wolf, "Inventing Society," *American Ethnologist* 15, no. 4 (1988): 752–761; and James Ferguson and Akhil Gupta, "Beyond Culture: Space, Identity, and the Politics of Difference," *Cultural Anthropologist*, forthcoming; also in *Culture, Power, Place: Explorations in Critical Anthropology*, ed. James Ferguson, Akhil Gupta, and Roger Rouse (Boulder, Colo.: Westview Press, forthcoming).

48. Akhil Gupta, "Space and Time in the Politics of Culture," paper presented at the 87th Annual Meeting of the American Anthropological Association, Phoenix, 1988, 5 ("The peasant is the archetypal native, inhabiting a sedentary space that is distinguished by its boundedness, whether that boundedness is due to its purported economic self-sufficiency or the enclosure of its moral universe"; and Arjun Appadurai, "Putting Hierarchy in Its Place," *Cultural Anthropology* 3, no. 1 (1988): 36–40.

49. Thus the whole tradition in American sociology stemming from William I. Thomas and Florian Znaniecki, *The Polish Peasant in Europe and America*, vols. 1–2 (Chicago: University of Chicago Press, 1918), vols. 3–5 (Boston: Badger Press, 1919–1920), esp. vols. 4 and 5; discussed by Eli Zaretsky in the introduction to his edited and abridged volume (Chicago: University of Illinois Press, 1984), 25–31.

50. Clifford, *Predicament of Culture*, 339n.

51. Borneman, "Race, Ethnicity, Species, Breed," 45–47, suggests that in contrast to Europe, where political centralization was of greater concern, in the United States the creation of shared cultural-identity markers took precedence over state building.

52. Higham quotes Robert Wiebe and Henry James here. Higham, *Send These to Me*, 183–184.

53. Howard N. Rabinowitz, "Race, Ethnicity, and Cultural Pluralism in American History," in *Ordinary People and Everyday Life: Perspectives on the New Social History*, ed. James M. Gardner and George Rollie Adams (Nashville: American Association for State and Local History, 1983), 28; Higham, *Send These to Me*, 198–230.

54. Stephen Steinberg, *The Ethnic Myth: Race, Ethnicity, and Class in America* (New York: Atheneum, 1981), esp. 261.

55. Higham, *Send These to Me,* 228–229, refers to the tendency in the 1960s toward "interpreting pluralism as a repressive condition and a delusive theory," and the opposing group of American intellectuals "still desirous somehow of upholding both equality and diversity." Higham ends with the assertion that an underlying consensus about basic values is indispensable to a decent multiethnic society and exhorts scholars to help "revitalize a common faith amid multiplying claims for status and power" (p. 232).

56. See the work of Dadabhay, Chakravorti, and others.

57. Anzaldua, *Borderlands,* esp. 78–80; Anna Tsing, "Temporary Wives: Dayak Women Sojourn in the Greater Asian Political Economy," paper, Association of Asian Studies, 1988 (she makes a good case for such an analysis). Nagata, "What Is a Malay?" 343, 346, argues against the "situational selection of ethnic identity" being associated with "personal insecurity or marginality," seeing it instead as positive adaptation to fluid situations.

58. Werner Sollors, *Beyond Ethnicity: Consent and Descent in American Culture* (New York: Oxford University Press, 1986), 13–14.

59. Renato Rosaldo ridicules the "zero culture" stereotype in "Ideology, Place, and People without Culture," *Cultural Anthropology* 3; no. 1 (1988): 81.

60. See Rutherford, "Bengalis in America," 1984, for transnational reconstructions of family, community, and ethnicity.

61. Salman Rushdie, *In Good Faith* (London: Granta, 1990), 3–4.

62. Parmatma Dhillon, El Centro, 1990.

63. Stanley Lieberson and Mary C. Waters, *From Many Strands: Ethnic and Racial Groups in Contemporary America* (New York: Russell Sage Foundation, 1988), 249–250.

64. *Ibid.,* 264–268; Stanley Lieberson and Mary C. Waters, "The Rise of a New Ethnic Group: The 'Unhyphenated American,' " *Items,* Social Science Research Council 43; no. 1 (1989): 7–10.

Bibliography

Unless otherwise specified, interviews were conducted by the author and took place in California; when others took a significant part in the interview, they are named in parentheses. For specific interview dates, contact the author; many people were interviewed several times and indicating month and day seemed cumbersome. People's names appear as they themselves spell them.

Interviews with Descendants

Abdulla, Ali and Lucy Singh. Fresno, 1982; telephone, 1983.

Bhatti, Ganga Singh and Josephine Lucero Bhatti (with Marianne Singh Andrews). Live Oak, 1989 (by Tejinder S. Sibia).

Canaris, Rose Chell. Calexico, 1987 (by Lupe Beltran).

Chand, Harry. Like Oak, 1982, 1983.

Chand, Harry J. Sebastopol, 1988.

Chell, Robert and Karmen. Holtville, 1981 (once with C. M. Naim), 1983 (with John Leonard), 1990 (Robert only).

Chell, Silveria. Holtville, 1981 (with Lala Garewal, Mary Garewal Gill, and Robert Chell).

Dad, Victor. Phoenix, Arizona, 1988.

Deol, Kishen Singh. Riverside, 1981.

Dhalliwal, Sally. Holtville, 1982.

Dhillon, David. El Centro, 1990 (with Jayasri Hart).

Dhillon, Irene. El Centro, 1990 (with Jayasri Hart).

Dhillon, Kartar. Berkeley, 1987.

Dhillon, Parmatma. El Centro, 1990 (with Jayasri Hart).

Dhillon, Surain S. Encinitas, 1990.

Dhillon, Uttam. San Diego, 1988 (with Gurdit and Dharmo Dhillon).

Dillon, Blanche. Vancouver, Canada, 1988.

Dillon, Joan. San Francisco, 1982.

Dillon, Lola, and Celia Dominguez (daughter). Holtville, 1981 (with Ernesto Vargas).

Dillon, Teja and Kay Sighera Dillon. Fresno, 1982 (with Sarah Leonard).

Din, Raymond. El Centro, 1981.

Din, Sophia. Brawley, 1981 (with Ernesto Vargas).

Fairfield, Pauline Garewal. Yuba City, 1982 and 1983 (letters).

Garcia, Isabel Singh. Yuba City, 1982, 1983, 1988.

Garewal, Gene. Yuba City, 1983 (letter).

Garewal, Lala. Holtville, 1981 (with Silveria Chell, Robert Chell, and Mary Garewal Gill).

Garewal, Teresa. Holtville, 1981 (with Ernesto Vargas).

Gill, Nika Singh. Holtville, 1981.

Gill, Mary Garewal. Holtville, 1981 (once with C. M. Naim), 1982, 1983, 1984, 1990 (once with Jayasri Hart).

Hernandez, Elizabeth Deen. Burbank, 1981.

Kakar, Karmelita. San Jose, 1982.

Khan, Mohammed Afzal and Irene Khan. Willows, 1988.

Khan, Mohammed Aslam. Butte City, 1988.

Khan, Robert. Phoenix, Arizona, 1990.

Khan, Salim and Olga Dad Khan. Sacramento, 1982.

Lang, Barbara Singh Quade. Tucson, Arizona, 1989 (telephone).

Mallobox, Joseph. El Centro, 1982, 1990 (with Jayasri Hart).

Mia, Fatima Din. Pacoima, 1983 (telephone).

Mohamed, Mary and Betty. El Centro, 1981.

Mohamed, Niaz, Jr., and Sally. Brawley, 1981 (with C. M. Naim), 1990 (with Jayasri Hart).

Mohammed, Robert. Yuba City, 1982 (with Lillian Palmer, sister), 1988 (once alone, once with Lillian Palmer).

Montgomery, Verdie Abdullia. Citrus Heights, 1982 (with Emma Smiley).

Netervala, Amelia Singh. Los Angeles, 1988, 1989 (with Rosa Reyes Singh), 1990.

Nichols, Nora Singh. Casa Grande, Arizona, 1989 (telephone).

Parker, Jovita Singh. Leucadia, 1987 (telephone).

Perry, Rose Singh. Pasadena, 1983 (telephone).

Poonian, Janie Diwan. Yuba City, 1982, 1983 (with Mary and Leela Rai).

Puri, George. Los Angeles, 1984.

Rahmatulla, Ishmael. Glendale, Arizona, 1988.

Rai, Chenchel. Yuba City, 1981 (with Naranjan S. Atwal and Bob Singh).

Rai, Mary Singh. Yuba City, 1981, 1983 (with Leela Rai and Janie Diwan Poonian), 1988.

Ram, Raymond. Firebaugh, 1983.

Rasul, Ali. Yuba City, 1981.

Resendez, Caroline Shine Sunghera and Nellie Soto Shine. Huntington Beach, 1982.

Saikhon, Norma. Brawley, 1981 (by Ernesto Vargas).

Sandhu, Charn and Anna Singh Sandhu. Calipatria, 1981 (both twice, Anna once); 1982, 1984, and 1987 (Anna); 1990 (Anna, once with Jayasri Hart).

Sandhu, Pritam. Calipatria, 1987 (letter), 1989, 1990.

Sanga, Bobby Singh. Brawley, 1987 (by Lupe Beltran).

Sanga, Fernando. Brawley, 1981 (once with Ernesto Vargas, once with C. M. Naim).

Sareeram, Louis. Sacramento (but interviewed in El Centro), 1981.

Sedoo, Puron and Laura Sedoo. Fresno, 1982 (with Sarah Leonard).

Sekhon, Lucy. San Diego, 1982.

Shine, Carmelita Singh. Chico, 1988.

Sidhu, Alfred. Sacramento, 1982 (once by telephone).

Sidhu, Bernice. Brawley, 1981 (with Ernesto Vargas and Sarah Leonard).

Sidhu, Lydia Soto. El Centro, 1990.

Sidhu, Ray and Isabel Sidhu Villasenor (sister). Yuba City, 1982.

Singh, Bachint Kaur (Mrs. Toga Singh). Imperial, 1981, 1982, 1984, 1990.

Singh, Bob Baldev. Yuba City, 1980, 1981 (with Sam Leonard), 1983.

Singh, Charlie. Yuba City, 1982 (letter).

Singh, David. Long Beach, 1987 (telephone).

Singh, Francisco. Kingsburg, 1983.

Singh, George, and Carmen Singh Sharma (sister). Davis, 1990 (by Tejinder S. Sibia).

Singh, Harmon. Holtville, 1981 (with C. M. Naim, Mr. and Mrs. Oscar Singh).

Singh, Hortencia. El Centro, 1981 (with Ernesto Vargas).

Singh, Jane. Berkeley, 1981, 1982.

Singh, John Diwan. Casa Grande, Arizona, 1989 (telephone).

Singh, Joseph Romero. Santa Ana, 1981 (telephone).

Singh, Kaser. El Centro, 1981 (by Ernesto Vargas).

Singh, Mike. El Centro, 1990 (once with Rosie Lusier, once with Jayasri Hart).

Singh, Mola and Susanna Mesa Rodriguez Singh. Selma, 1982, 1983 (once with Yolanda Singh).

Singh, Oscar Harr. Holtville, 1981, 1990 (with his wife and Jayasri Hart).

Singh, Mrs. Otto Gil. Woodland, 1981.

Singh, Rudolfo, and Munsha Singh (father). Imperial, 1981 (with C. M. Naim).

Singh, Sawarn. El Centro, 1984.

Singh, Yolanda. Santa Ana, 1983.

Sunga, Bagga S. Brawley, 1981 (once with C. M. Naim), 1982, 1984.

Uddin, Juanita. Rimpau Station, 1983 (telephone).
Walsh, Helen Ram. Hercules, 1988, 1990 (telephone).

Interviews with Others

Anderholt, Joseph and Dorothy Brown. Holtville, 1981 (once with C. M. Naim), 1982, 1983 (with John Leonard), 1984, 1990 (once with Jayasri Hart).
Bailey, Jim. El Centro, 1981 (once with Julia Youngblood).
Brinkman, Irene. Imperial, 1981.
Bryant, Kenneth. Vancouver, Canada, 1988.
Dannenberg, Danny. El Centro, 1981.
Ewing, William. El Centro, 1981.
Free, Harry M. El Centro, 1982.
Gibson, Margaret A. Sacramento, 1982.
Gonzalez, Hema. Oakland, 1982.
Goodman, Michael. Berkeley, 1982.
Grether, E. T. Berkeley, 1982.
Griffin, Allen. Brawley, 1981.
Harris, Elizabeth. Holtville, 1981 (with Robert and Karmen Chell).
Hughes, Herbert. Holtville, 1981 (with C. M. Naim).
Jacobson, Carl and Lorelei Griffin Jacobson. Brawley, 1981.
Jacoby, Harold. Stockton, 1981, 1982, 1983, 1984.
La Brack, Bruce. Stockton, 1981, 1984, 1989, 1990.
Lehnhardt, William. Brawley, 1981.
Patzloff, R. E. Holtville, 1981.
Savage, Keith. Holtville, 1981.
Singh, Inder. Tarzana, 1981.
Smith, Sherman. Brawley, 1981.
Taylor, Paul Schuster. Berkeley, 1982.
Thornburg, William. Holtville, 1982.
Vatuk, Ved. Berkeley, 1982 (telephone).
Waiches, Rev. Vincent. Holtville, 1982.
Wheat, Irma. El Centro, 1981.
Williams, Jack. Calexico, 1981.
Womack, Roy. El Centro, 1981.

Books and Pamphlets

Allen, James Paul, and Eugene James Turner. 1988. *We the People*. New York: Macmillan.
Allen, Ruth. 1931. *The Labor of Women in the Production of Cotton*. Austin: University of Texas Bulletin 3134.

Anderholt, Joseph J. 1989. *Desert Dairies: Catalyst for the Development of Imperial Valley*. Imperial: Imperial County Historical Society.

Anderholt, Joseph J., and Dorothy M. Anderholt, eds. 1984. *The History of the Imperial Valley Swiss*. Holtville: Imperial Valley Swiss Club.

Anzaldua, Gloria. 1987. *Borderlands/La Frontera: The New Mestiza*. San Francisco: Spinsters/Aunt Lute.

Arrom, Silvia. 1985. *The Women of Mexico City 1790–1857*. Palo Alto: Stanford University Press.

Bagai, Leona. 1968. *The East Indians and the Pakistanis in America*. Minneapolis: Lerner Publications.

Barth, F., ed. 1969. *Ethnic Groups and Boundaries: The Social Organization of Cultural Difference*. Boston: Little, Brown.

Barth, Gunther. 1964. *Bitter Strength: A History of the Chinese in the United States, 1850–1870*. Cambridge: Harvard University Press.

Beach, Walter G. 1971. *Oriental Crime in California*. New York: AMS Press. Originally published 1932, Stanford University Publications.

Bean, Frank D., and W. Parker Frisbie, eds. 1978. *The Demography of Racial and Ethnic Groups*. New York: Academic Press.

Bean, Walton. 1973. *California: An Interpretive History*. 2nd ed. New York: McGraw-Hill.

Brass, Paul. 1985. *Ethnic Groups and the State*. London: Croom Helm.

Briggs, Vernon M., Jr. 1973. *Chicanos and Rural Poverty*. Baltimore: Johns Hopkins University Press.

Briggs, William J., and Henry Cauthen. 1983. *The Cotton Man: Life and Times of Wolford B. ("Bill") Camp*. Columbia: University of South Carolina Press.

Brunner, Edmund deS. 1929. *Immigrant Farmers and Their Children*. New York: Doubleday, Doran.

Buchignani, Norman. 1982. *Anthropological Approaches to the Study of Ethnicity*. Ontario: Multicultural History Society of Ontario.

Buchignani, Norman, Doreen M. Indra, and Ram Srivastava. 1985. *Continuous Journey: A Social History of South Asians in Canada*. Toronto: McClelland and Stewart.

Buss, Fran Leeper. 1980. *La Partera: Story of a Midwife*. Ann Arbor: University of Michigan Press.

Cahen, Alfred. 1968. *Statistical Analysis of American Divorce*. New York: AMS Press. Originally published 1932.

California Department of Health Services. 1971. *Vital Statistics of California*. Sacramento: Department of Health Services.

California Labor Commissioner. 1966. *Licensed Farm Labor Contractors of California*. Sacramento: Office of State Printing.

California Legislature, Senate. 1953. *Seventh Report of the Senate Fact-Finding Committee on Un-American Activities*. Sacramento: California Senate Printing Office.

California Reporter. 1910–1960.

California State Board of Control. 1920, 1922. *California and the Oriental*. Sacramento: State Printing Office.

California State Commission of Immigration and Housing. 1918. *Report on Fresno's Immigration Problem*. Sacramento: State Printing Office.

Chan, Sucheng. 1986. *This Bittersweet Soil: The Chinese in California Agriculture, 1860–1910*. Berkeley: University of California Press.

Clifford, James. 1988. *The Predicament of Culture: Twentieth-Century Ethnography, Literature, and Art*. Cambridge: Harvard University Press.

Collier, Jane Fishburne, and Sylvia Junko Yanagisako. 1987. *Gender and Kinship: Essays Toward a Unified Analysis*. Stanford: Stanford University Press.

Coy, Owen C. 1919. *Guide to the County Archives of California*. Sacramento: California Historical Survey Commission.

Cray, Ed. 1973. *Burden of Proof: The Case of Juan Corona*. New York: Macmillan.

Daniel, Cletus E. 1982. *Bitter Harvest: A History of California Farmworkers*. Los Angeles: University of California Press.

Daniels, Roger. 1962. *The Politics of Prejudice*. Berkeley: University of California Press.

Daniels, Roger, and Spencer Olin. 1972. *Racism in California: A Reader in the History of Oppression*. New York: Macmillan.

Darling, Malcolm Lyall. 1930. *Rusticus Loquitur, or the Old Light and the New in the Punjab Village*. London: Humphrey Milford, Oxford University Press.

———. 1947. *The Punjab Peasant in Prosperity and Debt*. 4th ed. New York: Oxford University Press.

Das, Rajani Kanta. 1923. *Hindustani Workers on the Pacific Coast*. Berlin: Walter de Gruyter.

Dhillon, Mahinder Singh. 1981. *A History Book of the Sikhs in Canada and California*. Vancouver: Shromani Akali Dal Association of Canada.

Dyke, Bennett, and Warren T. Morrill, eds. 1980. *Genealogical Demography*. New York: Academic Press.

Elder, Glen H., Jr. 1974. *Children of the Great Depression*. Chicago: University of Chicago Press.

Farr, F. C. 1918. *The History of Imperial County, California*. Berkeley: Elms and Frank.

Fox, Richard. 1985. *Lions of the Punjab*. Berkeley: University of California Press.

Gamio, Manuel. 1971. *The Life Story of the Mexican Immigrant*. New York: Dover.

Garcia, Mario T. 1981. *Desert Immigrants: The Mexicans of El Paso, 1880–1920*. New Haven: Yale University Press.

Gardner, James M., and George Rollie Adams, eds. 1983. *Ordinary People and Everyday Life: Perspectives on the New Social History*. Nashville: American Association for State and Local History.

Gibson, Margaret A. 1988. *Accommodation without Assimilation: Punjabi Sikh Immigrants in an American High School and Community*. Ithaca: Cornell University Press.

Goldschmidt, Walter. 1947. *As You Sow*. New York: Harcourt, Brace.

Government of India. 1974. *Towards Equality: Report of the Committee on the Status of Women in India*. New Delhi: Ministry of Education and Social Welfare.

Griswold del Castillo, Richard. 1979. *The Los Angeles Barrio, 1850–1890: A Social History*. Berkeley: Univerity of California Press.

Hannah, Harold W. 1951. *Law on the Farm*. New York: Macmillan.

Hatch, Elvin. 1979. *Biography of a Small Town*. New York: Columbia University Press.

Hershman, Paul, and Hilary Standing, eds. 1981. *Punjabi Kinship and Marriage*. Delhi: Hindustan Publishing Corporation.

Heston, Wilma H., and Mumtaz Nasir. 1988. *The Bazaar of the Storytellers*. Islamabad: Lok Virsa.

Higham, John. 1984. *Send These to Me: Immigrants in Urban America*. 2nd ed. Baltimore: Johns Hopkins University Press.

Hindustanees' Welfare and Reform Society of America. n.d. *Constitution and By-Laws of the Hindustanees' Welfare and Reform Society of America*. Imperial: n.p.

Hobsbawm, Eric, and Terence Ranger, eds. 1983. *The Invention of Tradition*. New York: Cambridge University Press.

Imperial County Pacific Telephone and Telegraph Company. 1918, 1925. Both in Pioneers Museum, Imperial.

Imperial Valley Business and Resident Directory. 1912–1913. El Centro and Pasadena: Albert R. Thurston.

Imperial Valley College. n.d. *General Catalog 1981–1982*. Imperial: Imperial Community College District.

Imperial Valley Directory. 1924, 1926. Los Angeles: Los Angeles Directory Co.

Jacobson, Paul H., in collaboration with Pauline F. Jacobson. 1959. *American Marriage and Divorce*. New York: Rinehart and Company.

Jacoby, Harold S. 1956. "A Half-Century Appraisal of East Indians in the United States." University of the Pacific Faculty Research Lecture, Stockton, May 23.

Japanese Agricultural Association. 1918. *The Japanese Farmers in California*. San Francisco: Japanese Agricultural Association.

Jensen, Joan M. 1988. *Passage from India: Asian Indian Immigrants in North America*. New Haven: Yale University Press.

Jordan, Terry G. 1982. *Texas Graveyards: A Cultural Legacy*. Austin: University of Texas Press.

Kessinger, Tom. 1974. *Vilyatpur 1848–1968*. Berkeley: University of California Press.

Keyes, Charles F., ed. 1981. *Ethnic Change*. Seattle: University of Washington Press.

Kidder, Tracy. 1974. *The Road to Yuba City: A Journey into the Juan Corona Murders*. New York: Doubleday.

Kikumura, Akemi. 1981. *Through Harsh Winters: The life of a Japanese Immigrant Woman*. Novato, Calif.: Chandler and Sharp.

Kingston, Maxine Hong. 1977. *The Woman Warrior: Memoirs of a Girlhood among Ghosts*. New York: Knopf.

Kirk, George. ca. 1982. *Memoirs of a Cow County Judge*. n.p., n.d.

Kitano, Harry H. L. 1976. *Japanese-Americans: The Evolution of a Subculture*. Englewood Cliffs, N.J.: Prentice Hall.

Kitano, Harry H. L., and Roger Daniels. 1988. *Asian Americans: Emerging Minorities*. Englewood Cliffs, N.J.: Prentice-Hall.

Komarovsky, Mirra. 1940. *The Unemployed Man and His Family*. New York: Dryden Press.

Kramer, Mark. 1980. *Three Farms*. Boston: Atlantic Monthly Press.

Kurian, George, and Ram P. Srivastava, eds. 1983. *Overseas Indians, a Study in Adaptation*. Delhi: Vikas.

La Brack, Bruce. 1988. *The Sikhs of Northern California 1904–1975: A Socio-Historical Study*. New York: AMS Press.

Laslett, Peter. 1966. *The World We Have Lost*. New York: Scribner.

Laslett, Peter, and Richard Wall. 1972. *Household and Family in Past Time*. Cambridge: Cambridge University Press.

Leonard, Karen. 1978. *Social History of an Indian Caste: The Kayasths of Hyderabad*. Berkeley: University of California Press.

Lieberson, Stanley, and Mary C. Waters. 1988. *From Many Strands: Ethnic and Racial Groups in Contemporary America*. New York: Russell Sage Foundation.

Light, Ivan. 1972. *Ethnic Enterprise in America*. Berkeley: University of California Press.

Los Angeles City Directory, including San Pedro and Wilmington. 1910 on. Los Angeles: Los Angeles Directory Company. Microfilm, University of California, Los Angeles.

McLeod, W. H. 1976. *The Evolution of the Sikh Community*. Oxford: Clarendon Press.

————. 1986. *Punjabis in New Zealand: A History of Punjabi Migration 1890–1940*. Amritsar: Guru Nanak Dev University.

McWilliams, Carey. 1978. *Factories in the Field: The Story of Migratory Labor in California*. Salt Lake City: Peregrine Smith.

Malik, Iftikhar Haider. 1989. *Pakistanis in Michigan: A Study of Third Culture and Acculteration (sic)*. New York: AMS Press.

Masumoto, David Mas. 1987. *Country Voices: The Oral History of a Japanese American Family Farm Community*. Del Rey: Inaka Countryside Publications.

Maxson, Charles Hartshorn. 1930. *Citizenship*. New York: Oxford University Press.

Mayer, Adrian C. 1959. *A Report on the East Indian Community in Vancouver*. Vancouver: Institute of Social and Economic Research, University of Vancouver, British Columbia.

Mears, Eliot Grinnell. 1978. *Resident Orientals on the American Pacific Coast*. New York: Arno Press. Originally published ca. 1928.

Meister, Dick, and Anne Loftis. 1977. *A Long Time Coming*. New York: Macmillan.

Melendy, H. Brett. 1981. *Asians in America: Filipinos, Koreans, and East Indians*. New York: Hippocrene Press.

Miller, Barbara. 1981. *The Endangered Sex: Neglect of Female Children in Rural North India*. Ithaca: Cornell University Press.

Misrow, Jogesh C. 1971. *East Indian Immigration on the Pacific Coast*. San Francisco: R and E Research Associates.

Miyamoto, Kazuo. 1964. *Hawaii: End of the Rainbow*. Rutland, Vt.: Tuttle.

Moore, Sally Falk. 1986. *Social Facts and Fabrications*. New York: Cambridge University Press.

Mukerji, Dhan Gopal. 1923. *Caste and Outcast*. New York: Dutton.

Nash, Gerald. 1985. *The American West Transformed*. Bloomington: Indiana University Press.

Nutini, Hugo G., and Betty Bell. 1980. *Ritual Kinship: The Structure and Historical Development of the Compadrazgo System in Rural Tlaxcala*. Princeton: Princeton University Press.

Odens, Peter. ca. 1970. *Pioneerland Below the Sea*. Calexico: Calexico Chronicle.

————. 1977. *The Desert's Edge*. Benson, Ariz.: Border Mountain Press.

Pacific Reporter. 1910–1960.

Pettigrew, Joyce. 1975. *Robber Noblemen: A Study of the Political System of the Sikh Jats*. Boston: Routledge and Kegan Paul.

Pisani, Donald J. 1984. *From the Family Farm to Agribusiness: The Irrigation Crusade in California and the West, 1850–1931*. Berkeley: University of California Press.

Poli, Adon. 1942. *Land Ownership and Operating Tenure in Imperial Valley, California*. Berkeley, Calif.: U.S. Bureau of Agriculture Economics.

Pratap, Raja Mahendra. 1947. *My Life Story of Fifty-Five Years*. Dehradun: World Federation.

Puri, Harish K. 1983. *Ghadar Movement*. Amritsar: Guru Nanak Dev University Press.

Reed, Lester. 1967. *Oldtimers of Southeastern California*. Redlands: Lester Reed.

Register of Sikhs in the U.S. and Canada. 1972. Redwood City: Sikh Foundation U.S.A.

Rubel, Arthur J. 1966. *Across the Tracks*. Austin: University of Texas Press.

Runsten, David, and Phillip LeVeen. 1982. *Mechanization and Mexican Labor in California Agriculture*. Monographs in U.S.–Mexican Studies, No. 6, University of California, San Diego.

Rushdie, Salman. 1990. *In Good Faith*. London: Granta.

Sanford, John. 1953. *The Land That Touches Mine*. New York: Doubleday.

Saran, Parmatma, and Edwin Eames, eds. 1980. *The New Ethnics*. New York: Praeger.

Saund, Dalip Singh. 1960. *Congressman from India*. New York: Dutton.

Scheuring, Ann Foley, ed. 1983. *A Guidebook of California Agriculture*. Berkeley: University of California Press.

Seller, Maxine Schwartz. 1981. *Immigrant Women*. Philadelphia: Temple University Press.

Servin, Manuel P. 1970. *The Mexican-Americans: An Awakening Minority*. Beverly Hills: Glencoe Press.

Shammas, Carole, with Marilyn Salmon and Michel Dahlin. 1987. *Inheritance in America from Colonial Times to the Present*. New Brunswick: Rutgers University Press.

Sharan Kaur. n.d. Bombay: Amar Chitra Katha, India Book House Education Trust.

Shideler, James H. 1957. *Farm Crisis 1919–1923*. Berkeley: University of California Press.

Sidhwa, Bapsi. 1988. *The Ice-Candy Man*. London: William Heinemann.

Singh, Jane, ed. 1988. *South Asians in North America: An Annotated and Selected Bibliography*. Berkeley: Center for South and Southeast Asia Studies. Occasional Paper No. 14.

Singh, Khushwant. 1956. *Train to Pakistan*. New York: Grove Press.

Smith, William C. 1970. *Americans in Process: A Study of Our Citizens of Oriental Ancestry*. New York: Arno Press. Originally published Ann Arbor: Edwards Bros., ca. 1937.

Sollors, Werner. 1986. *Beyond Ethnicity: Consent and Descent in American Culture*. New York: Oxford University Press.

Stahl, F. A. 1928. *Rolling Stones*. Glendale, Calif.: Wetzel Publishing.

Steinberg, Stephen. 1981. *The Ethnic Myth: Race, Ethnicity, and Class in America*. New York: Atheneum.

Tandon, Prakash. 1968. *Punjabi Century 1857–1947*. Berkeley: University of California Press.

Taylor, Paul Schuster. 1929. *Mexican Labor in the United States: Racial School Statistics California, 1927*. Berkeley: University of California Publications in Economics, vol. 6, no. 4.

———. 1928–1930. *Mexican Labor in the United States: Imperial Valley*. University of California Publications in Economics, vol. 6, nos. 1–5.

———. 1933. *Mexican Labor in the United States*. Berkeley: University of California Publications in Economics, vol. 12, nos. 1–2.

Taylor, Ronald B. 1973. *Sweatshops in the Sun: Child Labor on the Farm*. Boston: Beacon Press.

Thomas, Sherry. 1981. *We Didn't Have Much, but We Sure Had Plenty: Stories of Rural Women*. New York: Anchor Press.

Thomas, W. I., and F. Znaniecki. 1918–1920. *The Polish Peasant in Europe and America*. Boston: Gorham Press. 5 vols.

———. 1984. *The Polish Peasant in Europe and America*. Abridged ed. by Eli Zaretsky. Chicago: University of Illinois Press.

Thompson, Paul. 1978. *The Voice of the Past: Oral History*. London: Oxford University Press.

Thurston's Imperial Valley Directory. 1914–1915. El Centro and Pasadena: Western Map and Publishing Company.

———. 1917–1918. Los Angeles: Albert G. Thurston.

———. 1920–1921. Los Angeles: Albert G. Thurston. All directories are in the Imperial County Library in El Centro.

Tostlebe, Alvin S. 1957. *Capital in Agriculture: Its Formation and Financing Since 1870*. Princeton: Princeton University Press.

U.S. Congress. Senate. 1911. *Immigrants in Industries: Reports of the Immigration Commission*, pt. 24; *Immigrants in Industries: Recent Immigrants in Agriculture*, pt 25; *Japanese and Other Immigrant Races in the Pacific Coast and Rocky Mountain States*, vol. I, *Japanese and East Indians*. Washington: Immigration Commission.

U.S. Congress. Senate. Committee on Immigration. 1926. *Ratification and Confirmation of Naturalization of Certain Persons of the Hindu Race: Hearings on Senate Joint Resolution 128*. 69th Cong., 2nd sess., December 9 and 15. Washington, D.C.: Government Printing Office.

———. 1944. *To Permit the Naturalization of Approximately Three Thousand Natives of India: Hearings on S. 1595*. 78th Cong., 2nd sess., September 13 and 14. Washington, D.C.: Government Printing Office.

———. 1945. *To Permit All Persons from India Residing in the U.S. to Be Naturalized: Hearings*. 79th Cong., 1st sess., April 16. Washington, D.C.: Government Printing Office.

U.S. Department of Commerce, Bureau of the Census. 1912–1914. *Thirteenth Census of the United States: Population, 1910*. Washington, D.C.: Government Printing Office.

———. 1913. *Thirteenth Census of the United States Taken in the Year 1910: Abstract of the Census with Supplement for California*. Washington, D.C.: Government Printing Office.

———. 1921–1923. *Fourteenth Census of the United States: Population, 1920*. Washington, D.C.: Government Printing Office.

———. 1951–1953. *Seventeenth Census of the United States: Population, 1950*. Washington, D.C.: Government Printing Office.

———. 1982. *Twentieth Census of the United States: Population, 1980*. Washington, D.C.: Government Printing Office.

U.S. Statutes at Large. 1915–1917. "An Act to Regulate the Immigration of Aliens to, and the Residence of Aliens in, the United States." P.L. 874–899. 64th Cong., 2nd sess., vol. 39, pt. 1, chap. 29.

————. 1921–1923. "An Act Relative to the Naturalization and Citizenship of Married Women." P. L. 1021–1022. 77th Cong., 2nd sess., vol. 42, pt. 1, chap. 411.

Velez-Ibanez, Carlos G. 1983. *Bonds of Mutual Trust: The Cultural Systems of Rotating Credit Associations Among Urban Mexicans and Chicanos.* New Brunswick: Rutgers University Press.

Wagoner, Jay. 1978. *Arizona's Heritage.* Santa Barbara: Peregrine-Smith.

Waris Shah. 1973. *The Adventures of Hir and Ranjha,* trans. Charles Frederick Usborne. London: Peter Owen.

Waters, Mary C. 1990. *Ethnic Options: Choosing Identities in America.* Berkeley: University of California Press.

Weaver, Mrs. Wiley M. 1915. *Imperial Valley 1901–1915.* Los Angeles: Board of Supervisors of Imperial County.

Wright, Harold Bell. 1911. *The Winning of Barbara Worth.* Chicago: Book Supply Company.

Woodruff, Philip. 1953. *The Men Who Ruled India: The Founders.* London: J. Cape.

Articles

Allen, Katheryn Martin. 1945. "Hindoos in the Valley." *Westways* 37: 8–9.

Anand, Rajen S. 1986. "Charn Singh Sandhu Dead at 96." *India-West,* January 31, 26.

Appadurai, Arjun. 1988a. "How to Make a National Cuisine: Cookbooks in Contemporary India." *Comparative Studies in Society and History* 30, no. 1: 3–24.

————. 1988b. "Putting Hierarchy in Its Place." *Cultural Anthropology* 3, no. 1: 37–49.

Applegate, Joe. 1981. "Fire in the Valley." *Reader* (San Diego) 10, no. 31 (August 6).

Avruch, Kevin. 1987. "The Emergence of Ethnicity in Israel." *American Ethnologist* 14, no. 2: 327–339.

Banerjee, Cynthia. 1976. "Isabel Singh." *Arizona Daily Star,* December 3.

Barth, Fredrik. 1960. "The System of Social Stratification in Swat, North Pakistan." In *Aspects of Caste in South India, Ceylon, and Northwest Pakistan,* ed. E. R. Leach, 113–146. Cambridge: Cambridge University Press.

Bentley, G. Carter. 1987. "Ethnicity and Practice." *Comparative Studies in Society and History* 29: 24–55.

Bertaux, Daniel. 1981. "From the Life-History Approach to the Transformation of

Sociological Practice." In *Biography and Society*, ed. Daniel Bertaux, 29–45. Beverly Hills: Sage.

Bloch, Louis. 1926. "Report on the Mexican Labor Situation in the Imperial Valley." *Bienniel Report 1922–24*, 113–127. California Bureau of Labor Statistics.

Borah, Woodrow, and Sherburne F. Cook. 1966. "Marriage and Legitimacy in Mexican Culture: Mexico and California." *California Law Review* 54, no. 1: 949–1008.

Borneman, John. 1988. "Race, Ethnicity, Species, Breed: Totemism and Horse-Breed Classification in America." *Comparative Studies in Society and History* 30, no. 1: 25–51.

Brar, Balwant Singh. 1978. "The East Indians in Sutter County." *Sutter County Historical Society News Bulletin* 17, no. 2: 13–24.

Brass, Paul. 1985. "Ethnic Groups and the State," in *Ethnic Groups and the State*, ed. Paul Brass, 1–56. Sydney: Croom Helm.

Brown, Emily. 1982. "Revolution in India: Made in America." *Population Review* 25, nos. 1 and 2: 41–47.

Buchignani, Norman, and Doreen Indra. 1989. "Key Issues in Canadian-Sikh Ethnic and Race Relations and Their Implications for the Study of the Sikh Diaspora." In *The Sikh Diaspora*, ed. N. Gerald Barrier and Verne Dusenbery, 141–184. Delhi and Columbia: Manohar and South Asia Publications.

Chan, Sucheng. 1988. "Asian Americans: A Selected Bibliography of Writings Published Since the 1960s." In *Reflections on Shattered Windows*, ed. Gary Y. Okihiro, Shirley Hune, Arthur A. Hansen, and John M. Liu, 214–237. Pullman: Washington State University Press.

Chock, Phyllis Pease. 1987. "The Irony of Stereotypes: Toward an Anthropology of Ethnicity." *Cultural Anthropology* 2, no. 3: 347–368.

Cohen, R. 1978. "Ethnicity: Problem and Focus in Anthropology." *Annual Review of Anthropology* 7: 349–403.

Comaroff, John L. 1987. "Of Totemism and Ethnicity: Consciousness, Practice and the Signs of Inequality." *Ethnos* 52, nos. 1 and 2: 301–323.

Conzen, Kathleen Neils. 1980. "Historical Approaches to the Study of Rural Ethnic Communities." In *Ethnicity on the Great Plains*, ed. Frederick C. Luebke, 1–18. Lincoln: University of Nebraska Press.

Cooke, W. Henry. 1972. "The Segregation of Mexican-American School Children in Southern California." In *Racism in California*, ed. Roger Daniels and Spencer C. Olin, Jr., 220–228. New York: Macmillan. Originally published in *School and Society* 67 (1948): 417–421.

Dadabhay, Yusuf. 1954. "Circuitous Assimilation among Rural Hindustanis in California." *Social Forces* 33: 138–141.

D'Andrade, Roy G. 1984. "Cultural Meaning Systems." In *Culture Theory*, ed. R. A. Shweder and R. A. Levine, 88–119. New York: Cambridge University Press.

Das, Taraknath. 1925. "Stateless Persons in the U.S.A." *Calcutta Review* (3rd series) 16, no. 1: 40–46.

Das, Veena. 1973. "The Structure of Marriage Preferences: An Account from Pakistani Fiction." *Man* 8, no. 1: 30–45.

Desai, Prakash, and George Coelho. 1980. "Indian Immigrants in America: Some Cultural Aspects of Psychological Adaptation." In *The New Ethnics*, ed. Parmatma Saran and Edwin Eames, 363–386. New York: Praeger.

Desbarats, Jacqueline. 1979. "Thai Migration to Los Angeles." *Geographical Review* 69, no. 3: 302–318.

Dhillon, Kartar. 1989. "The Parrot's Beak." In *Making Waves, an Anthology of Writings by and about Asian American Women*, ed. Asian Women United of California, 214–222. Boston: Beacon Press.

Domin, Dolores. 1974. "Some Aspects of British Land Policy in Punjab After Its Annexation in 1949." *Punjab Past and Present* 8: 19–25.

Dusenbery, Verne A. 1981. "Canadian Ideology and Public Policy: The Impact on Vancouver Sikh Ethnic and Religious Adaptation." *Canadian Ethnic Studies* 13, no. 3: 101–119.

Elder, Glen. 1981. "History and the Life Course." In *Biography and Society*, ed. Daniel Bertaux, 77–115. Beverly Hills: Sage.

Ellinwood, Dewitt C., Jr. 1976. "An Historical Study of the Punjabi Soldier in World War I." In *Punjab Past and Present: Essays in Honour of Dr. Ganda Singh*, ed. N. Gerald Barrier and Harbans Singh, 337–362. Patiala: Punjabi University Press.

Elliott, James F. 1988. "Cotton: Love Story Across Cultures," n.n. (Tucson), April, 5–6.

Everest, Hari Singh. 1972. "Letter to the Editor," *Sikh Sansar* 1, no. 1: 31.

Ferguson, James, and Akhil Gupta. Forthcoming. "Beyond 'Culture': Space, Identity, and the Politics of Difference." *Cultural Anthropology*. Also forthcoming in *Culture, Power, Place: Explorations in Critical Anthropology*, ed. James Ferguson, Akhil Gupta, and Roger Rouse. Boulder, Colo.: Westview Press.

Ferraroti, Franco. 1981. "On the Autonomy of the Biographical Method." In *Biography and Society*, ed. Daniel Bertaux, 19–27. Beverly Hills: Sage.

Fieldbrave, Theodore. 1934. "East Indians in the United States." *Missionary Review of the World* 57 (June): 291–293.

Foster, George M. 1953. "Cofradia and Compadrazgo in Spain and Spanish America." *Southwestern Journal of Anthropology* 9, no. 1: 1–27.

———. 1969. "Godparents and Social Networks in Tzintzuntzan." *Southwestern Journal of Anthropology* 25: 261–278.

Friedberger, Mark. 1983. "The Farm Family and the Inheritance Process: Evidence from the Corn Belt, 1870–1950," *Agricultural History* 57, no. 1: 1–13.

Frisbie, W. Parker, Frank D. Bean, and Isaac W. Eberstein. 1978. "Patterns of Marital Instability among Mexican Americans, Blacks, and Anglos." In *The Demography of Racial and Ethnic Groups*, ed. W. Parker Frisbie and Frank D. Bean, 143–163. New York: Academic Press.

Fuller, L. Varden. 1939. "The Supply of Agricultural Labor as a Factor in the Evolution of Farm Organization in California." Ph.D. dissertation, University of California, Berkeley. Also in U.S. Congress. Senate. Committee on Education and Labor. *Hearings Pursuant to Senate Resolution 266*. Exhibit 8762-A. 76th Cong., 34d sess., 1940, 19777–898.

Garcia, Isabel Singh. 1983. "They Are too Hindus." *Valley Herald* and *Independent Herald* (Yuba City), April.

Garcia, Mario T. 1979. "On Mexican Immigration, the United States, and Chicano History." *Journal of Ethnic Studies* 7, no. 1: 80–88.

———. 1980. "The Chicana in American History: The Mexican Women of El Paso, 1880–1920—A Case Study." *Pacific Historical Review* 40, no. 2: 315–337.

Gee, Emma. 1976. "Issei Women." *In Counterpoint: Perspectives on Asian America*, ed. Emma Gee, 359–364. Los Angeles: Asian American Studies Center, University of California, Los Angeles.

Gibson, Margaret A. 1987. "Punjabi Immigrants in an American High School." In *Toward an Interpretive Ethnography of Education: Educational Anthropology Today*, ed. George D. Spindler, 281–313. Hillsdale, N.J.: L. Erlbaum Associates.

Gonzalez, Gilbert G. 1989. "The Americanization of Mexican Women and Their Families during the Era of De Jure School Segregation, 1900–1950." In *Social and Gender Boundaries in the United States*, ed. Sucheng Chan, 55-79. Lewiston, N.Y.: Edwin Mellen Press.

Gonzalez, Juan L., Jr. 1986. "Asian Indian Immigration Patterns: The Origins of the Sikh Community in California." *International Migration Review* 20, no. 1: 40–54.

Gonzalez, Rosalinda M. 1983. "Chicanas and Mexican Immigrant Families 1920–1940: Women's Subordination and Family Exploitation." In *Decades of Discontent: The Women's Movement 1920–1940*, ed. Joan Jensen and Lois Scharf, 59–84. Westport, Conn.: Greenwood Press.

Greenwood, Leonard. 1966. "El Centro's Community of Sikhs Dying Out." *Los Angeles Times*, December 28, pt. 2.

Gregor, Howard F. 1963. "Regional Hierarchies in California Agricultural Production: 1939–1954," *Annals of the Association of American Geographers* 53: 27–37.

Habakkuk, H. J. 1955. "Family Structure and Economic Change in Nineteenth-Century Europe." *Journal of Economic History* 15, no. 1: 1–12.

Hadwiger, Don F., and Clay Cochran. 1984. "Rural Telephones in the United States." *Agricultural History* 58, no. 3: 221–238.

Hareven, Tamara. 1971. "The History of the Family as an Interdisciplinary Field." *Journal of Interdisciplinary History* 2: 399–414.

Hatch, Elvin. 1975. "Stratification in a Rural California Community." *Agricultural History* 49: 21–38.

Hess, Gary R. 1982. "The Asian Indian Immigrants in the United States, 1900–1965." *Population Review* 25, nos. 1 and 2: 29–34.

Higgs, Robert. 1978. "Landless by Law: Japanese Immigrants in California Agriculture to 1941." *Journal of Economic History* 38: 205–225.

———. 1979. "The Wealth of Japanese Tenant Farmers in California, 1909." *Agricultural History* 53, no. 2: 488–493.

"Hindus Fight Exclusion." 1913. *New York Times*, December 7.

"Hindus Too Brunette to Vote Here." 1923. *Literary Digest*, March 10, 13.

Hirata, Lucie Cheng. 1979. "Free, Indentured, Enslaved: Chinese Prostitutes in Nineteenth-Century California." *Signs: Journal of Women in Culture and Society* 5: 3–29.

"Historical Notes." 1982. *Valley Grower* (Imperial Valley Vegetable Growers' Association, El Centro), Summer, 23-25.

Ichioka, Yuji. 1977. "*Amerika-san*: Japanese Prostitutes in Nineteenth-Century America." *Amerasia Journal* 4, no. 1: 1–21.

———. 1980. "*Amerika Nadeshiko*: Japanese Immigrant Women in the United States, 1900–1924." *Pacific Historical Review* 48: 339–357.

———. 1984. "Japanese Immigrant Response to the 1920 California Alien Land Law." *Agricultural History* 58, no. 2: 157–178.

"Imperial Valley Firsts." 1982. *Valley Grower* (Imperial Valley Vegetable Growers' Association, El Centro), Summer, 38.

"In Memory of the Honorable Dalip Singh Saund." 1973. *Sikh Sansar* 2, no. 3: 89.

Iwata, Masakazu. 1962. "The Japanese Immigrants in California Agriculture." *Agricultural History* 36, no. 1: 25–37.

Jacoby, Harold S. 1958. "More Thind Against Than Sinning," *Pacific Historian*, 11, no. 4: 1–2, 8.

———. 1980. "Some Demographic and Social Aspects of Early East Indian Life in the United States." In *Sikh Studies*, ed. N. Gerald Barrier and Mark Juergensmeyer, 159–171. Berkeley: Graduate Theological Union.

———. 1982. "Administrative Restriction of Asian Indian Immigration into the United States, 1907–1917." *Population Review* 25: 35–40.

Johnson, Annette Thackwell. 1922. "The 'Rag Heads'—A Picture of America's East Indians." *The Independent* 109, no. 3828 (October 28): 234–235.

Jones, Idwal. 1939. "Mr. Har Chand." *Westways* 1: 16–17.

Juergensmeyer, Mark. 1982. "The Gadar Syndrome: Ethnic Anger and Nationalist Pride." *Population Review* 25, nos. 1 and 2: 48–58.

Kay, Margarita A. 1980. "Mexican, Mexican-American, and Chicana Childbirth."

In *Twice a Minority: Mexican American Women*, ed. Margarita B. Melville, 52-65. St. Louis: Mosby.

Keyes, Charles F. 1981. "The Dialectics of Ethnic Change." In *Ethnic Change*, ed. Charles F. Keyes, 3–30. Seattle: University of Washington Press.

Krom, Howard A. 1970. "California's Divorce Law Reform: An Historical Analysis." *Pacific Law Journal* 1: 156–181.

Kulkarni, Diane. 1984. "Immigrant a Strength and Inspiration." *Ogden Standard-Examiner* (Utah), April 30.

La Brack, Bruce. 1982. "Immigration Law and the Revitalization Process: The Case of the California Sikhs." *Population Review* 25: 59–66.

———. 1988. "Evolution of Sikh Family Form and Values in Rural California: Continuity and Change 1904–1980." *Journal of Comparative Family Studies* 19, no. 2: 287–309.

La Brack, Bruce, and Karen Leonard. 1984. "Conflict and Compatibility in Punjabi-Mexican Immigrant Families in Rural California: 1915–1965." *Journal of Marriage and the Family* 46, no. 3: 75–87.

Lacher, Irene. 1990. "No Fear He May Offend." *Los Angeles Times*, May 25, E1, E6.

Leonard, Karen. 1982a. "A Note on Given Names and Chicano Intermarriage." *La Red* 52: 4–5.

———. 1982b. "Marriage and Family Life among Early Asian Indian Immigrants." *Population Review* 25, nos. 1 and 2: 67–75.

———. 1984a. "The Pahkar Singh Murders: A Punjabi Response to California's Alien Land Law." *Amerasia Journal* 11, no. 1: 75–87.

———. 1984b. "The Pioneer Sikhs: Religious Tolerance." *Sikh Samachar* 8, no. 3: 13–15.

———. 1985. "Punjabi Farmers and California's Alien Land Law." *Agricultural History* 59, no. 4: 549–562.

———. 1988a. "Ethnicity Confounded: Punjabi Pioneers in California." In *Sikh History and Religion in the 20th Century*, ed. J. O'Connell, M. Israel, and Willard G. Oxtoby, with W. H. McLeod and J. S. Grewal, 314–333. South Asian Studies Papers, No. 3. Toronto: Centre for South Asian Studies, University of Toronto.

———. 1988b. "South Asian Immigrants: Then and Now." *San Jose Studies* 14, no. 2: 71–84.

———. 1989a. "Immigrant Punjabis in Early Twentieth-Century California: A Life History." In *Social and Gender Boundaries in the United States*, ed. Sucheng Chan, 101–122. Lewiston, N.Y.: Edwin Mellen Press.

———. 1989b. "Pioneer Voices from California: Reflections on Race, Religion, and Ethnicity." In *The Sikh Diaspora: Migration and the Experience Beyond Punjab*, ed. N. Gerald Barrier and Verne A. Dusenbery, 120–139. Delhi and Columbia, Mo.: Manohar and South Asia Books.

————. 1990. "Political Skills on a New Frontier." *South Asia* 12, no. 2: 69–81.

————. Forthcoming. "Finding One's Own Place: The Imposition of Asian Landscapes on Rural California." In *Culture, Power, Place: Explorations in Critical Anthropology*, ed. James Ferguson, Akhil Gupta, and Roger Rouse, Boulder: Westview Press.

————. Forthcoming. "Historical Constructions of Ethnicity: California's Punjabi Immigrants."

————. Forthcoming. "Ethnicity and Gender: South Asian Identity in the United States." In *Ethnicity, Identity, and Migration*, ed. Milton Israel and N. K. Wagle. Toronto: Centre for South Asian Studies, University of Toronto.

————. Forthcoming. "Intermarriage and Ethnicity: Punjabi Mexican Americans, Mexican Japanese, and Filipino Americans."

Leonard, Karen, and Chandrasekhar Tibrewal. Forthcoming. "Asian Indians in Southern California: Occupations and Ethnicity." In *Comparative Immigration and Entrepreneurship: Culture, Capital, and Ethnic Networks*, ed. Ivan Light and Parminder Bhachu. New Brunswick, N.J.: Transaction, forthcoming.

Lieberson, Stanley, and Mary C. Waters. 1989. "The Rise of a New Ethnic Group: The 'Unhyphenated American.'" *Items* (Social Science Research Council) 43, no. 1: 7–10.

Littleton, C. Scott. 1964. "Some Aspects of Social Stratification among the Immigrant Punjabi Communities of California." In *Culture Change and Stability*, ed. Ralph L. Beals, 106–116. Los Angeles: Department of Anthropology, University of California, Los Angeles.

Lockley, Fred. 1907. "The Hindu Invasion." *Pacific Monthly* 17: 584–595.

McLeod, W. H. 1989. "The First Forty Years of Sikh Migration." In *The Sikh Diaspora*, ed. N. Gerald Barrier and Verne Dusenbery, 29–48. Delhi and Columbia, Mo.: Manohar and South Asia Publications.

M'Crae, Lee. 1916. "Self-Exiled in America." *Missionary Review of the World* 39: 525–526.

————. 1918. "'Birds of Passage' in California." *Missionary Review of the World* 16, no. 12: 910.

"Man and Girl Found Slain in Lonely Cabin." 1934. *Wide World Magazine*, 336.

Mansukhani, Gobind Singh. 1974. "The Sikhs Today." *Sikh Sansar* 3, no. 2: 41–50.

Maskiell, Michelle. 1990. "Gender, Kinship and Rural Work in Colonial Punjab." *Journal of Women's History* 2, no. 1: 35–72.

Mazumdar, Sucheta. 1984. "Colonial Impact and Punjabi Emigration to the United States." In *Labor Immigration under Capitalism*, ed. Lucie Cheng and Edna Bonacich, 316–336. Berkeley: University of California Press.

Mears, Eliot Grinnell. 1926. "The Land, the Crops and the Oriental: A Study of Race Relations in Terms of the Map." *The Survey* 56, no. 3: 146–149, 203, 206.

Medick, Hans, and David Warren Sabean. 1984. "Interest and Emotion in Family and Kinship Studies: A Critique of Social History and Anthropology." In *Interest and Emotion: Essays on the Study of Family and Kinship*, ed. Hans Medick and David Warren Sabean, 9–27. New York: Cambridge University Press.

Millard, Ann V. 1982. "Women's Reproductive Histories and Demographic Change: A Case from Rural Mexico." *Women in Development Working Papers* 8 (Michigan State University).

Millis, H. A. 1912. "East Indian Immigration to the Pacific Coast." *Survey* 28, no. 9: 379–386.

Mintz, Sidney W., and Eric R. Wolf. 1950. "An Analysis of Ritual Co-Parenthood (Compadrazgo)." *Southwestern Journal of Anthropology* 6: 341–368.

Morrill, Warren T., and Bennett Dyke. 1980. "Ethnographic and Documentary Demography." In *Genealogical Demography*, ed. Warren T. Morrill and Bennett Dyke, 1–9. San Francisco: Academic Press.

Murarka, Bina. 1980. "Prejudice in Yuba City—Genuine Problem," *India West*, December 26, 8.

Murarka, Ramesh. 1980. "The Sikh Farming Community of California." *India West*, December 12, 8.

———. 1981a. "Rattan Singh Sahota—Incredible Saga of One Man's Journey to America." *India West*, May 15.

———. 1981b. "Pratap S. Brar—Pioneering Spirit Overcame 37 Years of Loneliness." *India-West*, July 3, 12.

Nagata, Judith A. 1974. "What Is a Malay? Situational Selection of Ethnic Identity in a Plural Society." *American Ethnologist* 1: 331–350.

Narayanan, R. 1972. "Indian Immigration and the India League of America." *Indian Journal of American Studies* 2: 1–29.

Narroll, Raoul. 1964. "On Ethnic Unit Classification." *Current Anthropology* 5: 283–312.

Oberoi, Harjot A. 1988. "From Ritual to Counter-Ritual: Rethinking the Hindu Sikh Question, 1884–1915." In *Sikh History and Religion in the Twentieth Century*, ed. Joseph T. O'Connell, Milton Israel, and Willard G. Oxtoby, with W. H. McLeod and J. S. Grewal, 136-158. Toronto: Centre for South Asian Studies, University of Toronto.

Okihiro, Gary Y. 1988. "The Idea of Community and a 'Particular Type of History.'" In *Reflections on Shattered Windows*, ed. Gary Y. Okihiro, Shirley Hune, Arthur A. Hansen, and John M. Liu, 175–183. Pullman: Washington State University Press.

Penalosa, Fernando. 1968. "Mexican Family Roles." *Journal of Marriage and the Family*, 680–689.

Portes, Alejandro. 1990. "From South of the Border: Hispanic Minorities in the United States." In *Immigration Reconsidered: History, Sociology, and Politics*, ed. Virginia Yans-McLaughlin, 160–184. New York: Oxford University Press.

Posadas, Barbara M. 1981. "Crossed Boundaries in Interracial Chicago: Pilipino American Families Since 1925." *Amerasia Journal* 8, no. 2: 31–52.

———. 1989. "Mestiza Girlhood: Interracial Families in Chicago's Filipino American Community Since 1925." In *Making Waves*, ed. Asian Women United of California, 273–282. Boston: Beacon Press.

Puri, Harish K. 1980. "Ghadar Movement: An Experiment in New Patterns of Socialisation." *Journal of Regional History* 1, no. 1: 120–141.

Rabinowitz, Howard N. 1983. "Race, Ethnicity, and Cultural Pluralism in American History." In *Ordinary People and Everyday Life: Perspectives on the New Social History*, ed. James M. Gardner and George Rollie Adams, 23–49. Nashville: American Association for State and Local History.

Reed, Howard S. 1946. "Major Trends in California Agriculture." *Agricultural History* 20: 252–255.

"A Retrospective on a Stalwart Sikh (Sardar Puna Singh)." 1974. *Sikh Sansar* 3, no. 3: 96.

Rogers, Susan Carol, and Sonya Salamon. 1983. "Inheritance and Social Organization among Family Farmers." *American Ethnologist* 10, no. 3: 529–550.

Rosaldo, Renato. 1988. "Ideology, Place, and People without Culture." *Cultural Anthropology* 3, no. 1: 77–87.

Rosenthal-Urey, Ina. 1984. "Church Records as a Source of Data on Mexican Migrant Networks: A Methodological Note." *International Migration Review* 18, no. 3: 767–781.

Schrager, Samuel. 1983. "What Is Social in Oral History?" *International Journal of Oral History* 4, no. 2: 76–98.

Sergeant, John. 1984. "Respected Sikh Elder Passes Away in Fresno." *India West* 24, June 15.

Shontz, Orfa Jean. 1927. "The Land of 'Poco Tiempo.'" *Journal of Social Casework* 8, no. 3: 74–79.

Sidhu, Gurnam Singh. 1972. "Saga of the American Sikh." *Sikh Sansar* 1, no. 4: 99–105.

Sihra, Nand Singh. 1913. "Indians in Canada." *Modern Review* (Calcutta) 14, no. 2 (August): 140–149.

Singh, Saint Nihal. 1909. "The Picturesque Immigrant from India's Coral Strand." *Out West* (Los Angeles) 30: 42–54.

Singh, Sardar Puna, adapted by Jane P. Singh. 1972. "My Early Years in America." *Sikh Sansar* 1, no. 4: 109–110.

Smith, Daniel Scott. 1973. "Parental Power and Marriage Patterns." *Journal of Marriage and the Family* 35, no. 3: 418–428.

Street, Richard Steven. 1989. "The Sikhs: Ethnic Farmers." *California Farmer*, January 21, 8–9, 40–41.

Sundaram, Viji. 1989a. "From Salt of the Earth to Rare Old Salt." *India West*, April 7, 31, 33.

———. 1989b. "Sareeram Becomes First Indian Admiral in Navy." *India West,* April 7, 1, 31.

Sunoo, Sonia S. 1978. "Korean Women Pioneers of the Pacific Northwest." *Oregon Historical Quarterly* 79: 51–63.

Swierenga, Robert P. 1980. "Ethnicity and American Agriculture," *Ohio History* 89: 323–344.

Taylor, Paul S., and Edward J. Rowell. 1938. "Patterns of Agricultural Labor Migration within California." *Monthly Labor Review* 47: 980–990.

Taylor, Paul S., and Tom Vasey. 1907. "The Labor Problem." *California Fruit Grower*, August 24.

———. 1936. "Historical Background of California Farm Labor." *Rural Sociology* 1: 281–295.

Thompson, Paul. 1981. "Life Histories and the Analysis of Social Change." In *Biography and Society,* ed. Daniel Bertaux, 289-305. Beverly Hills: Sage.

U.S. Congress. Senate. Immigration Commission, 1907–1910. 1911. "The East Indians on the Pacific Coast." in *Report,* 61st Cong. 2nd sess., doc. 633. Washington, D.C.: Government Printing Office, 321–349.

Vatuk, Sylvia, and Ved P. Vatuk. 1969. "Protest Songs of East Indians on the West Coast, U.S.A." In *Thieves in My House: Four Studies in Indian Folklore of Protest and Change,* ed. Ved Vatuk, 63–80. Varanasi: Vishwavidyalaya Prakashan.

Weber, Devra Anne. 1972. "The Organizing of Mexicano Agricultural Workers: Imperial Valley, and Los Angeles 1928–34, an Oral History Approach." *Aztlan* 3, no. 2: 307–347.

Wenzel, Lawrence A. 1968. "The Rural Punjabis of California: A Religio-Ethnic Group," *Phylon: Atlanta University Review of Race and Culture* 29: 245–256.

Wolf, Arthur P. 1984. "Family Life and the Life Cycle in Rural China." In *Households,* ed. Robert McC. Netting, Richard R. Wilk, and Eric J. Arnold, 279–298. Berkeley: University of California Press.

Wolf, Eric R. 1988. "Inventing Society." *American Ethnologist* 15, no. 4: 752–761.

Yang, Eun Sik. 1984. "Korean Women of America: From Subordination to Partnership, 1902–1930," *Amerasia Journal* 11, no. 2: 1–28.

Yans-McLaughlin, Virginia. 1990. "Metaphors of Self in History: Subjectivity, Oral Narrative, and Immigration Studies." In *Immigration Reconsidered: History, Sociology, and Politics,* ed. Virginia Yans-McLaughlin, 254–290. New York: Oxford University Press.

Primary Sources

Theses, Papers, and Other

Baptism, confirmation, and marriage records. 1915–1947. Holtville Catholic Church.

Berner, Loretta. n.d. "Sketches from 'Way Back.'" Unpublished short story, Long Beach.

Blackburn's Map of the Imperial Valley. 1943. Office of the County Clerk, El Centro, Imperial County.

———. 1955. Wells Fargo Bank, Holtville.

Bradfield, Helen. 1971. "The East Indians of Yuba City: A Study in Acculturation." Master's thesis, Sacramento State College.

Carroll, Elizabeth J. 1973. "A Study: East Indian (Sikh) Women Students at Yuba College." Ed He 690, USC, May.

Chadney, James Gaylord. 1976. "The Vancouver Sikhs: An Ethnic Community in Canada." Ph.D. dissertation, Michigan State University.

Chakravorty, Robindra. 1968. "The Sikhs of El Centro: A Study in Social Integration." Ph.D. dissertation, University of Minnesota.

Chima, Lal Singh. 1972. "Sikhs Marriage in India and California." Paper presented at the Southwestern Anthropological Association, Long Beach, Calif., March 29–April 1, 1–10.

Christensen, Marlin, Jim Thompson, and Phil Crump. 1966. "Four Day Community Study of Yuba City, California: A report by three Peace Corps Volunteers." University of California, Berkeley.

Clarke, Susan. 1932. "Holtville, Gateway to California: The First City of Imperial Valley." Master's thesis, University of Southern California.

Cramp, Kathryn, Louise F. Shields, and Charles A. Thomsen. 1926. "Study of the Mexican Population in Imperial Valley, California." Bancroft Library, University of California, Berkeley. Mimeographed.

Darnell, William Irvin. 1959. "The Imperial Valley: Its Physical and Cultural Geography." Master's thesis, San Diego State College.

Dhillon, Kesar S. 1976. "Interview, October–December, 1976," by Jane Singh, Oakland. Gadar Collection, South/Southeast Asia Library, University of California, Berkeley.

Ferguson, James. 1989. "Cultural Style on the Zambian Copperbelt: Micro-political Foundations of Localism and Cosmopolitanism." Social Relations colloquium, University of California, Irvine, October.

Fernandez, Bonifacio. 1953. "East Indian Contributions to Agricultural Development in Central California." *Development Problems in Selected California Areas*, 130–147. University of California, Berkeley, Institute of Governmental Studies Library. Mimeographed.

Finley, Robert L. 1974. "An Economic History of the Imperial Valley of California to 1971." Ph.D. dissertation, University of Oklahoma.

Fujioka, Shiro. 1957. "Traces of a Journey." Translated by Mabel Saito Hall for Sucheng Chan from *Ayumi No Ato*. Japanese, published in Los Angeles by Kanko Koenkai.

Ghei, Kiren. 1988. "Hindi Popular Cinema and the Indian American Teenage Dance Experience." Seventeenth Annual Conference on South Asia, Madison, Wis., November 4–6.

Gray, James. 1966. "The American Civil Liberties Union of Southern California and Imperial Valley Agricultural Labor Disturbances: 1930, 1934." Ph.D. dissertation, University of California, Los Angeles.

Griswold, Robert Lawrence. 1979. "The Character of the Family in Rural California, 1850–1890." Ph.D. dissertation, Stanford University.

Gupta, Akhil. 1988. "Space and Time in the Politics of Culture." Paper presented at the American Anthropological Association, Phoenix.

Harriss, Elizabeth, with John Polich. 1975. "Bibliography of Imperial Valley: and Its environs." San Diego State University, Imperial Valley Campus, Regional Studies Series, vol. 1. San Diego State University Press. Typescript in Arizona Western College Library.

Hatfield, James R. 1968. "California's Migrant Farm Labor Problem and Some Efforts to Deal with It: 1930–1940." Master's thesis, Sacramento State College.

Imperial Valley Khalsa Diwan. Articles of Incorporation. December 14, 1947. El Centro Sikh Temple (in the temple office).

Index to Great Register, General Elections 1958, Sutter County. Yuba City Library, Special Collection.

Jacoby, Harold S. 1978. "East Indians in the United States: The first half-century." Manuscript.

Kaur, Nand. "Interview, May 21, 1972," with Jane Singh, Yuba City, California. Bancroft, South and Southeast Asia Library, University of California, Berkeley.

Khan, Salim. 1981. "A Brief History of Pakistanis in the Western United States." Master's thesis, Sacramento State.

Khush, Harwant Kaur. 1965. "The Social Paritcipation and Attitudes of the Children of East Indian Immigrants." Master's thesis, Sacramento State College.

Kurtz, Carol Cameron. 1984. "The Sikhs of Yuba City, California: A Study in Ethnic Geography." Master's thesis, California State University, Hayward.

La Brack, Bruce. 1980. "The Sikhs of Northern California: A Socio-Historical Study." Ph.D. dissertation, Syracuse University.

———. 1987. "Overseas Sikhs and the Economy of Punjab: Remittances Before and After 1984." Paper, 16th Annual Conference on South Asia, University of Wisconsin, Madison, November.

La Brack, Bruce, and Juanita Bellew. ca. 1976. "Health Care and the East Indian." Yuba City, Yuba-Sutter Health Department, n.d.

Loosley, A. C. 1927. "Foreign Born Population of California, 1849–1920." Master's thesis, University of California, Berkeley.

Maskiell, Michelle. 1987. "Women's Work and the Household Economy in Panjab." Paper at 16th Annual Conference on South Asia, Madison, Wis.

⭑ Miller, Allan P. 1950. "An Ethnographic Report on the Sikh (East) Indians of Sacramento Valley." South/Southeast Asia Library, University of California, Berkeley. Manuscript.

Misrow, Jogesh Chander. 1915. "East Indian Immigration on the Pacific Coast." Master's thesis, Stanford.

"The New Puritans: The Sikhs of Yuba City." 1985. Film, Graduate School of Journalism, University of California, Berkeley.

Pendleton, Edwin C. 1950. "History of Labor in Arizona Irrigated Agriculture." Ph.D. dissertation, University of California, Berkeley.

Registrar's records, Imperial Valley College, 1934–1982.

Rutherford, Dorothy Angell. 1984. "Bengalis in America: Relationship, Affect, Person, and Self." Ph.D. dissertation, American University.

Samras, Kharaiti Ram. 1936. "Hindus in the United States: Their Part in the Economic Development of the West." Carey McWilliams Collection, University of California, Los Angeles, Minorities Miscellaneous File, Index 1, box 16.

San Quentin Prison Registers. California State Archives, Sacramento.

Santry, Patricia Josephine. 1981. "An Historical Perspective of the Factors Preventing Sikh Assimilation in California, 1906–1946." Master's thesis, California State University, Fullerton.

Schwartz, Jerome L. 1961. "Statistical Survey of the Aid to Needy Children Program in Imperial County, California." Imperial County Family Health and Welfare Project: El Centro. Imperial County Library. Typescript.

Shankar, Richard Ashok. 1971. "Integration Goal Definition of the East Indian Student in the Sutter County Area." Master's thesis, Chico State University.

⭑ Shroff, Beheroze. 1984. "Sweet Jail: The Yuba City Sikhs." M.F.A. 16-mm color film, University of California, Los Angeles.

Singh, Jane. 1982. "People of South Asia in America, 1899–1984." National Endowment for the Humanities Exhibit and Open Forum, Oakland Public Library, November 13.

Smith, Daniel Scott, and Michael S. Hindus. 1971. "Premarital Pregnancy in America, 1640–1966: An overview and interpretation." Paper, American Historical Association.

"Survey of Race Relations." Hoover Institution Archives, Stanford, California. Boxes 26–29, 35, 37.

Taylor, Paul Shuster. "Collection of Notes, etc., concerning Mexican Labor in the U.S., about 1927–1932." Bancroft Library, University of California, Berkeley. 2 cartons.

———. "Field Notes for his book, Mexican Labor in the United States, 1927–1930." Organized, transcribed, and edited by Abraham Hoffman. Bancroft Library, University of California, Berkeley. 1 carton.

Taylor, Paul Schuster, and Irving William Wood. "Correspondence and Papers,

1934–1937." Bancroft Library, University of California, Berkeley. 1 carton and 1 oversize portfolio.

"Union Sugar Company Black Book of Field Sheets." 1950, 1960–1961. El Centro Office. Shown in 1981 by Jim Bailey and Julia Youngblood.

U.S. Department of the Interior, War Relocation Authority. 1945. "Japanese Population of Imperial Valley." Washington, D.C.: Community Analysis Section.

U.S. Government, Los Angeles District Court. "Bankruptcy Records." Indexes I, II, and III (1907–1917, 1917–1925, 1925–1932), Laguna Niguel Federal Archives. Includes Los Angeles, Riverside, Orange, San Bernardino, San Luis Obispo, Santa Barbara, Ventura, and San Diego, and Imperial counties (the last two counties only until 1929).

U.S. Government, San Diego District Court. "Bankruptcy Indexes, 1929–1932." San Diego and Imperial counties, established March 6, 1929.

U.S. Government. War Relocation Authority. "Japanese Population of Imperial Valley." Washington, D.C.: Community Analysis Notes, no. 12 (April 9, 1945).

U.S. National Archives, Record Group 29. "Census of U.S. Population, Imperial County, California, 1910." Manuscript census.

U.S. Postmaster General. "Register of Money Orders Issued," 2 vols., January 2, 1909, through November 5, 1910, and July 16, 1912, through December 18, 1913. Holtville City Hall.

Watanabe, Chizuko. 1983. "The Japanese Immigrant Community in Mexico: Its History and Present." Master's thesis, California State University, Los Angeles.

Wenzel, Lawrence Allen. 1966. "The Identification and Analysis of Certain Value Orientations of Two Generations of East Indians in California." Ph.D. dissertation, University of the Pacific.

Wood, Ann. 1966. "East Indians in California: A Study of their Organizations, 1900–1947." Master's thesis, University of Wisconsin.

Newspapers and Journals

I am indebted to Joseph Anderholt, who supervised the clipping of stories featuring "Hindus" from the first three newspapers below in the Pioneer Museum, Imperial.

Brawley News, 1910–1984 (also in the Brawley City Library).

El Centro Progress, 1910–1984.

Holtville Tribune, 1910–1984.

Imperial Valley Press (in its office).

India West (published by Ramesh and Bina Murarka from Fremont, Calif.), 1970–1990.

Card File, Collection on the Hindus from local newspapers (*Appeal Democrat, Marys-ville Star*), 1910 on, Yuba City Library.

County Record Offices

I consulted the Vital Statistical Records (birth, death, and marriage records) kept by the County Recorders; additional records are specified. The California counties are listed first.

Colusa County, Colusa, California.
Fresno County, Fresno, California.
Imperial County, El Centro, California.
   Civil Case Indexes, 1910–1980. Office of the County Clerk.
   Criminal Case Indexes, 1910–1946. Office of the County Clerk.
   General Index to Plaintiffs, 1907–1919. Office of the County Clerk.
   General Index to Deeds, Grantors, 1916–1931. Recorder's Office.
   General Index to Deeds, Lessees, 1923–1931. Recorder's Office.
   General Index to Defendants, 1919–1931. Office of the County Clerk.
   Lessee-Lessor Index, 1916–1923. Recorder's Office.
   Naturalization Petitions, 1930–1980. Office of the County Clerk.
   Probate Records. Civil Cases, 1910–1960. Office of the County Clerk.
   Vital Statistical Records, 1910–1980. Office of the County Recorder.
Kings County, Hanford, California.
Los Angeles County, Los Angeles, California.
   Book of Deeds, Grantees/Grantors, 1912–1922. Recorder's Office.
Orange County, Santa Ana, California.
Placer County, Nevada City, California.
Riverside County, Riverside, California.
Sacramento County, Sacramento, California.
San Bernardino County, San Bernardino, California.
San Diego County, San Diego, California.
San Joaquin County, Stockton, California.
San Mateo County, Redwood City, California.
Santa Clara County, San Jose, California.
Sutter County, Yuba City, California.
Tulare County, Visalia, California.
Yuba County, Marysville, California.
Dona Ana County, Las Cruces, New Mexico.
Maricopa County, Phoenix, Arizona.
   Marriage Licenses, 1910–1960. State Archives.
   Probate Records, 1941–1951. State Archives.

Cemeteries

Auburn Cemetery.
Brawley Cemetery.
City Cemetery, Sacramento.
Evergreen Cemetery, El Centro.
Floral Memorial Park, Selma.
Greenwood Memory Lawn, Phoenix.
Masonic Cemetery, Sacramento.
Odd Fellows Lawn Cemetery, Sacramento.
Sacramento Memorial Lawn Cemetery.
St. Mary's Cemetery, Sacramento.
Sierra View Cemetery, Yuba City.
Valley View Cemetery, Selma.

Index